Knowing Music, Making Music

BENJAMIN BRINNER

KNOWING MUSIC, MAKING MUSIC

Javanese
Gamelan
and the
Theory of Musical
Competence
and
Interaction

The University of Chicago Press
Chicago & London

Benjamin Brinner is associate professor of music at the
University of California, Berkeley.

The University of Chicago Press, Chicago 60637
The University of Chicago Press, Ltd., London
© 1995 by The University of Chicago
All rights reserved. Published 1995
Printed in the United States of America
04 03 02 01 00 99 98 97 96 95   1 2 3 4 5
ISBN: 0-226-07509-5 (cloth)
      0-226-07510-9 (paper)

Library of Congress Cataloging-in-Publication Data

Brinner, Benjamin Elon.
   Knowing music, making music : Javanese gamelan and the theory of
   musical competence and interaction / Benjamin Brinner.
        p.   cm. — (Chicago studies in ethnomusicology)
     Discography: p.
     Includes bibliographical references and index.
     1. Musical ability.   2. Gamelan.   I. Title.   II. Series
   ML3838.B76   1995
   78'.9598'2—dc20   95-30177
                                                          CIP
                                                          MN

for Lisa,
Maya, Omri, and Devon

Contents

A gallery of photographs follows page 86

ILLUSTRATIONS

Acknowledgments

I owe an immeasurable debt to my three principal teachers, K. R. T. Wasitodiningrat (Pak Cokro), I. M. Harjito, and the late R. Ng. Martopangrawit for the many hours they spent with me sharing their knowledge and artistry, and patiently enduring my attempts at emulating their playing. One lifetime is not enough to absorb all that they have offered. I have also learned a great deal from other teachers, including Mloyowidodo (now K. R. T. Widadanegara), Djoko Sungkono, and Wakidi in Java; I Wayan Konolan, I Nyoman Windha, and the late I Wayan Saplug in Bali; and Taiseer Elias and Jamal Is'id in Israel. The little I know about Javanese dance I learned from the late Martati, whose gracefulness I sorely miss. To Widiyanto I owe a special debt of gratitude for many lessons learned in the course of our friendship.

Among the many other musicians who have contributed to my understanding of Javanese, Balinese, and Arab musics I would especially like to thank Suhardi, Tarnopangrawit, Dalimin, Paimin, and other musicians at the Mangkunegaran, Ki Sutino Hardokocarito and the members of Hardo Budoyo, Dr. I Wayan Dibia, Ni Made Wiratini, Walid 'Id'is, and Ghidian Qaimari.

This book has its roots in my dissertation, which took shape through the careful readings and copious comments of Judith Becker, whose writings did much to spark my interest in Javanese music, and Bonnie Wade, my teacher, adviser, and colleague. I am also grateful to Bonnie for her support and advice—including comments on an early draft—which have been crucial at many stages in the writing of this book. Amin Sweeney, another teacher turned colleague, has been an inspiration and has pushed me to finish this book so that I could find time for our joint study of Malay oral narratives. John Blacking took an interest in the project at an early stage. I am truly sorry that I did not have the opportunity to discuss it with him further. Though my contacts with Hardja Susilo over the years have been too brief, they have also stimulated my thinking.

The present shape of the book owes much to the many helpful suggestions offered by Michael Tenzer and an anonymous reader for the University of Chicago Press. I thank them and the editors, T. David Brent and Jane Lightner, who shepherded the book through this process. I would like to thank Sarah Weiss for her comments on a draft of this book, David Wessel for introducing me to the field of cognitive science and for reading the theoretical chapters on musical competence, Andy Sutton for trailblazing and friendly advice, Dalia Cohen for creating opportunities for me in Israel, and Ann Pescatello for advice and encouragement. Without the assistance of Nyoman Werti I would have had far less time to write this book.

Friends in the American *gamelan* world who have served as sounding boards for my ideas and have enriched my thinking with their own experience include Alex Dea, Laurie Kottmeyer, Kitsie Emerson, Greg McCourt, Henry Spiller, and Carter Scholz. Carter made my life much easier by designing the Kepatihan font that I have used for cipher notation. During my first sojourn in Java, Laurie Sears, Carol Block, and Joan Suyenaga were instrumental in leading me to people and sharing their own knowledge.

I owe a debt, too, to my students in Jerusalem and Berkeley who impelled me to think harder about issues I thought I understood. Among them Roberto Andreoni, Amatsya Bar Yosef, Anthony Brown, Ruth Charloff, Mark DeWitt, Bill Evans, Elisabeth LeGuin, Alan Mason, Ketty Nez, George Ruckert, and Andrew Weintraub were directly involved in courses such as the seminars on musical interaction and Javanese theory and practice that helped me shape this book.

The research for this book has been supported by a number of grants and institutions, including a Fulbright Doctoral Dissertation Research fellowship for my work on *pathetan* in Central Java 1982–83 and, ten years later, a Fulbright Faculty Research Abroad fellowship for a project on musical memory in Java and Bali. The University of California at Berkeley has also supported various aspects of this project, including several short research trips to Israel, through grants from the Committee on Research and the Center for Middle Eastern Studies. My parents' generous support in times of need has been no less important.

I am grateful to Dr. Sri Hastanto and Dr. Rahayu Supanggah at STSI Surakarta and Dr. I Made Bandem at STSI Denpasar, who sponsored my research in 1992–93, and R. M. Ng. Ronosuripto, who facilitated my work at the Mangkunegaran palace in Surakarta. I would also like to acknowledge the Lembaga Ilmu Pengetahuan Indonesia, which approved my research in 1982–83 and 1992–93, and the staff at AMINEF in Jakarta, who made the last trip much easier.

Last, but certainly not least, I am grateful to and for my three wonderful children, Maya, Omri, and Devon, who have put up with a father terminally linked to his computer at odd hours of the night and day, and Lisa, who has had to share our life with this book far longer than I had hoped. I cannot imagine how I could have done this without you.

Technical Notes

PRONUNCIATION

Approximate Indonesian pronunciations of letters that differ significantly from English:

    a is like "a" in father

    e is like "a" in say or short "e" in the

    i is like "ee" in see; in a closed syllable it is like "i" in sit

    o is like "o" in lode without a glide

    u is like "oo" in food

    c is like "ch" in church

    ng is like "ng" in singer

    ngg is like "ng" in finger

    g is always hard

    k at the end of a syllable is a glottal stop

Pronunciation of Javanese terms is similar, with the following additions:

    é is like "a" in late

    e is like the short "e" in the or debacle

    è is like "e" in bed

    a is like "a" in father unless it is final

    a is usually pronounced "aw" as in law at the end of a word; if the vowel preceding this is also "a," it is likewise pronounced "aw"

    d and t are pronounced with the tongue close to the teeth, while for dh and th the tip of the tongue touches the roof of the mouth.

    For further details on Indonesian see *An Indonesian-English Dictionary* by John M. Echols and Hassan Shadily (Ithaca: Cornell University Press,

1989); for Javanese see *Javanese-English Dictionary* by Elinor Clark Horne (New Haven: Yale University Press, 1974).

NAMES AND TITLES

Names are spelled according to the usage of their bearers. Thus, Muljono and Djoko rather than the modern Mulyono and Joko or the alternative Mulyana and Jaka. I have avoided the use of honorifics—not out of disrespect but because they do not sit well in the discourse of the Western academic world. To do it right would entail either false democratization of a highly status conscious society—adding the same title, Bapak or Pak, in front of all the mens' names—or the unwieldiness of full titles such as Raden Ngabei (Martopangrawit) or Kangjeng Raden Tumenggung for (Wasitodiningrat) that can change every few years if the individual has active connections with a royal court.

NOTATION

Javanese *gamelan* music is most clearly and economically represented by a system of cipher notation (used for most of the examples in this book) that has been widely adopted in this century. The pitches of *sléndro* are indicated 1 2 3 5 and 6 in ascending order with no a priori hierarchy; *pélog* pitches are numbered 1 2 3 4 5 6 7. Pitches an octave higher have a dot above the number, while a dot below signifies pitches an octave below the middle register. Since *gamelan* tuning varies greatly both in absolute pitch and in the relative size of intervals, cipher notation provides a flexible representation that does not imply a specific tuning. Duration is indicated by graphic spacing: beats are equidistant on the page, and subdivisions are grouped with horizontal beams similar to Western notation. Musical units are almost exclusively binary and end-weighted so the last beat in a group of four is stronger and more important than the preceding ones. Like tuning, this trait is also poorly represented by staff notation. For the benefit of those readers who are unaccustomed to cipher notation I have included a few examples in staff notation as an approximate translation. The transcriptions are highly selective, excluding rhythmic nuances and indications of dynamic levels and tempo.

A Sketch of Central Javanese Gamelan

A *gamelan* can range from a handful of portable instruments played by three or four musicians to a large array with as many as twenty-five instrumentalists and ten to fifteen singers. The instruments of a *gamelan* constitute a matched set with a more or less unique tuning that inhibits the transfer of instruments other than tunable drums and stringed instruments from one ensemble to another. This uniqueness is reflected in the practice of naming a *gamelan*; the principal gongs may also have individual names and receive offerings. A large *gamelan* is beyond the means of most musicians—although iron and brass instruments offer cheaper substitutes for the more desirable bronze instruments—and is usually owned by a wealthy patron, a shadow play puppeteer, or an institution such as a bank, school, or government office.

In one form or another the ensemble music of *gamelan* has been enjoyed and performed by Javanese from social levels ranging from beggars in the streets to kings. A broad, ever-changing tradition of indefinite antiquity encompasses an array of socially and regionally defined variants. Within the swirl of modern life, with its inescapable overlay of pop music, *gamelan* and associated performance arts continue to be valued by a fairly broad sector of the public and evince relatively moderate responses to modernization and outside influences.

The terms *klenèngan* and *uyon-uyon* denote performances of *gamelan* alone, without dance or theater. These typically occur at family celebrations such as weddings, circumcisions, and birthdays but in this century have also spread to radio broadcasts. Public *gamelan* concerts other than *gamelan* competitions are a rarity. *Gamelan* music is also integral to traditional Javanese theatrical genres and to modern innovations that have grown out of these genres. The types of theater that are most prominent and most important for this book are *wayang kulit*, shadow theater using flat puppets carved of water buffalo hide, and *wayang wong*, in which actors sing, dance, and act. Both types of theater involve substantial improvisation, drawing on a large, well-known stock of plots, characters, modes of speech, verbal formulas, musical compositions, and choreographic elements. The term "puppeteer" hardly begins to do justice to the many roles and complex competence of the *dhalang* who is the central performer in *wayang kulit*. He (or occasionally she) creates the story, narrates, speaks for the puppets in a range of voices, and moves them as well as singing and directing the *gamelan*. The *dhalang*'s role and his interaction with musicians will be discussed toward the end of this book. In the closely related genre of *wayang wong*, too, a *dhalang* participates and controls certain aspects of the performance although his role is far more circumscribed since the actor/dancers speak their own lines and make their own moves.

Gamelan accompanies many types of dance in various social contexts and with connotations ranging from exquisitely refined female court dances invested with mystical meaning through displays of martial prowess or feminine beauty to performances with links to prostitution. Some types of dance overlap with theater, representing *wayang* episodes and even including a *dhalang* in a drastically reduced role.

In this brief overview the instruments of a *gamelan* are presented according to instrument type and principal musical function (time-marking instruments, basic melody instruments, elaborating instruments, drums). For notated examples and more detailed descriptions of the individual idioms, see Sutton 1982 or 1993. Gongs of various sizes, pitches, and timbres provide a regular rhythmic framework for most *gamelan* music, marking phrases and groups of phrases or adding syncopated drive. All have bosses and are carefully tuned to specific pitches. A *gamelan* usually includes two very large hanging gongs (*gong ageng*) about a yard in diameter that are lower in pitch than all the other instruments and are very sonorous with a distinctive amplitude vibrato (see Giles 1974). One or the other of these is played at the end of most musical cycles. One to six slightly smaller and higher-pitched gongs (called *gong suwukan* or *gong siyem*) are played to mark cycles in the shortest pieces or to emphasize certain phrase endings. The smallest hanging gongs commonly used are *kempul*. They are about one and a half feet in diameter, range in number from three to eleven, are pitched slightly higher than the *gong suwukan*, and are used to mark smaller musical units. *Kenong* are horizontally suspended gongs pitched in the octave above the *kempul* and struck with a harder mallet, producing a longer, more ringing tone. In most pieces *kenong* strokes mark phrase ends. The *kethuk* is a single, small, horizontal gong with a dull, damped sound that is played in a syncopated manner marking the middle of a beat or a group of beats. The smallest gong, *kempyang*, is played singly or in a pair to mark even smaller temporal divisions; it has a ringing sound one and a half or two octaves higher than the *kethuk* with which it is paired. Occasionally one finds two smaller hanging gongs, *engkuk* and *kemong*, which are used instead of the *kempyang* to demarcate further subdivisions.

A *bonang* consists of ten, twelve, or fourteen small gongs suspended horizontally in two rows. Unlike the other gongs of the *gamelan*, the *bonang* is played melodically and is usually one of the leading instruments in the ensemble. A smaller *bonang panerus* tuned an octave higher is usually played twice as fast in close relationship to the melody of the main *bonang*. In some areas a slow abstraction of the melody is played on a large *bonang panembung*, tuned an octave lower.

Most *gamelan* have several trough-resonated metallophones in three sizes: *saron demung*, *saron barung*, and *saron peking*. Each is an octave higher than the previous one and usually has seven keys.[1] The *saron* are all struck with wooden mallets producing a clear, ringing tone that fades quickly. In most pieces musicians play the *balungan* melody on the two larger *saron* and a simple elaboration of this melody on the small *saron peking*. Other elaborations may also be played on the larger *saron* in certain circumstances.

The other metallophones in a *gamelan* differ from the *saron* because they have thinner keys suspended over individual resonators and these keys are struck with padded mallets producing a softer, more sustained sound. The *slenthem* has seven keys and is usually assigned the *balungan*. Its soft but rich tones, one octave lower than the largest *saron*, provide a foundation for the other melodic instruments. The multioctave *gendèr barung* has twelve to fourteen keys that are smaller than those of the *slenthem*. It is in many ways the heart of the *gamelan* (see Sumarsam 1975). Using two padded mallets, the *gendèr* player produces a smooth, polyphonic elaboration of the main melodic flow of the piece that blends subtly with the other instruments and provides continuous underpinning for the more percussive sounds of the *saron* and *bonang*. The smaller *gendèr panerus*, tuned an octave higher, is similar in construction. It is also played with two mallets, but most of the time the player's two hands

1. Some *saron barung* have nine keys; others may have only six.

pélog: 1 2   3   4 5 6 7   or 1 2   3   4   5   6   7
               | | | | | | | | | | | | | |
               | | | | | | | | | | | |
sléndro: 1   2   3   5   6   1   2   3   5   6

Fig. 1 Common correspondences between sléndro and pélog tunings

interlock to create a single melody that ripples along at maximum density.

Additional elaborating instruments are made of materials other than bronze. Three of these are played at the same speed as the gendèr panerus: the gambang, a xylophone, is played in parallel octaves; the siter and celempung are zithers plucked with the thumbnails. Free-form melodies that range farther away from the main melody than any other part are played on the suling, an end-blown duct flute (see Brinner 1993). The leading melodic part is played on the rebab, a bowed spike fiddle, and is closely related to the vocal parts sung by female soloists and male chorus. Male solos and parts for female or mixed chorus also occur in some pieces. The kendhang, double-headed barrel drums of several sizes, are played by one or two drummers to control temporal aspects of a performance.

This brief list covers the main instruments of the typical full gamelan. A few other instruments are added for particular pieces, and some pieces are played on a subset of the full gamelan. Some ensembles such as gamelan gadhon and gamelan cokèkan include just a few of these instruments. The Central Javanese courts also have several types of ceremonial gamelan that differ significantly in instrumentation and repertoire.

The two tuning systems (laras) of Javanese music, sléndro and pélog, have five and seven pitches to the octave, respectively. A full gamelan is actually two separate sets of instruments with only rebab, kendhang, and the biggest gongs in common. The sléndro and pélog sets are normally played in alternation rather than simultaneously. They usually have one or two pitches in common; figure 1 shows two possible correspondences, with the spacing of the numbers approximating the interval sizes. Since there is no standard tuning, both the absolute pitch and the intervallic relationships within each scale vary and establish the character of particular sets of instruments. This intonational variety is heightened because the singers and the rebab player deviate from the fixed tuning of the gamelan. In certain sléndro passages they may even leave the scale temporarily, introducing intervallic structures typical of pélog.

Within these two laras the pitch system of Javanese gamelan is organized in terms of several complexly interrelated modes (pathet) that will be discussed at length in chapter 2. The essence of each mode is difficult to define: pitch relationships and stereotypical melodic patterns differ from one mode to the next, but no one pitch serves as the finalis or tonal center for a given mode. The three *sléndro* modes share the same pitch resources while the *pélog* modes tend to favor different pentatonic subsets of the seven available pitches. For the present it is sufficient to know that these *pathet,* which are associated with particular times of day, moods, and theatrical conventions, influence musicians' melodic choices, particularly when performing on instruments such as the *rebab* and *gendèr,* and that each piece is identified with a particular *pathet* but some pieces modulate.

The melodies that unfold within the framework of *laras* and *pathet* are realized differently in accordance with the various vocal and instrumental idioms. This results in a richly heterophonic flow of divergent lines moving at different speeds, but following similar paths and converging on focal pitches at phrase endings. The *balungan* played on the metallophones is just one aspect of this flow, prominent in volume because it is played in unison by several musicians but usually not in speed because it is relatively slow-paced. Since the *balungan* is played on instruments with a small range (about one octave), musicians generally consider the full scope of the melodic flow to be more accurately realized by other parts, in particular the *rebab* melody, which ranges over two octaves. Some of the instrumental parts are elaborations on the pitches of the *balungan;* others are related more directly to the essence of the melodic flow.[2]

There are four principal aspects to the temporal framework of Javanese *gamelan:* patterns of stress, metrical colotomic structures, density ratios, and tempo. As a rule *gamelan* rhythm is end-weighted, the greatest stress falling on the last beat of a four-beat unit (*gatra*) and the end of the second *gatra* "weighing" more than the first. The cyclical structures that pervade Javanese music are demarcated by hierarchically organized, end-weighted, colotomic patterns played on the different types of gongs (fig. 2). Within this framework all of the parts other than the rhythmically free vocal, *rebab,* and *suling* melodies stand in constant rhythmic relationships to one another. Some elaborating parts (*gambang, siter,* and *bonang panerus*) are played at the highest density while others (*bonang, gendèr, saron peking*) are played at half this speed. The rhythmic relationships between these high-density parts and the basic beat vary depending on the directions of the *kendhang* player, which are expressed

---

2. There is a vital debate, too extensive to discuss here, over the true nature of the *balungan* and the relationship linking different melodic elaborations to some abstract conception. See Sumarsam (1984b), Sutton (1979), and Supanggah (1988) for differing views.

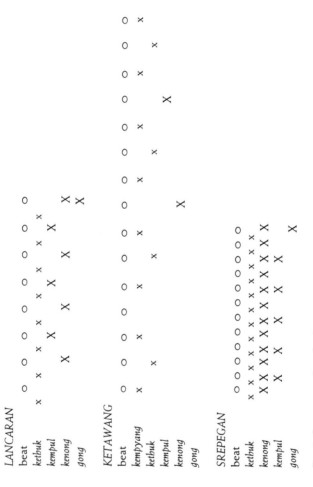

Fig. 2 Some examples of colotomic structures

Irama	Ratio (basic beat/fastest part)	Duration of a 32 beat cycle
Irama Lancar 1 : 2	X X X X X X X X X X X X X X X X xxxxxxxxxxxxxxxxxxxxxxxxxxxxxxxx	about 8 seconds
Irama Tanggung 1 : 4	X X X X X X X X xxxxxxxxxxxxxxxxxxxxxxxxxxxxxxxx	about 15 seconds
Irama Dados 1 : 8	X X X X xxxxxxxxxxxxxxxxxxxxxxxxxxxxxxxx	about 30 seconds
Irama Wiled 1 : 16	X X xxxxxxxxxxxxxxxxxxxxxxxxxxxxxxxx	about 1 minute
Irama Rangkep 1 : 32	X xxxxxxxxxxxxxxxxxxxxxxxxxxxxxxxx	about 2 minutes

Fig. 3 Irama ratios

through changes in tempo and pattern. Progressing from the fastest to the slowest of the five or six such relationships (irama) generally recognized by Javanese musicians, the duration of the beat is increased by a factor of two while the speed of the fastest parts varies little (see fig. 3).

The bulk of the Javanese gamelan repertoire is cast in a small number of colotomic forms. Collectively these pieces are called gendhing, a broad term that can be used in more restricted fashion to denote only those pieces with fully regular colotomic cycles of 8-, 16-, 32-, 64-, 128-, or 256-beat length. The melody of a gendhing may last one or more full cycles; within a cycle it almost invariably comprises two or four phrases (called kenongan because a stroke of the kenong marks the end of each phrase). Gendhing lampahan are pieces that are less regular and symmetrical, consisting of various combinations of 4-, 8-, 12-, and 16-beat units.[3] The temporal organization of other forms is looser, as we shall see in subsequent chapters.

Many other characteristics define the various genres of gamelan music. The relative prominence of vocal or instrumental parts is one variable, the leading melodic instrument another. In some genres certain parts are omitted altogether: in gendhing bonang, for instance, the bonang is the lead instrument and the singers and players of softer elaborating instruments are silent while in palaran the louder instruments and the rebab are not played.

3. This simplified definition will be refined in chapter 9.

Pieces also vary in affect. *Gamelan* music is called *karawitan*, usually glossed as a derivative of the root *rawit*, meaning elegant. The act of playing is seen as a means of attaining the desirable quality of *halus*-ness (refinement), and the sound is thought to be fitting for meditation. Yet there are a range of contrasting emotions expressed in *gamelan*, and a performance is generally built on contrasts between *regu* (stately) and *pernes* (lively, coquettish), between *soran* and *lirih* (loud and soft).[4]

4. See Brinner (1989/90).

INTRODUCTION

How do they do what they do? This basic question, asked in wonder or perhaps in envy, stems from an appreciation of other human beings' musicality. It implicitly motivates many studies of performance practice and style, though these may be couched in terms of constraints and rules—what one can and ought to do and not do. That this is not an easy question to answer becomes apparent if we turn it on ourselves as musicians and attempt to give a detailed account of how we perform, examining the many types of knowledge upon which we draw, the influence of situational factors, the unspoken assumptions, or the split-second judgments and reactions that are so difficult to verbalize.

Musical competence is an integrated complex of skills and knowledge upon which a musician relies within a particular cultural context. We can sketch the extent and nature of a competence by analyzing the conceptualization, distribution, and utilization of musical and music-related knowledge, particularly in terms of the interrelationships of different types of knowledge as they affect musicians' decisions in performance. These decisions rest on knowledge of how and what to play in circumstances that can be construed socially, musically, and contextually depending on different degrees of formality, simultaneous or consecutive nonmusical activities or events, and aspects of style, pitch environment, and so on.

Even a cursory comparison of musical traditions[1] reveals that significantly different demands may be made of musicians, different skills and types of knowledge may be emphasized and developed, and different standards and means of learning may be established for the assessment and enhancement of a musician's capabilities. Such differences are also manifest within a culture at varying levels of specificity. Understanding the full range of variation of these aspects of musical life is essential to our knowledge of specific musical cultures and of human music-making worldwide, yet in the twenty years since John Blacking broached the question "How musical is man?" (1973) scholarly attention to this complicated issue has been sporadic at best.

This book deals with the spectrum of competence as it varies in type and degree among musicians, taking a broad definition of this group: that subset of a society that possesses at least some of the skills and knowledge necessary to function in at least some of the musical situations typical for that society. Thus, it speaks not only to the experience of professionals or specialists identified as musicians (or some cognate) but also to that of amateurs and all members of musically inclusive societies in which distinctions are made not between musicians and nonmusicians, but between outstanding musicians and everyone else.[2]

Talent and competence are related but separable phenomena: a young musician may be talented (by whatever standard one chooses to apply) and yet not fully competent; conversely, an older person may be an experienced, knowledgeable, and capable musician without being perceived as exceptionally talented. Talent is just one of many factors that may influence the extent and rate of a musician's attainment of competence. Thus, arguments about the nature and mensurability of talent[3] need not cloud the discussion of competence as the term is used in this book—to denote the knowledge and abilities that can engender good, excellent, and superlative performances, rather than the potential for knowledge.[4]

The Chomskyian concept of linguistic competence and its offshoots

1. I use the word "tradition" in a loose and encompassing sense, not to connote venerable history, but to denote shared ways and standards of making music within consensual practical and theoretical frameworks.

2. This description fits the Venda, of course, the nation which John Blacking repeatedly praised for its inclusiveness, its basic assumption that all human beings are musical (1973).

3. For instance, McLeod and Herndon, who define talent as "an innate predisposition to competence," have suggested that it is a Western ethnocentrism (1980: 188), despite the occurrence of analogous concepts elsewhere.

4. "Competence" is not intended to bear the pejorative connotations sometimes associated with the term (e.g., an offhand dismissal of a musician as merely "competent," implying that he or she plays correctly but lacks some quality essential to greatness).

should not be taken a priori as the standard for the more inclusive concept of musical competence proposed here. I prefer to start with the assumption that these competences are essentially different, allowing the phenomenon of musical competence to be judged on its own merits while leaving open the possibility, indeed, the desirability, of comparing it with linguistic competence at a later date. Parallels between music and language are fraught with difficulties; a lengthy comparison of these fields of human activity is unnecessary here (see, e.g., Powers 1980 and Feld 1974). One obvious and crucial difference is that musical competence is usually more specialized in nature and limited to a subset of society while linguistic competence is generally conceived as universal. The two differ further in that the coordination and combination of simultaneous "utterances" are important aspects of musical competence while linguistic competence is exclusively concerned with consecutive statements. Finally, speech pervades nearly all facets of life while musical competence is far more limited in usage and often encompasses more distinctive specializations.

Since musical competence encompasses all the types of knowledge and skills that a musician may need, it is an organic rendering of the "systematics" of a musical tradition—the relationships between the things that are known. Grappling with the defining characteristics of a given competence should lead to an understanding of the inner workings of that musical tradition. It requires that we integrate our knowledge of disparate aspects of the musical tradition by attempting to understand the ways in which such integration takes place in the minds of practicing musicians. Thus, the study of musical competence takes us to the very heart of music-making, to the aesthetic judgments involved in the assessment of performers and the performances that they create, whether in formal "concert" settings or ritual acts, informal entertainment or rehearsals and other learning situations.

The study of musical competence also brings us to a consideration of musical interaction because the interactive knowledge and skills that musicians use in performing together constitute a central part of competence that is complexly entwined with other modes of social interaction. Furthermore, it is primarily in the interaction between musicians that competence is attained, assessed, and altered. A person may study and practice alone for hours on end, but certain aspects of musical practice can be absorbed and developed only through interaction with other musicians as a student, a peer, a follower or leader in an ensemble, even as a rival in a solo tradition. Competence entails not just what an individual knows but how much he or she projects that knowledge or acts on it in the company of others, leading with authority, influencing more subtly, or following meekly or with uncertainty. This musical persona may vary greatly in response to the other musicians present, their familiarity with one another, the degree of comfort they experience in a group setting, and the "chemistry" between them. Musical interaction is influenced, in turn, by musicians' assessments of each other's competence.

The interweaving of these two concerns leads to a variant of my opening question: How do musicians make music together? I am particularly interested in the ways we work together and influence one another when making music together. More aspects of competence are foregrounded in ensemble than in solo performance: differences of degree and type of competence as well as questions of authority, control, and relative independence are all of immediate concern. With the possible exception of aleatoric music and certain types of very free improvisation, ensemble performance tends to place more constraints on musicians, to be more conventionalized, than solo performance. My emphasis on ensemble performance also stems from the fact that Javanese musical practice, from which my primary analyses are drawn, is heavily weighted toward ensembles, with no context for solo instrumental performance. Musical interaction is particularly prominent in traditions, such as those of Java, that are typified by predominantly oral transmission and by a relatively high degree of flexibility in ensemble music-making. In these situations musicians often determine the actual course of a performance through their interaction; the sound product is a "trace" (Nattiez 1991: 12) of that give and take.

In most parts of the world, performers interact with their audience in ways which shape the flow of the performance. They may interact with patrons in particularly important ways or they may rely on specific audience responses. Interaction need not be limited to those physically present: images of composers absent or dead, great performers who have come before, and teachers who have set standards, expectations, and models may all be present in the minds of musicians and audience, exerting a powerful influence.[5] But for reasons of clarity and space the discussion here will focus on performers, taking a broad definition of performance and performers that encompasses not only the full range of professionals and amateurs in all contexts, but also conductors and other musically "mute" participants such as ritual or ceremonial officiants, dancers, and actors who play a part in shaping the performance.

---

5. Ali Akbar Khan's "presence" is so strong at his American school, for instance, that even when absent he is a shaping factor at his students' concerts at the college (George Ruckert, personal communication). Likewise, the American musicians of Gamelan Sekar Jaya who perform Balinese music under Balinese leaders perform markedly better when other Balinese musicians are present, even if the latter only sit and listen (Lisa Gold, personal communication).

Competence and interaction are intimately linked to a host of issues that have attracted the attention of scholars in a number of fields. I have found inspiration or corroboration in a wide variety of writings by ethnomusicologists, cognitive specialists, sociologists, and anthropologists. Ethnomusicologists who have directly addressed the topic of competence include Blacking (1971b), Laske (1977), McLeod and Herndon (1980), and Merriam (1964); many others have included pertinent information or thoughts on the subject in works devoted to other aspects of music. Causative and reflective links between social and musical organizations have been studied by sociologists such as Faulkner (1973) and by ethnomusicologists who are influenced by sociology (e.g., Neuman 1980). Research on issues of memory and the organization and interdependence of different domains of knowledge in the burgeoning field of music cognition is directly relevant to the themes of this book.[6] Some of the most recent contributions are gathered in an issue of *The World of Music* devoted to connections between ethnomusicology and cognitive psychology (Koskoff 1992). Of these, Davidson and Torff's model of "situated cognition" touches on some of the main ideas explored in the present book,[7] but barely mentions the crucial links between interaction and competence. Rather than embark on an extended survey of these references here, I shall comment wherever relevant in the following chapters.

In the course of research for this book I have been struck by the marginality of issues of competence and interaction in most scholarly works. Such references abound, but more often than not they are buried in discussions of other subjects. Sifting through large quantities of material, one finds brief statements such as "so and so leads the group," "a good musician must know," and so on. A deeper look inevitably reveals a far more interesting microcosm of connections, activities, and possibilities. By focusing on these aspects and delving into the expectations and demands typical of particular musical systems, we are bringing the musician to the fore, within the relevant social and cultural contexts. This in itself is a worthy goal,[8] but a study of one type of human action, music-making, may also reveal much about the cultural and social systems within which it occurs, as Harwood and others have noted.[9]

6. Basic music perception, a growing field of research (see, e.g., Dowling and Harwood 1986), is related but not central to the current endeavor and will not be discussed here.

7. I read their work late in the writing of this book.

8. Cf. Dane Harwood's call for moving "to an investigation of the individual music maker in cultural context" (1987: 508).

9. "It is through the flow of behavior—or more precisely social action—that cultural forms find articulation" (Harwood 1987: 506).

The focus on human beings and faculties serves as an anchor for an exploration of human artifacts: musical systems, compositions, instruments.

A focus on musicians must include consideration of the manner in which competence is attained because educational priorities and relationships between particular skills or areas of knowledge are manifested in processes of learning and transmission. Yet we know so little on this subject for most cultures. Henry Kingsbury's (1988) pioneering anthropological study of some of the central institutions and beliefs that shape the transmission of the Western concert tradition of "art music" is a notable exception. *Knowing Music, Making Music* was written in part as an attempt to offer a cross-culturally valid set of questions and subjects for further research into learning processes, a framework that will connect such research with other aspects of music.

The aims of this book, then, are to highlight the importance of competence and interaction as aspects of music-making; to build on previous work in these areas, examining assumptions, approaches, and results; and, finally, to suggest promising ways of dealing with these issues in focused studies and in more broadly comparative ones. Part 1 focuses on competence: three chapters dealing with theoretical issues of competence alternate with chapters on Javanese musical competence. Similarly, general theoretical discussion alternates with empirical analysis of Javanese music-making in the discussion of interaction in part 2. These two main threads of competence and interaction are woven together in the final chapter. The sketch of Central Javanese *gamelan* and the glossary should provide the reader who is not familiar with this music a basis sufficient to follow the arguments in the following chapters (for fuller introductions see Lindsay 1992, Sorrell 1990, and especially Sutton 1993).

The theoretical approaches and concepts presented here have been inspired by a wide range of musics and the scholarship on these musics. Brief illustrative examples are drawn from various types of music to provide a broader empirical grounding for the theoretical discussion than is available in a single musical tradition.[10] Unless otherwise noted, no historical connection between these musics is implied. They are juxtaposed not to exoticize one music and normatize another, but to bring into stark relief contrasting possibilities within the gamut of human musical activity and to lead, perhaps, to a reexamining of some basic assumptions through defamiliarization. The relative exoticness or nor-

---

10. More extensive analyses, focusing on key issues of competence and interaction, are planned as a companion volume.

mativity of a particular music will depend, of course, on the reader's background.

The concepts and approaches proposed in the general chapters of the book form the basis for an inquiry into the specifics of conditions and processes of Central Javanese *gamelan* performance that is based on oral and written sources, recordings, observed performances, and other materials and experience gathered during fieldwork in Indonesia and in the course of sixteen years of studying and performing with Javanese musicians. I began to grapple with issues of competence and interaction in my dissertation, but the scope has been substantially enlarged and the theoretical orientation developed. A wide variety of Javanese musicians have contributed directly and indirectly to this work. Some of the musicians whom I quote most frequently have been associated with institutions of education in the performing arts and have had extensive contact with foreigners; several have been respected and influential far beyond the circles of academically trained musicians and teachers of foreigners. In the course of my research I have had opportunities to observe, talk to, and perform with many other musicians. While their verbal comments are perhaps less memorable and quotable than those of the musicians whom I cite, my thinking on competence and interaction has been shaped by how they interact musically and socially and how they rate and respond to other musicians' competence. The musicians whom I quote cannot claim to speak for all Javanese musicians, yet taken together with the ones who contribute to this book through action rather than words they offer a representative spread which, if not inclusive of every "type" of musician (however one might define such), is at least suggestive of widely held views and areas of disagreement.

In attempting a "thick description"—Geertz's "exceedingly extended acquaintances with extremely small matters" (1973: 20)—of Javanese competence and interaction, I have found Henry Kingsbury's basic operational question "What is at issue?" helpful in focusing my inquiries. Whether reading between the lines of an instructional manual, interpreting musicians' comments or choices, or analyzing less than satisfactory interactions, I have asked what aspects of knowledge and communication are at issue, what musical values or meanings are coming into play. Certain items have been particularly pertinent for interpreting competence and interaction. These include my teachers' structuring of the knowledge that they wished to convey, problems that arise in performance such as failed communications or "black holes" into which coherence suddenly vanishes, and contrasting observations of Javanese and non-Javanese musicians grappling with similar situations in different ways.

The collision of Western and Javanese expectations and cognitive systems, which I have encountered in my own experience as a student, researcher, and teacher of Javanese music and in the attempts of other non-Javanese to come to terms with the values and thought processes associated with Javanese *gamelan*, has been a particularly fruitful source for the study of competence and interaction, validating the utility of bimusicality championed by Mantle Hood (1960) as an approach to the study of a foreign musical tradition. The most direct access to a different way of thinking and making music, one based on different assumptions and expectations about human action and sensation, is gained by making an intense, long-term effort to absorb those ways of music from within, attempting to get inside other peoples' heads and fingers. The failures and obstacles encountered in the course of this endeavor are often as enlightening as the successes, provided one is able to step aside and observe oneself and others, analyzing the problems that arise from clashing assumptions, perceptions, demands, and capabilities, few of which are made explicit. Understanding a music "on its own terms" (whatever that might mean) is a highly problematic and ultimately unattainable goal, as contemporary writings in anthropology demonstrate with regard to culture.[11] Comparison of some sort is inevitable but need not require a constant search for Western analogs. As a musician trained in several types of music current in the West, I did not leave all my cultural baggage at the door and approach the study of Javanese music as a tabula rasa. I have been careful to distinguish between my own perceptions and experiences and those elicited from Javanese, for they certainly differ. My experiences appear to be similar to those of other non-Javanese who have devoted considerable time and effort to this music, but here, too, I do not assume uniformity.

Any comparative study of musical traditions or systems must rest on the assumption that there are bodies of practice and collections of artifacts that can be termed "music" across linguistic, cultural, and social boundaries. In other words we can talk about partially analogous realms of action, thought, and sensation relating to acoustic phenomena in various cultures under the rubric of "music." I make this assumption while acknowledging that there are few, if any, terms that can be mapped precisely from one language or tradition to another.[12] A definition of musical competence should be flexible enough to incorporate types of

---

11. See Clifford and Marcus (1986) or Clifford (1988).

12. See Kingsbury (1988: 143–49, 158–63) and Nattiez (1991: 41–68) for two recent takes on the problematic nature of defining "music" cross-culturally.

knowledge that are clearly outside the domain of music in some cultures but crucial to musical performance in others: knowledge of dance movements or ritual procedures are common examples. Likewise, interaction should be understood in a broader sense—the many contexts in which musicians join dancers, actors, healers, and priests in a web of give and take that propels and paces a temporally defined progression of events. To be a musician in most cultures, one must know considerably more than "musical" things. A complete model of musical competence could reasonably be expected to include such things as mystical or ritual knowledge, an ability to gauge listeners' tastes, skill in negotiating with patrons, and so on.

It should be taken as axiomatic that virtually every aspect of music-making to be discussed here varies just as the concept of music does. Important differences separate one culture or society from another, one group from another, and even one individual from another within these groups: "participants in a performance do not necessarily share a common experience or meaning; what they share is only their common participation" (Bruner 1986: 11). Rather than repeat this disclaimer ad nauseam, I ask the reader to bear this variability in mind.

This book is written on the assumption that there is a complex of knowledge and practice subsumable under the rubric of Javanese culture. That such a rubric is not merely a political or scholarly invention is evident in a widespread and well-developed sociocultural sense of identity—of which *gamelan* is a powerful emblem—and in extensive Javanese concern with the essence, gradations, and limits of Javaneseness. The reality of this culture is also recognized by other Indonesians who live under Javanese cultural hegemony. On the other hand, Javaneseness subsumes a variety of experience and knowledge and varying degrees of command of that knowledge, evident in geopolitical attributions and codifications of difference (see Sutton 1991a); this holds even within the dominant court-centered culture of Surakarta. The limited usefulness of a concept of an "average" Javanese musician is demonstrated in chapter 4: differences in competence are related to the social and cultural contexts in which particular musicians have attained competence and interacted in performance. While avoiding a rigid typology that would contrast court and village musicians, for example, in a manner far too simplistic to reflect the complexities of real life, I have indicated the dimensions of variation in competence and some of the correlations between sociopolitical associations and musical experience. I hope that my discussion of musical competence will contribute to the understanding of the nature of difference within this not-so-monolithic Javanese culture. One of the main points in my analysis of Javanese competence and interaction is the accommodation of different types and levels of competence within an encompassing musical world.

Javanese music does appear to be a coherent world for most of its practitioners, and I shall present it as such while recognizing the significant differences that may obtain between musicians' knowledge—their coherent worlds (cf. Clifford 1988: 31). There are other kinds of music performed in the ethnically Javanese parts of Java, including various popular styles that have links to Indian film music and to American and European musical styles. Yet relatively few *gamelan* musicians appear to be significantly competent and active in other types of music. Some exceptions are noted in the discussion of multiple competence.

This investigation of Javanese *gamelan* music is primarily synchronic: my goal has been to investigate musical competence and interaction as they are currently played out in Central Java. It is not really possible to divorce synchronic from diachronic since "cultural change, cultural continuity, and cultural transmission all occur simultaneously in the experiences and expressions of social life" (Bruner 1986: 12). Not wishing to evoke a timeless present or to imply an undue degree of stability, I have noted aspects and issues of competence that have changed in this century and possible agents of change, but these comments do not amount to a full-fledged history of Javanese musical competence(s). Almost all of the musicians with whom I have discussed issues of performance seem to have little understanding of how things came to be the way they are (before their own lifetime) and relatively little interest in such questions. This is not to say that a historically motivated analysis of competence is either unnecessary or impossible. In my estimation of the sources available at present it is more difficult to achieve and less relevant to musicians' interests than the essentially synchronic analysis that I have pursued. Such a history would also expand the scope of the present work greatly, precluding the discussion of musical interaction that is an essential complement to competence, because it would need to deal with colonial history, the impact of the modern world, and cultural politics on local, national, and international levels.

In particular, the role of educational institutions in the formation and alteration of competence in twentieth-century Java deserves far lengthier discussion than I could provide here. The experiences of the many non-Indonesians who have turned to the study of Javanese music have likewise been shaped by educational and political agendas and institutions that are probably completely invisible for many of the participants. These, too, merit closer study, perhaps as part of a larger exploration of the trend toward the study of non-Western musics that has grown enormously since the 1960s.[13] While I could not do justice to the development of Indonesian performing arts schools under the influence of Dutch colonial institutions, nationalist movements such as Taman Siswa, and various non-Indonesian cultural and educational models, I have sketched some ways in which government-sponsored performing arts schools have taken over the roles of royal court performing ensembles in chapter 4. I also contrast traditional methods of transmission with the rationalized, notation-based approaches to formulaity developed at such institutions (chap. 6) and discuss changes in interaction induced by innovations in theater created at the academy (chap. 9).

13. Ruckert has contributed important insights into this trend in the realm of North Indian music (1994). Relevant documents for *gamelan* include Sorrell (1990) and various issues of the journal *Balungan*.

PRELUDE: TWO PERFORMANCES

A RECORDING SESSION

On an intensely hot May morning at the beginning of the dry season in
Central Java, seven musicians converge on a small house in Solo for a
recording session. Coming by pedicab, bicycle, and motorcycle, they
gather in the front room for tea and small talk. When everyone has
arrived, they move into the adjoining room and seat themselves on mats
at a small set of Javanese instruments, a *gamelan gadhon.*

After words of welcome from the host and a brief discussion of the
program, one musician tunes the *rebab*[1] and then plays a brief melodic
formula to identify the mode of the upcoming piece and test the tuning
of the strings and the placement of his fingers. Satisfied with the tuning,
he begins the introductory phrase of the first piece. The drummer joins
him for the last five beats, cuing other musicians to enter on the last
note of this phrase, which is marked by a stroke on the gong. The group
begins to play more or less in unison, but as the drummer gradually
slows the tempo, the *gendèr* and *gambang* players begin to subdivide the
beat by two, then by four and eight, filling in every rhythmic crevice,
while the *rebab* player begins to ornament the melody and deviate from
the beat (see appendix). The singer waits for the others to settle into a
slow tempo before adding her voice, following the *rebab* melody in loose
imitation and languid disregard of the beat. Finally, the *suling* player adds

1. See "A Sketch of Central Javanese *Gamelan*" for descriptions of instruments and other
introductory material. Javanese terms are also defined in the glossary.

high trills and cascading phrases in similarly free rhythms. The whole ensemble is now playing, bathing the room in an exquisite richness of sound, thick enough to feel and sweet enough to distract from the intense heat that is building inside the unventilated concrete room.

The first composition, a rarely performed piece titled Gendhing Lungkèh, lasts more than half an hour. During the next few hours the musicians play several other compositions of similar length, pausing briefly to eat and chat between pieces. Several times in the course of each piece the pace changes seamlessly, individual musicians adjusting the rhythmic density of their own parts in concerted action that is led with the subtlest of hints by the drummer and the *rebab*. Despite the difficulty of these rarely performed pieces, only one or two of the musicians read notation while playing; a few of the others consult notation briefly between pieces.

How do they know what to do and when to do it? Offering short answers to these questions would trivialize the extent of the musicians' accomplishments and the complexity of their cooperative efforts. They will be answered at length in the following chapters. Here I simply wish to demonstrate how this musical encounter can be better understood by considering issues of competence and interaction.

I convened this recording session as part of a research project on musical memory, not as a test of competence or as an experiment in musical interaction, but it turned out to be both of the latter despite the contrived nature of the occasion. At other performances there are usually more musicians and listeners in a larger performance space. The *gamelan* performance is usually just one of several activities, lasting several hours longer than this recording session with less manipulation of the choice of musicians and pieces by a nonperformer. The choice of pieces would be determined by the leading musician(s), who would take into consideration the occasion (certain pieces are traditionally played at celebrations of weddings or births, for instance) and his assessment of the taste of the audience and the abilities of his fellow musicians with reference to the parts that they happen to be playing on that occasion. In spite of these differences the session did turn out to be a "laboratory" of sorts, validating observations I had made on other occasions that were less influenced by my presence. A few salient aspects of this occasion will serve to introduce issues that will be discussed more fully in subsequent chapters.

These musicians know "the music" differently. The *rebab* player, Wahyapangrawit, is a master musician who knows hundreds of compositions in great detail. While he probably could have played Lungkèh at a moment's notice, he requested that I notify him before the session to ensure a better performance. One day's warning was sufficient for him to review the pieces for this session and revive his memory of the overall form, the basic course of the melody, and the idiosyncratic aspects of the *rebab* realization of each piece. By contrast, Tukinem, one of the most prominent singers in Central Java today, gave a beautiful rendition of each of these pieces without any specific preparation. In fact, she claimed that she does not know them and that she knows very few pieces, meaning that she would not be able to perform them alone. As *rebab* player on this occasion, Wahyapangrawit bore chief responsibility for expressing the melodic potential of the composition and guiding other musicians in the execution of their own parts. Tukinem followed the *rebab* melody, drawing on her large stock of vocal phrases and texts as well as her knowledge of how these phrases correspond to *rebab* melodies and to the forms of Javanese music. Tukinem says that she also listens to other parts, in particular the slow *balungan* melody that is played on the *slenthem* at a steady rate of one note for every one or two beats (in Gendhing Lungkèh and most other *gamelan* compositions). It is this melody that is represented in the notation; it is sparse enough and the notation economical enough to allow long pieces to be represented in a condensed fashion on one or two pages. All of the musicians who participated in this performance except Tukinem can read notation, but most use it only for reference when learning or reviewing a piece, not for performance.

The *gendèr* player, Sukamso, was not as familiar as Wahyapangrawit with Lungkèh, so he referred to *balungan* notation occasionally while playing, glancing briefly at it to absorb a fairly large chunk—sixteen-beat phrases lasting a bit more than thirty seconds—then looking away until it was time to grasp the next segment. He was able to grasp the gist of the piece in this manner because most of these segments were familiar from other pieces and because the *balungan* constitutes a type of shorthand. It does not directly represent the part to be played on the *gendèr*, but it evokes certain possibilities. To interpret the piece in an acceptable manner—there is no single correct rendition—Sukamso drew on many types of knowledge, including other pieces with analogous passages, a stock of patterns and their common usage, and a highly developed sense of Javanese modal practice, all the while monitoring the *rebab* player's melodic choices in order to create and sustain compatible interpretations of the piece.

The drummer's primary focus and responsibility is controlling the temporal flow of the performance with the utmost smoothness and instigating shifts in tempo with a few well-paced strokes. He plays a key role even in pieces such as Lungkèh which have very sparse *kendhang* parts.

Since a given drum pattern can be used for many different compositions, a drummer can know a piece in considerably less melodic detail than *rebab* and *gendèr* players do. He must know the form and idiosyncratic rhythmic aspects of the piece, maintaining a clear conception of the flow of the piece in performance. One prominent drummer showed me a minuscule notebook in which he had condensed the drumming requirements for virtually the entire repertoire by limiting the information for each piece to the melodic introduction, a schematic representation of the form, and comments on or notation for any atypical aspects such as a short phrase or a special transition between sections. In this session, however, the *kendhang* was played by Wakidjo, a widely recorded and emulated drummer who is also a fine *rebab* player. His knowledge of the piece clearly extends beyond the minimum necessary for his role, and he was far more actively engaged than the sparse drum part might indicate: seated in the middle of the room, he followed the lines of the various parts, keeping track of the melody as it ran its course through the form and silently lifting a finger to mark off the largest phrases for the benefit of those of us who were listening to the performance.

Wakidjo's influence over the other musicians was greater at certain points in the course of the piece. As the end of each large phrase and section was approached, he carefully controlled a retard leading to the last beat, then reestablished the tempo in concert with the *gendèr* player. He cued the transition from the first section of the piece to the second by accelerating. This brought everyone back to the initial tempo and caused the *gendèr* and *gambang* players to perform shorter melodic cells at a lower rate of subdivision. As the second section began, he slowed the tempo down again with a few deftly timed strokes. Finally, after several repetitions of the second section he cued the end of the piece by accelerating and then retarding the beat and switching to a special ending pattern on the drum. The smoothness of these interactions was due not only to Wakidjo's mastery but to the other musicians' competence: expecting certain cues at particular "places," they were ready to respond to the subtlest of messages.

Although the musicians all paid attention to the *balungan* while performing Lungkèh, only Suyadi actually had to know it note for note because he played it on the *slenthem*, providing the foundation for the other more elaborate parts. He has memorized an exceptionally large number of pieces, as is appropriate for his usual roles at the radio station, where he plays the leading melodic instruments *bonang* and *rebab*. Knowledge of each of these parts strengthens his ability to play the other parts. On the other hand, Tarnopangrawit, the *suling* player, was able—like Tukinem—to perform Lungkèh without knowing it because his part follows after the others and is only loosely tied to them (Brinner 1993). This strategy is possible, but less satisfying, when applied to *gambang*. Other musicians find it irritating when applied to *gendèr* because the *gendèr* part is so central to the conception of the piece.

We can extend our understanding of differing types of competence by learning a bit more about these musicians and the contexts in which they have performed. Ranging in age from late twenties to seventies, they all know each other; most have performed with one another in various groupings, but they had never performed together in this particular configuration. Some of them come from villages, but most live in Solo, where their performing careers are all centered. They play Solonese style, and some of them—notably Tukinem, Wakidjo, and Wahyapangrawit—are famous enough to serve as exemplars of it through recordings, broadcasts, and live performances. The others, while less famous, are well-known among musicians in the area. They derive their competence from a wide array of experiences.

Wahyapangrawit is currently the head of the *gamelan* at the government radio station, and Wakidjo is also prominent in this organization. Most of the others have also played there as regular employees, reporting to work daily for live broadcasts and prerecorded performances. As a result they have performed all genres of *gamelan* music including various types of theatrical performances that utilize *gamelan* and they have covered vast amounts of material. This in turn has required more rehearsals and more frequent use of notation for learning new pieces than most Javanese musicians would encounter. It has also afforded them many more recording opportunities and frequent invitations to play at private celebrations. Upon reaching mandatory retirement age, radio musicians tend to gravitate toward the two royal courts of Solo, where they have played frequently over the years.[2]

All of the musicians at this recording session, with the exception of Sukamso, perform regularly at one or both of the courts. This brings them into contact with repertoires and performance practices that are not commonly known outside court circles. However, they have not been immersed in this milieu to the same extent as previous generations since court musicians no longer form as large, vibrant, and hereditary a community as they did in the earlier years of this century when many of them lived in the same neighborhood and the courts supported a much more frequent schedule of performances. Thus, these musicians

---

2. Musicians from the radio station often participate in the regularly broadcast concerts at the two Solonese courts.

today are familiar with court practices but do not consider them an exclusive touchstone for authenticity of knowledge and practice.

Much of the musical legacy of the courts has been transferred to two government institutions for performing arts education, a high school conservatory and a college-level academy,[3] where Sukamso has studied and taught. Wahyapangrawit and Wakidjo acquired their knowledge outside these schools but recently have joined the faculty as guest teachers because of their expertise and reputations. As a result of his education Sukamso has a far more explicit theoretical model of musical practice than the other musicians at my recording session. His competence also extends to many other types of *gamelan* music—including contemporary innovations and traditions from other parts of Indonesia—that are beyond the realm of their experience.

Most of these musicians have obtained their knowledge largely through performance rather than formal instruction. Tarnopangrawit started his education as a dancer, then learned to play in a children's group sponsored by a local noble; he has had very little formal training but extensive experience in many performance contexts. Several others have learned from older family members or taught younger ones. For instance, Wakidjo has younger brothers who are also successful musicians while Paimin began his career by performing with his older brothers.

One of the most common contexts for *gamelan* performance is theater, particularly shadow plays. In addition to his position at the radio station, Wahyapangrawit plays *rebab* for Anom Soeroto, the most famous *dhalang* in Java today. Shadow plays involve interaction that is fundamentally different from other types of *gamelan* performance. As a *rebab* player Pak Wahya must have extensive knowledge of a large repertoire of pieces with their theatrical associations so that he can respond to a cue at a moment's notice by playing one of several hundred pieces. He must know the piece well enough to sustain a conception of it with almost no support from other musicians while the *dhalang* narrates (only the *gendèr* joins with him in this effort). Other musicians who participated in my recording session also have extensive experience in theater. Tarnopangrawit, for instance, was a musician in an itinerant troupe that performed *kethoprak*, a type of theater with human actors that differs from *wayang kulit* in musical conventions and repertoire.

---

3. Sekolah Menengah Karawitan Indonesia (SMKI) and Sekolah Tinggi Seni Indonesia (STSI), respectively. These institutions used to be known as Konservatory Karawitan (KONSER or KOKAR) and Akademi Seni Karawitan Indonesia (ASKI).

Neither the gathering nor the seating of these musicians was straight-forward. One musician had felt some discomfort at a previous session involving many of the same musicians because he had made some mis-takes which made him look bad in front of his inferiors. I did not learn this directly from him but through a chain of three intermediaries—a social interaction that is fairly typical in Central Java. Another of the musicians had to be soothed at the last minute with a letter because he felt that he had not been invited as officially as the others. He felt slighted, too, since some of the others had been displeased with his *rebab* playing at the previous session and had suggested that he take a less important role in this one. To my mind this was probably more of an issue than the problem of the invitation. In a sense we were both victims of a status game: he had helped me convene the previous recording ses-sion and had delighted me by gathering some of the very best musicians at short notice, but having brought in these higher-status musicians it was no longer appropriate for him to take a leading role. Had I asked him to convene the second session, I would have slighted the higher-status musicians.

Only after these matters of relative status were smoothed out was it possible to proceed with the recording. Moving from the sitting room to the *gamelan* was in itself an elaborate social choreography with musical overtones. It was clear that Tukinem would sing, Wakidjo would drum, and Tarnopangrawit would play *suling* because these three are well known for their mastery in these roles. Matching the others to the re-maining instruments was less straightforward since each of them could have played any of these instruments well. The roles that these musi-cians play vary with context and the status and competence of the other musicians present; those who were relatively low in the social hierarchy in the group that I recorded are recognized as leaders in other groups. As the youngest musician, Paimin "knew his place" and after polite hesi-tation sat at the least prominent instrument, the *gambang*, while others shuffled their feet in the doorway, trying to defer to their colleagues with words or actions such as sitting at the gong or retreating to an adjacent room. Two of the musicians had to be personally invited to play specific instruments. Some of this seeming awkwardness was un-avoidable, a typical acting out of deference and suppression of self-interest that is fundamental to being Javanese. Some was the residue of the problematic *rebab* playing at the earlier session noted above. There was also some consternation over the presence of an "extra" musician, who had not participated in the previous session. This person had been invited at the behest of one of the leading musicians to improve the level of performance and to enable Tarnopangrawit to concentrate on *suling* rather than splitting his attention between gong and *suling* as he had done at the earlier session. In the end everything worked smoothly and an arrangement was achieved that most musicians judged optimal for this group. All of this shuffling and adjusting depended on mutual assessments of competence and status modulated by personality traits such as relative extroversion or humility. Such delicate webs of social stances and acts are predicated on the assumption that all concerned understand and abide by the same conventions. Occasionally I have seen these conventions ignored by an aristocrat, for example, who pushes lower-class musicians aside verbally or physically to take a leading instrument. Through real or feigned ignorance of these conventions a non-Javanese student of *gamelan* may push his or her way into seemingly vacant positions of responsibility within an ensemble that would have been filled if the play of mutual deference had been allowed to run its usual course.

Since the pieces had been mentioned to most of the musicians when they were invited to the session, the initial discussion was primarily a transition into the business of making music. Conflicting opinions did emerge, however, regarding the optimal sequence of performance. One musician, younger and lower in status than several of the others, spoke out with uncharacteristic lack of deference in favor of an order that seemed motivated mainly by the hope of postponing the most difficult piece on the list so that we would run out of time before playing it. Another musician said that he enjoyed the challenge of playing such difficult pieces. The first musician was overruled, and the order was set in accordance with the conventions that govern the sequence of pieces in most performances.

The illuminative power of an analytical approach based on issues of competence and interaction can be demonstrated by considering an incident that occurred toward the end of the session. At the end of the second phrase of Gendhing Montro Kendho, the *gendèr* player, Muljono, stopped the others to say that the notation he was reading differed from the way they were playing the piece. While he argued with the *slenthem* player, Wahyapangrawit (who was playing *rebab*) hummed through the phrase and decided to play it as it stood in the notation that Muljono was reading.[4] The issue of authority arises here in two overlapping conflicts: notation against aural memory and one musician against others. Muljono was reading from a widely used collection that bears a double stamp of authority: it is published by the academy (STSI) and compiled

---

4. The melody they had been playing was in fact taken from another piece that is closely related to Montro Kendho.

by Mloyowidodo, one of the oldest living musicians in Solo, who is a recognized authority on *gamelan* repertoire. It is doubtful that Muljono's argument would have carried as much force if the notation had been a lesser musician's handwritten collection. Once he pointed out the discrepancy, the authority to decide which version to follow clearly rested in the hands of Wahyapangrawit by virtue of his preeminence as a musician and as head of the radio *gamelan*.

The interactive capabilities of Javanese musicians—the ability to lead with conviction, on one hand, and to adapt rapidly and flawlessly, on the other—are demonstrated by the fact that the conception of the *rebab* and *slenthem* players was strong enough to carry the piece without apparent problems through the first two phrases. Despite the discrepancy with the notation Muljono adjusted with lightning rapidity to the *rebab* and *slenthem* parts. This might have gone on longer had he not referred to the notation. Furthermore, if this had not been a recording session where the quality of the sound *product* was of paramount importance, he would likely have ensured the smoothness of the *process* by continuing to play, simply accepting the *rebab* and *slenthem* players' conception of the piece.

SHADOW PLAY

A few weeks later, in a small village many miles to the south of Solo, a *dhalang* and his troupe of musicians travel to the house of a spiritual leader to mark the beginning of the Javanese year with a *wayang kulit* performance. The instruments are brought in by truck and set up in the main room of the host's house. In the center of the room a large screen is stretched above two banana logs in which the puppets will be placed. The front wall of wooden panels has been removed so the performance space now extends out into the flat empty yard in front of the house.

Village children gather round the *gamelan* to watch the *dhalang's* teenage son make his debut in an abridged performance. Hendro has been studying at the conservatory in Solo, where students receive training in *gamelan*, dance, and *wayang*. He has received methodical training there, but the real feel for *wayang* comes from growing up in a *dhalang's* household—in the eyes of many Javanese this is a hereditary profession. This afternoon he demonstrates considerable mastery of most aspects of the *dhalang's* art. His vocal skills are not yet fully developed, however, and this causes some interesting interaction with the musicians. Toward the end of the performance he starts to sing one of his songs one pitch too high. The musicians follow without noticeable disruption by transposing the accompaniment to this song and all the ensuing pieces into a mode that is not usually initiated at this point in the performance. This brings up two issues of competence: localized knowledge and authority. The musicians switched to *pathet manyuri*, a mode that is common locally but not used by city musicians—it is an aspect of a fairly restricted regional competence (Widiyanto, personal communication). Furthermore, the mode is not officially recognized by the urban arbiters of standards in Javanese performing arts, whose authority derives from (1) institutional associations (they have taught, performed, or trained at a palace or academy), (2) location in urban centers, (3) possession of an explicit theoretical apparatus, and (4) the fixity and prestige of print.

Following Hendro's performance there is a brief *klenèngan*. In the early evening the musicians are served a meal in one of the other houses; then, donning their performing clothes, they walk over to the *gamelan* and begin to play, replacing the recorded music that has been booming from loudspeakers. They play several pieces while the audience gathers.

The audience comes from miles around, walking, boating across the lake, or riding on bikes, motorcycles, vans, or trucks down tortuous dirt roads that wind around. Invited guests sit on metal chairs arranged in rows inside the house. The uninvited gather in the street, and as the show begins they edge closer until they fill the yard and begin to seep into the spaces between the instruments of the *gamelan*. All night long people come and go—the crowd easily exceeds a thousand in the early hours of the night, then thins out around three in the morning and swells again as reinforcements arrive with the approach of dawn. This is a ritual occasion, and people derive benefit from attendance aside from any interest they may take in the performance itself.

Most of the musicians at this performance are villagers who live in the area and perform *wayang* regularly with this *dhalang*, Ki Sutino. Urban musicians tend to view villagers with some disdain: village *gamelan* is generally a pejorative categorization that implies a cruder playing style and a smaller repertoire with "wrong" variants of pieces "derived" from the courts and city. Yet, if one judges the musicians in this troupe not against some foreign (i.e., urban) standard but for what they are—specialists in a localized *wayang* tradition—they are highly competent. A concert piece such as Gendhing Lungkèh which I recorded in Solo is simply not a part of their musical world.

During the dry season they may perform together all night as many as twenty-five nights a month. With this shared history they have become a cohesive troupe, fully accustomed to each other and to Sutino's musical tastes and expectations as well as his means of communicating these expectations. Certain roles and relationships within the group are more important than others for the proper functioning of the ensemble.

The people who play these roles often are connected to the *dhalang* by family ties, reflecting the high degree of familiarity and mutual under- standing that is considered necessary for a good performance. Sutino's regular *gendèr* player is his adopted son and has worked with him for years. He is fully attuned to the pacing of Sutino's singing so that he can properly accompany the many ametrical mood songs that occur throughout a performance. He is also adept at creating a soft, fluid back- drop that is appropriate for the narration and dialogue. This man is an intuitive musician who has an idiosyncratic playing style. He does not explain what he does, preferring simply to demonstrate, in striking con- trast to Sukamso, who participated in my recording session, has a highly explicit knowledge of *gendèr* playing, and is the author (1992) of a lengthy analysis of multiple interpretations of one of the better known pieces in the repertoire.

No less important is the link between *dhalang* and drummer. When- ever the *gamelan* accompanies puppet movement, the drummer is the key intermediary between *dhalang* and *gamelan*. He translates the *dhalang's* cues and guides the other musicians through various changes of tempo and volume, starting and stopping the *gamelan* at the command of the *dhalang*. In addition to these coordinative functions the drummer ampli- fies puppet movement with sound effects, which requires that he antici- pate the *dhalang's* moves. While the *dhalang* has the upper hand in this partnership, he depends on the drummer to support his puppet move- ments and is likely to perform better when he knows what to expect from the drummer—patterns that are a mixture of regional and personal conventions, peppered with spontaneous invention.

This *wayang* performance, like most others, began shortly after dark and lasted until the first light of day. Some musicians stayed awake the whole time while others gave in to fatigue here and there. For the most part this did not hamper the performance noticeably, but the drummer, who teaches school during the day, was so tired that he actually fell asleep while playing and had to be relieved. As dawn approached, one of the *saron* players repeatedly fell asleep with his mallet poised on the instrument, but whenever the drummer cued the beginning of a piece he awoke instantaneously, demonstrating the well-honed reflexes and "automatic" knowledge of pieces that are the trademark of an experi- enced *wayang* performer.

The *dhalang* shaped his story in accordance with conventions that govern the overall framework of the story as it unfolds through three acts constructed from standard scenes. Sutino bent these conventions to his will, pacing the play to suit the solemn occasion. There was rela- tively little joking and rather more philosophizing than usual, which extended the first act well beyond the length that theoretical tracts on *wayang* dictate. The musicians were not confused by this, since important junctures in the progress of the play were marked by particular musical pieces and scene types. Sutino made all of the large-scale musical decisions, choosing which pieces to play and regulating their tempo and duration. In doing so, he exploited the full range of interactive devices that every *dhalang* uses to communicate with his musicians including rhythms tapped with a small wooden hammer, phrases sung as introductions to certain pieces, and allusions to the names of other pieces that were woven into his improvised narration. These communications were smooth and effective because the musicians knew at least approximately what he wanted before he cued them. Their extensive experience with the conventions of *wayang* enabled them to follow the course that Sutino charted through the night, drawing on a large and varied musical repertoire to accompany the *wayang* effectively.

Part One

Knowing Music

CHAPTER ONE

MODELING MUSICAL COMPETENCE

These pieces contain all you need to know.
If you know how to play X then you must know how to play Y.

In one form or another these statements surfaced frequently in my lessons and encounters with Javanese musicians who tried to make sense of what I (and other non-Javanese) could and could not play. Both statements convey assumptions about the nature of competence. Taken at face value, the assurance that a particular group of compositions constitutes a repository of knowledge sufficient to master the rest of the repertoire is false—the innumerable quirks and twists of Javanese music preclude a fully systematic approach to performance based on knowledge of a few pieces. Interpreted more leniently, it does reflect the general usefulness of a formulaic approach to Javanese *gamelan*, one that enables good musicians to perform pieces such as Lungkèh that they may rarely if ever have played before.

Similarly, the second statement is more than an expression of a hierarchy or learning progression of compositions (or instruments and styles, for that matter). Piece X is being named as an index of accomplishment and ability. Often this occurs when a student has performed X passably but then is incapable of performing Y, which is similar and may even be easier to play. This has implications beyond knowledge of repertoire: by the time one can play piece X, one is expected to have mastered particular knowledge and skills. It is tacitly assumed that becoming competent involves the absorption of knowledge in a flexible, transmutable manner that allows transferal of knowledge gained in one musical context to other analogous contexts.[1] Analogy is one of a musician's most powerful tools, channeling the application of generalized music-making procedures to specific frameworks according to perceived similarities between these frameworks. A Javanese drummer can perform Lungkèh "on sight" because it is analogous to numerous other pieces as far as the drumming is concerned.

Musicians' conceptions of what is musically difficult and which knowledge is the key to performance ability are intriguing, particularly when they are at odds with the perspective of an outsider to the complexes of thought and experience that constitute the musical tradition. Such conceptions are just one of many avenues for comprehending a conglomerate of knowledge and skills whose extent and complex structure may well be obscured, at least in part, to the very people who attain it.[2] Observing musicians in action and analyzing my own successes and failures have been no less significant in this search.

The provisional result of this search is a definition of musical competence as *individualized mastery of the array of interrelated skills and knowledge that is required of musicians within a particular tradition or musical community and is acquired and developed in response to and in accordance with the demands and possibilities of general and specific cultural, social, and musical conditions*. This definition leaves open the relationship of competence to performance and is flexible enough to allow us to consider both ideal and actual competences, stressing norms and constraints without precluding individual differences and socially or culturally instituted distinctions. Competence within a community is not an immutable set of facts, for it can differ in accordance with instrument or repertoire as well as age and a host of other factors and it can improve with experience, in the course of performance, and over longer stretches of time in response to the accumulated experience of performing. Thus, while we need to elicit communal ideals, we must also assess particular individuals' knowledge, remaining alert to variant learning progressions and recognizing that these ideals not only derive from individual articulations but influence them in turn.

This definition states that knowledge is contextual, not absolute, in recognition of the fact that most people learn to make music and go on to perform in social settings, in reaction to and in contact and coopera-

---

1. Cf. Davidson and Torff (1992: 129).

2. Writing about rock musicians, Bennett notes that "playing techniques need not be products of formal institutional socialization, and therefore. . .a player cannot be expected to provide a formalized account of play activity. The special awareness of a playing episode means that a player is not in a position to *objectively* analyze what is being done in order to do it" (1980: 191). Cf. Sloboda (1988: xiii).

tion with other humans.[3] It relates the shaping of musical competence both to sociologically and psychologically defined environments of interpersonal relations and to shared conceptual frameworks and practices that are cultural and social in nature. The term "community" is used here in addition to "tradition" to circumvent questions of continuity and transmission. It denotes a group of people who share enough common musical goals and means to enable interaction in performance and audition without a strong sense of adapting to "foreignness." A musical community may be coterminous with the inhabitants of a particular locale, region, or larger sociocultural unit or it may be relatively widespread and therefore interleaved with members of other musical communities. People often refer to a "jazz community," for instance, that spans many regions and is found side by side with, but separate from, other musically defined communities (Dasilva, Blasi, and Dees 1984: 48). Slobin has directed attention to the many groups that are not locally or regionally bounded, acknowledging that members of a community can be widely dispersed but not isolated from one another thanks to electronic media and worldwide transportation networks (1992: 9).

Competences are sometimes viewed simply as "stocks of knowledge" or checklists of things to learn and know. Some sociologists have explicitly characterized social competence in this manner (e.g., Schutz 1976 or Turner 1988), and most Javanese writings about *gamelan* contain a list of types of knowledge, an approach which has also been adopted by Hood (1988). But a checklist tells little of what actually transpires in the mind when acquiring and using these stocks of knowledge. Brief lists of the main types of knowledge necessary for a musician are too schematic while comprehensive ones—if we could compile such—would be too cumbersome, burying inner relationships in a mass of detail. Most important, lists obscure the situational aspect of knowledge.

Rules and conventions, sometimes formalized in a grammar, offer greater order and more powerful explanations than simple lists. McLeod and Herndon emphasize this approach to the analysis of musical knowledge when they link competence to "an idealized conceptualization of possible rules setting a style" (1980: 188). A number of scholars have attempted to formulate such rules, generally constructing grammars that generate well-formed musical utterances. The theory for Western tonal music proposed by Lerdahl and Jackendorff (1983) is the most ambitious of these. Outside the field of Western music most grammatically oriented analyses have been more limited in scope. The most fully elabo-

---

3. Cf. Davidson and Torff (1992: 127).

rated and tested model of musical production of which I am aware is Kippen's study of Hindustani drumming improvisation (1987, 1992). In the study of Javanese music, grammatical approaches to formulating improvisational practices and compositional structures include Sutton 1978, Becker and Becker 1979, Becker 1980, and Hughes 1988 (the only one to include some perceptual testing). It has not been demonstrated that the complexities of an entire musical system can be successfully encompassed in a rigorous set of rules, nor is it clear that such an approach reflects human thought processes just because it produces acceptable results; this is the essence of the ongoing debate over the ability of artificial intelligence to mimic not just the manipulation of symbols but actual thought processes (Gardner 1987: 172–77).

The emphasis in grammars is generally perceptual or generative with respect to some fairly limited corpus. Individual ability to perform is not usually addressed, despite the close relationship between performative competence and generative processes for musicians who improvise to any sizable degree. To the extent that human agency is acknowledged at all, it is only in the role of idealized listener or performer. In the quest for an encompassing understanding of the cognitive demands or challenges posed by a given set of musical practices, we need not assume either a gray, robotic sameness or a lowest common denominator. Rather, our research ought to reflect the gradations and distinctions manifest in any group of musicians, the range of different ways of knowing that underlie various performative capabilities and choices and serve as foundations for exceptional ability and artistry.

To understand how we as humans manage to make music in such complex and varied ways, it is necessary to go beyond lists and rules. Few have attempted a comprehensive treatment of the subject. Blacking took a preliminary stab at the problem, identifying human interaction and "the opportunities which different cultural systems offer for the development of musical talent" (1971b: 19) as crucial factors in the formation of competence. But he was overly concerned with linguistic comparisons and with distancing himself from Western concepts of genius to do much more than stake out a few assumptions and offer some relevant data from his fieldwork with the Venda. Feld has outlined some basic questions concerning the identity of music-makers, patterns of acquisition of musical knowledge, the influence of ideologies of talent on this acquisition, stratifications of competence, and the differences between production and reception skills (1984: 386–87).

The most extensive attempt at modeling musical competence that I have encountered is Laske's *Music, Memory, and Thought* (1977) in which the author proposes a blueprint for the new field of cognitive musicology, identifies the need for studying musicians' competence, and points to the importance of considering process and product, both separately and in terms of the links between them.[4] The heavy influence of computer science and psychology is evident in his formalistic method and his focus on information processing theory which lead to such unfortunate and inherently unmusical formulations as "actual music understanding systems, i.e., human musicians" (1977: 12). Laske also clearly equates musical and linguistic competence, ignoring the many differences between these realms of activity and translating definitions of psycholinguistics to constitute psychomusicology (1977: 25ff.). The strict dichotomy between process and product which Laske posits is convenient for theorizing but far removed from reality. He recognizes the importance of studies of acquisition (1977: 12), but he appears to take a "goal-state" approach to competence itself: he implies that it does not change once it is attained, and he does not differentiate between types of competence within a musical community or tradition.[5] By contrast, I think it essential to consider how competence varies in type and degree within a musical community as the result of individual motivation and ability in response to community options and demands. Furthermore, I see the relative explicitness or intuitivity of various components as one of the most important dimensions of variation in the constitution of particular competences (see the discussion of "ways of knowing" below) while Laske assumes that competence as a whole is tacit (1977: 10).

The approaches advocated in this book differ in several other ways from those of Blacking, Laske, and Feld. I do not posit a unitary competence either for a given culture as Laske implies or for humanity as Blacking envisioned when he wrote that "we must look for the facts which will lead us towards a theory of universal musical competence" (1971b: 33). I see social stratification, which dominates Feld's agenda, as just one of a broad range of social considerations that influence the shaping of musical competence. Laske's theory does not recognize that extensive aspects of competence are socially constructed and evaluated through interpersonal interaction, that musicians, in their roles as teachers, stu-

---

4. I discovered this monograph (which does not appear to have reached a wide audience) only at a late stage of my own work long after deciding to focus on the dichotomy between procedural and declarative knowledge that is also central to Laske's model.

5. Laske contrasts analyses of initial state (plans, resources, "musical systems"), goal state (produced music, scores), and intermediate state ("the link between initial musical states and goal states"). Both initial and goal state deal with musical competence which is "unobservable knowledge" (1977: 7–8).

dents, fellow performers, or auditors, are constantly judging competence in comparison with general standards or particular musicians.[6] Finally, I reject the static, ahistorical views of competence implied by
Blacking, Laske, and Feld, preferring a flexible view of competence as
an entity that changes throughout individual lives and over the history
of a community and tradition, as something that can be grasped at a
given moment as a frozen representation of a dynamic, multidimensional flow.

APPROACHES TO MODELING KNOWLEDGE

Musical competence is one of a number of distinct cognitive domains
each of which comprehends a distinct body of knowledge and skill
(Gardner 1984: 259). Scholars in the field of artificial intelligence have
given considerable thought to the modeling of domain-specific competence while attempting to emulate various kinds of human expertise.
Among the explanatory tools proposed are semantic nets, schemata, and
models that favor some mix of declarative or procedural knowledge.[7]
Semantic nets, in which "information is represented as a network of
nodes connected to each other by labeled arcs, each node representing
an object, event, or concept, and each arc a relation between nodes"
(Pressing 1988: 152), offer a means of mapping the layout or structure
of knowledge. Information encoded in these networks is activated by
associations spreading along arcs in a particular region of a network
(Hayes-Roth 1977: 260). Schemata such as rule models, scripts, and
frames offer more localized tools that can be applied to various aspects
of musical cognition. Sloboda, Laske, and others have invoked production systems (in which rules are organized into a program rather than a
grammar) to explain the ways in which humans master particular music-
making tasks.[8] These endeavors usually require such extensive abstraction or the selection of tasks so minute that the results have questionable
relevance to an understanding of the knowledge and activity of real musicians in real situations. If we do not view music (or culture) as thoroughly systematic, the "rigor" advocated by researchers such as Laske

6. The terms "teacher" and "student" are used here in the broadest sense to denote those
who manifest knowledge and those who learn from such manifestations.
7. See Pressing (1988: 151–52) for a brief evaluation of the utility of some of these concepts for modeling improvisational skills in music. Gjerdingen explores schemata in Western
music as he tries "to find a better tool for understanding how knowledgable listeners perceive
many of the sublimely beautiful musical phrases of the eighteenth and nineteenth centuries"
(1988: x).
8. See Sloboda (1985: 216) and Laske (1977: 136ff.).

(1977), Rahn (1983), and Pressing (1988) is not necessarily desirable. Bourdieu's critique of such endeavors is pertinent:

> So long as he remains unaware of the limits inherent in his point of view on the object, the anthropologist is condemned to adopt unwittingly for his own use the representation of action which is forced on agents or groups when they lack practical mastery of a highly valued competence and have to provide themselves with an explicit and at least semi-formalized substitute for it in the form of a repertoire of rules. (1977: 2.)

An interpretative, ethnographic approach based on observed conduct and musicians' concepts and concerns is far more likely to produce an understanding of musical competence that is rooted in human experience.

While none of the approaches enumerated above is sufficient in itself, each can be useful within the context of an encompassing model of competence. Their comparative utility and limitations can be illustrated with regard to the modeling of discrete musical pieces. The grammars proposed by Becker and Becker (1979) and by Hughes (1988) are examples of rule models that generate certain types of Javanese pieces.[9] Such models can represent the interrelationships of pieces with considerable elegance and rigor, but they may also reach great complexity without necessarily reflecting the individual creative decisions or historical processes that shaped the pieces in question or the ways in which musicians conceive of these pieces when learning or performing them.

Scripts and frames can easily be adapted to describe a musical piece—whether fully composed or partially improvised—as it is realized by musicians in performance. A script is a sequence of procedures to be executed. Much of the script of a musical piece may be encoded in the score, if one is used. Lower-level scripts are invoked for the production of individual notes while higher-level scripts incorporate the procedures of performance practice. A hierarchical formulation of this sort does not account for contextual, associative, and symbolic aspects of the piece. Some of these aspects can be captured in frames that "describe collections of attributes of an object . . . [and consist] of slots filled with attributes and associated values" (Pressing 1988: 152). Frames may provide apt models, for example, for the ways in which musicians conceptualize pieces in a repertoire that has complex internal classifications and external associations.

---

9. Pressing defines rule models as "common features shared by a set of rules which form the basis for a production system" (1988: 151). See Perlman (1983) for a critique of the Beckers' model.

These ways of modeling knowledge have dynamic and static qualities that have come to the fore in debates about the relative appropriateness of declarative and procedural models for emulating human intelligence: "Declarativists felt that intelligence rests on a highly general set of procedures which can be used widely, coupled with a set of specific facts useful for describing particular knowledge domains . . . the proceduralists felt that human intelligence is best thought of as a set of activities that individuals know how to do" (Gardner 1987: 161–62). Elsewhere Gardner has glossed declarative knowledge as "know-that" and procedural knowledge as "know-how" (1984). These contrasting concepts are useful so long as we acknowledge that they frequently overlap: an instrumentalist knows, for example, that a particular fingering will produce a certain pitch—fingering charts are declarative tables of all the available fingerings and corresponding pitches—but there are also procedural aspects to the conceptualization of pitches that are intimately linked to the production of these notes both in isolation and in combination (see Sloboda 1985: 218–19).

In the brief history of comparative musicology and ethnomusicology attention has shifted from declarative knowledge of diverse musical cultures, that is, "hard musical facts" such as tuning, scale, and mode, which occupied stage center from the late nineteenth century to the mid-twentieth, to procedural aspects of music, which have been the primary focus of most ethnomusicological work in recent decades. There has also been significant work on the affective aspects of music in particular societies. If we wish to achieve a full picture of what musicians know and how they know it, these complementary perspectives must be integrated. The computer-inspired perspectives outlined here have fairly rich explanatory powers, but they are not fully satisfying: they lack an element of feeling or expression, particularly important in an affective art such as music, that finds no easy parallel in the realm of artificial intelligence. This is perhaps the most difficult aspect of competence to capture in words. While the basic "correctness" or acceptability of a performance may depend on the proper application or execution of procedures within declarative frameworks, feeling and emotional charge are the unquantifiables that distinguish one performance from another qualitatively.

WAYS OF KNOWING

We know things in different ways: intuitively or explicitly, actively or passively, as a way of doing something, as probabilities or as immutable facts, and so on. Distinctions of this sort are essential characteristics of a competence and are manifested in the accessibility of things that we know, in our ability to act on them or talk about them, rationalize and classify them, or trust them to work for us with little or no conscious control. They may influence assumptions that underlie sociocultural constructions of competence, contributing to definitions of the relative importance of different types of knowledge and relationships between distinct musical competences that exist within a given musical community (as we shall see later with regard to the ranking of musicians at one Javanese court). By incorporating these different ways of knowing as they apply within and between domains of knowledge, we enrich our understanding of musical competence, adding dimensions of variability to a model that might otherwise remain little more than an idealized list of lists.

Knowledge that is active is accessible for use while passive knowledge enables a person to understand and respond to something without being capable of producing it. This distinction, commonly invoked with regard to linguistic competence, is an especially useful tool for investigating musical competence because it can be applied to a wide variety of situations. In a given musical tradition, for example, distinctions between different types of competence or specializations may involve varying degrees of active and passive knowledge of particular parts of a general musical competence. Within an ensemble, musicians who play different instruments may need to know each other's parts in a passive sense, without actually being able to produce them actively. In this sense, conductors and instrumentalists in a symphony orchestra exemplify complementary competences: conductors must have at least a passive knowledge of the technique and capabilities of each instrument while each player must have active command of all performative knowledge pertaining to his or her instrument. Conversely, conductors actively use their knowledge of conducting technique while orchestral players must have a passive knowledge of this technique in order to understand and respond to the conductor's indications, but are not called upon to perform the conductor's role. A similar complementary relationship exists in North Indian music: vocalists and players of melodic instruments must have at least a passive understanding of the intricacies of drum cycles and patterns that are the active domains of drummers while the latter may not be able to play a melodic instrument or sing but must know a good deal about melody.

Active/passive distinctions may also clarify the relationships between musical and nonmusical domains within a competence. A Javanese drummer needs at least a passive knowledge of dance in order to coordinate *gamelan* and dance while dancers must be able to recognize the different drum patterns, which are linked with specific dance movements. Some dancers master drumming at a performance level, but as dancers they only require a semiactive knowledge of drumming, often expressed in the ability to recite patterns using mnemonic drum syllables.

The accessibility of a person's knowledge is also manifested in its explicitness, the degree to which that person is aware of knowing something, is aware of the internal organization of that thing, and is capable of expressing that knowledge in some way. The contrast between explicit and intuitive (or tacit) knowledge is not the same as the distinction between active and passive. Explicit knowledge involves a clear mental representation but has nothing to do with the ability to act on that knowledge.[10] A person can have explicit passive knowledge of an instrumental idiom—for example, knowing how the instrument ought to be played without being able to play it. Conversely, a musician who has intuitive knowledge of the performance practice associated with some ritual is unable to express the ordering of this knowledge in words or otherwise externalize it, but is capable of acting on this knowledge, playing the appropriate music for each stage of the ritual.[11]

Degrees of explicitness for a culture as a whole may be revealed in terminology, although gaining access to the articulation of musical knowledge is a challenge that varies widely from one culture to the next, depending in part on the ways in which writing is used. This does not boil down to a simplistic distinction between literate and oral societies, for even in a highly literate culture some fundamental aspects of musical competence may not be explicit.[12] Baroque manuals on continuo playing, for instance, make scarcely any mention of interaction, despite the general articulateness and explicitness of this literature regarding other aspects of performance practice and the clear necessity of interactive skills occasionally hinted at by authors (Elisabeth LeGuinn, unpublished manuscript).

The existence of terminology does not guarantee that the terms will be known by all musicians. We can take three hypothetical musicians' use of tune names as an example: musician A knows the names of tunes

10. Sloboda appears to fuse these two distinctions and implies that explicit knowledge is active while implicit knowledge is passive, thereby missing a useful cognitive distinction. He writes about the "dissociation between implicit knowledge (in this case of metre) that children display in their enactive repertoire (such as singing the songs they know) and the explicit ability to isolate and use such knowledge in tasks of perception and judgment. In this case, children of five have implicit knowledge of metre but seem not to be able to use this knowledge explicitly" (1985: 208).

11. In her research on Balinese ritual music Lisa Gold has found that this is often the case (personal communication).

12. See Sweeney (1987) for a discussion of the complexity of this issue.

and calls them out (active knowledge); B recognizes the names and associates them with the proper tunes when player A says them, but otherwise is more likely to hum or play a bit of a tune than to name it (passive knowledge); musician C has no use for titles, but recognizes the tunes as soon as A or B begins to play, and joins in. In many traditions these three musicians can play together with little trouble. Musician C has a less explicit grasp of the repertoire than musicians A and B, who have explicit knowledge of titles, A's being active and B's mainly passive. This scenario could occur in Java or Bali, but it is just as likely among Middle Eastern musicians or performers of British or North American fiddle tunes. Distinctions of this sort can obtain between groups as well as individuals. The explicitness of knowledge of stereotyped sound patterns, for instance, varies both within and between musical communities, as we shall see in chapters three and four.

Explicit knowledge enables a person to communicate with others in a symbolic manner, via names or other denotations of pieces, melodies, patterns, dance steps, notes, and playing techniques. Because symbolic representations are generally more compact than the items that they represent, symbolic communication is more efficient than actual performance (assuming that both parties to the communication are sufficiently competent). Notation is generally a far more systematic means of symbolic communication than language, but both require explicit knowledge rather than a purely intuitive grasp. A singer who cannot read notation but who knows which key is comfortable for a particular song can effectively convey that to accompanying instrumentalists through explicit knowledge of pitch names.

Explicitness is not limited to verbalization and notation. The ability to simplify a complex musical pattern for the sake of demonstration depends on an awareness of the workings of such patterns that is as explicit as notation or verbal explanation. Two musicians who are both capable improvisers may lack precise terminology to describe the underlying processes of improvisation, but if asked to explain these processes the one whose knowledge is largely intuitive will simply produce more improvisations while the one who has explicit awareness of these processes may find a musical way, perhaps augmented verbally, to convey that knowledge. There is a significant methodological issue here: the fact that a musician is not explicit about his or her knowledge at any given time cannot be taken as proof that that knowledge is intuitive. The musician may feel, for example, that the interlocutor is incapable of absorbing the information or that one ought to undergo a lengthy process of personal experience to arrive at this knowledge rather than having it spoon-fed. Assessment of the explicitness of aspects of competence is further complicated by the possibility that a musician who has not had occasion to analyze competence in the normal course of a performing career may be drawn into theorizing in conversation with a researcher either out of genuine interest or out of a sense that some answer must be given. I do not mean that such theorizings should be discounted. On the contrary, they may well be more interesting and directly relevant than reiterated platitudes that have spread from theorists to teachers to students through rote memorization. But the researcher ought to attempt to clarify the source of these thoughts to the extent possible.

Explicitness does not necessarily increase with learning, because procedural knowledge can become "second-nature," becoming internalized and receding from conscious, detailed control to a level where a person can utilize it automatically:

> The change from *controlled* processing to *automatic* motor processing as a result
> of extensive skill rehearsal is an idea of long standing . . . and it undoubtedly
> improves movement quality and integration . . . [Automaticity is] a stage at
> which it has become possible to completely dispense with conscious monitor-
> ing of motor programmes, so that the hands appear to have a life of their
> own, driven by the musical constraints of the situation. (Pressing 1988: 139.)

Pressing specifically links automaticity with relatively low level motor control, but it must also occur with regard to nonmotoric aspects of performance. For example, an accomplished musician performing in an ensemble probably does not need to devote conscious attention to orienting his or her part to other parts at every moment. This is something the performer can leave to automatic control, attending to it only intermittently. Gruson writes about the passage from conscious to automatic control within the learning process in a study of pianists' rehearsal practices, taking a somewhat broader stance than Pressing by speaking of "behavioural sequence" rather than a motor program (1988: 108). Likewise, Hayes-Roth notes that "once a knowledge structure has acquired a unitary representation, its prior constituent . . . representations can be activated only by activating and decomposing the unitary representation. Therefore the information about the complete structure should be more accessible than any part of that information" (1977: 264). A renowned Balinese *gender* player goes so far as to say that one's knowledge of entire pieces should be automatic: you really know a piece when you can play it in your sleep (I Wayan Loceng, personal communication).

Automaticity is not synonymous with intuitivity. The musician who plays something intuitively is not surrendering all conscious control but is employing a number of conscious thought processes—of which we know nearly nothing—in addition to the constant, low-level automaticity on which all musicians rely to get their bodies moving at the right speed and in the right direction at a particular moment.

Yet another dimension of knowing is captured in the contrast between procedural and declarative knowledge, discussed earlier in this chapter, that opposes factual knowledge—knowing, for example, that a particular fingering produces a certain pitch—and knowing how to do something, a procedure or set of procedures for moving from one fingering to another. Several writers on musical cognition have had recourse to this distinction, which is commonly invoked in the field of artificial intelligence (where conflicting claims have been made for the primacy of one type of knowledge over the other). Laske relies extensively on the declarative/procedural dichotomy for his model of musical competence, but here as elsewhere his theory is too heavily biased toward the interpretation of notation to have much relevance outside the world of written music, in which compositional structures predominate and performance takes second place. He writes that "structures result from musical activity" (1977: 3), ignoring the fact that these activities also take place with reference to structures.

These contrasting pairs—active/passive, intuitive/explicit, conscious/automatic, procedural/declarative—apply to individual domains and subdomains of competence as continuously variable attributes rather than strict oppositions. A musician may be able to express certain aspects of a domain in words or musical action, but not know the domain explicitly in its entirety. Likewise, a musician may not have the confidence and knowledge to perform a piece without the example of someone who knows it better or who is more competent in general. Thus, a more flexible usage of these terms, allowing for a continuum, provides a more generally useful tool.

Active manifestation of knowledge often depends on social and psychological aspects of context: a particular musician may be confident enough to play a leading role or explain musical practice in a group of less competent musicians, but suddenly lose confidence and assertiveness in the presence of someone *judged more competent.* The last phrase is emphasized in order to point out the crucial role of social and technical perceptions, the importance of the not-so-confident musician's assessments of others present. The assessment of greater competence may be a function of higher social status or authority, not necessarily indicating that the inhibiting individual is more proficient or knowledgeable in the domain in question. Issues of this sort, involving psychological and social forces, will be discussed in part 2 of this book.

DOMAINS OF COMPETENCE

These ways of knowing apply to particular domains[13] of musical competence. Any attempt to model competence requires that we start with
working definitions of the component clusters of knowledge and skills
that constitute a competence though these may be redefined at later
stages. The following set of domains is offered in this provisional spirit:
it tends toward comprehensiveness and universality but attains neither.
This is not necessarily a shortcoming since generalizing beyond a certain point erases the very diversity that we are attempting to grasp. The
sequence of presentation has no significance since these domains are
linked to each other in a variety of ways and can predominate or recede
to the background of consciousness from one moment to the next.[14]

The domains of knowledge in a given musical competence may differ
from these suggested generalizations in emphasis and in extent (the
amount and type of material that a particular domain includes). It is
conceivable, for example, that knowledge of a particular ensemble's performance practice and knowledge of its repertoire are inextricably entwined and together constitute a body of knowledge separate from other
domains. Particular categories may not be relevant in some musical communities while other aspects of musical competence, particularly "nonmusical" ones, that are important to a particular musical community
may have been omitted here. Nonetheless, this list provides a basis for
discussion.

sound quality: Since sound is the primary material of music, whatever
the definition or extent of the realm of creative activity that we identify
as "music," the characteristics of musical sound constitute a primary domain of competence. Musicians master contextual distinctions of appropriate and inappropriate qualities of sound, as they vary along dimensions of loudness, timbre, manner of production, and pitch. Some of
this knowledge is declarative: for example, the array of available sounds,
perhaps with associated labels, or the association of sound qualities with
particular instruments, genres, or contexts. Knowledge of the production of sound, on the other hand, is largely procedural, consisting of
specific vocal and instrumental techniques, but it is also linked to declarative and affective aspects of competence by the need to match personal
conceptual models and communal norms of sound quality. In some musi-

13. In the context of general human cognition, the subsidiary types of knowledge that
constitute musical competence might be termed "subdomains," but since the present discussion
is limited to music, they will simply be called "domains" here.

14. These links will be discussed further in the next section; here only a few of the most
common are noted.

cal traditions this domain is common to all musicians while in others instrumentalists have relatively little in common with one another or with singers in this regard.

sound patterns: Perceptual and performative knowledge of patterning is as fundamental as knowledge of sound quality. Reporting on studies of cognitive development, Gruson states that "one of the most consistent findings that emerges from the research on skills is that as an individual learns a skill, he or she acquires the ability to process increasingly larger and more complex units of meaningful, skill-related information" (1988: 91). The invention and performance of sound patterns in composition or improvisation is procedural knowledge. Declarative knowledge of patterns ranges from brief ornaments, through stock phrases, to complete pieces. These patterns may be associated with names and other symbolic representations and with a wide variety of nonmusical concepts, practices, and entities.

symbolic representation: While all knowledge must take some form of mental representation, explicit systems of symbolic representation constitute an important domain of competence, comprising mnemonic syllables used for the vocalization of instrumental parts, pattern names, and, of course, the many different types of written notation.

transformation: Procedural knowledge of transformative processes, such as transposition, augmentation, diminution, and variation, may be linked to sound patterns of all sizes including stock phrases, specific pieces, and general melodic or rhythmic parts.

interaction: Interactive procedures include both the ongoing adjustments of intonation, timing, and other aspects of sound production mentioned above and the more prominent or significant mutual influence that generally occurs among performers and between performers and audience. Knowledge of cues and appropriate responses has declarative and procedural aspects. Since such knowledge is often context-sensitive, it is closely linked with the domain of performance context (see below).

orientation: This domain includes declarative knowledge of common points or lines of reference (a concept that will be developed in the discussion of interaction in part 2) within a given type of music, such as tonal center, chord progression, time line, metrical cycle, colotomic pattern, and procedural knowledge of how to coordinate with that reference. Mastery of this domain is vital to interaction.

ensembles: This domain includes ensemble structure, constituent parts and relationships between parts, and functional and contextual associations linked to particular repertoire, instruments, idioms, and sound qualities.

repertoire: Musical pieces are known not just as individual extended sound patterns but also in relation to groupings of pieces according to criteria of affect, text, usage, instrumentation, structure, rhythmic or melodic characteristics, and so on. Issues that arise in this domain include ownership or attribution and restrictions on performance according to context, occasion, performers, or audience, as well as other traits that are not performative in themselves but may influence when, where, and by and for whom a piece is played.

performance context: Specific occasions, places, instruments, ensembles, repertoire, and modes of appropriate behavior for performers and non-performers are linked in this domain. The contextual determination of which ensemble is to be played creates further links among basic concepts of sound quality (such as the indoor/outdoor distinctions that exist in various cultures), idiomatic knowledge of specific instruments, and other contextual aspects such as the distinction between music for listening and music for dance.

meaning or symbolism: Beliefs concerning the powers of music may or may not be an essential element of a musician's performative competence. Aspects of this domain may include association of certain sounds, patterns, pieces, or instruments with particular deities, beliefs, or practices. This domain may overlap the previous two since a musician may need to know which pieces are sacred, require special preparation, or are proscribed save for certain people or occasions.

Other clusters of knowledge directly pertinent to musical competence may include nonmusical performance forms such as

language arts: Such knowledge is often of central importance and includes texts, both fixed and improvised, and poetic meters together with their correspondences with particular compositions or melodic and rhythmic patterns or usages.

dance, theater, religious rituals, and social occasions: Whether the occasion is a communal dance or a sacred ceremony, musicians often set the pace and control aspects of the event, requiring—at the very least—a knowledge of the sequence of events and the appropriate actions. A dance master or a spirit medium clearly needs to command additional capabilities and domains of knowledge. Musicians may train as dancers or at least know movement patterns and choreography well enough to accompany or even lead dancers.

A domain may have fuzzy boundaries or it may contain a clearly delimited group of entities. For some musics, for example, melodic practice may be defined in terms of a group of modal categories and this group in turn may be closed or open-ended, challenging musicians in very different ways. A closed group of entities such as Javanese *pathet* or Persian *dastgah* offers a finite partitioning of knowledge, a clear goal for mastery, though musicians may continue to develop their expertise within these partitions. An open-ended group, such as Hindustani *raga*, invites exploration and innovation on another level, and there is likely to be no sense of ever finishing one's studies or encompassing the whole of such a domain.

A domain may have a well-ordered internal structure of subclasses of knowledge. Common internal organizations include symmetrical classifications of repertoire for purposes of performance or transmission and simple hierarchical formulations of roles or functions within an ensemble. Subclasses of knowledge may be conceptualized as having prototypical elements. Such focal points offer a handy encapsulation of knowledge—"this piece contains all you need to know"—that can be important both for the learning process and for performance practice.

THE ORGANIZATION OF COMPETENCE

The links between domains are at least as important as the domains themselves. Musicians piece knowledge together consciously and unconsciously as they learn, adding new items to those already known and drawing connections between items and groups of items. We can learn something about the resultant groupings and links through the metaphor of a multidimensional map. If current thinking about associative networks is on track, then such a map may prove to be more than just a metaphor.

A full mapping of any one competence is a daunting task, and attempting a prototypical map with universal pretensions is completely premature at this point. Nonetheless, thinking in terms of such a project can lead to a fresh understanding of the structure of musical knowledge within a given community. To illustrate the complexity of the undertaking, a fragment of a hypothetical array of knowledge is represented in figure 4. It shows links between sound quality and three other domains: modal aspects of melody making, interactive knowledge, and vocal and instrumental idioms. The arrow linking "Interactive Knowledge" to the procedural aspects of "Sound" indicates the ongoing low-level adjustments that musicians make in intonation, volume, timbre, articulation, duration, and timing in order to match, complement, or contrast with each other to maintain a desirable sound. Modal practice is linked to declarative knowledge of available pitches, including hierarchical relationships between these pitches, to procedural knowledge of sound pro-

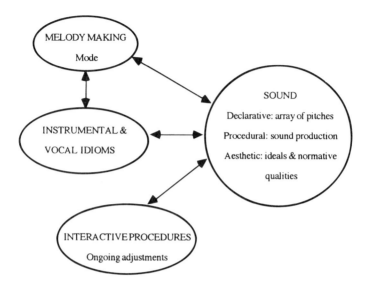

Fig. 4 Some links between the domain of sound and related domains

duction inasmuch as individual pitches may be produced in special ways
to suit modally defined situations, and to knowledge of the affective
aspects of musical sound because of the expressive and emotional associations integral to many modal systems. Modal knowledge is also closely
bound to knowledge of vocal and instrumental idioms, which are linked,
in turn, to the three aspects of "Sound."

Some domains may bridge, overlap, or encompass other domains.
Compositional and improvisational knowledge draws together some of
the most central domains of a competence. Mode, which I have just
described as a subdomain of "Melody-making," might be conceived in
other circumstances as the linkages in a complex of separate domains
concerning pitch sets, other melodic constraints and preferences, categories of repertoire, and contextual factors.

Such superordinate/subordinate relationships between domains raise
questions concerning large-scale structuring of knowledge. Both hierarchical and heterarchical organizations of competence have been proposed. Adler models musical competence for amateur bluegrass banjo
players as a hierarchy without questioning the suitability of such a structure (1979: 199). On the other hand, Hayes-Roth has suggested that
"the structure of information in an assembly may be heterarchical" in
distinction to older theories that see the "organization of information
into successively larger units as the imposition of successively higher
order structural characteristics on a fixed set of functional units" (1977:

265). More recently Pressing has argued that the hierarchical models favored by many psychologists are too narrow in scope and that heterarchical models incorporating parallel processing are probably more accurate (1988: 136). In his generalized model of improvisation he postulates that the "control of event production is heterarchical, and may potentially shift rapidly from one cognitive control area to another" (1988: 161).

Such conclusions should be informed by study of coherent epistemological structures recognized by musicians. Equilibrium, symmetry, hierarchy, and other harmonious arrangements of knowledge formulated by musicians may be more reflective of cultural concepts of organization than of actual cognitive organization, but such arrangements are nonetheless important so long as we are prepared for discrepancies between neat cognitive models and messy reality. It is also possible that members of a community maintain conflicting conceptualizations of the same competence.

By contrasting named and unnamed aspects of a musical tradition, we may gain a sense of underlying cognitive distinctions and structures. We must keep in mind, however, that some aspects of music-making may be so basic as to be taken for granted and that language does not necessarily structure cognition or fully reflect a person's powers of differentiation. Cognitive research on classification of colors, for example, has shown that explicitness of cultural categories (i.e., nomenclature) does not necessarily correlate with powers of discrimination evidenced by members of that culture (Lakoff 1987: 24–30).

The organization of knowledge for transmission is one of the most readily accessible conceptualizations of competence. For example, musical competence may be structured in terms of essential and progressively more esoteric knowledge, reflecting not only an order of learning but a path of spiritual progression or maturation. Socially motivated control of access to knowledge is often implicit in such a structure. Such possibilities require consideration of how musicians attain competence and the ways in which competence differs between musicians within a community, for these differences are the result and often the goal of socioculturally determined methods of musical education, as we shall see in chapters 3 and 5.

CHAPTER TWO

JAVANESE MUSICAL COMPETENCE

The complexity and diversity of Javanese musical competence makes its essence difficult to encapsulate. In addition to the many "exceptions" that belie the systematic relationships within and between some domains, individual differences and variation between localized traditions are fundamental to the nature of Javanese musical competence. The closer we approach definition of individual competences, the more we find that such a definition must vary with the dialectic of individual achievements and consensual ideals. For the sake of clarity I shall defer consideration of these exceptions and differences to a later chapter, beginning instead with an idealized universal Javanese competence that will then serve as a basis for comparing individual musicians.

The following discussion is based on observed practice and musicians' expressed or implied ideals, principally within the community of musicians centered in Surakarta, as well as on publications by Javanese musicians and foreign scholars. I have attempted to assess the nature and extent of the actual competence of particular musicians through interviews, peer evaluation, and observation in lessons, rehearsals, and performances. This is supplemented by my experience studying and teaching *gamelan,* in the course of which I have had the opportunity to compare the skills and problems of non-Javanese with those of Javanese, noting who adapts best to what and which situations are more problematic.

DOMAINS OF COMPETENCE

Javanese writers on *gamelan* generally list domains of musical knowledge, including tuning systems, modes, repertoire, temporal aspects of performance practice, and instrumental roles in the ensemble. Some of these, such as tuning systems, are fairly limited and self-contained bodies of knowledge while categories such as mode are far more complex and on further inspection are seen to comprehend or bridge several domains of knowledge. Such lists tell nothing of the relationships between these types of knowledge.

Mantle Hood has gone a step further by proposing a hierarchy progressing from general to specific: tuning system, mode, colotomy, *balungan*, fixed melody, instrumental and vocal idioms, local style, group empathy, and personal style (1988: 150). This list is problematic in several ways. Local style is not a domain of competence in the sense of an independent body of knowledge, an ingredient to be added to some base competence as Hood's recipe implies: each domain of competence is likely to have both localized content and substantial overlap with other competences, as we shall see in the next chapter. By specifying a hierarchy, Hood is forced to impose irrelevant priorities. As with other formulations of Javanese musical knowledge this simple hierarchy reflects the author's ideas about the appropriate structure of a model more than the reality it purports to describe. The simplicity of such schemes is deceptive: analysis of musicians' conduct and mutual evaluations shows that the organization of musical knowledge is far more complex with more components and many nonhierarchical links between domains.

A multidimensional approach to the domains of competence in terms of the different ways of knowing discussed in the previous chapter—the procedural/declarative, explicit/intuitive, and active/passive contrasts or continua—circumvents these problems. The first contrasting pair is particularly useful: much of Javanese music-making can be explained in terms of a reciprocal relationship between declarative and procedural knowledge. Procedural knowledge operates within a set of declarative frameworks, and these procedures, in turn, affect and alter those frameworks. Thus, this distinction is the primary dimension for the account of Javanese musical competence offered here, fleshed out by references to the other continua. Among these, the distinction between active and passive knowledge is particularly pertinent to a richer understanding of Javanese musical competence, as I suspect it is for other musical traditions as well. Variation along the explicit/intuitive and active/passive dimensions is of more importance for the differentiation of types of competence and individual competences than it is for defining an idealized body of knowledge.

Declarative Frameworks

Sociocultural function and *context* are among the most far-reaching declarative frameworks that Javanese musicians must learn to navigate or manipulate. Whether the occasion is a private celebration such as a wedding, a court performance, or a private gathering of musicians, social function and context influence the choice of pieces played and their style, duration, and sequence, as well as the social and musical demeanor of the musicians. At the night-long *tayuban* (dance parties) popular earlier in this century, for instance, the sequence of pieces was determined by the choices made by the male guests as they got up to take a turn—according to descending social rank—with a professional female dancer. Pieces were not only shorter than at other types of performances but also livelier and louder, so much so that a practical guide for musicians (Djakoeb and Wignyaroemeksa 1913) suggested that musicians should maintain their strength by taking turns on the louder instruments and leaving the softer-sounding instruments unmanned because the absence of the latter would not be missed in the general merriment.

Extramusical influence is more noticeable still when *gamelan* is performed in conjunction with other performance arts that involve specific repertoires and performance conventions. A basic and largely intuitive aspect of a musician's competence is the ability to select the options appropriate to a given theatrical situation. If the musician plays a leading role in the *gamelan*, this knowledge must be active; otherwise, musicians must at least have sufficient passive knowledge of the conventions to allow them to interpret the leading musicians' choices in light of the contextual framework. The same is true for choreographic knowledge: leading musicians must know the key formations in order to keep track of the dance and coordinate the musical accompaniment. When an unmetered piece is played for the dancers' entrance, for instance, the musicians must extend or abbreviate it to fit the dancers' pace and the dimensions of the performance place. Their estimation of the dancers' arrival depends on knowledge of the opening formation of the dance (Martopangrawit, personal communication).

Knowledge of these contextual frameworks guides musicians in making appropriate choices of musical and social conduct. It is not necessary to posit a large number of distinct domains, each focused on a single performance genre or context, because there is substantial overlap. While the conventions of *wayang kulit* form a system that is distinct from the practice of *wayang wong* (theater with human actor/dancers rather than puppets), the two also have much in common. Musicians may specialize in one and need little additional experience or training to become proficient in the other. Likewise, a musician may perform in widely differing social contexts, but certain formal frameworks for interaction with hosts, fellow musicians, and audience will serve, with some modification, for all of these contexts.

Another type of nonmusical framework, *sung texts*, is important not so much for the overall course of events as for a single piece or section of a piece. Familiarity with the poetic meters and their associated melodies is a central part of vocalists' competence. It also figures prominently, if passively, among the types of knowledge that instrumentalists must master, for these meters and melodies are fundamental to many parts of the repertoire.

The domain of *symbolic representations* includes knowledge of systems for encoding performance information in gestures, pattern names, drum syllables, and graphic notation. Like text, this domain bridges the musical and extramusical areas of declarative knowledge because of the close relationship between movement patterns, drum syllables, and dance and theater. Since these representations are used both for personal reference and for teaching, they have mnemonic and communicative importance.

One of the major changes in Javanese musical competence during the past century has been the gradual encroachment of written notation on a fundamentally oral tradition, first in personal manuscripts and later in widely available printed form. The social upheavals following World War II, Indonesian independence, and the ensuing breakdown of much of the system of feudal patronage and oral transmission created a much greater need for means of preservation and rapid transmission. The establishment of formal educational institutions in the arts has spurred the use of notation as have associated projects of documentation and preservation of various repertoires.

The extent of dependence on the common system of cipher notation is difficult to estimate today.[1] Returning to Central Java in 1993, I found the use of notation more pervasive than in 1983. It is used extensively in formalized instruction, but some musicians still get by without reading notation at all. Experienced musicians do not use notation in performance but may refer to it at other times to refresh their memories. As various groups seek to resurrect or maintain aspects of the court traditions that are no longer a central part of court musicians' competence,

---

1. See Becker (1980) for a history of Javanese notation. Ten years later Sutton (1991b) suggests that the effects of notation have not been as extensive as Becker predicted.

it becomes increasingly necessary to resort to notation—particularly, vocal notation—for rarely performed pieces. At the same time musicians at STSI have actually reduced their reliance on notation over the past decade or so as they have become aware of its shortcomings (Supanggah, personal communication).

By far the most commonly notated part in the *gamelan* is the *balungan*. Supanggah summarizes the effect of notation on *balungan*: "With the rapid development of the written tradition, this balungan tended to become 'fixed' (standardized), and it developed not only as a memory-aid but also as a[n] educational tool, an aid in performance, and a means of disseminating karawitan" (1988: 9). Indications for colotomic instruments are often added to the *balungan*. The elaborating parts are rarely notated, with the exception of some instructional materials developed at the conservatory and academy in Surakarta.

Nominal and gestural systems of representation have received less scholarly attention. Musicians need not master all of these symbol systems in order to achieve competence. Some musicians use a fairly extensive collection of names for *gendèr* patterns as a sort of shorthand, for instance, while others only know a few names; there are also musicians who do not resort to any pattern names at all.[2] Gestural communication includes hand signals for pitches and for the principal drum strokes. In addition to the interactive use of these signals to assist confused players in performance, Mloyowidodo told me that musicians used to learn and practice melodies with reference to drum patterns by humming the melody and reproducing the gestures symbolizing the drum strokes.

Drum syllables are widely known and are used particularly by dancers because they are linked to choreographic patterns. Even dancers who are not technically competent in drumming can reel off complex patterns of drum syllables. Together with named dance patterns this language of drum syllables serves as an efficient means of communication in the creation, arrangement, and transmission of choreography. At a dress rehearsal in the United States, for example, a Javanese dancer who had just flown into town was able to communicate a lengthy and fairly complex dramatic choreography in condensed form to a Javanese drummer with whom he had never performed. Using pattern names supplemented with some drum syllables, they were even able to cross stylistic boundaries: although dancer and drummer came from different regions of Central Java, each had sufficient knowledge of the other's tradition—

2. See, for instance, the comparison between three *siter* players in Astono (1990: 69). Two used pattern names and were aware of the connections with nominal systems for other instruments, while the third musician was unaware of these pattern names.

thanks to training at performing arts institutions—to find appropriate parallels and substitutions between dance and drumming "languages."

Much of the more musical declarative knowledge mastered by a Javanese musician centers around *repertoire*, including two principal frameworks: the *individual composition* and the array of options and conventions governing the combination of these compositions in *performance sequences*. A composition is almost never fixed in detail, but as a framework for performance it has a number of relatively fixed features that limit the potentially infinite productions of Javanese musical procedures. Foremost of these is form. The number of forms is small, and most are cyclical and defined by a particular colotomic structure. Musicians must be familiar with all the forms and their colotomic articulations, as these constitute the principal temporal frames of reference. Particularly in the larger forms, where a cycle may last several minutes, it is essential that the musicians maintain orientation within the cycle. The explicitness of this knowledge varies: some musicians function well on an intuitive level, unable to write out or dictate the characteristics of a particular form, but able to play appropriately within it in the context of performance. There is also variation along the active/passive continuum, related once again to a musician's role in the ensemble. Both the drummer and the musicians who play the colotomic gong and *kenong* should have active general knowledge of all the forms and should know the form of each piece in particular. However, this is more crucial in the case of the drummer, because the gong and *kenong* players can rely on the drum pattern for orientation but a lost drummer is in deep trouble.

A composition is also defined by *laras* (scale or pitch system) and *pathet* (mode). Knowledge of these frameworks is as central to general musical competence as knowledge of form. At the most basic level, the distinction between *sléndro* and *pélog* scales affects every part in the *gamelan* as a framework for performance: most *gamelan* contain parallel sets of instruments tuned to *sléndro* and *pélog* which are placed at right angles (space permitting), and musicians shift back and forth as they alternate between *sléndro* and *pélog* pieces in the course of a performance. *Gamelan* limited to one tuning are common, too, and some village musicians who have extensive exposure to one tuning through association with such an ensemble may develop a lopsided competence, knowing more pieces and feeling more at home in one tuning than the other. This is often the case with groups that regularly accompany a *dhalang* (puppet master) who owns a *sléndro gamelan* for shadow play performances (Widiyanto and B. Subono, personal communication).

Explicit knowledge of pitch names is probably almost universal now, but according to Mloyowidodo there were still many illiterate musicians in the early decades of this century who simply hummed melodies and did not use pitch names (personal communication). Theoretical knowledge about pitch systems does not appear to be a salient aspect of competence.

Knowledge of *pathet* is more systematized and complex than knowledge of *laras*. Although knowledge of *pathet* is absolutely essential to performance, it has proven elusive for Javanese and foreign theorists who would encapsulate it in some tidy formulation.[3] This is due in part to a failure to distinguish between *pathet* as a relatively fixed and restricted declarative framework for performance and *pathet* as a far more variable and flexible set of procedures for conducting oneself melodically. Declarative knowledge of *pathet* is systematically conceived in terms of a matrix of six *pathet*, organized in two parallel sets of three modes. This matrix governs many aspects of musical knowledge and practice. The modal classification and characteristics of a composition are among the principal determinants of how a musician will realize his or her conception of a piece in a particular performance and as such constitute a framework for the procedures of performance. The often overlooked inadequacies of this neatly symmetrical conceptual model as a representation of musical practice will be discussed below.

A piece is defined broadly by form and mode, more specifically by contextual and textual aspects, and most specifically by melody. Melody is a multifaceted phenomenon manifested on one level as a fixed melody (*balungan*) played in unison by a number of musicians and on other levels as a heterophonically realized melodic path[4] performed idiosyncratically by each of as many as nine or ten musicians. The *balungan* may exist in a number of versions, one of which will emerge in a given performance, generally determined by the player of the *slenthem*, the most important *balungan*-playing instrument. The individualized elaboration of a melody is relatively free and open to formulaic treatment—matters which are procedural—but certain passages are more fixed, that is, they belong to the framework of the piece. The melodic path of a piece is often linked, for example, with the characteristics of poetic texts. Musicians should know the basic melodic path and the relatively fixed *balungan* which is one manifestation of this path, but the degree to which they must be familiar with these varies in accordance with the parts that

---

3. Scholars who have written about *pathet* include Kunst (1949), Sindoesawarno (1987), Hood (1954), Martopangrawit (1984), Kartomi (1973), McDermott and Sumarsam (1975), Schumacher (1980), and Hastanto (1990).

4. This is called "inner melody" by Sumarsam (1984b) and *lagu* by Suhardi (Sutton 1979).

they play in the ensemble. The importance of this point will become clearer in the analysis of the ranking of court musicians presented in chapter 4.

The *sequence* in which pieces are performed is subject to a number of constraints and influences, dependent in part on extramusical context and in part on musical considerations. The spontaneity of many programmatic decisions renders this a significant domain within the *gamelan* competence. Programs are rarely planned in all aspects, but emerge in performance from the decisions and interactions of the leading players. Mode and form play a classificatory role as frameworks here, each piece in the repertoire usually fitting in one modal category and one formal category. Leaders choose pieces from the appropriate categories according to conventions of program sequence. There is a traditional progression of musical modes linked to time periods, and, likewise, there are rules regarding the sequence and compatibility of musical forms within the medleys or "suites" that constitute the bulk of most performances (Brinner 1989/90). The order is further affected by considerations of balance that depend to a large extent on the character of the piece and the particular way in which it is performed. Leading musicians must have active, though perhaps not explicit, knowledge of these constraints in order to make appropriate choices while musicians playing other parts will have better chances of anticipating and correctly interpreting the leaders' cues if they, too, have some knowledge of this domain, however passive and intuitive. Less common but also important is the particularized competence characteristic of and limited to a closely knit group of musicians who have developed habitual sequences of pieces that are not linked in the general competence.

The multiplicity of relationships and aspects possible for a given domain, already apparent in the preceding paragraphs, bears further discussion. Form and mode are recognized as domains in Javanese theoretical discourse and ethnomusicological literature, but each term carries different connotations depending on context, reflecting relationships with other domains. Mode, for example, is a framework for melodic analysis and realization of a single piece, but it is also a classifying framework for repertoire and a set of procedures for playing. Likewise, form can be a framework for melody, dance, and puppet movement within a given piece but it is also a classifying principle to be applied to the entire repertoire. Together, mode and form create one of the most important and frequently invoked conceptual matrices of Javanese music (see below and Brinner 1995).

The other major framework for music-making is the *ensemble*. The group of musicians with their individual competences, the matching of particular musicians to the instruments, and even the array of instruments available may all vary greatly. Often the roles within a group are fluid, changing from one performance to the next and even within the course of a performance. Ideally the capabilities of individual musicians should suit their assignment to the various instruments because the division of labor in a *gamelan* is linked to specific instruments. But musicians often choose their places only as the result of a complex social interaction and an optimization of roles is often attained only gradually by adjustment in the course of performance, as we shall see in chapter 10.

General knowledge of the characteristic parts played on each instrument in the *gamelan*, the temporal relationships between these parts, and the associated responsibilities and possibilities is basic to any musician's competence. This knowledge provides guidelines for appropriate personal and interpersonal conduct, including which part to take and how active a role to play in making the decisions that affect the ensemble and the course of the performance. Nearly every Javanese treatise on *gamelan* contains some classification and discussion of the roles and responsibilities associated with each instrument.[5] Knowledge of one's companions' competences is perhaps as important, but one would be hard-pressed to find any discussion in written sources. Yet this is the basis upon which each musician assesses the validity of other musicians' cues, responses, and other musical, gestural, and verbal communications and performances: hearing musician A play something unexpected at a given point in the performance, musician B may ignore, try to correct, respond to, or give in to A, depending on his or her assessment of A's competence relative to general standards and to the respective roles of A and B in the *gamelan* at that moment.

Ensemble roles are also linked to context, whether it be the social affiliation or setting or the accompanying nonmusical performance form. In chapter 4 we shall see how court rankings of musicians differ in several important ways from the division of responsibilities in other groups. Shifting from shadow play to dance to *klenèngan*, the leading roles and relative importance of the roles associated with particular instruments change and requirements for knowledge of repertoire and performance practice shift to different members of the ensemble. A basic element in musicians' competence is the ability to adapt to the myriad variations associated with these contexts.

---

5. See Martopangrawit (1984), Soekanto (1966), or Poerbapangrawit (1984), for example, and the discussion in chapter 4.

Procedural Knowledge

The primary procedural domains concern *pitch, time,* and *idiom.* Procedures in the domains of pitch and time have received so much attention as systematic complexes and so little attention has been paid to the many nonsystematic aspects that Javanese music-making is perceived by some foreigners as thoroughly formulaic.[6] There are indeed numerous procedural aspects of performance—including the many types of sound patterns which can be reused, transposed, transferred from one situation to another, and otherwise altered—that can be understood systematically, but formulaity or rule sets do not explain all aspects of performance.

Pitch procedures include characteristics of melodic flow and ways of hearing and knowing melody in its many facets and locating one's self within that flow. This knowledge is general in application[7] unlike knowledge that is specific to a given piece and therefore more declarative in nature. The domain of pitch also includes aspects of mode because Javanese *pathet* is not only referential in the classificatory and compositional senses but also procedural: a musician must know modally specific ways of moving melodically. Such knowledge is most important for leading melodic instrumentalists and singers.

Several *temporal* aspects of competence also fall within the procedural category. Leading musicians, particularly drummers, master the many options for altering tempo and *irama,* both as general procedures and as characteristics of specific pieces. Other musicians must know the significance of changes in speed of the basic pulse: whether to ride out a temporary change in speed, retaining the ratio between their parts and the basic pulse, or to shift *irama* by halving or doubling the density of their parts with reference to the basic pulse. Knowledge of relative rhythmic densities is a link to the domains of ensemble and idiom.

The instrumental and vocal *idioms* of the *gamelan* vary greatly in complexity (see Sutton 1982, 1993). Some passive knowledge of the idioms of leading parts is essential: even a musician who is unable to drum at all will certainly recognize the main drum cues and know how to respond to them (an important link to the domain of interactive knowl-

6. See Becker (1981) on rhythmic expansion of melodic patterns, Sutton (1978) on variation of patterns, and Forrest (1980), but see also Pemberton's criticism of ethnomusicological obsession with pattern and regularity in studies of Javanese *gamelan* (1987: 27).

7. These aspects of *gamelan* have been discussed extensively in publications such as Sumarsam (1975, 1984b), Sutton (1978, 1979, 1982), and Forrest (1980), which contain numerous examples of idiomatic instrumental patterning and the interrelatedness of the parts in Javanese *gamelan* performance.

edge to be discussed shortly). Active knowledge of an idiom begins with basic playing techniques and appropriate playing style. For the more complex idioms, a higher level of competence is evidenced by command of all the options inherent to the instrument, including a stock of patterns, ways of manipulating these patterns, and knowledge of their proper usage. The patterns themselves are more procedural than declarative because they are ways of doing—moving from one pitch place to another. Such knowledge may be highly formulaic, but in the case of better musicians it also includes a problem-solving orientation toward ways of creating idiomatic parts to bridge difficult or unusual passages in aesthetically pleasing ways.

The relative explicitness of a musician's idiomatic knowledge becomes evident in lessons or in remarks made to other musicians. Some musicians—particularly those associated with academic institutions—employ a nominal symbol system that enables them to capture and transmit the formulaic gist of a passage (involving both framework and procedures) in a few words. A musician whose grasp is intuitive can only play through the passage in question to communicate his interpretation. Such is the difference, for instance, between the *gendèr* players introduced in the Prelude. Both can perform idiomatically on the *gendèr*, but the one who is a teacher at the academy can verbalize at length about what he does, comparing alternatives and justifying his choices, while the *wayang* musician's teaching abilities are far more limited because he does not do these things.

The domains of pitch, time, and idiom are linked to interactive and transformative domains. *Interactive* procedures, which are the heart of *gamelan* competence and performance, include ways of leading and following, cuing and responding, influencing and imitating. Because frameworks of performance are often only loosely predetermined and a performance is never planned down to the last note, it is the network of interactive procedures—the ways and means of communication—that enables musicians to perform with little or no rehearsal or overt verbal communication.

In this flexible and unpredictable musical world musicians often find it necessary to give or take hints from others. Most musicians with whom I studied spoke of the need to correct and guide other musicians, to show them the way during performance. The inverse of this responsibility is the ability to *ngèli,* to float along on the stream of the melody, picking up from other musicians' parts what one does not yet know or has forgotten. The ability to hear and act on hints of the melody from other parts is an essential skill for learning and survival because the repertoire is large, some pieces are rarely played, and many pieces differ from one locale to another. This knowledge is neither passive nor purely active: the musician uses interactive skills to construct an appropriate performance by drawing on other musicians' active knowledge of the particular piece and his or her own knowledge of instrumental idioms and correspondences between these idioms.

Cuing and all the related procedures constitute a complex domain that is discussed at length in the second half of this book. This domain of competence requires, for example, that players of leading melodic instruments have active knowledge of the introductions to hundreds of pieces. Other musicians need only a passive knowledge of these introductions so that they can recognize them and join in the performance. Performers must also know when to give or expect other cues with regard to frameworks of piece and context. Those who are not playing leading roles must be able to interpret the cues and respond appropriately.

Transformative competence includes the ability to transfer and adapt knowledge from one context to another. *Gamelan* melodies ranging in length from short fragments to entire pieces are frequently transposed to different degrees of the scale, moved from one mode to another, or transferred from *sléndro* tuning to *pélog*, and each such transformation entails adjustments.[8] Some transpositions or tuning changes require no change in production (hand movements) but only in orientation to their different sound. Patterns are easily moved from one scale degree to another and from one tuning to another on instruments such as *siter*, *gambang*, and *gendèr panerus* because unaltered kinetic patterns produce different sounds when the pattern is started on different strings or keys. Other instruments require more complex transformations, either because of the layout of pitches on the instrument or because of other idiomatic constraints. Since the gongs of the *bonang*, for instance, are arranged in a nonscalar layout, many transpositions require change in kinetic patterns. Idiomatic constraints come into play with *gendèr* patterns, for which only selected transpositions are traditionally sanctioned. This is one of the reasons that *gendèr* is more difficult to master than *gambang* or *gendèr panerus*. The *rebab* is another case in point: the fingering positions in the *pélog* modes *pathet lima* and *pathet barang* are the same but produce different absolute pitches since the *rebab* is tuned one pitch lower in *pélog pathet lima*. Theoretically this should enable easy transferal of patterns, but the differing functions of the pitches in these

8. See, e.g., Martopangrawit (1984: 191) and Supanggah (1988: 6).

modes complicates the procedure: pitch 3 is integral to *pélog pathet lima* while the same fingering in *pélog pathet barang* produces a flat 4, which is a rarely played auxiliary pitch.

Some transformations are actually translations in the literal sense of carrying over musical material from one framework to another, from one composition to another, or from one performance context to another (adapting a shadow play piece to dance performance practice, for example). Players are constantly translating from other instrumental and vocal idioms to their own instrument as they interact with other musicians. Finally, transformation of musical material from a fast *irama* to a slow one and vice versa—that is, from one set of rhythmic densities to another—takes place in virtually every performance of every piece and, once again, any competent musician knows how to do this.

Such transformations offer musicians some of their chief avenues of innovation (Brinner 1995). New pieces are created by transposition to a different mode, by transferal to another tuning, and by changing the colotomic structure of an existing piece, and with it the drumming and performance practice. Some translations—such as the recolotomization of a piece to create a new one—require substantial reorientation for the performer, but this does not appear to pose a problem for most musicians. Musicians at the prime minister's household in Surakarta delighted in creating transformations of this sort in the first half of this century, partly out of boredom with the traditional repertoire (Mloyowidodo, personal communication) and perhaps also as a way of establishing an exclusive in-group repertoire.

Aesthetic Sensibilities

Javanese musical competence rests on some fundamental aesthetic sensibilities that are not clearly declarative or procedural. Less susceptible of analytical formulation than frameworks and procedures, they contribute to an appropriate Javanese "feeling," permeate all levels of performance, and must be absorbed through extensive experience. The confluence of these sensibilities, which include *rasa* (feeling or sensation), sound-quality, timing, and balance, is epitomized in the sounding of a gong, struck with just the right force and an unquantifiable but essential delay which balances the timing, tension, and gravity of the stroke with all that has preceded it.

The concept of *rasa* is frequently invoked by Javanese musicians to subsume uncodifiable and therefore unteachable aspects of "playing with feeling" that set a masterful musician apart from those who merely have some level of technical ability. Praise for foreigners who are proficient in the technical aspects of *gamelan* performance is often tempered by a comment on the lack of proper feeling. For example, in a research report from STSI Surakarta, the renowned teacher and musician Martopangrawit is quoted as saying that foreigners do not possess Javanese musicians' *rasa* and only learn the corporeal aspects of *karawitan* (Waridi 1985/ 86: 17–18). Even with regard to native Javanese, musicians distinguish between *kemampuan garap* and *kemampuan rasa*, the ability to interpret a piece correctly[9] and the ability to evoke the proper *rasa*, or feeling; many feel that the latter ability is more important than the former (Widiyanto, personal communication).

A flexible sense of pitch is needed to accommodate the different tunings of the various *gamelan* ensembles that each musician encounters in the course of his or her performance experience. Relative pitch, stretched or compressed octaves, and nonharmonic intervals played on instruments with predominantly nonharmonic overtone structures pose problems for foreigners who have a sense of absolute pitch or a fascination with forcing rational analysis on the vagaries of Javanese tunings.[10] But these theoretical concerns, derived from the venerable Pythagorean preference for mathematically simple tunings based on the harmonic properties of vibrating strings, are irrelevant for practicing Javanese musicians, who learn to sense, appreciate, and adapt to individual tunings without the aid of mathematical models or even a complex terminology or categorization. As singers or *rebab* players move from one *gamelan* to another, they make minute adjustments of intonation necessary to effect a compromise between their own senses of *embat* (intonation) and the fixed tuning of the particular *gamelan*. Other musicians, playing on instruments with fixed tunings, must still orient their ears to the individual tuning of a *gamelan* but need not actively produce a particular intonation.

Since the process of ending a piece (*suwuk*) involves many domains of competence, it is a fitting example with which to conclude this portion of the chapter. The most common way of ending a piece is to accelerate slightly, then slow the pace gradually and smoothly until the last beat, which is stretched while the *pesindhèn* (female vocalist) sings a final melisma. A stroke from the gong player is timed to suit this melisma and marks the end of the piece, the other musicians sounding their final notes just after the gong stroke. Aesthetic sensibilities are involved in the creation or replication of a consensus on timing, particularly in the

9. See the discussion of *garapan* below.

10. The chain of attempts to formulate a mathematical model for Javanese tunings leads from Kunst (1949) through Hood (1966) and Surjodiningrat, Sudarjana, and Susanto (1972) to more recent proposals by Rahn (1978) and Polansky (1985). Perlman has analyzed the philosophical thrust of these attempts (1992) while Vetter's summation (1989) begins to right the balance by putting the concerns of *gamelan* tuners and performers first.

unmeasured stretching of the final portion of the last beat, the precise placement of the final gong stroke relative to the vocal phrase, and then the slight delay before the other players strike their final notes. Frameworks of various sorts come into play, including the form of the piece, which dictates appropriate moments in the cyclical structure for producing or expecting cues to speed up and slow down, and the binary temporal relationships between the basic pulse and the faster moving parts. The latter framework is an essential referent for all performers, but in the course of a *suwuk* it undergoes extreme deformations as it is first compressed, then drastically stretched, and finally dissolved. Interactive procedures are important here, too, as players strive to maintain a consensus regarding the overall rate of deceleration governing the beat and its subdivisions. The musicians must also invoke their interactive knowledge of the drum cues governing these tempo changes. Passive knowledge of the vocal idiom enables musicians to anticipate the probable timing of the singer's final melisma, thus preparing a concerted sounding of the final note of the piece. None of this is problematic for competent Javanese musicians although it is never explicitly taught. The complexity of this process becomes apparent when teaching non-Javanese to play *gamelan*: novices generally have great difficulty sensing the proper elongation of the beat and the appropriate delay of the gong.

THE ORGANIZATION OF COMPETENCE

Explicit Javanese classifications of items within domains exhibit several common traits despite the diversity of content across domains. There is a propensity for symmetry, balance, tripartite divisions, and identifying a set of items with a prototypical member of that set. These traits come together in organizational schemes which I have dubbed cultural matrices (Brinner 1995).

A cultural matrix is a set of categories created by the intersection of two or more dimensions—sets of distinctions which can be musical, dramatic, choreographic, social, geographical, or political in nature. One of the most commonly invoked matrices, expressing relationships between the six main *pathet*, is the product of two dimensions: the two tuning systems intersect with a tripartite modal progression which has temporal significance (see fig. 5).

This matrix works best as a framework for the selection of repertoire appropriate to the traditional performance progression. In its fullest form this progression alternates between the two *laras* of *sléndro* and *pélog*, passing from one pair of *pathet* to the next (*sléndro nem* and *pélog lima, sléndro*

TUNING

SEQUENCE	Sléndro	Pélog
first	Nem	Lima
second	Sanga	Nem
third	Manyura	Barang

Fig. 5. Matrix of Javanese modes (*pathet*)

sanga and *pélog nem, sléndro manyura* and *pélog barang*).[11] Boundaries between groups of related items are clear, and almost all pieces are attributed unambiguously to one modal category or another. The matrix is symmetrical, but this orderliness comes at the expense of comprehensiveness, for the "subsidiary" mode *pélog manyura* or *pélog nyamat* is ignored. (In practice, pieces in this mode are performed together with *pélog nem* pieces, which they most closely resemble.)

The relationships between *pathet* become less straightforward when applied to modal characteristics of specific pieces. It is sometimes difficult to justify the classification of a piece in *sléndro nem* rather than *sléndro manyura*, for instance, because the fairly clear boundaries that obtain when fitting items into the *pathet* sequence of performance become fuzzy and categories overlap when the characteristics of individual pieces are analyzed. The difference between pieces in *pélog lima* and *pélog nem* is so obscure that some musicians ignore the fuzzy boundary and group them together as *pathet bem*.[12]

This situation has caused great difficulties in Javanese music scholarship as people have failed to distinguish first between procedural and declarative aspects of *pathet* and second between two different *pathet*-related frameworks. One framework influences the sequence of events by classifying repertoire in a largely unequivocal manner, assigning each piece to one *pathet*. It is the cumulative result of the assignment of pieces, generation after generation, to particular *pathet* for the purposes of producing a performance sequence. Deducing the modal characteristics of *pathet* from this classification is fraught with difficulties because a wide range of potentially conflicting considerations may have affected the evolution of this classification through periods of changing stylistic ideals and modal concepts.

11. This pattern is followed in nighttime performances of music or theater when a full *gamelan* is available. If only one tuning is available, the modal sequence is followed in that tuning.

12. But see Hastanto (1990) for the most cogent attempt to differentiate these two *pathet*.

The second type of *pathet* framework gives a much more complex and sometimes uncertain "placement" of pieces *vis-à-vis* possibilities of interpretation on the elaborating instruments. It is based on the recognition that there are more and less typical pieces in each *pathet*. A competent musician should be able to make the less typical ones, even the ones that appear to "belong" in a different *pathet*, sound "in" the *pathet*. This is something that Martopangrawit emphasized repeatedly in our discussions. In other words, *pathet* is only partially inherent in a piece and must be actualized by a performer's choices of elaborating patterns and intonation (for vocal and *rebab* melodies). This is a fundamentally different perspective from the ahistorical analysis undertaken by Western scholars such as Kunst (1949), Hood (1954), and Becker (1980) who have conflated the two frameworks, acting on the assumption that all pieces in a modal category share certain attributes and that the attributes are manifest in the *balungan*.[13] However, in current practice—and presumably in the past, too—the *balungan* is no more than a skeleton; it remains for the musicians who perform the elaborating parts to bring this skeleton to life and "flesh it out."

Application of the *pathet* matrix to domains of procedural knowledge is still more problematic, because links between *pathet* do not follow the structure of the matrix. If the parallels inherent in the six *pathet* matrix held true for performance procedures, one would expect links between patterns in *sléndro manyura* and *pélog barang*, on one hand, and between those in *sléndro sanga* and *pélog nem*, on the other. But practice is not so straightforward: *sanga* and *manyura* patterns are used in various mixtures in both *pélog barang* and *pélog nem*, and a *gendèr* player can analyze each passage in a piece in terms of its *manyura* or *sanga* character, choosing patterns accordingly.[14]

A prototype effect is evident here (Lakoff 1987)—some elements in the set of modal procedures (patterns typical of *sléndro sanga* and *manyura*) are more central than others and serve as conceptual models for those other elements. Similar prototype effects are observable in other domains: *gendèr* patterns and procedures associated with the two intermedi-

13. The most egregious example is Hood's doctoral thesis, in which he "corrects" the classification of certain pieces in a manuscript collection on the basis of the presence or absence of a few key formulae in the *balungan* of these pieces (1954).

14. This is the explicit basis of modal pattern usage as taught in the performing arts schools (see McDermott and Sumarsam 1975 or Martopangrawit 1984), particularly on the *gendèr*, which serves as the referent for most theoretical discussions (see Hastanto 1990, for instance). I do not know the extent of similar conceptualizations among other musicians. Modal practice is similar but more loosely regulated for most of the other elaborating instruments. Relationships are more complex and patterns less transferable in the idioms of the voice, *rebab*, and *suling*.

ate *irama* (tempo/density levels) are more central than those associated with the faster and slower levels. The latter can be derived by contraction or expansion from these prototypical elements. This particular prototype effect is probably more pronounced for foreign students of *gamelan*, who are usually introduced to the most expansive *irama* at an advanced stage of study.

On close inspection many of the explicit classifications of Javanese musical knowledge are illogical. Parallel tripartite divisions of the *gamelan* and vocal repertoires into large, medium, and small pieces are not consistently determined, for example. But the mnemonic utility of these classificatory devices must also be considered. Grouping knowledge in familiarly patterned matrices enables musicians to learn and keep track of large quantities of information. The importance of such patterning should not be underestimated in an oral tradition: prior to this century written records played a negligible role in the maintenance and transmission of musical knowledge in Java, and their role today is still secondary to oral means of transmission. From this point of view, discrepancies and inconsistencies are less important than the basic noetic utility of classification systems.

Domains of competence are linked in myriad ways. Knowledge of repertoire, for example, is multifaceted. Pieces are known both as independent entities and in relation to other pieces, either through analogy or through direct derivation. Performance becomes possible through calls on declarative knowledge of the relevant contextual frameworks and of specific, nonsystematic aspects of the individual composition in conjunction with procedural knowledge relating to melodic flow, idiomatic patterns, modal practice, interaction, and various transformative possibilities. Each piece within the repertoire is known as a framework having melodic and formal characteristics and, perhaps, contextual associations that can be realized in a variety of ways by application of relevant procedures within the framework of the particular performance.

It is theoretically possible to learn to play the *rebab* parts of many pieces without knowing the underlying patterns or to learn the patterns without knowing a single piece, but neither possibility is at all likely in practice. These two domains of knowledge—*procedural knowledge of idiomatic patterning* and *predominantly declarative knowledge* about a certain piece—mesh and reinforce one another. Yet these two interdependent types of knowledge must be mastered with some degree of separation. A competent musician must know the specific quirks of individual pieces, but can call on general knowledge of an instrumental idiom for a stock of patterns to speed the learning, recall, and re-creation of the several hundred pieces he or she must be able to perform from memory at a moment's notice. *Transformational knowledge* is called into play, too, as patterns are joined together in various combinations, played at different speeds in condensed and expanded forms, and varied or substituted during the many repetitions of a piece. These three domains do not suffice for actual performance. Most of the other domains are invoked continuously or repeatedly. The need to adjust vocal and *rebab* intonation, for example, calls on aesthetic sensibilities and a transformational procedure: a singer knows melodies as contours and adjusts intervallic sizes to personal conceptions and the tuning of the accompanying instruments. Other interactive procedures are constantly called into play as well.

Some domains may be so closely linked that they function as integrated units. Perhaps the clearest example of such higher-level groupings is the ability to create an appropriate part on *rebab, gendèr,* or any other elaborating instrument in the *gamelan.* Known as *garapan* (literally cultivation), this superdomain involves knowledge of repertoire, idioms, transformational procedures, and *pathet* frameworks and procedures.

Successful *garapan* depends upon aspects of competence that are generally applicable approaches to the utilization of knowledge rather than specific to a particular domain. Chief among these is flexibility, an ability to adapt knowledge, expectations, and actions to changing situations and requirements. Analysis and analogy are two further generally applicable tools a musician must master in the course of learning *garapan* and acquiring competence in *gamelan* performance.

For some Javanese musicians, particularly those involved with performing arts schools, knowledge of *garapan* is explicit: analysis of typical and problematic passages can be discussed orally and in writing.[15] For many other fully competent musicians, however, this knowledge is not readily verbalized and may not even be explicit enough to enable such musicians to produce examples out of context. Yet the processes of *garapan* must be at work in their minds, because rather than knowing a fixed part for each instrument for each of several hundred pieces, these musicians create or re-create the parts as needed in accordance with the changing circumstances and sequence of events in a particular performance. They manipulate stocks of patterns, working from declarative knowledge of a particular piece and following their understanding of modal frameworks and procedures, typical melodic progressions, and idioms. In this endeavor they are guided by analogies with pieces of similar form, character, mode, and so on. Their understanding of these frameworks and procedures is shaped through interaction with other

15. See Sukamso (1992) and Suraji (1991b), for example.

musicians in performance rather than through formal instruction or theoretical discussion.

The importance and prevalence of these interpretive tools can be inferred from problems that arise in performance. A musician may be criticized for choosing the wrong *céngkok* (elaborative pattern) due either to mistaken analysis (a "misreading" of the passage) or to poor analogy (choosing an inappropriate model for emulation). For example, a piece that begins and ends in *pathet sanga* may contain passages which "modulate" to the other two *sléndro* modes. A musician may fail to analyze these modulations and mistakenly interpret these passages using *pathet sanga* patterns rather than ones from the appropriate mode. Or a particular piece may require that parts such as the *gendèr* or *rebab* melodies diverge from the *balungan*. In this case specific knowledge of the piece is required: standard procedural knowledge applied to general frameworks would lead a performer astray, as he or she would analyze the passage in terms of analogous passages in other pieces. Likewise, a drummer may mistakenly choose to cue an *andegan* (a pause in the middle of a cycle in which a brief solo is sung) at a point which is structurally analogous to places for *andegan* in similar compositions but which is inappropriate for the piece in question.

It is essential to realize that these analyses and analogies may only be mistakes with respect to the practice and norms current at a particular time and place. Should the "mistakes" be repeated frequently enough, they are likely to cease to be mistakes and to become common practice instead, either as an accretion to previous practice or as a replacement for it. Martopangrawit explained the increased use of *andegan* in this manner and also made the dire prediction that the use of *pamijèn* (elaborative patterns specific to one piece) would only survive in America in the near future because only his foreign students expressed interest while younger Javanese musicians were not interested in specific declarative knowledge of individual pieces, preferring systematic application of procedures (personal communication).

COMPETENCE IN PERFORMANCE

This emphasis on flexibility and the procedures of *garapan* brings us to another view of Javanese musical competence: as it is used in performance. Competent *gamelan* performance involves using a set of procedures (ways of conducting[16] oneself musically) within a given set of cir-

---

16. "Conduct" is used here in preference to "behavior"; see Dasilva, Blasi, and Dees, who have argued for this choice (1984: 157, fn. 1).

cumstances to produce an acceptable sequence of events. The set of circumstances encompasses context in its most inclusive sense: time, place, function, available instruments and musicians, and so on—in other words, specific instances drawn from the general classes of possibilities that constitute a performer's declarative knowledge. Through association with expected sounds and acts this set of circumstances influences the sequence of events that constitutes a particular performance. This sequence of events is the act of performance as it unfolds: a dynamic framework for the procedures of performance that is created by those very procedures. The sequence is acceptable to the extent that it matches the declarative knowledge of the requirements for those circumstances. On one level this unfolding may be viewed as a single sequence, but in any ensemble situation it is actually built up of simultaneous action sequences produced by individual musicians; the number of strands increases when music is linked with dance, theater, ritual, or some other activity. The ability to control this sequence when appropriate or to predict it and "go with the flow" when a performer is not in a position of control is a primary aspect of competence.

The epistemological status of different aspects of a musician's competence determines the utility of that competence in performance. Passive knowledge is sufficient if—by virtue of one's role/instrument—one is not called upon to initiate actions but only to respond to other musicians' actions. Interactive skills enable musicians with relatively limited knowledge of repertoire to play adequately with more experienced musicians as long as they play roles which allow them to float along with the others. For this reason the repetitive and derivative elaborating melodies played on *bonang panerus, siter,* and *gendèr panerus,* which are the fastest parts in the ensemble, are considered easy to play despite their high speed.

Explicitness of knowledge enhances a musician's performance capabilities chiefly in instructional situations. Explicit knowledge of the names of the various songs sung by a *dhalang* in theatrical performances does not directly enhance a musician's ability to accompany these songs since they are never referred to by name in performance but are cued in other ways. Likewise, a musician can perform perfectly well without knowing the names for *gendèr* patterns that are used principally by academically trained musicians. But explicit knowledge allows a person to convey aspects of competence to others, and knowledge of terminology or theoretical constructs, for example, may add to a musician's prestige or aura of competence, enhancing his or her standing as an authority (a point to which we shall return in later chapters).

The relative automaticity of a musician's knowledge is a third variable. Beyond the usual low-level types of "automatic" skills such as hand movements there are larger combinations of patterns such as the many interactively determined external calls on knowledge that are invoked by other performers. The split-second responses required in shadow play performance (discussed in chap. 9) are a particularly clear case of the independence of automaticity and explicitness. Whether or not a musician is able to give explicit explanations out of context, he or she must have an automatic command of performance options in order to react virtually instantaneously to the *dhalang's* cues.

All the above distinctions pertain to the representation and storage of knowledge in memory, the accessibility of this knowledge, and the control a person has over it. Active knowledge enables a person to recall readily items that if known passively could only be evoked by external information and associations. Explicit knowledge is labeled or otherwise "packaged" in mental representations that allow a greater degree of conscious control and reflection than is available for intuitive knowledge and therefore a greater capability of drawing on knowledge out of context. Automaticity bypasses conscious control of access to memory and allows a musician to play faster than he or she can think.

A simplistic approach to the question of memory and competence holds that the more a person stores in memory, the more competent he must be. But a rich "memory bank" is not enough—one must also have quick and flexible access to be able to utilize this memory bank in performance. Summarizing prior research on memory, Gruson writes that

> long-term memory is hypothesized to contain an internal representation of . . . familiar patterns together with information concerning appropriate associated actions. Furthermore . . . the information is organized hierarchically. A number of patterns may, therefore, be represented in a single familiar configuration in long-term memory. Experience is proposed as the process through which one's knowledge base and cognitive structure are built up. (1988: 92.)

The importance of internal links is recognized here, as is the complementary pairing of declarative and procedural knowledge. But this formulation is not sufficient: one must also develop grouping skills, learning how to interpret new input meaningfully.

A Javanese *gendèr* player hearing another musician play something new can probably construct an equivalent pattern in his or her own style far more rapidly than a "verbatim" repetition that includes the other musician's nuances. Inexact, interpretive repetition is not only an aesthetically motivated strategy to make one's playing distinctive (see Sutton 1982: 26) but the direct result of typical Javanese contexts for transmission of musical knowledge. By contrast, exact emulation is precisely what most foreign students produce with the aid of tape recordings and transcriptions, creating a false impression of competence and building up a stock of patterns that is not immediately flexible in usage. This flexibility must be built up, too. My own experience playing *gendèr* (which I have seen duplicated in the case of other non-Javanese) involved learning the parts to various pieces note for note with the aid of recordings, developing passive recognition of recurring patterns but not the active access or the flexibility which would allow me to break these patterns down and recombine them in new contexts or even to substitute one pattern for another in familiar contexts in the course of performance. Only after being given explicit instruction in the formulaic aspects of *gendèr* playing by Harjito was I able to develop the basic cognitive skills of *garapan*: (1) analyzing context and producing the appropriate sound patterns by analogy with pieces I already knew and (2) grasping new patterns as variants or combinations of old ones, or in contrast to known patterns. In my case, the availability of names for basic patterns definitely facilitated access to these patterns. The interpretive skills were then available to be applied to the *gambang*, which I learned far more easily despite the lack of named patterns, not only because the idiom is easier but because I had already learned generally applicable procedures for making appropriate analogies, substitutions, and transformations of basic patterns and had become familiar with the frameworks within which these operations take place.

In performance, musicians access knowledge within the flow of events. This access is influenced by the relevant declarative frameworks that create an individual's reality of the moment. In addition to perceptions of what is taking place at that moment this reality may include past and future—memory traces of the sequence of events which has led to that moment and potential interpretations and continuations of other performers' actions. Such access is different from out-of-context calls on explicit knowledge that require the person to construct a set of circumstances mentally and then imagine a sequence of events. Thus, for instance, when musicians were first tested for teaching positions at the conservatory in Surakarta, they had to display far more explicit knowledge of the conventions of *gamelan* accompaniment to the shadow play than would be required in actual performance situations. Given the location and leading character of a hypothetical scene, they were required to name the appropriate piece (Wasitodiningrat, personal communication).

If our memories are structured as semantic nets in which each item is a node linked by associative arcs to a number of others, then Javanese performance involves the incremental arousal of mutually reinforcing nets of knowledge. These nets create a context for choosing among appropriate options and anticipating other performers' choices. The examinees in the above example had to invoke these nets consciously rather than flow through the experience of a familiar sequence of events that facilitates recall by association. Of course, this was precisely the point of the exam—to find performers whose knowledge was explicit enough to enable them to teach well by conveying knowledge out of context.

At present we know far too little about mental representations of musical knowledge. The prevalence and widespread recognition of many types of patterning clearly speaks for the probability that "chunking" individual notes into larger groups is predominant in the perception, learning, and retention of Javanese music, but how are these groups encoded and accessed—as pure sonic "images," as kinetic patterns, as named entities? Nominal systems offer a highly economical means of access to knowledge, while melodic and rhythmic essences offer an unmediated impression on memory and kinetic patterns offer direct access to reproduction of sounds remembered. All of these possibilities must be considered in a search for mental representations in Javanese music.

Chunks of knowledge can, by frequent association, be grouped into larger sequences, forming scripts for a stereotypical course of action or set of moves. Obvious examples in Javanese performing arts include dance and puppet movement sequences that are standardized but not completely fixed. The drummer who is responsible for interacting with dancers or puppets and coordinating the *gamelan* with their movements can anticipate those movements and reproduce a compatible script of drum strokes.

But are pieces also known as scripts? We noted earlier that a piece may be known somewhat abstractly in terms of form, melodic shape, and contextual associations and demands. In performance, a player's knowledge is probably not highly segmented and analytical. There is some evidence that a piece is known as a linear sequence with options for repeating, altering, or straying from parts of this sequence. It is unusual to isolate small sections of a piece for teaching or rehearsal; instead, cyclical repetition affords repeated opportunities for getting it right. Early cipher notation was written in a run-on fashion (see fig. 6a); the graphic convention of arranging the layout of notation to reflect musical form, each phrase or phrase group as a line and four-beat groupings (*gatra*) set off by spaces (fig. 6b), is a relatively recent invention and does not seem to have imparted a strongly sectional conception of pieces to most musicians. In my admittedly limited experience, I have found that musicians have difficulty leaping into the middle of a piece to recall and discuss or perform a particular passage even with the aid

a. Older run-on layout

$\cdot 1 1 \cdot 1 1 2 3 5 6 5 3 2 1 2 \quad \cdot \hat{1} 1 \cdot 1 1 2$

$3 5 6 5 3 2 1 2 \hat{1} 3 2 1 2 \cdot 1 2 6 3 5 6 1$

$6 5 2 \hat{3} 2 1 2 \cdot 2 1 6 5 3 3 \cdot 5 6 1 2 \textcircled{1} \cdot 1 1$

b. Newer symmetrical layout

$\cdot 1 1 \cdot \quad 1 1 2 3 \quad 5 6 5 3 \quad 2 1 2 \hat{1}$

$\cdot 1 1 \cdot \quad 1 1 2 3 \quad 5 6 5 3 \quad 2 1 2 \hat{1}$

$3 2 1 2 \quad \cdot 1 2 6 \quad 3 5 6 1 \quad 6 5 2 \hat{3}$

$2 1 2 \cdot \quad 2 1 6 5 \quad 3 3 \cdot 5 \quad 6 1 2 \textcircled{1}$

$\hat{}$ = *kenong* marking end of phrase

$\bigcirc$ = *gong* marking end of cycle

Fig. 6 Notation layouts

of notation. But they appear to have no difficulty maintaining a mental representation of lengthy pieces in the course of various "deforming" transformations such as temporal expansion or change of instrument or tuning. We can deduce from this that mental representations of pieces are characterized by a high degree of continuity and linear integrity, but are flexible and abstract enough to allow for a wide variety of realizations.

There must be some differentiation within this continuity, however, for there are points at which the path can branch off in several directions. Perhaps the mental representations of a piece should be viewed as a continually evolving tree or net of converging and diverging possibilities that musicians follow and, at times, control as leading roles shift with context.[17] Choices made in performance create a particular permutation of the basic characteristics of the piece that emerges from countless possible realizations.

We must distinguish between short pieces that are easily grasped as a single entity and long ones that may strain the limits of human memory. A Javanese piece may be as short as an eight-note cycle, repeated every four seconds, or so long that it spans several 128-beat cycles, repeating only after eight to twelve minutes. The dividing line between these extremes probably varies with the musician, more experienced players being able to grasp longer and more complex chunks. Knowledge of the shorter, faster pieces can pass from consciously controlled processing to automaticity: when playing one of the short *sampak* or *srepegan*, which are repeated seemingly endlessly in the course of a shadow play performance, musicians need not think about the next note—they need only be alert and ready to respond with split-second reflexes to cues to stop or alter the piece. Such automaticity does not seem possible for the more extended pieces. In some of these there is a real danger of

17. The converging and diverging paths of related *pathetan* are discussed extensively in Brinner (1985).

losing one's place or drifting into another piece. This concern was raised by most of the musicians with whom I studied. It is particularly problematic when playing an extended section in which the *balungan* notes are widely spaced in time and large segments of the piece are also common to other pieces. Reinforcement of memory by other players is essential in such situations: the presence of others forms a safety net so that if one person starts to drift or forget, several others will probably be able to maintain the piece while the drifter gets back on track.[18]

A person can develop and maintain several representations of an item in memory. My teacher I. M. Harjito differentiated between his kinetic and auditory memories of the *gendèr* part for Sendhon Rencasih when he talked about the commonly acknowledged difficulty of playing this piece. He found the sounds of the piece confusing because it is a transposition of the more commonly performed Sendhon Pananggalan (transposition in *gamelan* music inevitably involves changes in intervallic relations akin to those produced by a modal change in Western music). He said that when he felt he was in danger of losing his place because of the altered intervals of the transposed melody, he would concentrate on the kinetic patterns of the hand movements that produce the piece. Clearly he knew the piece in at least two different ways and had sufficient control to separate the two. This is something that every Javanese musician who plays a melodic instrument can do on some level, since kinetic patterns are constantly being shifted from one pitch to another or from *sléndro* to *pélog* with strikingly different sonic results, but I am not sure that most musicians would be able to maintain the separation between kinetic and auditory pattern for as large a chunk of music as Harjito could. This separation requires the rejection of the auditory feedback that a musician usually relies on as a confirmation of his or her processes of sound production.

Another instance of multiple representations is more typical. On one level the distinction between the basic *sampak* and *srepegan* pieces in a given mode is clear: since they can be performed independently and differ in colotomic structure and performance practice, they must be known as separate entities. However, they share such aspects as melodic contour and drumming patterns and must also be known as two transformations of a single piece in order to enable the seamless shifts from one to the other which occur frequently in theatrical performances (see fig. 7). Similarly, pieces that are derived from a common vocal melody may

---

18. The interactive safety net is discussed in the next part of the book. My current research concerns the ways in which musicians learn, remember, forget, and recall long and confusing pieces.

Fig. 7 Srepegan and Sampak Manyura

have overlapping conceptualizations, that is, multiple mental representations. These are examples of the phenomenon of fuzzy boundaries: while the domain of repertoire might be assumed to consist of discrete items, some pieces can be viewed both as separate items and as related manifestations of a single item.

When a musician says "this piece contains all you need to know," several assumptions about the nature of competence are implicit: the existence of prototypes, finite domains, and systematic transferability. Among the things to be known, some are more representative than others; the piece in question is such a prototype. Some domains of competence are finite in the sense that a set amount of knowledge, which can be derived from this one piece, is representative of the entire universe of possibilities. Finally, musical performance is systematic enough to enable one to apply the knowledge gained from this prototypical piece to other pieces.

The systematic applicability of procedures to analogous frameworks is also implied by the assessment that "if you know how to play X, you must know how to play Y." Sometimes assumptions about the sequence of competence acquisitions are also implied. For example, *rebab* and *gendèr* are considered to be particularly difficult instruments which are usually studied only after attaining some competence on most of the easier instruments and gaining substantial experience in most aspects of *gamelan* performance. Foreign students who begin to play these instruments in their first or second year of study fail to match these expectations and, in a sense, have to backtrack as they progress.

The discussion of competence in this chapter has focused on ideals of competence, on generalizations and abstractions. Actual competences feature idiosyncratic links and groupings deriving from individual experience: associations formed when a certain piece was first heard and impressions made by hearing particular performers or playing with them. Since much knowledge is not explicitly taught but deduced by each musician, we should expect diverse personal "theories" which—articulated or not—may be used to organize individual knowledge. It is precisely this individual variation that makes an abstract model of potential competence useful as a basis for analyzing and comparing individual realizations of this potential. The next two chapters explore some of the ways in which actual competence varies and the implications of these differences for performance.

CHAPTER THREE

INDIVIDUAL COMPETENCES

A substantial variety of competences is often recognized and fostered by a musical community. Musicians do not know all aspects of a tradition to the same degree. Distinct competences may be linked to roles within an ensemble, to instruments or repertoires, to levels of accomplishment, or to contexts and functions: a religious specialist knows things that a dance musician does not and vice versa. Such differences may be developed in specialized training or result more haphazardly from a musician's particular experiences; they may be recognized in competitions, occupational rankings, and so on. Ultimately these differences of competence may tell us more about the nature of musical competence than direct investigation and enumeration of the domains that constitute the general competence of a musical community. In view of the recognized differences that are integral to most musical systems and communities, McLeod and Herndon's hypothesis that "a normal member of a community, culture, or group, has knowledge about all aspects of his/her communicative system" (1980: 185) hardly seems tenable. This formulation, which McLeod and Herndon attribute to sociolinguistics, may be appropriate in the realm of language, but in the many musical communities that recognize and depend on a variety of musical specializations it is tautological, applying only to the shared core competence which it defines.

Competence also varies *regionally, historically,* and—within a regionally and historically defined community—according to *experience.* "Region" is used loosely here in recognition of the importance of physical proximity and face-to-face exposure in most music communities as a basis for the development of the distinctive variations in repertoire, style, and other aspects of music-making that tend to evolve when a music community is spread over large areas. "Historical" variation encompasses style as it develops and changes, but includes changes in other aspects of musical knowledge and practice such as the distribution of competence within the community.[1] "Experience" is to be understood here as the product of age, education, and association. In other words, a musician has the potential to enlarge his or her musical knowledge and ability through contact with others over time and the exact "shape" of that competence will be influenced by the other musicians with whom he or she has contact as student, auditor, co-performer, and even teacher. It will also be affected by the musician's ability and desire to hear and respond to what others do. The predominance of "influences" as a narrative device in jazz musicians' accounts of their personal development is a particularly clear example of the significance of individual experience in the formation of competence, but it is certainly not an isolated one.

The different ways of knowing discussed in previous chapters provide dimensions of variation that form the basis for socially and culturally defined distinctions of types and degrees of competence, particularly when these distinctions are applied to specific domains and roles. For example, leading musicians may need or be expected to know considerably more than other members of an ensemble, but their knowledge may differ in kind as well as in extent, being more active and explicit, while musicians who play other roles have less extensive knowledge of some aspects of competence and have only passive knowledge of other aspects. The explicit knowledge of musicians who are recognized as teachers in a community is likely to be unusually extensive. Other musicians may know many of the same things but in a more intuitive manner since they do not need to encapsulate this knowledge for transmission to others. Conversely, some teachers are valued more for their explicit knowledge, particularly pertaining to theory, than for their active command of performative skills and knowledge.

The extent of a person's knowledge has been mentioned several times in the last paragraph. This concept may be clear intuitively, but can it be quantified and if so how? There are probably no universally applicable answers to these questions, but in a given musical community the indig-

---

1. McLeod and Herndon are too restrictive in their choice of style as the primary defining element of competence (1980: 188).

enous methods of recognizing, ranking, or otherwise assessing musicians manifest the aspects of competence that are important within that community and suggest how these aspects might be measured. These culture-specific assessments are especially revealing when based on a breakdown of the competence into component domains and a relative weighting of these domains.

One way to assess the extent of competence is to measure it domain by domain, as with the active/passive and intuitive/explicit assessments. Taking a spatial metaphor of breadth and depth, we can say that musician X has a broad knowledge of the repertoire, while musician Y knows fewer pieces but has a deeper knowledge of those few pieces. A similar comparison might be made substituting modes, drumming patterns, or some other item. In any case, breadth expresses the number of items or classes of items known and depth measures the degree of detail, refinement, or explicitness of a musician's knowledge in a given domain.

The relative weight or importance accorded each domain also characterizes a musician's competence. Perhaps mastery in the domain of sound quality, exemplified by extraordinary tone and intonation, is enough to compensate for a musician's relatively small repertoire or simple playing technique. If such comparisons are made frequently within a musical community and the terms of comparison are consistent, then we have evidence of the relative weight of these domains in that community. For instance, technical mastery and emotional depth are often cited as contrasting poles with regard to musicians in the Western concert tradition. Is this juxtaposition merely a journalistic ploy trotted out by critics, or does it reflect more widely held conceptions about these aspects of competence, perhaps even a sense of mutually exclusive goals? A comparative study of musicians' assessments of concert pianists or violinists might teach us something about the relative values of these and other domains.

Given these rough methods of measurement, refined by indigenous standards and terms of appraisal, we can begin to piece together a picture of the different types of competence within a community and their importance to the structuring of music-making within that community. Differences based on experience and age are to be expected, for instance, but how are these accommodated within a given community? Are there roles within an ensemble for musicians who are significantly less competent than others because they have less experience or less aptitude? The roles of drone player in a Hindustani ensemble and gong player in a Sundanese *wayang* troupe—which are often filled by a disciple of the soloist and by a child of one of the other performers, respectively—come immediately to mind, but there must be many more such opportunities in other music communities for breaking in a student or enabling a younger relative to begin a performing career, or for taking advantage of family resources to augment an ensemble.

Is there a general competence for a given music, from which all the limited or specialized competences are drawn? If so, a musician who has truly mastered the tradition—who "knows the score"—would be one who has command of this encompassing competence. Alternatively there may be separate competences that overlap but do not form a whole that a single person can master. While the various specializations in the Western concert tradition are based on many shared elements, it is highly unlikely that one person could master all or even most of the specialized competences in the orchestra, save in the essentially passive way that a conductor does. Yet the specialized competences of orchestral players overlap more with one another than with the competence of musicians who specialize in the performance of medieval European music. By contrast, the nature of Javanese *gamelan* is such that musicians do have the possibility of attaining a global competence, though most do not fully attain it. There is little differentiation of historically defined competences among current musicians although there are musical competences linked to other styles that have little overlap with *gamelan* competence.

Such examples point to the need for some basic distinctions that will allow characterization and meaningful comparison of different competences within and between communities (see fig. 8):

global competence encompasses all the performance possibilities within a musical community;

specialized competence is characterized by significant differentiation from other competences within the community;

a *core competence* consists of the shared knowledge, the area of overlap or intersection between different specializations, which may serve as a common basis for communication and specialization;

a *discrete competence* is more intensely distinctive than specialized competence because it has little or no overlap or common ground with other competences.

Further distinctions can be made to reflect an individual's competence relative to culturally defined standards and maxima:

well-rounded competence denotes mastery of most aspects of a global competence, exemplified by the ability to play all instruments or all repertoire though not equally well;

limited competence denotes partial knowledge.

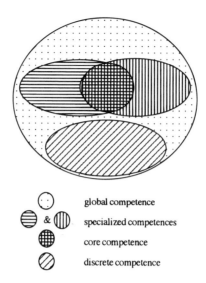

global competence

& specialized competences

core competence

discrete competence

Fig. 8 Types of competence

Every competence is limited in some sense, of course, but some are more limited than others. The word "limited" is used here to denote a competence whose extent is markedly less than others in depth and breadth, consisting perhaps of the core competence with little additional knowledge of a specialized nature. This level of competence is sufficient for some roles and contexts, but is surpassed by many musicians. The analysis of some musics may call for additional distinctions such as *novice*, *amateur*, and *professional* that can be used to qualify the types suggested above by denoting levels of attainment and communal recognition.

All of these distinctions are useful tools, not ends in themselves. They should be used with regard for synchronic differences and diachronic changes within a given musical community. They are valuable only to the extent that they are linked to the experience of particular individuals and help us to understand the nature and distribution of musical competence within and between communities.

Distribution of Competence

Who knows what? is one of the fundamental questions that must be asked in any localized study of competence. This question can be posed for all members of a community to determine the distribution of musical competence among musicians and nonmusicians. All members of a community may be knowledgeable and involved in making music, although certain specialists surpass the common competence. Examples of universally distributed competence are reported by Blacking among the Venda in South Africa (1971b: 4, 46), by Turino for Aymara men in Peru (1989: 18), and by Pertl for Tibetan monks (1992: 90). In other communities musical competence is more limited in distribution, reserved for or relegated to some subset of society. In such cases we need to know whether this musician subset of society is defined by hereditary distinctions or other nonmusical constraints on individual choice or aptitude such as gender, class, religion, or ethnicity.

The question Who knows what? can then be asked again with reference to this musician subset to obtain a picture of the types of competence—well-rounded, specialized, discrete, and core—recognized in a given community. As with the distribution of musical competence in general, we should question the patterns of distribution of these types of competence, looking for social distinctions that arise from or lead to distinctions of musical competence. How and why have competence archetypes such as court musician, village musician, drummer, or folk singer developed in particular communities? We need to learn more about how such distinctions of competences are fostered and accommodated in musical communities. Neuman's work on Hindustani musicians (1980) is exemplary in this regard.

Since the attainment of musical competence is a function of a musician's experience, the distribution of competence within a society is directly related to the degree of freedom a musician has in shaping that experience. The distribution of musical competence is likely to be more constrained, more predictable, and slower to change in communities with stronger social divisions and greater linkage of the role of musician to particular socially defined niches. Conversely, communities with fewer social strictures or less restrictive definitions of who can be a musician will almost certainly display a less predictable distribution of competence.

Musical competence is directly linked to social distinctions because it enables a person to participate in social associations among music-makers and between the music-makers and the audience; this association intersects with social attitudes that may act as incentives or constraints for individual initiative. Social distinctions often influence or determine who may achieve musical competence and who may not. For some, a musical calling is ordained by external forces beyond an individual's control: such people are born into the occupation, just as others are barred by reason of birth. Lane (1860) and Racy (1983a) report on specialized competences in nineteenth-century Egypt that were defined by gender, repertoire, instruments and ensembles, contexts, and status. Social determinism is rarely complete, however: while an individual can only alter or suppress attributes such as heredity, gender, ethnic origin, religious affiliation, and socioeconomic standing with great effort, if at all, extraordinary individuals do manage to surmount barriers imposed on the basis of these factors.[2] On occasion they break down these barriers, paving the way for others to follow. Musical competence can thus empower a person to associate outside and "above" his or her social group. In the United States, as in many other countries, the role of entertainer has afforded members of many minorities, in particular African-Americans, a way to transcend many social and economic barriers.

Set against these social strictures and incentives is the concept of talent, widely held to be the primary determinant of musical competence. Merriam briefly surveyed the treatment of talent in the ethnomusicological literature in 1964, contrasting societies that believe in fundamental equality of human capacities with those that believe in unequal distribution of talent, the presence of such talent usually being ascribed to heredity:

> The concept [of unequally distributed talent] . . . determine[s] who will or
> will not become a musician and who will or will not be encouraged along
> these lines. Further, it affects the potential for music within the society;
> among the Anang, it may be presumed that the potential sources from which
> the society can draw to provide musicians are substantially greater than in
> Basongye society where the number of possible musicians is sharply restricted
> by the concept of individual inheritance of "talent." (1964: 68.)

He also adopts Linton's distinction between ascription and achievement, suggesting that we differentiate between societies in which the role of musician is ascribed to certain individuals and societies in which individuals must achieve this role of their own accord (Merriam 1964: 131), but failing to clarify the connection between talent and ascription. A quarter of a century later Merriam's student Henry Kingsbury has taken up the question of talent in the context of an American conservatory, focusing on a predominant cultural attitude toward the potential for competence by titling a chapter "Cream Rises." While one may or may not accept the full thrust of Kingsbury's definition of talent as "a representation of differentials of potential for certain socially valued behavior, differentials that are believed to be ordained not in social order but rather by the inherent nature of people" (1988: 63) or his indictment of conservatory musicians' attitudes, it is hard to deny that assessed talent

---

2. Ankica Petrovic has reported on Yugoslav women who cross gender barriers by adopting male social and musical roles (colloquium at U. C. Berkeley, January 1991).

is the basis for initial and continued access to the best means of attaining competence in Western conservatories, just as it is in some other traditions.

As we examine the distribution of musical competence within a community of musicians, it is useful to posit two contrasting poles of undifferentiated, *uniform competence* and fully differentiated, *disjunct competences.* Musical communities tend toward uniformity when most musicians share a common competence that includes most aspects of musical knowledge. In such situations global and well-rounded competences are not only possible but widespread and differences in competence result from individual experience (and talent) rather than from specialized training. In the context of a nearly uniform competence, differences are mainly a matter of focus, the emphasis of one domain relative to others, rather than of specialization or differentiation. Conversely, disjunct competences arise when musical knowledge is segmented in such a way that different specialists have little or nothing in common. As the incidence of specialization rises and the core competence common to all musicians decreases, individual competences become more discrete or disjunct and a musical community tends toward differentiated competence.

These concepts of uniformity and differentiation are theoretical extremes that provide a means of comparing different musical communities and talking about diachronic changes within one community. It is unlikely that either pole is ever attained: we can only talk about truly uniform competence by ignoring musicians who are still in the process of attaining competence; on the other hand, a musical community whose competence is fully differentiated hardly qualifies as a community from a musical point of view since there is no common ground. The conceptual "space" separating these poles is multilinear. Locating a particular musical community closer to one pole or the other therefore entails considering a number of variables. A particular degree of disjunction or uniformity does not necessarily characterize an entire music-making community since different mixes, groupings, and rankings of competence often occur within one musical complex.

Distinctiveness may be downplayed in communities tending toward egalitarianism such as the Venda, whose competence is in fact differentiated according to gender and age. In other societies the distinctiveness deriving from differentiation of competence is a desirable attribute and even a focus of creative activity. For example, Jacqueline Cogdell DjeDje's analysis of responses by three black Catholic congregations to gospel music shows a process of differentiation whereby disparate attitudes toward a particular way of making music are linked to the marking and maintenance of social distinctions (1986). While this analysis does not refer specifically to competence, the processes described are relevant. DjeDje borrows the concept of differentiation from the sociologist Eisendtadt:

> Differentiation describes the ways through which the main social functions or the major institutional spheres of society become disassociated from one another, attached to specialized collectivities and roles and organized in relatively specific and autonomous symbolic and organizational frameworks within the confines of the same institutionalized system. (1964: 376; quoted in DjeDje 1986: 241.)

Esoteric knowledge and practice can become cultural and social goals in their own right for schools, patrons, religious sects, teachers, or performers who distinguish themselves from all others through their way of making music. The development of distinctive traditions by rival Japanese schools of *koto, shamisen,* and *shakuhachi,* or Hindustani *gharanas,* or Central Javanese courts exemplifies this to varying degrees. A segmentation of competence is achieved by developing differing notation systems (such as tablatures) for each instrument, differing versions or interpretations for the same instrument, and strong social associations through pupil-teacher allegiances and guilds. Even when such means of differentiation are not involved, hierarchies of specialization are usually established. These are based, to some extent, on evaluations of the relative difficulty of the competences in question. Each specialization can be "located" relative to others, as when a violinist is placed in concentric groupings of increasingly narrow definition: in common perceptions of relative difficulty and importance "classical" is higher than popular, string players are higher than wind players, violinists are higher than other string players, and solo violinists are higher than orchestral players.

MULTIPLE COMPETENCES: BIMUSICALITY AND POLYMUSICALITY

When Mantle Hood argued for bimusicality (1960), he was breaking new ground only with regard to ethnomusicological training—musicians all over the world regularly master more than one competence for other reasons: as a result of living in a mixed community, out of economic, religious, or political necessity, or simply because of their curiosity about and attraction to other ways of making sounds. Whether it be different instruments and roles within a single complex of music-making practices or more distinct musical traditions, musicians frequently attain considerable mastery of two or more musical competences. The Japanese court musicians who added competence in European music to their native competence in *gagaku* as part of the political and cultural transformation of Japan during the Meiji restoration in the late nineteenth century offer one example of the capacity of the human mind and body to bridge extreme disjunctions in musical knowledge and skills. Davis has described some Caribbean examples that occur in sacred contexts, coining the term "native bi-musicality." She distinguishes between communal and individual bi-musicality, but does not explore the implications for competence or interaction among these individuals or embark seriously on the theoretical and comparative venture that she proposes (1987). These cases of multiple competence are interesting not only in their own right, but also as evidence of the extent of human mental and physical capacities and of the relationships among competences and between sociocultural complexes and contexts.

The many kinds of multiple competence fall into four categories with very different implications for social and cultural motives, influences, and results. First, there are the multiple competences that exist within one overall competence. For example, orchestral players who play several instruments or perform in significantly different roles and contexts as soloists or in chamber ensembles have done so by acquiring an additional body of specialized knowledge to add to a substantial core competence. The percussionist in a symphony orchestra is a case in point: because of stylistic preferences and developments in symphonic composition over the course of the last century, percussionists have been forced to expand their competence to such an extent, mastering a far greater variety of instruments and playing techniques than any other orchestral musician, that this competence has become a set of related competences. Study of such multiple competences reveals areas of overlap that form the core competence of a given community. Common learning sequences and career trajectories may also emerge, revealing musical and social priorities. Consider, for example, the added skills and knowledge of repertoire required of orchestral players who move to a solo career seeking fame and greater income as well as artistic challenge and satisfaction.

A second type of multiple competence bridges different communities or traditions within a larger tradition. Motivations for the development of such competences include potential appeal to a broader audience and reinforcement or reflection of large-scale ethnic, national, linguistic identities. Such reasons impel many Palestinian musicians to learn the repertoires of neighboring regional variants of the encompassing Middle Eastern tradition. An ethnomusicological inquiry into Western musicians' motivations for developing multiple competences that include different historical styles, repertoires, and practices is long overdue and would surely turn up other motivations that would further our understanding of attitudes toward culture, society, creativity, and taste.

A third type of polymusicality occurs within a social conglomerate that has a composite identity but is culturally heterogeneous. This type of multiple competence is evidence of culture contact between "subcultures." It deserves study for what it may reveal about value systems and intergroup relationships: members of one group may learn the other's music in order to "serve" it, as Gypsies and Jews did in Eastern Europe and as Armenians, Jews, and Greeks did in Egypt and other parts of the predominantly Arab Middle East. American popular musics offer many further examples of such border-crossings.

The most disjunct type of multiple competence encompasses completely unrelated competences associated with fundamentally different spheres of human association. Here the musician is a cultural and social outsider, often brought to the new musical tradition by social and political pressures. The above-mentioned Japanese court musicians who were required to master Western music in addition to *gagaku* offer a striking example of disjunct multiple competence. The forced adoption of Spanish or Portuguese church music throughout Latin America is another (Davis 1987). The reasons impelling increasing numbers of musicians in North America, Europe, and Japan to study completely foreign musical traditions during the past few decades have yet to be evaluated, but we are already surrounded by experiments in fusion undertaken by some of these musicians (see, e.g., Ruckert 1994 or Zhang 1994).

Over an extended period of time such disjunct competences do have the potential of leading to a fusion that engenders a new competence. The two competences in the Japanese example have yet to merge to the extent that competences have merged in various parts of Latin America. Davis foresees something of this sort occurring in the Caribbean (1987: 52). The musical mélange created in the United States in the twentieth century exemplifies the lessening of differences between discrete traditions and competences. Musicians who have training and performance experience in both symphonic and jazz traditions are not uncommon. While these competences still differ significantly, there is more overlap today than ever before.

What effect does the learning of one competence have on another competence? What is carried over from one competence to another, from one subdomain to another? Does affinity between discrete competences substantially enhance transferal of skills? One of the most interesting aspects of multiple competence is the assumption that studying one competence will improve another. In Western conservatories, for example, keyboard training is required of wind and string players as a basis for development of harmonic understanding and skills. In more disjunct competence mixes we find rock musicians studying classical music in order to gain the ability to read notation and classically trained musicians looking for improvisatory capabilities in rock:

> The rock musicians I studied . . . tended to stand in awe of those who were academically trained, and many were planning to obtain or were actually in-volved in gaining so-called classical skills. Similarly, there are some academi-cally trained musicians who passionately seek the ability to play by ear, to improvise, and to communicate with popular musicians . . . a newly flexible musician is among us. (Bennett 1980: 216–17.)

It is also fairly common for Arab musicians to turn to Western musical training for instrumental technique, particularly associated with the vio-lin, which they transfer to the performance of Arab music on violin and 'ud. One Arab musician who has followed this path writes somewhat bleakly of the artistic dilemmas that await him and his fellow travelers (Elias 1990/91).

In the process of learning one type of music to enhance another, mu-sicians are liable to be influenced by aspects other than those they set out to adopt. El-Shawan writes about the Arab Music Institute estab-lished in Cairo in 1929: "The inclusion of training in both Western art music and [Arab music] in the Institute's curriculum has contributed to the changing of the characteristics which were considered desirable in professional musicians . . . a close familiarity with both Western music and [Arab music] gradually became part of the ideal of a 'good' musician" (1980:96). Working with Arab musicians in Israel, I have found that those who have sought Western musical training have significantly dif-ferent expectations regarding intonation, ornamentation, and ensemble unity and blend compared with musicians who do not have this training.

There is no guarantee that components of a multiple competence are mastered to equal degrees. One competence may be rarely attained but highly valued, perhaps precisely because of the fact that it is rarely at-tained. Baily gives an example from Afghanistan—where local and North Indian competences are mastered to distinctly unequal degrees— of a prominent musician who was literate and knew North Indian *sargam* (a syllabic system of pitch representation), noting that "this highly edu-cated 'musicality' no doubt helped him to establish and maintain his dominant role amongst the musicians of Herat" (1988: 120). In this case, as in many others, the foreign competence is only partially mastered relative to the standards of the source community (India in this case), but that is sufficient by local standards.

A major challenge for future research in musical cognition is the study of factors affecting the potential for particular multiple competences. Common sense says that musicians who have already mastered similar knowledge in their own tradition are likely to learn the next competence more rapidly. But does it matter which aspects of two traditions are closest? We need to ask whether an instrument common to both traditions offers a smoother bridge than common approaches to ensemble organization, for instance. Musical and nonmusical motivations need to be explored further, too.

In this chapter I have suggested some ways of conceptualizing differences of competence within a musical community. Types of competence are characterized by the items that musicians know and the way that they know these items. Varying degrees of overlap or shared knowledge determine the relative integration or disjunction of a musical community and tradition. Similar concerns are relevant to the study of multiple competences. The dimensions of diversity outlined here serve as the framework for the exploration of differences of competence among Javanese musicians in the next chapter.

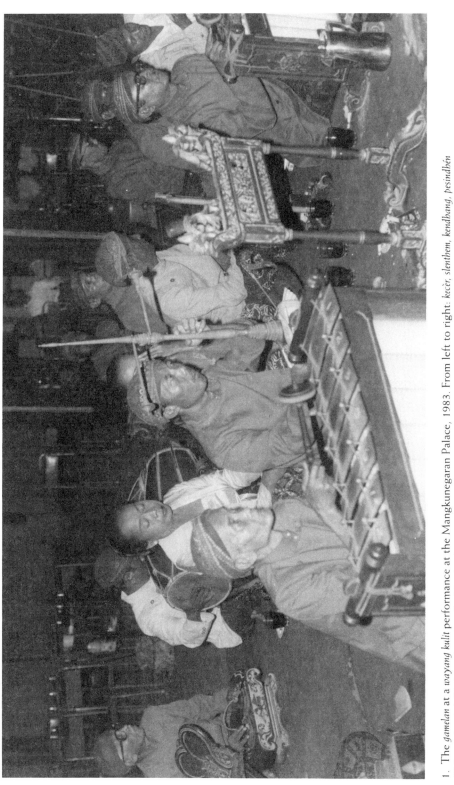

1. The *gamelan* at a *wayang kulit* performance at the Mangkunegaran Palace, 1983. From left to right: *kecèr, slentbem, kendhang, pesindhèn* (Tukinem), *rebab* (Dalimin), and *gendèr* (Turahyo).

Plate 11. The Iban RUK (BLK) Anthropomet

3. Turahyo playing *kendhang gendhing* and *ketipung*, *rebab* in background.

4. Turahyo (*kendhang*), Harjito (*gendér*), and Martopangrawit (*rebab*).

5. Mloyowidodo playing *suling*.

6. Martopangrawit playing *gambang*.

7. Tarnopangrawit playing gong.

8. Djumadi playing *rebab*.

CHAPTER FOUR

WHO KNOWS WHAT?

The ability to play *gamelan* is a specialized competence which is attained by a minority of Javanese. The aspects of musical competence that appear to be most widespread among nonmusicians are familiarity with the choral vocal parts (*gérongan*) of the most popular pieces and perhaps a sense of temporal aspects, which enables them to participate in the interlocking handclapping (*keplok*) that accompanies certain pieces.[1] Musicianship does not appear to be viewed primarily as a hereditary competence, although musicians often learn from relatives (as we noted in the Prelude) and there have been families of musicians associated with the courts. The innate or ascribed nature of competence is not nearly as strong for musicians as it is for *dhalang*. Many believe that only those born into the family of a *dhalang* can aspire to success, but this does not stop students who are not so blessed from enrolling in *wayang* classes.

For Javanese men there are few overt social limitations regarding who may or may not become a musician. Other than the minority of strict Muslims, who tend to shun *gamelan* for religious reasons, men from most social backgrounds play *gamelan*. Some ensembles are formed along class and occupational lines, but it is also possible to find sanitation workers sitting down to play with nobility. Although there may be few among

1. Martopangrawit criticized this participation as a recent development that was part of a general decline in order and standards (personal communication)

the upper classes who attain competence today, training in *gamelan* was considered an important element in the education of a cultivated person in the recent past. In performance, however, there was a status distinction: in court performances nobles danced and commoners played music, although some nobles including kings could also play (Martopangrawit, personal communication).

The situation for women is more complex and deserves careful scrutiny. A division between amateurs and professionals that is difficult to define for men appears to have real social significance for women. Today there are many women who participate in sexually segregated amateur ensembles called *ibu-ibu* groups. There, without any threat to their reputations, they may play all the instruments of the *gamelan*, although usually at a relatively low level of competence and under the leadership of a male musician who often takes the role of drummer. Outside such groups the opportunities for women to attain competence appear to be more limited than for men. Female relatives of a *dhalang* are most likely to be able to play *gamelan*.

Professional performance by women is almost completely limited to two roles: singer and *gendèr* player. A social stigma associated with the role of female singer keeps some higher-class women from pursuing this profession despite the star status attained by some singers.[2] This stigma, based on the close and sometimes flirtatious association between female singers and male musicians, is evident, for example, in self-conscious efforts to upgrade the status of singers by substituting the term *warang-gana* for the traditional term *pesindhèn*, which bears negative connotations. This stigma does not apply to *gendèr* players, who generally are not expected to engage in flirtatious interaction with male musicians and, in fact, often come from the inner circle of *dhalang* families and perform mainly with relatives (Sarah Weiss, personal communication). A late-nineteenth-century author writes of the superiority of women as *gendèr* players, preferring their supple wrists to a man's heavy hands (Kusumadilaga 1981: 49). A distinction between male and female *gendèr* styles is recognized, and men seem to find it improper to play in female style even though they may value that style (Wasitodiningrat and Sarah Weiss, personal communication).

Musical competence is of limited use as a means to gain wealth, recognition, and elevation of social status. Successful *wayang* drummers can be paid relatively well, but other musicians earn relatively little and there are no starring roles for musicians. Compensation for performance in court *gamelan* ensembles is now purely symbolic, but there is an aura

2. See Sutton (1984b) for a discussion of the role and status of female vocalists.

which still attracts some musicians, particularly villagers, to come to the court. In the past, musicians of humble origin who did well at court could achieve recognition and reward in excess of what they might have expected elsewhere. The late Mardusari is an example of a highly re-spected artist who rose to fame and status at the Mangkunegaran court earlier in this century because of her abilities as a singer and dancer. Today such transitions are possible mainly for *dhalang, pesindhèn,* and a few dancer/actors.

The concept of talent which Kingsbury (1988) has found to be the predominant element in the assessment of competence and prediction of potential in the American conservatory system (and by implication in Western musical training as a whole) does not figure as centrally in Javanese musicians' assessments of musical competence. This is not to say that some musicians are not recognized as better than others, but some aspect of a person's experience or character is far more likely to be invoked as the reason for a person's success as a musician. I have heard musicians mention character (*watak*) far more often than talent (*bakat*) as an essential element in the way a person plays.

LOCALIZED COMPETENCE:
SOCIOCULTURAL DISTINCTIONS

Global competence, embracing the universe of a musical tradition, can be viewed as an absolute construct if one takes a general theoretical stance, as we did in the last chapter, or the perspective of an insider who is ignorant or intolerant of diversity, but actual competences can only be global within sociogeographically defined communities that create and maintain cultural distinctions based on concentric local and regional loyalties, identities, and interests. These distinctions between one's own group and outsiders create a matrix for the conceptualization and loca-tion of self versus others in and outside the community. Matrices based on sociogeographically defined stylistic distinctions are also important cognitive devices for structuring musical knowledge: musicians attribute certain pieces and practices to categories labeled in accordance with particular places and groups of people.

Sociocultural milieu shapes evaluations of competence. An experi-enced Javanese court musician steeped in the many intricacies of special court performance traditions views matters very differently from an aca-demically trained musician, whose perspective differs, in turn, from that of a villager who plays in *wayang* performances twenty nights or more each month of the *wayang* season or from an urban musician who has not undergone training at the court or academy. Some musicians have more systematic conceptions of the patterning that characterizes many aspects of *gamelan* performance. This leads to situations in which city musicians, for example, claim to play more correctly than village musicians because their choice of patterns is more consistent, following *pathokan* ("rules") that are "ignored" by the village musicians. The establishment of institutions for education in the performance arts may well have intensified such comparisons and claims of correctness as formalized knowledge is promulgated through standardized curricula, teaching methods, and textbooks.

In such cases the assessment of relative competence is a matter of perspective. When a musician from one sociocultural community judges a member of another community to be ignorant, he is assuming that there is a universal competence—his own. But in fact there can be many localized competences and the urban musician's "rules" may simply not be part of the particular village competence. A generalized ideal competence is manifested in "localized" or "particularized" competences. The limitations of a generalized formulation quickly become apparent when confronted with reality because it is abstracted from the contexts and events that are determined by particular individuals acting in particular places.

The large-scale regional diversity of Java encompasses communities with historically interrelated *gamelan* styles but distinctive competences. Significant differences set Central Java apart from West Java (home to a separate ethnic group, the Sundanese, with a distinct cultural identity, language, and musical traditions) and, to a lesser extent, from East Java.[3] Within Central Java people distinguish four major court traditions of Surakarta and Yogyakarta, urban traditions from those same cities and from Semarang, and rural traditions from areas such as Klathèn, Boyolali, or Wonogiri. These communities of shared competence may in fact be far more complexly constituted than the shorthand of geographical or socioeconomic labels implies, with significantly different competences existing side by side. This is due in part to a high degree of mobility in the last half century that has brought many villagers to the cities and has also led to the breakdown of musicians' allegiances to the individual courts. In recent years, radio broadcasts and widely available cassette recordings have been the most important agents in the spread of aspects of localized competence beyond local boundaries. Such movement is not new, however: we know, for example, that musicians and

3. See Koentjaraningrat (1985) for a Javanese anthropologist's survey of the major cultural divisions and Sutton (1991a) for a comprehensive study of regional diversity in music in Central and East Java.

other performers deserted one royal court to seek employment at another on several occasions in the late eighteenth century (Ricklefs 1974: 230).

The difficulty of precisely defining local traditions derives from the complexities of political allegiances and demographic developments in Java. There has been a constant give-and-take between palaces, cities, and villages. Over the past centuries the royal courts have drawn musicians and particular repertoires and practices from villages and cities and these musicians have mingled and returned home, further spreading musical knowledge and resources. The political domains of the four Central Javanese principalities are geographically intertwined. The minor court of the Paku Alam is located within the city of Yogyakarta, not far from the palace of the senior ruler, the sultan. The proximity of Mangkunegaran and Kasunan palaces in Surakarta is similar. Contact between members of different communities has been facilitated by the fact that these two cities are not far apart and the territories ruled by the four courts are a patchwork quilt. Court alliances, often based on marriage diplomacy, have been accompanied by gifts of compositions, practices, and performers that have created strong ties in dance and music between the major house of one city and the minor house of the other.

In this century, educational institutions and mass media have further complicated the picture. Schools for performing arts founded by the courts have served as magnets which draw students from great distances, who then take these court practices home with them, establishing outposts of court-related practice in rural areas. Government conservatories and academies have continued this and have also served as catalysts and repositories for the collection, preservation, and transmission of local and regional traditions. Finally, the advent of radio broadcasts and cassette recordings has muddied boundaries and distinctions, removing the need for face-to-face contact as a basis for transmission.

Yet, despite these influences to the contrary, distinctive traditions persist and form the basic matrix for musical knowledge in Central Java. The desire for distinctiveness has been an important motivating force in the history of Javanese music, expressed in rivalry between the courts and accounting for many of the special features which separate the competences of different musical traditions and communities. Even within the limits of the city of Surakarta, musicians move in different circles and develop distinctive competences. The clearest examples are to be found in the courts because their power and resources in earlier days enabled them to support the creation and maintenance of a wide variety of distinctive ensembles, repertoires, and practices, including special ceremonial ensembles with specific repertoires, particular arrangements of pieces to accompany court dances, and special musical repertoire and practices for shadow plays.

Even within one tradition, significantly different competences have existed: at the height of royal patronage of the arts at the major court in Surakarta, several different groups of musicians were employed, each with its own duties. At one point the musicians of the Kadipatèn, the crown prince's residence, asked to be excused from performing on the ceremonial *gamelan sekatèn* because it was not within their competence (Warsadiningrat 1987: 147). Other, less exalted groups also have special pieces or ways of performing, but they do not have the institutional longevity of the courts and so the distinctive aspects of their competence do not attain the level of arcaneness that the court competences have. Musicians in rural areas, too, still maintain some of the specific repertoire and practices which developed in the relative isolation of the past.

A sense of community and shared knowledge exists in time as well as space, of course, and so the changes that inevitably occur in many aspects of musical competence accumulate and differentiate between earlier and later "versions" or "phases" of a competence. If change is rapid or drastic enough, a person's knowledge can easily become obsolete within a lifetime. Smaller changes or shorter time spans can create discrepancies between the competence of younger and older musicians, discrepancies that may be augmented by differences of taste and different patterns of association. Some older Javanese musicians complain that the young ones are not interested in large portions of the *gamelan* repertoire. In 1983, for example, Mloyowidodo (who was then seventy-two) complained that he was forgetting pieces he no longer had the opportunity to perform. In 1993 I found him sounding the same complaint but he had been given a forum to revive some of these pieces by teaching them to musicians at the Mangkunegaran palace. On the other hand, new pieces are added and ways of performing a piece also change, though most changes seem to stay within a circumscribed range of traditional options. These diachronic differences in competence are more difficult to study because of insufficient documentation of earlier practice and because the old and new are not brought into striking juxtaposition as frequently as differing contemporaneous styles are.

TYPES OF COMPETENCE WITHIN A COMMUNITY

Within each sociogeographically defined cultural community, Javanese musicians recognize a number of fundamental differences in musical competence dependent on roles in the *gamelan*. These distinctions are structural (relating to the ensemble framework) and procedural (relating to knowledge of idiomatic performance). It is common to distinguish between singers and instrumentalists whose skills differ considerably. Among the singers there is a further clear distinction between the male chorus and female soloists, while among instrumentalists the distinction between "front row" and "back row" players, based on placement of instruments and relative complexity of parts, is reflected in differing degrees of competence. Sindoesawarno defines this commonly invoked distinction in the following manner:

> A "musician of the front" means a musician who plays the gender, rebab, kendhang, slenthem, bonang, etc.; a "musician of the back" plays instruments that do not embellish the lagu, such as saron, kethuk, kempul, kenong, and gong. The terms "front" and "back" indicate a gradation, the front being higher than the back. The gender and rebab are the instruments that have the greatest freedom to make cengkok and wilet [patterns and variations] and these two instruments are played by musicians of the front. (1984: 398.)

Such informal typification of competence is the rule in Java. Aside from certain court rankings that will be noted presently, there are no formal ranks or stages of competence comparable, for instance, to the ranking within Japanese musical guilds.

The ways in which Javanese musicians distinguish between different types of competence are significant, but more significant still is the substantial core common to these competences. On the continuum stretching from uniform to fully differentiated or disjunct competences, Central Javanese *gamelan* traditions certainly fall closer to the uniform end than to the disjunct one. There are no truly discrete competences in the realm of Central Javanese *gamelan*. The core competence extends well beyond the fact that every musician can play instruments of the "back rows" (the colotomic and *balungan* instruments): there is a shared body of conceptual frameworks and procedures that constitute the bulk of musical knowledge. Compared with ensemble traditions in many other cultures relatively little additional knowledge is required for most specializations.

Many musicians progress beyond this core competence to master the more specialized knowledge of "front row" instruments or particular repertoires and associated performance practices. Each instrument requires specific idiomatic knowledge and technical skills. The demands associated with some instruments are greater and are augmented by the need to develop active mastery of performance practice and interactive procedures that are contextually determined. Instruments associated with leading roles are more difficult to master because a musician must know how to fulfill the role appropriate to his or her instrument (or vocal part), making decisions that affect the course of the performance for the entire ensemble. A few contrasting examples of specialized competence will suffice to illustrate this point. It is essential to remember that minimal requirements are discussed here. Many players surpass these by mastering the specialized knowledge of several instruments or performance contexts.

Drummers must master a large body of specialized knowledge and skills, particularly if they perform in dance and theater. They need to know the basic building blocks (the patterns of movement and appropriate drum patterns) as well as the larger sequences in order to control the temporal flow of the *gamelan*. A large body of procedural interactive knowledge specific to particular contexts must also be mastered. Drumming differs so greatly from one context to another that musicians actually distinguish between specializations in dance, *wayang*, and *klenèngan* drumming. Each requires different patterns, similar but not identical vocabularies of strokes, and particular tempi and changes of speed. Slightly different drums are used, and the basic touch, sound quality, dynamics, and overall feel of these three drumming styles differ.[4] This complexity is balanced, to some extent, by the fact that the same drum patterns apply to many different pieces.

A drummer needs comprehensive knowledge of the possible ways to perform each piece, including all the performance possibilities such as temporal transformations and transitions within and between pieces. Much of this knowledge need only be passive because he steers the other players through the transitions that require them to transform their parts. His active knowledge of patterns and processes of transformation can be used and reused ad infinitum, one pattern being used for all the pieces within a given type. For example, several hundred pieces are based on a sixty-four-beat cycle subdivided into four phrases that can be performed with a single drumming pattern.[5] A drummer needs to know the basic melody and some aspects of melodic *garapan* in order to orient himself to the piece, but since he does not actively use this knowledge by producing melody he may know the repertoire in a very different way than players of melodic instruments do. Some drummers, such as Wakidjo, whom we met in the Prelude, are proficient on other instru-

4. The division into three types of drumming is a simplification. There are actually several different kinds of dance drumming, and theatrical drumming differs depending on whether shadow play (*wayang kulit*) or theater with dancer/actors (*wayang wong*) is being performed.

5. Once again this is a simplification. There are often several appropriate patterns for a given piece, but with very few exceptions each of these can be applied to many pieces.

ments and also have extensive active knowledge of the melodic aspects of the repertoire.

The *gendèr* is another instrument of central importance that requires so much specialized knowledge that this competence is sometimes divided into two specializations, somewhat akin to the division in drumming: the requirements for a *gendèr* player in theater differ from those in *klenèngan*, although the overlap between these two roles is greater than for the different types of drumming (the role of the *gendèr* is less prominent in dance). For theatrical performances the *gendèr* is played almost continuously to accompany the *dhalang*'s songs and provide background for narration and dialogue. This requires close coordination and empathy with the *dhalang* as well as knowledge of a special repertoire of songs and mastery of improvisational skills. In *klenèngan* the *gendèr* and *rebab* provide the fullest realization of the basic melodic flow of the piece and share the responsibility of indicating the appropriate *garapan*. The modal implications of the *gendèr* part are particularly important for the ensemble. But unlike a *bonang* player, who must lead the *balungan* by playing a part that is usually closely linked to each pair of *balungan* notes, a *gendèr* player does not need detailed knowledge of the *balungan* of pieces for full *gamelan*. Martopangrawit and Mloyowidodo both stressed that it is enough to know the sequence of *sèlèh* (goal tones) and the appropriate patterns (*céngkok*) for proceeding from one *sèlèh* to the next (personal communication).

The competence required to play subsidiary elaborating instruments such as *gendèr panerus* or *siter* contrasts with the specialized competences associated with these leading instruments. The *gendèr panerus* offers a handy example since it requires a playing technique similar to the larger *gendèr* but has fewer patterns, is less stringently constrained, and makes far fewer demands on a player's knowledge of repertoire. Given sufficient passive familiarity with leading idioms and the main frameworks and transformational procedures to follow the basic melodic flow of the piece, a musician can easily learn to manipulate a fairly minimal stock of patterns to provide a satisfactory *gendèr panerus* part. He can even do so without actually knowing the piece that he is performing because the idiomatic patterning of *gendèr panerus* (and *siter*) does not commit a musician to begin a cadential pattern leading to a *sèlèh* until it has been clearly foreshadowed on leading instruments such as the *gendèr*, *rebab*, and *bonang*.

The performance contexts that serve as a basis for distinguishing drumming specializations are also associated with distinct bodies of knowledge that are relevant for other musicians. While idiomatic knowledge does not differ as it does for the drummer, significant differences exist in the domains of repertoire and performance context that constitute frameworks for orientation and interaction. Items of repertoire specific to a given performance context must be learned, and the ways that pieces are performed can also differ considerably. Musicians who specialize in shadow play performance know a somewhat different repertoire from others and are attuned to different ways of manipulating and transforming pieces.

Specializations defined by performance context and repertoire are most clearly marked in widely disparate types of performance such as court dances and village shadow plays. Musicians who are fully competent in one have relatively little preparation for the other. However, even closely related performance genres can require significantly different competences. Many similarities in repertoire and performance practice link *wayang kulit* (shadow play) and *wayang wong* (theater with actors), for example, yet the *wayang kulit* repertoire includes longer pieces that are rarely if ever played in *wayang wong* while vocal pieces sung by actors to the accompaniment of the *gamelan* are central to a *wayang wong* performance but rare in *wayang kulit*. Even pieces that are commonly used in both contexts may be played differently: one master musician told me that he could never play *gendèr* to accompany the *dhalang*'s songs in *wayang wong* because they are performed so much faster than in *wayang kulit*.

A significant number of Javanese musicians attain or approach global competence by knowing all or nearly all of the vocal and instrumental idioms and the "standard" repertoire for all of the main performance contexts. Their actual performance capabilities may be more highly developed in some domains than in others. Ironically, global mastery often leads to atrophy of practical skills, since it accords a position among fellow musicians that is not commensurate with performance on the instruments that are low in the hierarchy. These master musicians may actually become less proficient than less competent musicians at playing instruments such as the *gambang* or *siter* that require a considerable degree of dexterity despite the fact that they may well have a better sense of the idiom. Due to the integrative nature of Javanese *gamelan*—individual parts are closely related in "intent"—a musician may develop and retain a rich knowledge of the idiomatic patterns for an instrument that he rarely plays, knowledge that is reinforced by hearing others play this instrument while he plays something else.

This disparity between knowledge and skill, which in many ways is also a matter of passive and active competence, reaches its epitome in *sindhènan*, the female vocal part, a domain of competence that many male musicians know without being able to perform. This passive competence expresses itself in several ways: in men teaching women to sing *sindhènan*, in the contention that *rebab* players, in particular, have a responsibility to show the *pesindhèn* the proper melodic path,[6] in a general sense of superiority to *pesindhèn*, whose musical knowledge is often derided, and in the propensity of male musicians to heckle a singer for the slightest glitch in one of her solos.

Qualifying and quantifying knowledge of particular domains is a way to assess the type and extent of musicians' competence. Distinctions between active and passive knowledge of particular domains can be crucial in differentiating competence types. A *rebab* player has active knowledge of modal procedures and the melodic path of particular pieces which a musician of more limited competence may know only in a more passive sense. Such passive knowledge is adequate for playing the colotomic or *balungan* instruments, but it must be activated—that is, made accessible as a basis for independent action—in order to progress to a higher level of competence that enables performance on the melodic elaborating instruments.

When Javanese musicians speak of knowledge, they often measure it in terms of depth. A person may have superficial knowledge of a large portion of the repertoire, allowing the performance of any of the simpler parts, but in order to deepen that knowledge (*mendalami*) it is necessary to come to know, in some abstract and inclusive sense, the range of melodic possibilities and the structural and modal characteristics of the piece from performative and classificatory perspectives. The musician must learn the correct realization of the piece (*garapan*) and master other procedural knowledge concerning musical and extramusical associations and implications, including knowledge of when the piece is to be played, how it is to be treated, and to which other pieces it may be linked.

The typical variations in knowledge of repertoire shown in figure 9 illustrate this manner of assessing relative competence in a two-dimensional representation of how many pieces a musician knows and how well he or she knows them. Musician A has maximal command of repertoire, knowing all of the pieces and all there is to know about each piece. Musician B's repertoire is not as broad or as deep, including fewer pieces and lacking some aspects of these pieces, such as the modal classification, appropriate drum patterns and performance practice, or particulars of *garapan* for the leading melodic instruments. Musician C's knowledge of the repertoire lies somewhere between the knowledge of A and B since C knows most of the repertoire, but some pieces are known in

6. Wasitodiningrat (personal communication), but many others also say this.

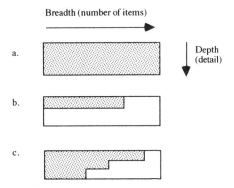

Fig. 9 Extent of knowledge

greater depth than others. Such simplistic measures can be refined by subdividing the repertoire or by specifying particular aspects of repertoire knowledge. A highly competent musician might know almost all the pieces in the traditional repertoire but few of the newer ones. A drummer might know the performance practice and drumming possibilities for most of the repertoire but have a more limited command of melodic interpretations or vocal parts of these pieces. From these examples we see that knowledge of repertoire is in fact multidimensional, since there are many aspects to each piece and these aspects link the domain of repertoire to other domains of competence. Knowledge of repertoire is also relative to a given locale and group of musicians, as we noted earlier. While some pieces are widely known, even closely associated musicians will know slightly different repertoires or different versions, performance practice, and contextual links for a given piece.

A picture of the relative salience of particular domains in Javanese musical competence emerges from musicians' distinctions, evaluations, and comparisons of different competences. On this basis, knowledge of *garapan* and repertoire seems to be valued over technical skills. Analysis of the competence requirements in actual performance situations is necessary to counter and supplement musicians' verbal judgments and, perhaps, to reveal aspects that may be taken for granted. Such analysis clearly indicates the preeminence of interactive knowledge in all performance situations, although this domain is not explicitly recognized to the extent that *garapan* and repertoire are.

Valorization of knowledge of *garapan* and repertoire over technical skills is manifested in a number of ways. For example, a *rebab* player who demonstrates a broad command of the repertoire and good choices of melodic patterns may be forgiven a less-than-beautiful tone and odd intonation while a musician who plays with technical facility but inadequate knowledge of the repertoire is unlikely to be judged as highly. A similar comparison can be made in *gendèr* playing: technical skills are important, but they take second place to knowledge of appropriate *garapan*.

As a rule, the technical demands of performance on an instrument do not correlate with the perceived degree of difficulty. Musicians generally consider some of the fastest parts relatively easy because they are derivative of the leading parts: the musician does not need to know as much about the specific piece or about general considerations of *garapan* so long as he or she has the interactive skills necessary to construct an appropriate part based on the leading musicians' parts. Thus, the *bonang panerus*, which is technically more difficult than the larger *bonang* because it is generally played twice as fast as the larger instrument, is considered a much easier instrument because its part is derivative (Wasitodiningrat, personal communication; Supanggah 1991). Conversely, the gong, although sounded less frequently than any other instrument, should be played by a musician with a command of the repertoire and a highly developed sense of timing.

Perhaps the most striking example of this logic is to be found in the rationale for the ranking of musicians in the Solonese *Kasunan* court in the early years of this century. The highly florid and complex patterns of the *ciblon* drum were assigned to a musician of medium rank because they were considered less refined, originating in village practice, while the leading musician played a very simple part on the *ketipung* drum. The leader's standing derived from his responsibility for all aspects of performance and the global competence necessary for this, including command of the entire repertoire with its internal classifications, conventions, and special instances of performance practice and extramusical associations.

Interactive considerations are also apparent in this ranking. The player of the leading melodic instrument, the *rebab*, was ranked beneath the player of another leading melodic instrument, the *bonang*, whose part is technically less demanding. Several older court musicians explained to me that the *rebab* player is the one who decides which pieces are to be played so he need choose only those that he knows well. The *bonang* player must know all the pieces that the *rebab* player knows so that he can play whatever the *rebab* player chooses. Moreover, the *bonang* part is more closely linked to the fixed melody of the composition so that the musician must know it in greater detail than the *rebab* player, who performs a semi-independent melody. Players of other technically difficult instruments are ranked lower still, because their parts either are clearly derivative of the leading parts or allow the musician more freedom, which in turn means less need to know and conform to the details of the piece. In balancing different skills and ways of knowing, we can see that knowledge of the repertoire may carry more weight than technical mastery and that the way in which the repertoire is known is also an important aspect of competence.

Another comparison will serve to illustrate these considerations further. The *rebab* and *suling* require more specialized technical skill than most other instruments, but only the *rebab* is considered a difficult instrument. This is due more to the knowledge than to the technical skill that is required. Viewed from the perspective of transformational procedures applied to the matrix of tuning systems and modes, the *rebab* and *suling* idioms are less systematic than most others because many patterns must be altered substantially when transposed from one pitch level to another or transferred from one tuning to another. Despite this, the *suling* is not considered particularly difficult, just different. Sound production is relatively simple, and the idiom is perhaps the least constrained of all *gamelan* instruments (Brinner 1993). A *suling* player has great freedom in choosing when to play a phrase and can wait to get his bearings from other parts, so he can easily participate in pieces that he does not know well. There are no mandatory *suling* patterns and no leadership responsibilities. The *rebab* poses greater technical challenges with regard to tone production and fingering. It also requires a much deeper knowledge of repertoire and *garapan* both because of the many melodic characteristics of particular pieces that must be faithfully re-created in performance and because of the responsibility that derives from the *rebab* player's role of melodic leadership.

Interactive and transformational procedures are key to most of the situations and evaluations described thus far. Sindoesawarno confirms the importance of transformational competence: "It is evident . . . that the rank of *gamelan* musicians is based, not only on the memorization of pieces, but also (and especially) on skill in creating cengkok and wilet [patterns and variations]" (1984: 398). Given a rudimentary knowledge of frameworks for performance, procedural knowledge is generally more essential to successful performance at a basic level than broader or deeper knowledge of the frameworks. A player can get by with active mastery of interactive and transformational procedures coupled with passive knowledge of basic temporal frameworks and ensemble roles.

This allows a beginning musician to participate in performance and gradually master the other aspects of competence. While a foreign student of *gamelan* who has learned how to play particular versions of *gendèr*, *rebab*, or *gambang* parts to a few pieces without understanding the operative procedures is generally at a loss when confronted with other pieces, a Javanese performer at a similarly rudimentary level of competence may well have enough sense of the basic procedures of performance to stumble along. Musicians develop the ability to float with the flow of the ensemble and perform pieces they have never played or even heard. Even at an advanced level of musicianship situations arise in which a musician is forced to "wing" a particular passage that he or she does not know or remember by applying procedural know-how.[7] Of course, the more knowledge of pertinent frameworks a musician uses in such a situation, the better. Pemberton's account of a *pesindhèn* coming late to a performance and adding a vocal part to a piece in the *gendhing bonang* genre that never includes vocal parts or any of the softer-sounding elaborating instruments is a perfect illustration of substantial procedural competence misused through failure to assess the relevant frameworks for performance (1987: 27). In this case the singer should have identified the compositional framework and associated ensemble roles, without knowing the particular piece, by noting that only the gongs, drum, and louder metallophones were being played.

To conclude this discussion, we turn to the accommodation of different types and levels of competence within an ensemble. An ensemble is the product of a particular matching of specific individuals—each with his or her own competence and character—to the various instrumental and vocal roles within a *gamelan*, each with its characteristic competence requirements, responsibilities, and possibilities for interaction. Within any *gamelan* ensemble there are differing degrees and mixes of competence, and these can be matched with the levels and types of competence associated with particular roles. Some roles require little beyond the core competence while others require varying degrees of specialized knowledge. A group is able to perform well so long as leading roles are filled by reasonably competent musicians and the less competent musicians have (1) enough declarative knowledge of contexts (musical and nonmusical) to orient themselves to the information they pick up from the leaders and (2) sufficient mastery of the basic interactive and transformational procedures to interpret this information. The social interaction that determines the apportionment of roles does not necessarily lead to such a straightforward matching of abilities to requirements, as we shall see at the end of this book.

Musicians are often linked to a particular instrument by personal choice or by their peers when they can in fact play other instruments quite well. In the past, court rankings such as the one mentioned above

---

7. See Pemberton (1987: 27).

formalized such assignments, although they were not always honored: Mloyowidodo, for instance, was often allowed to "rise above his station" in one of the Solonese court *gamelan* groups to play *bonang* by a relative who was the official *bonang* player (personal communication). Nor were these assignments necessarily based on purely musical considerations: Martopangrawit felt that he was passed over several times in favor of relatives of the *gamelan* leader before he gained rightful recognition as the *gendèr* player in another court (personal communication). He claimed to have caused one of the rivals who "usurped" his position to go insane, breaking under the pressure of knowing that Martopangrawit was sitting there listening and could play better than he could.

One of the most important things to recognize regarding the propriety of role assignment within an ensemble on the basis of competence is that competence is relative. A musician who fills a leading role in one ensemble may consider himself or be considered by others as an inadequate lead player when performing with a group of more competent musicians. For instance, the man who played *slenthem* in one group that I observed took the leading role of *bonang* player in another group. He was perfectly capable of playing *bonang* in either ensemble, but he bowed to the greater competence of the *bonang* player in the first group. Another musician played *bonang* in a court *gamelan* but would take the higher role of nonperforming leader in groups under his tutelage.

MULTIPLE COMPETENCE

Thus far I have focused on diverse types of competence within a community of musicians, ignoring the possibility of multiple musical traditions and communities. In reality, musicians from different communities come into frequent contact with each other and often form larger, more heterogeneous communities. In these environments other kinds of competence archetypes inform musicians' mutual assessments and accommodations. Academically trained musicians talk about the difference between their competence and that of *seniman alam*, "natural artists" whose competence is supposed to be intuitive. Village musicians are frequently contrasted unfavorably with court and urban musicians, the implication being that they know less or that their knowledge is imperfect. Musicians associated with differing court traditions come together and must find common musical ground. These meetings favor the development of various kinds of multiple competence.

Multiple competence involves the crossing of boundaries that separate specializations, traditions, communities, and performance arts. The sociocultural significance of multiple competence necessarily varies with the type of boundary crossed. Here we shall consider polymusicality within a tradition and among related and unrelated realms of music-making. Because of the high degree of integration among Javanese performing arts, multiple competence that includes the realms of theater and dance will also be discussed briefly.

Multiple competence in the narrowest sense of the word is the rule within Javanese *gamelan* traditions. This type of polymusicality is characterized by the mastery of different specializations within one sociogeographically defined cultural community. We have already noted that Javanese musical competence is characterized by a large core of knowledge that includes not only basic frameworks but also much procedural knowledge. This is why specializations linked to instrumental roles differ mainly in the domain of idiomatic knowledge and are relatively easy to attain since a musician does not need to begin his or her training anew. The well-rounded competence that is typical of most good Javanese musicians is based on this type of polymusicality.[8] Certain multiple competences are particularly common: most instrumentalists have extensive knowledge of vocal idioms and repertoire, for example. It is also common to find male singers who play *suling*; this gives them something to do in the many pieces and sections of pieces that do not require a male chorus. In small shadow play troupes, particularly in villages, the drummer or *saron* player often doubles on *rebab* so that he can accompany the *dhalang's* songs, which do not require *saron* and *kendhang*.

Another common type of polymusicality bridges different repertoires or performance contexts within the scope of one cultural community. Most musicians can and do perform for shadow play and dance as well as *klenèngan*, although individual musicians may have a better command of the repertoire and performance practice associated with one rather than another. Court musicians are required to acquire competence in special dance repertoires and several types of ceremonial *gamelan* with particular repertoires, instruments, and performance practice.

Within a tradition one competence may be viewed as a stepping stone to another or, alternatively, one competence may be perceived to encompass another. Susilo offers an example of hierarchically related competences when he writes that "competence in accompanying Solonese wayang kulit is more than sufficient preparation for performing in wayang wong theatre" (1984: 125). Mantle Hood has reported on a carefully graded Yogyanese progression for attaining competence in each of the instruments of the *gamelan* in turn (1988: 180–89), although it is not clear to what extent this prescription was ever realized in prac-

---

8. Cf. Vetter (1986: 148–49, 193).

tice. Supanggah gives a more concrete example of such a progression (1991): a student should start with the *kethuk,* a low-level colotomic instrument, in order to develop a sense of the time relationships that constitute *irama* before proceeding to play other instruments.

Multiple competence that bridges differing local or regional traditions is also common in Central Java, though perhaps less common than polymusicality within one of these traditions. One of the prime reasons for this is the diffusion of Solonese practice and repertoire through mass media and the widespread influence of the court- and government-sponsored educational institutions of Surakarta (see Sutton 1991a). As a result of this diffusion, many musicians outside the geographical area traditionally associated with the city of Surakarta are conversant with repertoire, idiomatic patterning, *garapan,* and various aspects of performance practice typical of this city.

Multiple competence of this sort has long been required of court musicians as a result of exchanges of practice and repertoire which were an important part of diplomatic relations between the four courts of Central Java. Wasitodiningrat, from the court of Prince Paku Alam in Yogyakarta, learned much of the repertoire and practice of the court of the Sunan in Surakarta because the Sunan's daughter married the Paku Alam. Musicians and other performers came to the Pakualaman from the Kasunan to perform the arts familiar to the princess and to instruct the Pakualaman musicians. In 1931 some of these musicians were sent to Surakarta to continue their studies, focusing on the special court repertoire of *bedhaya* and *srimpi* dances but learning many other aspects of Solonese competences through extensive exposure. This connection was mirrored by the transfer of dances and musical accompaniment from the Yogyanese Kraton to the Solonese Mangkunegaran, though the influence of Yogyanese practice and repertoire was not as pervasive at the Mangkunegaran as Solonese influence was at the Pakualaman.

If we follow Wasitodiningrat's career further, we can see the pivotal role of this unusual man in the mixing and dissemination of regional styles. As head of the *gamelan* at the Pakualaman he championed Solonese music and then continued this practice as head of the *gamelan* at the government radio station in Yogyakarta, thus reinforcing the position of the rival Solonese tradition in the Yogyanese heartland. On the other hand, Wasitodiningrat was one of the first faculty members at the first government institution for education in the performing arts, Konservatori Karawitan in Surakarta, where he taught Yogyanese traditions to a student body drawn from all parts of Java. He has a highly developed knowledge of different styles and has drawn freely on that knowledge in his own compositions, presaging the mixed stylistic palette that has become common for composers of more recent generations who work at academic institutions.[9]

It seems inevitable that a second competence, no matter how tirelessly championed or eagerly received and "mastered" in essence, will probably not be adopted in all its detail if the musician is not actively involved with primary bearers of the tradition over an extended period of time. One of Wasitodiningrat's protégés in Yogyakarta is probably as bimusical in Yogyanese and Solonese traditions as anyone, yet there are some relatively obscure pieces in the Solonese court tradition with which he is unfamiliar.[10] After his initial exposure under Wasitodiningrat's tutelage, radio broadcasts and recordings, which necessarily provide a selective portion of the tradition, have been his primary sources for Solonese practice.

The connection between village and court has developed in several directions. Villagers have come to serve as musicians at the courts for generations, supplementing their local competence with the special practices and repertoires of the court. I had the opportunity to observe a recent instance of this when Martopangrawit and Mloyowidodo, erstwhile court musicians, were invited to instruct the village musicians who had joined the Kasunan *gamelan* in the traditions of the court that had been lost through high turnover of personnel. Village musicians have also served as conduits bringing certain village traditions to the courts, where they have been transformed and absorbed. The creation of court performance genres based on village traditions of *topèng* masked dance (Ben Suharto, personal communication), *taledhèk* dance (Sutton 1991a: 25, fn. 5), and *ciblon* drumming style exemplifies this process. Presumably musicians returning to the villages have brought court practices with them, but many of those practices have not been absorbed into village traditions so these musicians must have maintained multiple competences, one for home and one for the court.

In recent years, institutions such as STSI Surakarta that have a mandate to encompass diverse musical traditions as part of the Indonesian government's political goal of creating a national culture have been instrumental in the development of multiple competences that bridge regional and social divisions, enabling students and faculty to learn a wider variety of styles and practices than previously possible. Ceremonial en-

9. See Becker (1980) for a study of much of Wasitodiningrat's creative output.

10. I was able to investigate this within the limited repertoire of Solonese *pathetan*, which is codified in a book of vocal notation by Martopangrawit. The Yogyanese musician was not familiar with a few of the *pathetan* that are specifically associated with the now defunct *wayang gedhog* shadow play. At least some of the Solonese musicians whom I recorded knew these *pathetan*.

sembles and items of repertoire previously studied only by court musicians have become part of the curriculum, and students are also required to study a number of regional styles. STSI has actually taken a custodial role in the preservation of court arts.[11] Students and instructors are encouraged to exploit elements of these styles for broader expressivity in their creative work (Brinner 1992). These meetings and blendings are facilitated by the fact that the student body itself is drawn from different regions of Java and other parts of Indonesia. These students also come into contact with local styles through field work and in turn become involved in the spread of their own particular blend of knowledge, as they are required to go out to towns and villages to teach *gamelan* and dance.

There have been other, nonacademic, mixtures such as Wasitodiningrat's compositions or the very popular works of the late Nartosabdho (Becker 1980). Exposure to this variety has created new possibilities for performance, but it has also raised expectations that cannot always be met. When a *gamelan* group from the Yogyakarta Kraton performed a shadow play in Los Angeles in 1990, for example, the *dhalang* called for a piece in Banyumas style at one point in the performance. The *pesindhèn* obliged, but the piece fizzled out because the musicians were not able to join in—the *dhalang* had overstepped the boundary of their regional competence.

Multiple competences that span related but different local or regional traditions are volatile mixes. Unless musicians have compelling reasons to maintain distinctions, fusion and elision of differences in neighboring traditions seem inevitable, with multiple competence eventually becoming a single, unified competence. The implications of this process have been hotly debated in Java, particularly with regard to the perceived disappearance of the identifying characteristics of Yogyanese musical traditions (see Sutton 1984a and 1991a).

The dynamics of multiple competences that cross ethnic boundaries are largely uncharted in Java. Little attention has been paid to the participation of the substantial Chinese minority in Javanese musical life, although Chinese patronage has been important at times in the flourishing of *gamelan* in the urban centers of Central Java. This is evident in some innovations in instrument design[12] and in the popularization of *wayang wong* at the turn of the century when Chinese-sponsored commercial

11. See comments by Hastanto, the director, in Devereaux (1989).

12. Wasitodiningrat told me of a Chinese-owned *gamelan* that included additional *gendèr* and *siter* tuned an octave higher than the smallest normal instruments of these types. He said that musicians did not know what to do with these innovative instruments (personal communication).

troupes gave many people access to court arts (Sumarsam 1992: 172). Some Chinese later moved into performance, too: Sumarsam names troupes of Chinese *wayang wong* performers active after Indonesian independence and notes that Chinese studied dance with Javanese court dancers (1992:161). We do not know whether these performers also were competent in the performance of other musics.

Given the long history of contact with European colonialism and commerce, one would expect a high incidence of multiple competence spanning the completely disjunct competences of European and Javanese traditions. This actually appears to be relatively rare. In colonial times the courts maintained Western musical ensembles in a compartmentalized fashion, staffed by a separate group of musicians, unlike the Imperial Japanese Court, which forced its musicians to master Western music during the Meiji reform in the second half of the nineteenth century. In his study of music in nineteenth-century Java, Sumarsam offers evidence of the low incidence of such bimusicality: "It was acknowledged in this early account [the *Djedjèrèngan* manuscript] of *tayuban* that a dancer who could sing both *gamelan* songs and European music was very rare" (1992: 162). More recently there have been musicians who perform in traditional *gamelan* and in hybrid *kroncong* ensembles or other Western or Western-influenced types of music.[13] Unlike some Arab musicians who turn to Western music for technical training and resources, Javanese musicians do not appear to be interested in enhancing their abilities through learning a completely foreign musical competence. If anything, the contrary is true: musicians may believe in mutually exclusive competences and fear that the diatonic Western scale will have a deleterious effect on Javanese intonation (Sutton 1991b and Perlman, personal communication).

Disjunct polymusicality of a different sort is fostered at performing arts institutions in various parts of Indonesia that train students in Javanese, Balinese, and Sundanese traditions. The political motivations for this are very different from those that brought European music into the courts of Central Java. The Indonesian national motto, "unity in diversity," provides twin goals of maintaining diversity and creating a common ground that have led to the inclusion of disparate traditions in instruction and to the encouragement of experimentation in the fusion of these traditions in new works.

In Java, the integration of music, theater, and dance requires that we

---

13. See Sutton (1991b); according to Wasitodiningrat the Solonese court *gamelan* leader Wiryadiningrat had a group of blind musicians in the 1930s who played both *gamelan* and *kroncong* (personal communication).

go beyond the realm of music to consider "cross-competences," those multiple competences that bridge several types of performance. The musical competence that we have considered thus far is a recognized entity among Javanese musicians, but it is also intimately related to competence in other types of performance art. Javanese books on *pedhalangan*, the art of shadow puppetry, emphasize the importance of musical knowledge as one of the principal domains in a *dhalang*'s training. At the very least a *dhalang* must know enough to sing in tune and in time, to move puppets in accordance with the musical accompaniment, and to cue the *gamelan* in a manner that makes musical sense. This is all part of traditional competence, but musicians often complain about *dhalangs'* lack of knowledge. On the other hand, it is not unusual for a *dhalang* to be competent enough to play *gendèr* or *kendhang*. The musician's knowledge of *pedhalangan* is the other side of this coin. Musicians who frequently accompany *wayang* usually have substantial knowledge of *pedhalangan*, which they use passively to form the appropriate expectations and responses to the *dhalang*'s actions. This competence may become active if the right opportunities arise.[14] The intertwinedness of these roles and competences is enhanced by the fact that a *dhalang* is often accompanied by members of his own family, who are likely to have gained experience and received training in *pedhalangan*.

Cross-competence spanning music and dance is also common, particularly through the link of drumming. Many dancers can drum for dance fairly well but may not know other pieces and styles so well. Often they are not completely ignorant of these other aspects of competence but lack the depth of knowledge that a full-time musician gains. Conversely, many musicians have extensive familiarity with dance movements and choreographies. For drummers who would accompany dance such knowledge is essential. Some theatrical dance styles require vocal competence and mastery of special repertoire such as *palaran* (see chap. 7) and other vocal-centered compositions. The Langendriyan dance drama makes extreme demands in this regard, but the more common *wayang wong* also requires substantial musical competence, since dancers are expected to improvise text to stock vocal melodies (see Susilo 1987). This multiple competence allows some dancers to become musicians as they grow older.

Polymusicality within a single tradition is facilitated by the basic similarities of the idioms of the *gamelan*, by the unity of concept provided

14. For example, four of the nine musicians of the Hardo Budoyo *wayang* troupe that performed at the Sattler Gallery in Washington, D. C., throughout the summer of 1991 were capable of performing *wayang* in their own right, albeit at varying levels of competence.

by a melodic flow that underlies varied surface manifestations, and by the fact that there are no solo instrumental repertoires and all members of the ensemble participate in each piece, with few exceptions. Multiple competence contributes in turn to this integration, and in this sense Javanese music constitutes a system: despite the many "quirks," the unpredictable moments that defy rule making, there is an underlying body of conceptual frameworks and procedures that constitute a large core competence. There is relatively little compartmentalization, and specialization is more a matter of emphasis and addition to a large core competence than a choice between mutually exclusive bodies of knowledge and skills. This same integratedness supports the development of cross-competences that span different performing arts. There can be little doubt that these cross-competences are beneficial to the integration of music and other elements in dance and theater performances.

CHAPTER FIVE

ACQUIRING COMPETENCE

A comprehensive study of competence must consider how musicians acquire competence in relation to the totality of musical life within their communities. This study must examine the ways in which aspects of musical competence are learned, the order in which they are learned, and the sources from which musical knowledge is obtained. Information about opportunities for interaction between more and less competent musicians and about the nature of this interaction is no less essential to the endeavor. This panoramic view encompasses not only musicians' initial study but also the changes that continue to occur throughout their lives. To reflect this broader perspective, I have used the term "experience" in previous chapters, stating that attainment of musical competence is a function of a musician's experience, that experience may be defined as the product of age, education, and association, and, finally, that the distribution of competence within a society is directly related to the degree of freedom a musician has in shaping his or her own experience. Thus, a comprehensive approach to the study of competence acquisition should examine the patterns, expectations, possibilities, and limitations associated with particular ages, the more or less formally instituted processes of education, and the other interpersonal contacts that may be gathered loosely under the rubric "association."

Since competence may be acquired over a span of many years, researchers rarely have the opportunity to observe directly and compile detailed individual histories of acquisition throughout this period.

Within the shorter time frame of most research, interviews with experienced musicians who have already reached a high level of competence are invaluable but cannot elicit all of the details of acquisition. The facts are so complex that memories of learning processes and experiences must be highly selective. There are seldom opportunities to corroborate detailed recollections of the past. However reliable or detailed these individual histories may be, it is also necessary to evaluate their commonalties, to assess their relevance as indices of more general patterns if we are to accomplish a full ethnomusicological study of competence within a musical community.

We can search for the patterns of learning and exposure to music and musical knowledge by extrapolating backwards and forwards in time, attempting to reconstruct how musicians used to learn by juxtaposing evidence gained in interviews with older musicians with observation of the ways that novice musicians learn in the present and attempting to predict their further development. These extrapolations must be tempered by sensitivity to the possibilities of change in every aspect of competence acquisition and by attention to the idiosyncratic aspects of each musician's experience. We are forced, furthermore, to focus on those aspects of individual experience that are more readily approached and susceptible of generalizations because some aspects of the perception and interpretation of external events may be difficult or impossible to observe and record.

The conditions of learning can be grouped under the rubrics of age, education, and association. *Age,* whether measured chronologically or more loosely understood as a socioculturally defined life stage (infant, child, adolescent, young adult, and so on), is both an index and a biological determinant of the development and degeneration of mental and physical abilities. Particular ages or age groups may be limiting or enabling factors in the acquisition of competence. At issue are culturally defined measures of physiological and psychological capacities such as the development of vocal cords, embouchure, breath control, hand size, attentional capacity, and expressive or spiritual maturity. The training of Tibetan *dung chen* players offers extreme examples of age-related limitations: the monks who are to play these large ceremonial trumpets begin their training at the age of six to eight years, before they can handle the large trumpets and so must learn to play other instruments first. But there is also an upper limit to their performance career, as the intense pressure and vibrations associated with playing the *dung chen* can cause teeth to fall out when musicians reach their late twenties (Pertl 1992: 96)!

Childhood is a privileged time for the acquisition of musical competence; this is often stated in negative terms when someone is judged too old to learn. The opinion that would-be concert pianists and violinists must start their training by the age of four or five is widely held, for instance, and is linked to observations and beliefs regarding the receptivity and pliability of youthful minds and fingers. The process of enculturation, the largely unconscious absorption of ways of being within a community or community of communities, is generally associated with early childhood. Surveying scholarship on learning for implications for musical learning, Sloboda concludes that a

> shared set of primitive capacities which are present at birth or soon after, . . . [a] shared set of experiences which the culture provides as children grow up . . . [and the] impact of a rapidly changing general cognitive system as the many other skills supported by the culture are learned . . . combine to yield a roughly similar sequence of achievements for the majority of children in a culture, and a set of roughly similar ages at which the various achievements occur. (1985: 196.)

At present we lack the comparative data to test the validity of this view. Ethnomusicologists and cognitive scientists need to give more attention to identifying and analyzing the "shared set of experiences" and "skills" that are characteristic of a given community or culture.

Acquisition is by no means limited to childhood—youth can also be a barrier to some competences or aspects of competence.[1] In many instances a certain degree of maturity or stamina is prerequisite to study of a particular repertoire or set of practices. The considerations may be related to physical development or to mental or spiritual preparation. But age-related access to particular aspects of a competence may also have little or nothing to do with assessment of an individual's actual capabilities or state of development, being determined instead by external sociocultural criteria. This is true of competences associated with rites of passage such as the music of various African initiation schools, which are learned by all members of an age group, and the biblical cantilation learned by Jewish males who begin to "perform" at the age of thirteen, regardless of musical aptitude or vocal development. Even in the relatively individualistic and multiform life of late-twentieth-century American society Bennett has found age-related limitations on the formation of a rock musician's identity (1980: 25).

In the area of *education*, the second component of experience, concepts of appropriate learning progression have received a fair amount of attention from ethnomusicologists, although much more can be said.

---

1. Laske defines acquisition as a childhood process, like the acquisition of linguistic competence, making no allowance for the many instances of later acquisition (1977: 30).

We have reports and analyses of a wide spectrum of institutions ranging from intensive and restrictive teacher-disciple relationships and hereditary schools to more casual or occasional associations and tapering off into the ill-defined but nonetheless "concrete" osmosis that appears to be the principal mode of transmission in some communities (e.g., Neuman 1980; Wade 1984a; Chernoff 1979; Moro-Myers 1988; Supanggah 1991). The subject is particularly accessible in societies that have formalized musical education, but it is too vast and the literature too varied to encompass here. One aspect particularly worthy of study is the institution of formalized musical education in many parts of the Third World under the influence of Western (including Eastern European) pedagogical institutions. This transformation of traditional learning processes, often motivated by desires for rationalization and standardization, may drastically alter the structure and content of musicians' competence. From reports such as Dibia's comments on changes in Balinese competence (Vitale 1990) and Marcus's analysis of changes in Arab modal practice (1989), we learn that recent education is generally characterized by newly formulated, uniform "standards" abstracted from multiform oral practice, ensconced and legitimated in writing, and by emphasis on declarative knowledge of cultural "facts" such as musical scales and meters rather than performative processes. The pace of learning, too, has changed: "The decline of apprenticeship [in Morocco] has been exacerbated by the spread of public education, which has turned more than a few prospective musicians away from the profession . . . and has made those that remain impatient with the loosely structured, extended process of apprenticeship" (Schuyler 1979: 26). It is a common lament in various countries that modern life does not allow prospective musicians the extended and intensive contact that was common in preindustrial times or before the advent of compulsory mass education.

Association, the most loosely defined component of experience, encompasses the many forms of interpersonal contact that initially shape and continue to alter a musician's knowledge. The nature of variation in competence is determined in part by patterns of association. When musicians cluster in hermetically isolated groups, homogeneous experiential histories are shared by members of each group but are distinctly different from one group to the next. The more freedom individual musicians have to associate, the more heterogeneous experience becomes and the less we can distinguish sharply delineated local traditions.

Association and education both depend on access to individual musicians and groups, to teachers or models, and to instruments, recordings, performance opportunities, and performances by others. A range of associations may allow a musician to continue to develop, taking a leading role in an ensemble of musicians who are less competent while playing a subsidiary role in another ensemble that is more competent. Merriam has remarked on the difficulty of access among Flathead Indians: "Youngsters who wish to sing and drum are given no training and must be extremely persistent in their efforts to join an established singing group" (1964: 131). Similar difficulties certainly exist in other societies and are perhaps more common for those who are not born into families of musicians. But issues of access also arise in educational systems based on disciple or apprentice relationships. Students may effectively be cut off from experiencing any version or vision of music-making other than that of their teacher (Ruckert 1994). We know far too little about these matters; aside from scattered anecdotes like Merriam's, this crucial perspective on musical life has been largely neglected.

In some communities an important consideration for an aspiring musician's access to musical experiences is the need for sufficient freedom from such pressing obligations as finding food, clothing, and lodging. Solutions have included the competitive scholarships common in many Western countries, extensive government support by Communist regimes of Eastern Europe, and joining a teacher's household or exchanging manual labor or other services in some Asian societies.

Access to different types of musical experience is linked to considerations of age and relative competence that may limit the kinds of music younger musicians hear and perform as well as the circumstances of contact. We need to know how younger musicians are initiated into performance, noting when such opportunities arise and whether the young musician first participates in age- or competence-delimited ensembles and contexts or directly in the "real thing." There may be special student concerts or performance opportunities within a standard performance context for musicians who are not yet fully competent. Ensemble roles that demand only a limited competence can provide initial access to the realm of professional music-making and a means of breaking in disciples and children. Access to competence-enhancing opportunities may continue to be an issue even at a relatively high level of competence: the heads of Japanese schools of music maintain control of performance opportunities even for their most advanced students, regulating when, where, and with whom they make public appearances (Michael Hattori, personal communication). Similar restrictions may have obtained in Egypt when guild masters had control over the members of their musical associations (see Racy 1988).

Limitations of access can create or maintain distinctive competence: certain knowledge may only be passed to members of a family or to disciples, as in some Indian *gharana*s. Conversely, increased accessibility can break down distinctions, as it has in Central Java with the loosening of restrictions on court knowledge and the spread of mass media. Worldwide, the advent of mass media and of mechanized transportation has greatly increased access to music from distant places and has changed the definition of musical community in the twentieth century (Slobin 1992). Exposure to a wider variety of musics has led to the expansion of some competences and has probably increased the incidence of multiple competences. This greater variety of experience has been countered to some extent by the narrowing of variety within some music-making communities as a result of the mass production and promotion of selected aspects of a tradition.

In order to begin to unravel the complexities of competence acquisition under varying conditions of age, education, and association, it is helpful to look at the following cross-culturally valid aspects: progression and pace, processes and methods, agents, contexts, and means of acquisition. Other formulations are possible, of course, but I believe that this one covers the main issues in a manner conducive to an ethnomusicologically informed understanding of the similarities and differences in competence acquisition around the world. Since learning is a vast topic, I can only outline these aspects here.

Progression and pace. The stages, materials, and experiences associated with competence acquisition vary in terms of uniformity and regulation, ranging from a single standard to diverse individual progressions of learning. Classification of repertoire according to degrees of difficulty commensurate with levels of performance ability is a prime example of an explicit structuring of both competence and acquisition. Such structures may not be motivated solely by a rationale of increasing difficulty. Ritual concerns and social considerations associated with authority and power over knowledge may be just as important determinants of the sequence in which musicians learn elements of a competence. The ordering of repertoire in certain Japanese *shakuhachi* schools is a case in point (Weisgarber 1968). A learning progression may also include the acquisition of several competences, with skills and knowledge from the earlier competences serving as stepping stones to the acquisition of more complex ones.

A progression usually includes both explicit instruction and intuitive processes of adoption, absorption, and adaptation. The type of material learned differs: explicit instruction often focuses on representational models that describe what a musician already knows but have little direct role in performance while the operational models that play a dynamic role in the control of performance must often be deduced by a student.[2] Middle Eastern musicians, for instance, can acquire explicit declarative knowledge of the theoretical aspects of modal and metric systems in formal instruction but practical procedural knowledge is usually acquired through exposure to the performances of other musicians.

Ethnomusicological literature does not overflow with analyses of learning progressions; even less attention is given to the pace at which musicians advance through these progressions, either in an ideal sense or in individual trajectories. We know little beyond the fact that some competences such as Hindustani music or Japanese *gagaku* are only acquired through lengthy training while others are acquired much more quickly. Yet this is certainly a compelling issue, both in its own right and as an indicator of the nature of a competence. The slower stages of attaining competence, if there be such, may tell us about the relative difficulty of the aspects of competence absorbed during that stage. Consider, too, the assumptions about proper pace evident in the following account of the development of an operatic singer who started as a contralto and gradually progressed to higher-pitched roles, saying that hers was "an old-fashioned career—everything was done not too quickly so the voice would not burn out early. I gave myself a lot of time to be sure my voice, body and mind had an equal chance to grow into the high dramatic Fach. Even when I was a contralto, everyone told me I was a high dramatic soprano, but to sing those roles then would have been a disaster" (Tucker 1991). Progression may also be regulated by rituals of initiation, examination, or performance or by other forms of audition. Issues of power and authority surface again when the pace of learning progression depends on the will of hierarchically placed musicians.

Process and methods. Most writers on non-Western music essentialize the process of transmission by stressing rote learning by ear in stark contrast to the notation-based transmission of European art music. In so doing they mask a great variety of learning methods, ignoring, for example, the degree of flexibility or freedom a student has in imitating a teacher, which varies greatly from one way of music-making to another. In most cases we do not know what sorts of musical, verbal, and kinetic modeling and correction have been proffered. Nor do we get an impression of the variety of demands placed upon the students—such as the length and number of sections to be learned—and the interactive settings in which these demands are fulfilled (individual or group lessons, observation or participation in performance, and so on). Some more recent writings such as Moro-Myers 1988 have begun to address these and

2. See Baily (1988: 114) for a discussion of operational and representational models. The juxtaposition with explicit/intuitive and declarative/procedural distinctions is mine.

other aspects of teaching methods, but we are still far from achieving a global survey or a theoretical framework for analysis and comparison.

Processes and methods of transmission are closely related aspects of one enormously complex phenomenon, processes being more fundamental than methods. Since a few basic processes are common to a wide variety of learning situations, this distinction enables us to ignore temporarily the distinction between directed learning (education within a pedagogical tradition) and other forms of "picking up" knowledge such as receiving tips from other musicians, listening to other performers, or accompanying them. Teaching and learning methods can then be understood in terms of the particular ways in which these basic processes are implemented and combined.

The basic processes of learning to make music include repetition, feedback, imitation, inference, and interpretation. The closely related processes of repetition and feedback, characterized by Sloboda as "the cornerstones of any procedural learning" (1985: 225), are particularly important to the acquisition of musical competence because of the inherent difficulty of capturing and reproducing evanescent musical soundings. It is rare that a person can learn—perceive and successfully reproduce—a long or complex sequence of transient sounds after one hearing. In most cases where such assimilation does take place it is made possible by extensive repetitiveness within the musical system, that is, by those aspects of musical systems that are often characterized as formulaic.

The process of repetition manifests itself in many ways. Through repetition a musician hones perception and strengthens it in memory. Repetition by a teacher or other model enables the student to focus and to correct perceptions. When extensive repetition is integral to a music, opportunities for learning through performance are dramatically increased. Cyclical structures, for example, offer numerous opportunities to perceive, remember, and then reproduce.

Imitation is a special instance of repetition: a pattern of sounds produced by one person is reproduced by someone else. The degree of accuracy expected by the teacher, by the student, or by some cultural consensus is of central concern here and should correlate with different types of competence. It is useful to posit a continuum ranging from "verbatim" repetition, which must match the model in every nuance, to fairly free modeling, which might consist of grasping a gestalt and then reproducing it in variant form.

Feedback is linked to repetition and imitation as a controlling function; as such it plays a key role in Pressing's sophisticated model of improvisation (1988). Consisting of evaluation and correction by the performer or by some external monitor, feedback is "essential to an adaptive system in order to prevent unsuccessful or potentially damaging productions from being formed" (Sloboda 1985: 225). Acquisition of competence involves developing standards and an ability to measure one's own output against those standards. Through development of internal standards and feedback the interactive ability to adapt the qualities of one's own sound (pitch, timbre, timing, volume, and so forth) to others should shift largely from conscious to automatic control. In the process, a musician develops an individual instance of a culture's aesthetics: what sounds good or right and what is affectively effective and appropriate, not in an abstract or uniform theoretical sense but as part of a contextually localized, applied understanding. This is precisely the "typicality" to which Schutz refers when he defines competence as stocks of musical experiences that serve as reference for a "player's anticipations of what he may or may not find in the composition before him," but he ignores the sophistication of the human capacity for feedback and adaptation when he states starkly that these anticipations may be fulfilled or exploded and "annihilated" (1976: 168), leaving no middle ground for adjustment and recalibration of standards and expectations.

The types of external feedback available in particular musical traditions or communities should have a direct bearing on the acquisition of competence and the nature of the competence itself. We need to know more about differences in external feedback between and within musical traditions in order to test this. Variables include the time frame (in the course of performance, directly following, or postponed), the medium (corrective musical demonstration, verbal comment, gestures), and the message (technical evaluation, general assessment, affective response).[3] Although it is extremely difficult to gain access to an individual's internal feedback mechanisms—even determining one's own requires an exceptional degree of awareness—we should also consider the influence of external factors such as instrument and ensemble types and performance frameworks on this internal feedback.

Inference and interpretation are essentially pre-performative mental processes. Inference refers here to the extension and application of knowledge and skills through the drawing of connections and analogies; interpretation involves adapting and re-creating musical practices, patterns, and the like within one's own frame of reference. Through inference an individual discovers order and utilizes that order to create and act upon analogies. Inference involves subsidiary processes of general-

---

3. Pressing proposes a classification of feedback that is problematic because it mixes a temporal dimension with the distinction between external and internal feedback (1988: 135).

ization and discrimination that have been studied by J. R. Anderson in various types of learning: "The generalization and discrimination mechanisms are the inductive components of the learning system in that they are trying to extract from examples of success and failure the features that characterize when a particular production rule is applicable" (1982: 394). The ways in which musicians extend and limit the analogies that shape their creative thinking can be understood in terms of these two processes. Through generalization the realm of application of a specific item of knowledge is expanded. Discrimination does the reverse, restricting the range in which a general procedure applies. Anderson has found that excessive use of these subprocesses—"overgeneralizations and useless discriminations"—is balanced by "strengthening," which gives preference to a particular application of a mental "program" (1982: 394–95).

Beyond direct, explicit instructions, corrections, or explanations proffered by a teacher or mentor, a musician is forced to rely on personal powers of deduction, developing an individualized understanding of the way things work in a particular music. Substantial portions of these understandings must overlap to enable musicians to work together in an ensemble. Even in solo performance the musician's inferences must at some points intersect audience understandings of the workings of the music. Modal improvisation, one of the thornier issues with which ethnomusicologists have grappled, can be understood or at least delimited in this way: a wealth of variants forces a student to deduce the "ground rules" and successful strategies of sound production, patterning, and manipulation—what is possible, what is preferable, and what is to be avoided. It also forces flexibility and develops transformational abilities (as we shall see in the next chapter). This method of acquiring competence is prominent in jazz and in various Middle Eastern and South Asian musics; it is also typical of Javanese *gamelan*. Confronted with multiple versions of important musical entities, a student must infer "ways in which improvisation or variation may occur by an appreciation of the intrinsic 'fuzziness' of the musical concept" according to Pressing (1988: 143), who cites Persian *radif* performance and Ghanaian drumming as examples. The musical products of such inference are rich expressions of the logic perceived in a musical system by its primary users, managers, and modifiers.

Like inference, interpretation depends on the construction of analogies, but while processes of inference are used to discover, delimit, and navigate a musical universe, processes of interpretation are applied to representations of other persons' intentions—to mental traces of past performances, to signs, such as mnemonics, gestures, and notation, and to verbal comments and instructions. Interpretation is a central concern of musicians and teachers in the Western art music tradition, because of the culturally pervasive dialectic between expressing one's own intentions and discovering or rediscovering those of the composer. In the circles of musicians who deal in "historical performance" the issue is framed somewhat differently, as a matter of authenticity. This is in effect an attempt to recapture a lost competence—all the orally transmitted knowledge that musicians required in the past to interpret the limited information about a piece conveyed in a notated representation.

Processes of repetition and imitation are present in all methods of learning and teaching, but are manifested and utilized differently. Simultaneous imitation, in which the learner plays along with a more competent musician, offers opportunities for perception, feedback, and correction that differ from those afforded by consecutive repetition. In simultaneous imitation the imitated model serves as a template against which each nuance of the imitation is matched, thus providing instantaneous feedback. In consecutive imitation, the learner must match his or her imitation against a remembered record of the model and that record may be elusive or subject to alteration if the model is complex. Thus, the amount of time elapsed between model and consecutive imitation is a crucial factor: in directed learning situations the student will most probably imitate the teacher on the spot, but when musicians learn through observation in performances they may not have an opportunity to reproduce what they have heard until hours or days later. For example, one Balinese musician whom I interviewed learned the leading instrumental parts of a particular repertoire without any direct guidance by observing the leading musician while he himself played a simple supporting part. He did not have a chance to imitate the leading part until he returned home and played the appropriate instrument in his neighborhood ensemble.

The degree of segmentation of the music to be learned, the number of repetitions, and the amount of verbal guidance or other feedback offered the student are the variables that shape particular learning methods based on repetition. In a study of pianists' practice habits, Gruson has shown that segmentation in practice, lessons, and rehearsals offers evidence of perceptions and conceptions of musical structure (1988). The method of segmentation is probably linked directly to the nature of musical competence and to the ways in which music-making is structured in a given tradition. For instance, the integrity of a composition is generally maintained in Javanese rehearsals so a piece is usually rehearsed in its entirety rather than in smaller segments. In contrast, many types of Balinese *gamelan* music are taught and rehearsed in incremental fashion. Reasons for this difference can be found in the contrasting constitution of ensembles and composition and arrangement of pieces in these two traditions. In essence, the speed, precision, and note-by-note fixity of *kotekan* (interlocking parts) played by groups of musicians within a Balinese *gamelan* require an intensive, segmented learning method for most pieces while the greater flexibility of the individual parts within a Javanese *gamelan* composition enables musicians to take advantage of the interrelatedness of these parts and the cyclical repetition inherent to most compositions to work things out in performance.

The incorporation of feedback in teaching methods may not be as clearly linked to musical structure as the use of repetition in the previous example, but the type and amount of feedback and the way that feedback is combined with other processes almost certainly influence the nature of competence and the manner of its acquisition. We can expect that feedback which is withheld or voiced indirectly (as it often is in Java) will have a less immediate and constraining effect on individual musicians' individually formed understandings of how to perform, than the explicit commentary that characterizes most Western teaching methods. Suanda notes that in Cirebon, an area in West Java bordering on Central Java, advanced musicians criticize, punish, and demand respect but refuse to teach, telling younger musicians to watch (1985: 92). He attributes a general loss of knowledge to this combination of negative feedback and refusal to assist in the transmission of knowledge (1985: 118, fn. 10).

Such culturally informed attitudes toward knowledge and teaching are sometimes ignored by researchers. When Pressing and Sloboda emphasize the importance of repetition and feedback in music learning, they assume the relatively smooth, socially sanctioned exchange of knowledge in an explicit manner that is typical of the Western tradition of art music. Yet teachers in some traditions refuse to play an example more than a few times because of a philosophical stance toward reception: a student who is really ready to receive a particular piece of knowledge should be able to perceive, retain, and emulate the teacher's example without explanation or extensive repetition. Some older Javanese musicians insist on demonstrating a particular piece or passage no more than two or three times (R. Supanggah, personal communication), and a similar attitude obtains in the Indonesian martial art form *pencak silat*: the teacher may agree to show a particular move only three times to an advanced student, with no possibility of returning later for comments or explanation (Gary Gartenberg, personal communication). In Morocco, Schuyler observes that "fear of competition may cause the master to be reticent and balky in passing on information. In turn, at times this reticence can provoke the very breach of trust that a master fears . . . Mutual distrust between teachers and students was one factor leading to the decline in the repertory of Moroccan art music in the early twentieth century" (1979: 25). Beyond any mystical interpretations such attitudes must be seen not only as expressions of power within a delimited realm of knowledge but as a way of forcing the student to rely on inference and a richly patterned, formulaically organized memory. Even in less extreme cases, when the student has repeated opportunities to hear a passage but that passage is played differently each time, an essentially inferential, interpretive, and creative process of learning and knowing is favored over rote memorization or verbalized explanations and instructions.

Agents, contexts, and means of transmission. The relationship between learner and teacher or model and the contexts in which these relationships are played out also merit consideration. A wealth of contextual knowledge and performance experience can be gained, for example, through apprenticeship to a master musician, a process that often involves a long period of subservience and may include playing a supporting part in performance. However, apprenticeship may severely limit access to other musicians, styles, and approaches within a musical community. There may also be strong sanctions against any innovation or deviation from the master's way of doing things.

Most other types of teacher-student relationships involve lesser degrees of control over a student and over the breadth of the student's exposure to musical life. Some musicians learn from a single source or pass through a hierarchy of teachers within a more or less formally instituted school, ensuring a fairly uniform approach and a competence with few internal conflicts. Others are exposed to contrasting approaches to music-making and teaching when they switch teachers or mix sources. They must cope with these differences as they search for coherence and synthesize their own competences.

Consider the institution of the master class, an important educational tool in the Western concert tradition in which complex relationships are played out. A teacher who is highly placed in a hierarchy of professional recognition listens to a series of promising young musicians who have been selected on the basis of the competence they have already achieved. The teacher offers his or her criticisms and suggestions, usually illustrated by direct demonstration on the instrument in question. The students then have an opportunity to apply the feedback and further instruction offered. The intensity and brevity of interactions in a master class, which often involves substantial public exposure, stand in stark contrast to the more private and long-lasting relationships that usually develop in private lessons. Comments and illustrations directed at the students and the students' efforts at improvement are observed by a third party, the auditors, who learn by watching someone else receive direct instruction and feedback and must retain that experience, applying it at a later time. Since master classes often draw an audience heavily populated with teachers who are probably less recognized or experienced than the spotlit master, instructional methods and attitudes toward teaching and learning are transmitted in addition to direct knowledge of the music and requisite performance skills.

Musicians also increase competence outside teacher-pupil relationships. In many musical communities, listening to other musicians is the primary type of learning relationship. This differs greatly from the mutual bonds of teacher and pupil because the musician who serves as a model, as a source of knowledge, is performing in context and may not even be aware of the person who is trying to learn from his or her playing. Musicians who might be hesitant to reveal the secrets of their art directly to a pupil are less likely to hold back in performance, particularly if there is a competitive atmosphere or any other reason to demonstrate competence. The auditor has none of the obligations to this model that a student has toward a teacher, but the feedback that a teacher can give is also lacking except in those cases where the learner is performing alongside the model. The cognitive challenges of learning in performance contexts also differ significantly from explicit lessons. There is no possibility of repetition or segmentation of the musical material to suit the needs of the learner. On the other hand, frames of reference, which may be lacking in a lesson, are explicit in performance.

The spread of inexpensive tape recorders and cassette recordings in the past twenty-five years has depersonalized the interaction between source and learner. In the short run, at least, the interaction is unidirectional and anonymous. The learning listener avoids the inhibitions and sanctions against mistakes or experimentation that may arise in face-to-face learning situations but also lacks the feedback that a teacher can offer. Recordings alter the nature of transmission in traditions such as Hindustani music as rote imitation becomes less problematic: it is possible to obtain repeated access to the improvisations of many master musicians without engaging in the long-term personal contact of a subservient relationship on which this tradition has rested for generations.

Interaction between model and listener differs in quantity as well as in kind because commercial recordings confer mass accessibility. Since recordings readily cross barriers of space and time, musicians long dead can be heard thousands of miles from the areas in which they lived and performed. The only socioeconomic barrier between a learner and such recordings is the lack of funds to purchase recordings or lack of contact with people who have recordings and playback equipment.

Recordings remove all constraints on segmentation and repetition. The auditor can hear passages as many times as necessary and can isolate segments of any duration. Some musicians even have access to equipment for altering playback speed, which allows them to capture nuances of performance and enables exact imitation.[4] This is detrimental to traditions in which competence is developed by inference from a group of variants or from ever-varying subjects. Such traditions may suffer from a lessening of variety as repeated playback of a single recorded performance supersedes exposure to many unique live performances.

There are few musicians in the world today who are completely untouched by the phenomenon of recorded sound, but the usage and influence of technology are by no means uniform. This point can be illustrated by a rough comparison of the uses of recordings in some of the dominant musical traditions of North America and Europe. Recordings are influential in the education of most musicians trained in the European tradition of concert music, offering exposure to a wide variety of performers and a much larger repertoire than one can find performed live in most locales and conveying nuances of interpretation that are highly valued by musicians. However, they do not supplant the notated scores that constitute the primary texts of this tradition. The use of recordings among jazz musicians reflects the differing nature of this music: recordings capture particular improvisations and, together with live performances, offer an important means of exposure to the improvisatory styles of those performers who constitute a musician's primary "influences." As in classical music, recordings are important because they offer access to multiple performances of a composition, but the emphasis is different here: the performances are likely to be far more divergent and, in the case of the standard jazz repertoire, the improvisations are of greater interest than the compositions themselves. For rock musicians recordings constitute the primary texts, perhaps even more so than for jazz musicians, but the incidence of multiple interpretations is much lower: most recordings represent singular performances that are imitated both as a source of repertoire and as a source of sound production skills. One of the central claims of Bennett's study of rock musicians is that the chief source for competence is the commercial recording due to the

4. Such devices are heavily marketed to popular musicians in the United States.

absence of an institutionalized system of instruction and the tendency for beginners to associate with equally inexperienced musicians (1980: 181–82). The continual reinvention of competence that he discerns contrasts strongly with the attributions and lineages of tutelage or influence that characterize the transmission of competence among classical and jazz musicians.

The significance of this comparison grows when one considers that many musicians have multiple competences covering two or even all three of these musical traditions, often using recordings in different ways for each type of music. While a classical musician may learn repertoire and interpretive approaches from recordings, a jazz musician uses recordings as a tool for developing or expanding improvisational skills and a rock musician may do a bit of both. Jazz and rock musicians improve competence by playing along with recordings. This is probably not nearly as common or important for classically trained musicians (with the exception of music-minus-one recordings, which afford an opportunity to perform in ensemble with highly competent musicians).

In addition to recordings, means of transmission include technical exercises, writings about music, and symbolic representations such as mnemonic syllables and notation. The use of specific technical exercises or pieces arranged in a pedagogically reasoned progression favors the development of technical skills independent of specific musical contexts. Through extensive repetition, low-level processes of music-making are grouped into higher-level cognitive units, enabling rapid, automatic production (Hayes-Roth 1977: 404; Gruson 1988) that can be put to very different uses. While Hindustani musical training, for example, relies on technical exercises to build improvisatory fluency, the exercises in Western classical training prepare a musician to meet the technical challenges of a wide variety of notated music. The contrast between these traditions and ones that rely on training solely through performance of "real pieces" from the repertoire has yet to be studied.

Writings about music impart knowledge that is explicit by definition, but the aspects of competence included are often peripheral to actual performance demands. Books that offer instruction in Arab music, for example, include notation of the basic scales that are characteristic of the modes (maqamat) but explicit knowledge of these scales is only tenuously related to knowledge of the processes required for appropriate performance of the maqamat (Marcus 1989). Similarly, instructional writings on Javanese music generally convey elementary declarative knowledge about the instruments of the gamelan, about basic musical forms and modes, and occasionally about topics such as special ceremonial ensembles or appropriate choices of pieces in shadow play perfor-mances.[5]

Some books are intended to replace a teacher and therefore include both written instructions for the processes of sound production and no-tated music with which the reader can practice the procedures learned from the instructions. There is a vast array of such self-help manuals available today, including some that take advantage of video and CD-ROM technology, but the motivation for such books was already ex-pressed in the title of a nineteenth-century guitar manual: *Winner's Perfect Guide for the Guitar, In which the Instructions are so clearly and simply treated, as to make it unnecessary to require a teacher* . . . (anon. 1861).

The issue of access, discussed above in connection with teachers and performance opportunities, arises again with respect to the availability of notation and the prevalence of literacy, the ability to interpret these records. Manuscript cultures are generally characterized by limited ac-cess to written materials and by greater variation in the items recorded and in the selection of these items (Sweeney 1987). Notation that was written down or copied by hand was likely to have a much more local-ized effect on competence than readily dispersed printed music. The advent of cheap photocopying has begun to erase this distinction. In Central Java, handwritten notation, which spread among musicians in the early decades of this century, began to be replaced by printed nota-tion in the middle decades; photocopied handwritten notation has re-cently begun to appear in large quantities (e.g., Suraji 1991a).

As a domain of competence musical literacy varies in importance with the ways in which notation is used in a given community and with the kinds of information encoded. Common use of notation in perfor-mance, rather than for reference, implies that literacy is a central skill, visual symbols are a main referent, and notation functions as a script for action. On the other hand, notation may be highly abstract and nonpre-scriptive; reading is then likely to be a less frequently used skill and may be relatively laborious. When the use of notation is fairly widespread but not a universal component of competence, a sharp division may arise between two groups of musicians, excluding those who cannot read from ensembles that rely on notation and from repertoire that is not commonly performed despite the fact that they are fully competent in every other aspect of the tradition. Such a division exists in certain parts of the Middle East, for example, where many musicians pursue success-ful careers relying solely on their ability to learn new pieces by ear but

---

5. Gitosaprodjo (1984) is a typical example of this type of writing. Martopangrawit (1984) is unusually rich in analytical detail but difficult to apply in practice.

numerous ensembles rely on notation to learn new repertoire quickly or to reintroduce older pieces that are not commonly heard, and thus inaccessible save through notation.[6]

In some traditions, the mastery of mnemonic sounds such as solfège systems and drumming syllables is important to competence not just for its own sake but also as a means of communication between teacher and pupil or between co-performers. In this latter sense, the musician acquires an intermediate category of knowledge that may not be used in performance but is a means of acquiring performance competence. Baily characterizes Hindustani drum syllables (bols) as a verbal framework "to which the individual [hand] movements for the various bols become progressively attached. The player is able to drop rehearsing the verbal framework when the motor representation, or motor programme has become well established" (1988: 117). Javanese drum syllables provide a similar means of learning and connecting knowledge: an auditory pattern becomes a frame of reference for a nonsounding dance movement pattern and also a representation of the sounding drum pattern that accompanies this movement. While essential to the acquisition of a drummer's competence, these syllables are never performed. Mnemonic systems used in various types of Japanese music serve an analogous intermediate function.

ASSESSING COMPETENCE

Musicians are evaluated constantly by teachers, peers, students, audience, and employers. These assessments of competence may be expressed explicitly in verbal evaluations or implied in musical responses and in the performance associations which others are willing to join, instigate, or maintain. As a person learns and becomes more capable, opportunities for performance and further advancement often depend to a great extent on other musicians' assessments of that person's competence.

The priorities and aesthetics of a musical community are expressed in the aspects of competence that are emphasized in such assessments. If quality of sound production and mastery of repertoire are most frequently mentioned, one can surmise that these aspects of competence are more highly valued than virtuoso display, to take a simple example. A more comprehensive analysis of cultural priorities requires that the terms of assessment be compared to observable utilization of musical knowledge within the tradition. The implications of attention to vocal

6. Bennett discusses limited literacy among rock musicians (1980).

quality, for example, differ depending on the range of variation among singers: if the differences between singers are relatively large, it is important to establish whether singers who do not approach a particular sound ideal are valued for other aspects of competence or by other segments of the community and why such singers cultivate a different sound. Likewise, assessments of individuals' knowledge of repertoire must be interpreted in light of the size and nature of that repertoire. If the repertoire is extensive, a musician who is noted for knowledge of the entire repertoire is being recognized as exceptional. If the repertoire is not large, such an assessment may simply be an acknowledgment that the musician has fulfilled one of the requirements of competence.

Assessments of musicians' competence are often expressed in classification systems. Institutionalized evaluations may actually accord a musician a rank or title in recognition of attaining a certain degree of competence. This is the case in Japanese schools of *shakuhachi, koto,* and *shamisen* and in degree-awarding conservatories of European music around the world. In less formal situations, people categorize competence in a looser manner. The stages of competence attainment may be openly expressed in the ranking of particular musicians; they are often implicit in other expressions of assessment. For most musical communities it should be possible to elicit an expected progression of degrees of attainment articulated in labels such as apprentice, professional, star, master, and guru, although assessments are not always so neatly ordered. Evaluations of intent, accomplishment, and potential are mixed in the following hypothetical assessments: musician A is a master, B is still learning, C shows great promise, D is an amateur, E is the best dramatic singer, and F can play anything. These comments also point to specialized competences.

Benchmarks are items or capabilities that a musician is expected to master in the course of attaining competence. The underlying premise of a benchmark is encapsulated in the statement "If you know how to play X, then you must know how to play Y." Whether it is a particular piece, a playing technique, an instrument, or some other aspect of musical competence, a benchmark is a prototypical representative of an entire class of similar items. Once attained it implies mastery of all items in that class or at least sufficient competence to master all such items. It usually implies mastery of items in other classes by association. Thus, benchmarks are evidence of optimal or typical learning progressions. They often constitute a set or gradated series of goals to be attained and as such offer a good means of ascertaining underlying conceptualizations of musical knowledge.

Special keys to knowledge often figure prominently in explanations of competence acquisition. A key is an item or group of items that is thought to contain the essence of an entire domain of knowledge, as in the opening quote of chapter 1: "These pieces contain all you need to know." While benchmarks are markers along the road to competence, implying an ordered progression, a key opens the door to knowledge. It is a means of enlightenment that gives the bearer access to all knowledge within a particular domain. I have encountered this concept in a number of cultures (without attempting to elicit it): some Javanese examples will be discussed in the next chapter; several Middle Eastern musicians have demonstrated keys to the modal system for me; a Balinese dancer/musician explained to me that her illiterate grandmother could remember sung poetry after one hearing because she possessed a key. In essence, the authors of method books for self-instruction in jazz improvisation are making a similar claim when they offer a system that is supposed to enable the student to master improvisation.

Attitudes toward other aspects of knowledge are also likely to surface in an analysis of the terms of assessment. Ideas about the finiteness, stability, and authenticity of knowledge are often implicit in evaluations of musicians and are likely to be related to general cultural beliefs about the finiteness of knowledge. We should be able to learn whether musicians believe that complete competence is attainable, whether it is possible to master the entire repertoire, a particular instrument, or all of the modes, or whether musicians strive for unattainable goals, delving ever deeper and viewing competence as a set of inexhaustible potentials.

There may be no universal limits to musical competence, only culturally defined ones, and these, too, are subject to question. Since actual measurement of the extent of an accomplished musician's competence is not feasible, the limits of competence can only be deduced from musicians' assessments of each other in comparison with the competence demonstrated in actual performance. McLeod and Herndon suggest biological limits in their sketch of an ideal competence within which all others are contained (1980: 186), but this is hardly a useful overall distinction, given the ever-mounting accomplishments of athletes who give us precisely measured instances of surpassing previous "absolute" limits. Biological limits are particularly irrelevant at a time when electronic technology, increasingly available and availed of by musicians in many different societies and musical contexts, circumvents many of these limitations. Electronic amplification has enabled musicians to exceed all prior limits of volume. Through electronic sampling musicians can use a synthesizer to produce and control timbres that would otherwise require difficult instrumental techniques or be limited by instrument construction to a small range. Multitracking, tape loops, and sequencing enable one person to play many "instruments" or parts at once.

Individuals may conceive of a stable ideal competence, but the ways of making music favored in a community or tradition change over the years, causing changes in musical competence and in the standards by which this competence is assessed. Younger musicians may no longer find it necessary or desirable to know all the aspects of music that older musicians know, and they may develop new ways of playing instead. As a result they do not measure up to the standards of their predecessors. Some older musicians keep up with these changes, but others do not and may even think it improper to do so. These others would be found wanting if judged by the new standards created by younger musicians. Such generational disparities of competence are a potential source of friction. A stable set of standards may also be differentiated according to age: I Wayan Loceng, a Balinese musician now in his mid-sixties, says that in recent years he has adopted a more restrained style appropriate to his age (Lisa Gold, personal communication). Similarly, the late I Wayan Saplug, another Balinese musician, told me that he could not play Galang Kangin, one of the most commonly performed pieces in the *lelambatan* repertoire, because it was not fitting for an old man to play the modern arrangement that is now in fashion.

Some of these issues can be illustrated by a brief look at the competence of jazz musicians. This competence has changed drastically and frequently in the short history of this musical tradition as new ways of improvising, new aesthetics, and new compositional frameworks have developed. Fundamental differences in the standards by which different groups of musicians and their adherents assess competence reflect the extent of the changes that have occurred. The innovations of Charlie Parker, one of the chief inventors of the bebop style of the 1940s, are the most famous example of radical change. The early rejections that he suffered at the hands of swing era musicians exemplify the evaluative impact of changes in style. Established jazz musicians have responded to these changes in different ways. Many continue to play in the style that was dominant when they first achieved competence. In the eyes of younger musicians and jazz historians, these older players have failed to progress and have receded into history, despite the fact that many continue to perform, pushed out of the field of view of an evolutionary narrative by younger generations playing newer styles. Some musicians, probably fewer by far, have adapted to these stylistic changes—their competence has continued to evolve. Coleman Hawkins, for instance, continued to adapt to changes in performance styles and contexts as he made the transition from vaudeville bands to the early jazz of the 1920s, then to the swing bands and finally bebop, playing with ever-younger musicians and altering his competence in ways that many other musicians, particularly his counterparts from the swing era, were reluctant to do.

Similar situations obtain in other musical traditions, although the changes are not necessarily as rapid or as drastic. It is fruitful to consider such changes not just as stylistic developments but as alterations of the substance and standards of competence, of the expectations regarding what a musician should know and be able to do, and also as a breaking or reshaping of old standards linked to the creation of new ones.

The standards upon which assessments are based may vary significantly within a community for other reasons besides stylistic change. This variation sometimes coincides with divisions between musicians and nonmusicians or with obvious sociological distinctions such as age, education, and class, but allowances must also be made for individual idiosyncrasies. Too often musical scholarship focuses solely on dominant styles, ignoring the individuals and groups who form and act upon divergent aesthetic preferences. Yet it is the dynamics of this activity that ultimately determine the norms of competence and the ways of making music. Attention to individual preferences must be balanced, of course, with acknowledgment of the influence of standards based on a broader consensus or promoted by figures with greater cultural authority. Such balance is lacking, for instance, in Bennett's claim that local groups of rock musicians create standards independently in an extremely localized manner:

> Lacking an institutionalized educational form and . . . experience with an established population of musicians . . . a *spontaneous* standard system which is wholly confined to each group's reality is constructed on the basis of the minimal level of virtuosity which the group has in common. This amounts to no more than an assessment of playing ability which is constructed around an individual by the uniquely formulated concept of musicianship which the group evolves. (1980: 29–30.)

While Bennett does argue elsewhere for awareness of the multiple aesthetics of musicians, listeners, and record producers (1980: 9–10), here he ignores the enormous importance of exposure to other groups in public performances and especially through broadcast and recording media. The use of studio recording techniques, in particular, sometimes establishes standards that are unattainable in live performance or with the equipment available to most musicians.

The meaning of an assessment depends on the authority and sociocultural agenda of the person making the assessment. Kingsbury has aptly highlighted the relativity of assessment and its social nature: "The validity of a given person's musical talent is a direct function of the relative esteem of the persons who have attributed the talent to the person in question . . . For a meaningful assessment of musical talent to take place, some listener must, at least implicitly, be able to claim a certain amount of critical knowledge and authority" (1988: 68–69). The compartmentalization of competences in Western music is such that some musicians disqualify themselves from judgment because of differences in specialization. "Both within and outside a conservatory, highly trained singers, for example, may hesitate to comment on the merits of pianists" (1988: 69).

Assessment may also be influenced by perceptions of the source of the performer's knowledge. Schutz notes the "prestige of authenticity and authority" accorded the socially derived and approved knowledge obtained from the great masters of European music (1976: 169–70). In other musical traditions, too, musical pedigrees deriving from teaching lineages or institutions can play important roles in the perception of competence. Thus, assessments of competence must be evaluated with regard to the sociocultural standing of the people involved. Because assessment is inherently interactive—even self-assessment involves mental constructions of others' actions and opinions—the topic will be considered further in the discussion of competence and interaction in the final chapter of this book.

CHAPTER SIX

MY EXPERIENCE IS MY TEACHER
THE ACQUISITION OF JAVANESE MUSICAL COMPETENCE

Claims of autodidactic acquisition of competence surface frequently in conversations with Javanese musicians. The independence conveyed in phrases such as "my experience is my teacher"[1] is tempered by naming specific musicians as sources for items of knowledge such as a variant on a pattern or a way of playing a certain passage. By asserting independence while acknowledging sources, musicians implicitly stress their own syntheses of these sources and solutions to the "puzzles" of performance without distancing themselves from the realm of musical consensus.

Transmission by osmosis and reinvention may well seem mysterious to someone accustomed to formalized learning situations in which most musical knowledge is acquired from a teacher, perhaps with auxiliary resources such as notation and books about music. Yet for most Javanese musicians acquisition of competence is relatively unfocused and unstructured because neither the curriculum nor the social contract of the learning process is fixed. While some younger musicians have received formalized instruction, this is usually not their primary learning experience but a means of ordering and filling in a competence substantially achieved through performance.

1. While I have heard this wording from musicians speaking in English who may have sought to mystify foreign students, the learning experience of other musicians seems to bear out the essential validity of the statement.

In this chapter we shall see how a Javanese musician's learning experience—to the extent that one can generalize about this highly variable aggregate of individual perceptions, interactions, and accomplishments—is influenced by the structures and performance practices of Javanese music and by the constitution of Javanese musical competence and how, in turn, the manner of acquisition favors the development of certain types of competence and ways of knowing. These issues are discussed in tandem rather than consecutively because we lack the historical evidence to ascertain whether the manner of acquisition gave rise to a certain competence or vice versa. Since acquisition of competence can extend throughout a person's active life as a musician and since a communally recognized body of knowledge is likely to change, too, the chapter concludes with a discussion of long-term developments in individual and communal competence as these intersect and diverge.

An early start on the acquisition of musical competence is both common and advantageous, although there are some good musicians who have managed to overcome the disadvantage of starting late. Sutton has described a case in which the son of a leading musician and teacher showed no overt interest in *gamelan* until his mid-teens, at which point he acquired a high degree of well-rounded competence with astonishing rapidity (1991b), indicating that extensive exposure offers an important passive basis on which active competence can be rapidly built.

Age-defined restrictions of association such as youth ensembles or nominal levels of achievement do exist but are not common. Instead, most musicians are absorbed into regular ensembles early in their careers. The incorporation of novice musicians is greatly facilitated by the spectrum of levels of difficulty within the idioms and repertoire of the *gamelan*. Instruments such as the time-marking *kethuk* or the *saron* (on which the *balungan* is played) pose no technical difficulties. Elaborating instruments of secondary importance such as the *bonang panerus* or *gendèr panerus* also provide opportunities for relatively inexperienced musicians because the parts played on these instruments derive from other parts, following behind them and affording musicians the opportunity to learn pieces through performance. They also can be played softly, and mistakes are not as detrimental to the performance as mistakes on more central instruments would be. The small repertoire of short, repetitive pieces used for theater and dance are good vehicles for learning. Precocious young children may even be allowed to drum for short battle pieces in a shadow play years before they have mastered the more complex drumming patterns for other pieces (Widiyanto, personal communication).

The loose nature of membership in many performing groups affords musicians a wide range of associations with other musicians. Even members of ensembles as official as the radio station or the court *gamelan* frequently perform in other ensembles. Group membership often fluctuates, and players readily trade places during performance, especially in long performances such as all-night shadow plays. Role assignments are often worked out on the spot,[2] and even the regular assignments of some more formalized ensembles do not prevent players from trading positions on occasion. Thus, musicians have the potential of gaining a broad range of experience by playing any of the parts in the *gamelan* and by hearing a wide variety of other musicians playing these parts.

Taking advantage of the wealth of opportunities available in the shifting ensemble associations of Javanese *gamelan* depends to a great extent on initial access to performance experience, which is often a function of who one is and whom one knows. Relatives who already play *gamelan* are a major asset. A member of a *dhalang's* family, for instance, has unparalleled access to instruments and to opportunities to hear and participate in performances from a very young age.[3] Most musicians whom I questioned noted some family member—usually an older brother, father, or uncle, occasionally an older female relative—who had given them initial instruction or a first opportunity to play one of the more difficult instruments.

Imitation is the primary method of acquiring competence, whether learning through osmosis or from a teacher. Imitation is not simply a matter of rote repetition. It is subject first to vagaries of perception and limitations of performative abilities, but cultural standards of replication are also a factor. While some communities demand a high degree of faithfulness to the model, Javanese musicians expect a certain amount of individual variability, particularly in the idiomatic patterning of the elaborating instruments: "A musician is not considered fully equipped if he merely imitates another in all details. His playing ideally should represent the tradition filtered through his own sensibilities, which . . . are not expected to be precisely like anyone else's" (Sutton 1982:26). The relatively broad Javanese tolerances of fidelity in imitation are also due to the general lack of extensive and specific feedback from a teacher or other more knowledgeable musician.

The circumstances of imitation directly affect the accuracy of reproduction. In the following comparison of simultaneous and consecutive imitation I use the terms "teacher" and "student" loosely (as in chap. 1)

2. See chapter 10 and Vetter (1986).
3. Suanda notes the same phenomenon for Cirebon, to the northwest of Central Java (1985: 91).

to denote those who manifest knowledge and those who learn from such manifestations, whether in a lesson, a rehearsal, or a public performance. *Simultaneous imitation*, in which the student plays along with the teacher, enables a close modeling because differences between model and imitation are immediately and starkly apparent, particularly when imitating rhythm or intonation for singing or playing the *rebab*. On the other hand, there is little time for observation and reflection while the model sounds. The opposite is true for *consecutive imitation*, where the student listens to the model before replicating it. Here external feedback is more important, since the model and the reproduction are not juxtaposed, but in Java such feedback is often sparse, particularly if the imitation has come close to the model. This encourages the proliferation of small divergences from the model.

Simultaneous imitation and consecutive imitation make strikingly different use of memory. Let us assume that the teacher presents a new piece or fragment of a piece, repeating it several times in succession. The student who imitates simultaneously will necessarily lag a split second behind the teacher at first, feeding auditory and visual perceptions into memory and immediately acting upon these perceptions, attempting to reproduce as many as possible of the sounds heard in a precarious balancing act that probably involves extensive use of "echoic memory"—what he or she has perceived in the instant just past. Extensive stereotypical patterning helps the student guess where the teacher is heading and encourages automaticity once such a path has been confirmed. In later repetitions of the piece, the student draws on memory, but this is constantly reinforced by the teacher's repetition of the piece. The student who imitates consecutively must first commit the performance to memory and then retrieve the remembered performance, using it as a template. In extreme cases feedback is purely internal and based on this memory because the teacher is no longer present or makes no comment. It is probably more common, however, for a Javanese teacher to sing out a note or two to guide the student who goes astray. This terse hint is rarely a full representation of the desired sound so it must be interpreted by the student and linked up correctly to a more complex remembered sound sequence. The student who imitates simultaneously has the luxury of constant guidance but lacks the time for reflection and analysis while the one who imitates consecutively must rely on memory without the external reinforcement of the teacher's playing but has more time to analyze and interpret the model as it is performed. It seems reasonable to expect a closer reproduction of the model in the first case, but more research on musical memory is required to verify this.

In consecutive imitation the teacher will often play a second part on another instrument. This additional part provides a frame of reference and affirmation of the larger scheme of the performance rather than direct note-by-note modeling. If the teacher plays *rebab* while the student plays *gendèr* or vice versa, he manifests the larger outline of the melody with the correct sequence of tonal goals and melodic contour. If the teacher plays the *balungan*, he provides a less detailed frame of reference and more general affirmation, but his part still includes information that can spark recollection.

Straightforward transmission is sometimes hindered by a teacher's attitude and method. The teacher may not offer a model for imitation, expecting that the student obtain the knowledge elsewhere and come to him only for correction or refinement. This was my drumming teacher's experience when he studied drumming: he was forced to learn the patterns from notation and from hearing other musicians because his teacher never touched the drum during lessons, making at most a slight motion with his hand to indicate main strokes but not filler strokes. On the other hand, a teacher may provide a model but little or no opportunity to imitate the model in his presence. This was often the case in the early years of this century when musicians would play for students but not listen to them (Wasitodiningrat, personal communication).

Only the more difficult elaborating parts are taught in actual lessons; other parts are almost always learned through imitation and deduction in the course of performance. The proper placement of the colotomic *kenong, kethuk, kempul,* or gong strokes can be deduced from the form of a piece and passive knowledge of the corresponding cyclical drum patterns. The musician then has time to absorb the melody from other musicians because the colotomic parts move relatively slowly in most pieces. When playing the *saron,* it is also fairly easy to pick up the *balungan* by watching the *slenthem* player, who often has a firmer grasp of the *balungan* than the others, and by listening to instruments that anticipate the *balungan* (see fig. 10).[4]

Learning through performance often requires extremely rapid cognitive processing. The time frame within which a musician gleans information from other parts and interprets it idiomatically on his or her instrument may be short, bordering on the instantaneous, so this procedure ranges between nearly simultaneous and slightly consecutive imitation. But *delayed imitation* is also an important part of the learning process as a musician attempts to reproduce something heard in earlier repetitions of the piece or in earlier performances.

---

4. The *bonang* and *bonang panerus* parts illustrated here are theoretical models. In practice a musician omits some notes.

Fig. 10   Anticipation of the *balungan*

In addition to the distinctions already drawn between simultaneous, consecutive, and delayed imitation on the basis of time elapsed between the model and reproduction, it is useful to distinguish *deductive imitation, selective imitation,* and *emulation,* which have differing implications for the conditions and quality of perception and reproduction. Deductive imitation involves idiomatic translation or transformation of an essence abstracted from perceptual input, distancing the reproduction from its model because of a conscious decision to differ or a need to translate from one idiom to another. By contrast, emulation is an attempt to reproduce the model as faithfully as possible, taking on another's musical persona, as it were. Emulation involves going beyond the bounds of common competence, entering domains of highly individual knowledge, and is most likely to occur when learning one of the more stylized idioms that afford room for individual stylistic expression and variation. Selective imitation is a middle ground: a musician may emulate only those aspects that he or she values in the model, without aiming for precise reproduction of every nuance.

Emulation may be most prevalent at an early stage of a musician's education. While lack of sufficient skill may cause a reproduction that does not match the model, the student is building a stock of idiomatic knowledge that becomes available for use in analogous musical contexts. This stock of knowledge can then serve as the basis for more selective imitation: when learning to play a new piece on one of the elaborating instruments, a student can deduce the gist of the part and reproduce it using his or her own versions of the patterns. Thus, it is likely that emulation gives way to selective imitation as a musician becomes more competent, although a more advanced musician may still seek to emulate particular aspects of another musician's playing. It is hardly conceivable that one could learn only through emulation, particularly given the predominance of multiple models and sources that most Javanese musicians acknowledge. At some point musicians must begin to "translate" into their own terms. Conversely, selective imitation and deductive imitation are probably difficult at an early stage of learning when the student has yet to acquire a sufficient command of procedures and stock of patterns to enable the perceptual distinctions and translation these modes of learning require.

These conjectures and the ones that follow are based on substantial observation and on comments by various musicians (including Supanggah 1991) and require validation through extensive research. In lieu of an exhaustive study of patterns of learning in Java that will require years of observation and analysis of a wide sample, I offer a meditation on my experiences and those of other foreigners, contrasted with the experiences of Javanese musicians in terms of respective accomplishments, capabilities, and difficulties.

Anecdotal evidence indicates that most Javanese musicians derive their knowledge from other musicians outside a formal student-teacher relationship, implying that the main channels of transmission are not directed by the person who serves as a model. Whenever experienced musicians perform, they are potential models and often unwitting ones for aspiring and established musicians, who listen and pick up whatever they can; even relatively mature musicians may adopt something that they hear. For the past twenty years the impersonality of this "surreptitious" transmission has been augmented by the widespread availability of commercial *gamelan* recordings, which allows individuals to emulate the playing of recorded musicians from a different time and place. The anonymity of this relationship is often mutual, since recordings never name musicians other than the leader and the vocalists, although musicians can identify some of the participants in a recording session because of acquaintance with the group or acute awareness of individual playing styles.

My own learning experience with regard to *gendèr* and *rebab* is not typical for a Javanese musician, but it serves well to highlight these issues through the contrasting approaches of my Javanese teachers and through my achievements and failures in response to these approaches. Wasitodiningrat, who taught me to play both of these instruments while I was his student in the United States, took a decidedly nonanalytical approach. He rarely used pattern names as a shorthand and gave almost no verbal guidance regarding the identity or proper usage of the patterns that were evident in his playing. Most of our lessons focused on *rebab*, because that was the instrument that he wanted me to play. Simultaneous imitation was the main method of transmission, as I endeavored to match Wasitodiningrat's playing as best I could on a second *rebab*. This was supplemented by simultaneous and consecutive imitation of recordings that I made in lessons; this private practice provided better opportunities to emulate the nuances of Wasitodiningrat's *rebab* playing and also allowed me to break the piece down into smaller sections, a method Wasitodiningrat did not use in lessons. As an aid to understanding and remembering I also made use of transcriptions taken from these recordings. When I knew the piece well enough to get through it, Wasitodiningrat would play *gendèr*, establishing crucial temporal, intonational, and modal frameworks for my *rebab* playing.

Through this process I achieved a largely unarticulated understanding of the *rebab* idiom that was sufficient for adequate performances of pieces that I knew and for fairly rapid acquisition of new pieces. When I continued my studies in Java with Martopangrawit, the methodology changed only to the extent that theoretical discussions augmented my understanding of the modal practice and interpretive possibilities of the instrument. Martopangrawit's playing differed in style from Wasitodiningrat's, but I did not emulate it as fully as I had Wasitodiningrat's: my ability to construct an acceptable *rebab* part that was not a slavish imitation of my teacher's playing was increasing thanks to extensive exposure to a variety of performers and performances and increased understanding of common melodic patterns in Javanese composition. When I returned to the United States and began to play with Wasitodiningrat again, I was torn between returning to an emulation of his playing and continuing the individual mixture which had developed mainly unconsciously through my various experiences in Java.

The experience of studying *gendèr* was strikingly different when I shifted from nonanalytical emulation of Wasitodiningrat in Berkeley to consciously deductive imitation in my studies with Harjito in Solo. Unlike *rebab* lessons, imitation was almost exclusively consecutive because only one instrument was usually available. When I arrived in Java, I had already emulated some aspects of Wasitodiningrat's *gendèr* style by learning to play a small number of pieces, chiefly from recordings (which I subsequently transcribed). I could discern patterns, but there was sufficient variety in their usage and the sample of pieces that formed the extent of my experience was so small that I was unable to apply this knowledge to other pieces except in the most straightforward and rudimentary cases. Furthermore, I lacked the degree of comfort and automaticity that I had achieved on *rebab* through extensive simultaneous imitation, because Wasitodiningrat was not particularly interested in teaching me *gendèr* and generally preferred "making a tape" to the time-consuming process of repeating a piece while I gradually came closer to matching his playing.[5]

Harjito took a radically different approach when I began to study with him: in the course of one or two lessons he taught me basic forms of the common *gendèr* patterns in *sléndro manyura*, explaining the appropriate tonal contexts for each pattern and—equally important—naming each pattern. At first I emulated his playing as closely as possible, but I soon began to mix and match his patterns with corresponding patterns that I was now able to excerpt from Wasitodiningrat's performances. As soon as he had taught me this basic stock of patterns, Harjito taught me two fairly long pieces that made use of these patterns in a stereotypical manner, without the modal ambiguities or other complications that occur in many pieces. Thus, I was provided with procedural knowledge—how to get from one goal tone to the next—and sample frameworks within which to apply these procedures. At a later stage, Harjito had me transpose most of the patterns down one pitch to create a parallel stock of *sléndro sanga* patterns and he also began to teach me pieces in *pélog* which made use of the same patterns transferred to another tuning. In both cases I reinforced and expanded the transformative knowledge that I had begun to develop intuitively under Wasitodiningrat's tutelage, learning to preserve kinetic patterns of sound production independently of the acoustic product. On this basis it was possible to proceed rapidly to the acquisition of many more pieces, which I began to learn through selective imitation rather than emulation. I recorded my teacher's playing less frequently (unfortunately) and almost ceased to transcribe, making brief notes instead while he played. Here the names of the patterns

---

5. He gave unstintingly of his time in *rebab* lessons, repeating pieces many times while I played along on a second *rebab* and enduring horrific dissonances in the first lessons before I was able to match his pitch.

provided an invaluable tool for recording the essence of his interpretation (*garapan*). As I progressed, deductive imitation became more and
more feasible: I could work out likely *garapan* for *gendèr* based on the
balungan, the *rebab* part, and analogies to *garapan* in similar contexts in
the growing body of pieces that my teacher was imparting. Thus, I could
anticipate Harjito's *garapan* and reserve most of my attention for those
places that did not match my expectations.

Many Javanese musicians surpass my achievements without benefit
of the extensive individual instruction I received. Since the primary
mode of learning is participation in actual ensemble performance, deductive imitation is of paramount importance when playing a piece or
an instrument that a musician has not yet mastered. Words such as *ngèli*
(float) and *ngawur* (blunder) are used to describe the ways in which musicians act in such situations. Such methods are supported by the interrelatedness of all the parts and particularly by the derivative nature of
many of those parts, as we have already seen. *Pesindhèn* can take advantage of the characteristic delay in their phrases to listen to the *rebab* or
the *gérongan* (male choral melody) for clues, and musicians playing the
faster elaborating parts can resort to the repetition of static "holding"
patterns, turning to more melodically directed playing only when reasonably certain of the direction that the melody is going. For example,
Widiyanto once showed me a *siter* pattern so neutral tonally that it could
be played in almost any context without clashing with other parts.[6]

In Javanese musical practice the predominance of cyclicity, the preference for group rehearsal over individual practice, the rarity of overt
external feedback, and a holistic approach to pieces in rehearsal all combine to create a characteristic learning situation that differs significantly
from many other traditions. The cyclical structures of the vast majority
of Javanese pieces provide extensive repetition that facilitates learning
both the pieces themselves and the standard ways of performing those
pieces. This is crucial for learning by osmosis, since it provides several
opportunities to hear something new, to memorize it, and to reinforce
this mental record. With further repetition a musician can reproduce
this new knowledge, get feedback, and correct and perfect it. This is
particularly important because the phenomenon of practice, the solitary
repetition of exercises and working out of problematic passages that is
central to any Western or Indian musician's training, is peripheral to a
Javanese musician's experience. An individual may practice *rebab, gendèr,*
or *kendhang* alone but is more likely to play in a group situation. Musical

---

6. See also the repetitive initial segments of the *gendèr panerus* patterns in Marsudi (1983).

exercises are unknown, and practice on all other instruments occurs only in performance.[7] Thus, nearly all reinforcement of knowledge takes place through concerted rather than solitary musical action.

This reinforcement occurs in the virtual absence of external feedback expressed verbally by one person to another. Criticisms and corrections are often restrained or withheld altogether on the assumption that apt students will eventually develop the sensitivity to recognize and correct their own mistakes. There is also a relatively high tolerance for mistakes—musicians are not oblivious to them, but attitudes toward performance are fairly informal in most contexts. Since feedback is mainly internal, repetition in ensemble provides a crucial opportunity to validate newly acquired knowledge by checking one's performance against that of the rest of the group. The heterophonic interrelatedness of the different melodic strands affords ongoing opportunities to do this. The musical consensus of the group is the most fixed and readily available reference that a musician has in an oral tradition. The widespread availability of commercial recordings in Java has not altered this appreciably, since it appears that playing along with these cassettes is not yet the norm.

When musicians do rehearse, they usually preserve the integrity of musical pieces, playing through from start to finish as they would in a full performance. Combined with the rarity of external feedback such as explicit discussion of problems, this can make the perfection of a difficult or little-played piece a time-consuming and mysterious process, as Vetter has documented for Yogyakarta palace musicians (1986: 194). The fact that a group can get through a piece that most of the musicians do not know well is a tribute to the strength of the interactive network of Javanese *gamelan*, to the pervasiveness of the required interactive competence, and to the colotomic structures that enable correct chunking by providing unambiguous frameworks for congruent perceptions and conceptualizations of musical form.[8] Non-Javanese students can learn to benefit from this manner of rehearsal, but they need far more time to approach the broad experience of performance procedures and interaction that enables Javanese musicians to operate in this manner. A Javanese musician teaching foreign students may eventually adapt to the necessity of breaking a piece up and repeating problematic sections in rehearsal. I noticed such a transformation in Wasitodiningrat's teaching

7. Suanda reports that Cirebonese musicians also learn through performance and never practice at home (1985: 90).

8. This is one of the hypotheses of my current research on musical memory.

between 1977 and 1984. While he did not abandon the Javanese way of rehearsal, he did begin to make concessions by repeating some problematic sections.

LEARNING PROGRESSIONS

The progression of competence acquisition in Javanese *gamelan* is not strictly gradated. It is most often conceived in terms of a loosely hierarchical order of instruments defined by a combination of technical difficulty, control over the *gamelan*, and mastery of related performance practice. The colotomic and *balungan* instruments constitute the base of this hierarchy, the simpler elaborating instruments such as *bonang panerus* and *gendèr panerus* are a step above, *bonang* and *gambang* are higher still, while *gendèr, kendhang,* and *rebab* top the list. Judith Becker has named the gong as the first colotomic instrument to be played, but Supanggah and others name the *kethuk,* which is a lower-level time marker, because mistaken *kethuk* strokes are certainly less disturbing than a misplaced gong stroke. Similarly, Suanda reports that mastery of the basic rhythmic instruments precedes study of the more complex melodic instruments and the drums in Cirebon (1985: 92); musicians begin with the simplest instrument, the *beri* (concussion plates), because "even if this instrument is played incorrectly during a performance, the error will not ruin the music, and the other musicians can correct the player" (Suanda 1985: 87).

Some fine musicians stop before completing the progression, never mastering all of the main instruments; such a person might play *gendèr* well, but not *rebab* or *kendhang,* for instance. Judging by the personal histories of a few musicians, it seems unlikely that a musician who has skipped over stages in the progression will be able to go back once he has reached the top of the hierarchy and has taken on leadership roles, because he will no longer have opportunities to play the "lower" instruments.

The vocal idioms are extraneous to this hierarchy. Female vocalists gain proficiency in a complex idiom that should rank at the apex of the instrumental hierarchy, but their competence is considered to be a realm apart and they rarely play any of the instruments. Aside from the social divisions that militate against women participating in professional *gamelan* performance outside of the roles of *pesindhèn* or *gendèr* player, there is no economic or status incentive to play an instrument since a good *pesindhèn* can earn ten times as much as an instrumentalist and be treated like a star to boot. Male vocalists are often regarded as distinct from instrumentalists, too, but their specialized knowledge is far less formidable than a *pesindhèn*'s and instrumentalists appear to view them as inherently less competent, perhaps because so many musicians and nonmusicians are familiar with the *gérong* parts to the more popular pieces.

There is no hierarchical progression for repertoire analogous to that for instruments. While many of the longest pieces are no longer learned and performed, every competent musician must master a large variety of pieces covering the entire spectrum of forms and genres, since each performance involves a selection of pieces from most parts of this spectrum. However, the order in which these pieces are learned appears to be almost completely haphazard and idiosyncratic, dependent mainly on the individual's associations and performance experiences and opportunities. Instructional pamphlets intended for public school instruction start with a group of pieces based on a cycle of eight or sixteen beats and lead up to thirty-two-beat cycles, but do not go beyond this very limited repertoire. Such an orderly progression is unlikely to be followed in the education of most musicians. But there does appear to be a consensus regarding the relatively greater difficulty of the longer pieces in the repertoire. Most prospective musicians probably pick up the shortest, most repetitive, and most frequently played pieces in shadow play performances at a very early stage. There are also a number of pieces of moderate length that are considered appropriate for beginning instruction, but these are not necessarily the easiest pieces. Ladrang Wilujeng and Ketawang Puspawarna, frequently chosen as first pieces for *rebab* students, require most of the fingering positions available on the instrument, including some shifts of position that pose significant technical challenges.

Repertoire and instrumental idioms are learned simultaneously. The order of acquisition is independent, but the knowledge acquired is interdependent. Although the links are not well defined, it is highly unlikely that a Javanese musician will learn to play the more difficult instruments without a fairly extensive knowledge of the repertoire. A musician does not usually "learn a piece" on one of the more difficult instruments but augments and deepens (*mendalam*) the knowledge acquired in playing that piece on the simpler instruments.[9] The systematic aspects of Javanese musical practice are crucial for the acquisition of instrumental idioms and repertoire. Many of the patterns and organizational principles found in the more complex idioms are closely related to those in the simpler idioms. Similarly, melodic and structural commonalties ease the learning of repertoire as they make it possible to learn new pieces by analogy to ones already known. Every piece contains phrases which

9. This is one of the areas in which patterns of competence acquisition by non-Javanese differ most from those of Javanese, as we shall see shortly.

occur in other pieces, and some pieces are known to be closely related to others.

It is particularly striking that other important domains of competence are rarely gradated or even mentioned in discussions of learning progressions. There is a general feeling that two of the six main modes, *pathet sléndro nem* and *pathet pélog lima*, are more difficult than the others, but musicians can hardly avoid playing pieces in these modes since most performances run through all six modes. In the course of learning repertoire and acquiring idiomatic knowledge it is inevitable that a musician will also learn about the important aspects of pitch, rhythm, interaction, and context. This is due in large part to the fact that learning takes place in performance, so that the learning process is in fact holistic to an even larger extent than Becker stated when she wrote that "the experience of the whole piece is learned first and only slowly does [a novice] learn to fill in the component parts" (1980: 23).

It is this learning through performance which explains the predominance of intuitive rather than explicit knowledge. For most musicians it suffices to know what to do, and when and how to do it. This knowledge has been distilled individually from observation and participation, and there is little need to make it explicit unless a musician takes on the role of teacher. It is quite possible for a musician to perform well on the most important and complex instruments of the *gamelan* without being able to make this knowledge explicit through speech or musical discourse abstracted from performance contexts.

The continuum from passive to active knowledge is more likely to be traversed in the course of a musician's studies. Musicians usually have passive knowledge of the idioms of the leading instruments long before they begin to play those instruments. As they progress through the instrumental hierarchy, they come to control aspects of other musicians' performance by virtue of the roles assigned to the leading instruments. Passive knowledge of interactive procedures and contextually determined options must then be made active in order to fulfill the obligations associated with these roles.

The Javanese learning progression is not uniformly articulated: individual musicians may well pass significant milestones in the course of acquiring competence, but there are no commonly recognized levels of attainment, with the exception of court rankings (which were based to some degree on relative competence) and the formalized curricula of the conservatories and academies which culminate in degrees. In other musical traditions the learning progression may consist of several stages linked to the mastery of particular items of repertoire or levels of technical skill as it does, for example, in various Japanese traditions and in the Western conservatory system; at the very least, the transition from apprentice or disciple to full-fledged musician is often recognized. This is generally not the case for Javanese musicians, probably because musicians can begin to participate in performance at a very early stage and because most aspects of musical education are informal, including the relationships between students and the people who serve as their sources of knowledge.

The only distinction commonly made by Javanese musicians is between front and back row musicians, as we noted in an earlier chapter. This distinction, derived from the positioning of instruments and applied to the roles associated with those instruments, can be extended to distinguish musicians who have a deep understanding of the tradition from those who follow along, doing no more than playing their roles adequately. A member of a *gamelan* group that went abroad on tour once complained to me that too many of the members of the group were back row musicians chosen for social reasons rather than for their musical competence. Some of them could, in fact, play front row instruments, but they were markedly less competent than the musician who was complaining.

Ability to participate appropriately in ensemble performance is a basic goal for Javanese musicians since there are no opportunities for solo performance. Some musicians do not appear to be motivated by much more than this, being content to remain at the bottom of the internal hierarchy of the ensemble, playing back row instruments. Many others are motivated to progress beyond this level, some turning to a particular instrument as a specialization while others move from one instrument to the next, eventually attaining the well-rounded competence which is typical of most of the best musicians. In domains other than instrumental idioms, different degrees of motivation are also notable, as some musicians seem content to play the common repertoire while others seek to go beyond this pool of widely known pieces.

Flexibility, analysis, and the use of analogies were identified in chapter 2 as central mental processes in the exercise of Javanese musical competence. They are also keys to the acquisition of that competence, for they provide the means of gaining experience by building on previous experience, of understanding present experience in terms of prior experience. Flexibility is fostered by the impermanence of the phenomena that an aspiring musician perceives and attempts to imitate. This impermanence is greater in Javanese music than in some other types of music because so many aspects of performance are variable and because Javanese musicians make very limited use of notation as a means of freezing the inherent transience of musical performance.

Analysis is generally implicit, since many musicians do not command the verbal or notational tools that would enable explicit analysis. Yet analysis is evident in the analogies by which musicians perform unfamiliar pieces. As such a piece is performed, it becomes familiar, entering the musician's stock of knowledge. By applying procedural knowledge to a stock of declarative knowledge of prototypical pieces and situations, a musician gains additional declarative knowledge, increasing his or her knowledge of repertoire. Only a small part of the repertoire is directly taught, even in the most formalized and thorough instruction. Most musicians do not get even this basis and learn nearly everything by drawing analogies from past experience, analyzing new situations in terms of what they already know. Musicians who refer to notation of elaborating parts are forced to think flexibly and in terms of analogies when they utilize their knowledge because so many aspects of performance are variable. Even published notation can stimulate flexibility, analysis, and analogy: by presenting basic patterns ordered according to the melodic context within which they are used, notation provides a stock of knowledge and a set of conditions that the musician must match with the varying conditions of actual pieces.

NON-JAVANESE *GAMELAN* STUDENTS

Comparison of non-Javanese and Javanese *gamelan* players underscores many of the salient features of Javanese competence and the acquisition of that competence. The learning progression of non-Javanese is often odd by Javanese standards, however amorphous those standards may be. For instance, some students jump fairly quickly to the most difficult instruments—particularly *gendèr*, but also *rebab, gambang,* or *kendhang*—without having built a foundation on simpler instruments. This leap may be due to excitement, impatience, or ambition unrestrained by Javanese self-effacement or by a large pool of more experienced musicians who take the leading roles as they do in Java. It may also be due to a *gamelan* teacher's need to fill these places in the *gamelan* or to the student's considerable competence and experience in a different musical tradition.

These unusual progressions are odder still when one takes into account the way in which repertoire is learned. Foreign students often learn elaborating parts to pieces that they have never heard before rather than building on previous experience of the piece (or similar pieces) as a Javanese musician would. For a Javanese musician a little "expert" knowledge implies a larger repertoire: by the time a Javanese musician can play *gendèr* at the level of a given foreign student, for instance, he or she probably already knows hundreds of pieces while the foreigner may know five. This disparity is evident when Javanese musicians overestimate foreign students' competence on the basis of their ability to play certain pieces.

The unusual degree of access to master musicians which foreign students often enjoy gives the false impression of a high degree of competence. Both in Indonesia and abroad, these students spend substantial amounts of time studying with some of the best musicians, learning to emulate fairly well within limits, often with the aid of tape recordings. Considerable specialized knowledge can be acquired in this manner, but key parts of the core competence are missing or only partially learned.

Foreign students generally lack the fundamental passive competence, gained by hearing *gamelan* played since early childhood, that provides the basis for later experience and refinement of competence. However diligently they might have studied abroad, students may arrive in Java having only heard a few recordings, their listening experience limited to the *gamelan* group in which they studied at home and to the playing of the one or two Javanese musicians who taught that group.

This limited experience is particularly evident in the domains of contextual knowledge and interactive competence. A foreigner is generally far less aware than a Javanese musician of what to do when. The ability to hear other parts and orient, derive, or confirm one's own part in relation to the ensemble is also not as fully developed as it is for most Javanese, because the foreign student will have acquired most of his or her knowledge in a fairly explicit manner while most Javanese musicians are forced much of the time to figure things out on their own.

Flexibility is often lacking or insufficient to cope with the many ways in which a piece may be played in Java. A foreign student usually will have learned to play each piece a certain way, perhaps with the ability to adjust to a few variations such as optional repeats and shifts in tempo and rhythmic density. Even foreign students who have gained substantial performance experience in Java are likely to be taken by surprise on occasion as they encounter an unfamiliar way of performing a particular piece or a new combination of pieces. This is not an indictment of the teaching methods employed by Javanese musicians outside Indonesia, who are certainly aware of these problems, but simply recognition of the fact that there are many aspects of competence that are difficult to teach and must be experienced repeatedly in a variety of performance situations.

Directed emulation is the primary mode of learning for non-Javanese students: the teacher serves as a model and generally determines most aspects of what the student learns. Emulation reaches an extreme when teachers come to rely heavily on tape recorders, having their students make a recording rather than working over a piece through time-consuming repetition. This approach appears to be limited to the instruction of foreign students. It enables rapid learning of particular versions of pieces but inhibits development of the flexibility which is paramount for successful maneuvering in the variable contexts of Javanese performance because a tape recording never varies the way a teacher plays from one lesson to the next and even from one repetition to the next within a lesson and because a tape recorder allows a student to stop and reverse time, segmenting a performance and reliving moments which would have elapsed irretrievably in live performances.

Variety may be lacking in another sense. When one Javanese musician serves as the sole source of knowledge for an entire ensemble, individuality may be squelched as he surrounds himself with fifteen or twenty musical clones. Such a situation can arise outside Java where *gamelan* is studied and played in relative isolation from a larger community. It is highly unlikely to occur in Java, as it contravenes the individuality and expected variety which are fundamental to musical life there. Wasitodiningrat underscored this when he recalled an exceptional occasion at which he played with several other Javanese musicians who had learned from the same sources. He remarked on how odd they found it to hear themselves playing very similar patterns on the different elaborating instruments (personal communication).

THE MEANS OF ACQUISITION

The bulk of Javanese writings about *gamelan* performance are elementary in scope and approach. They are certainly inadequate to equip a musician for actual performance, but they can supplement practical experience with declarative knowledge concerning types of pieces, ensembles, ensemble roles, the mechanics of creating a simple elaborating part, and perhaps something about expressive import or goals. A few texts, particularly Martopangrawit's theoretical treatise (1984), go into greater depth, but these are not a major means for the acquisition of competence either.[10]

An aspiring Javanese musician learns compositions from the regular repertoire in public group performance rather than through technical exercises or student pieces, as we have already noted. Most musicians also make use of some forms of symbolic representation for communicating and remembering musical knowledge. Nowadays knowledge of

10. Recent detailed analyses of particular pieces by Sukamso (1992) and Suraji (1991b) may alter this situation if they are utilized for instructional purposes.

repertoire is often initiated, assisted, or solidified by reference to notation or recordings, two forms of symbolic representation which have
dramatically altered the accessibility of musical information in Java, as
they have elsewhere in the world.

Most notation, whether handwritten or mass-produced, represents
the *balungan* and the colotomic parts. The layout emphasizes musical
structure: each line of notation is equal in length, corresponding to the
phrases or subphrases of the composition, which are almost always equal
in duration.[11] Within each line the four-beat groups (*gatra*) that are the
building blocks of Javanese instrumental melody are separated by
spaces.

Javanese notation serves first as a reference, an aid to memory, a vehicle for preserving the outlines of pieces. It is also a means of communication, transmission, and teaching, spanning time and space, and theoretically doing so with greater efficiency than oral transmission. When
notation is used archivally, as it has been for the past century, it alters
the basic orality of the tradition by introducing an element of perma-
nence or stability against which change can be measured and it raises
the issue of authority. Many musicians view the printed text as truth,
more worthy of trust than their own memories. Such an attitude can
lead to standardization and loss of the rich variety that once characterized the larger tradition as musicians abandon variants which differ from
the notation; in a few cases it can even legitimize typographical errors.
These problems are mitigated by the fact that some musicians have a
more sophisticated understanding of the limitations of notation and the
variety inherent in the dynamics of oral tradition while other musicians
do not use notation at all.

Notation has the potential to surpass oral transmission in influence
by reaching a greater number of people over a wider area. This leads to
far-reaching changes in regionally defined competences when versions
of pieces from one area supplant versions from another, perhaps as a
result of the higher authority accorded notation. The predominance of
Solonese music, which threatens to supplant most other local traditions,
is partially due to the quantity and availability of notation stemming
from this tradition. This in turn is a result of the publication activities
of government-sponsored educational institutions in Solo.

The fear that notation is a crutch that will cause musicians' abilities
to memorize and improvise to atrophy has been expressed repeatedly
by Javanese and foreigners alike. It is necessary to distinguish between

11. This layout was compared with the older run-on method of notation in chapter 2 (see
fig. 6).

balungan notation and notation of elaborating parts when evaluating this claim. The use of *balungan* notation is more widespread and has in fact changed the nature of performance to some extent. Notation is written on blackboards, stenciled, or photocopied for radio broadcasts by various groups either because new pieces are introduced with insufficient rehearsal for learning by ear or because the leaders of these groups do not trust the ability of the weaker musicians to follow when playing unusual repertoire.[12] However, in most performance situations the musicians do not need notation because they are not called upon to perform unfamiliar pieces. Furthermore, the conditions of performance are too variable to allow the convenient use of notation: most performance takes place without rehearsal, the repertoire is not selected ahead of time, and performance decisions are communicated through musical means rather than verbal instructions. Musicians must depend on their interactive knowledge to navigate in these circumstances; notation would be too distracting. Mloyowidodo, who is, ironically, the compiler of the most influential collection of notation, believes that connecting with the audience and connecting with the notation are mutually exclusive: one can focus either inward or outward. In his youth anyone caught using notation in performance was ridiculed and likened to a monkey looking in a mirror (personal communication).

Notation of elaborating parts is far more restricted in availability and in use. The abstraction inherent in such notation demands elaboration: performing notated parts requires reversing the process of abstraction through which the notation was produced, matching the numerically encoded information with the full-fledged manifestations of auditory experience and adding or substituting rhythmic and melodic nuances. This is a fairly arduous procedure that does not appear to form an important part of the education of many musicians other than students at the conservatories and academies. So long as the community of musicians refuses to accept stiff performances based on simplified notation, the improvisatory aspects of Javanese performance are not seriously endangered by notation. Dealing with these abstractions may actually encourage the development of elaborative skills.

Bennett has argued that recordings constitute a form of notation, a means of preserving (literally recording) aspects of musical performance for later decoding by other musicians as performance instructions (1980: 210). Compared with the symbols of written or printed notation, which

---

12. Tarnopangrawit, a longtime member of the radio station *gamelan*, told me that musicians were often given a few hours to memorize a blackboard full of new pieces for a broadcast that same day (personal communication).

must be interpreted systematically according to learned rules, audio recordings offer more directly accessible models for imitation, but they do not ensure precise replication and they do require some cognitive transformation in order to be exploited as sources of performance information. Javanese musicians use recordings in this manner less extensively than do the American rock musicians whom Bennett studied: the Javanese do not usually need to discover independently how to produce the sounds they hear on recordings because the array of possible sounds and sound-producing techniques is not as open to innovation as it is in the world of rock and because this array is learned early through plentiful contact with other musicians.[13] Javanese musicians who learn from tapes are not necessarily isolated from more experienced musicians; they are just augmenting what they learn in face-to-face contact.

The types of knowledge most often gleaned from *gamelan* recordings are items of repertoire, "arrangements" (new ways of playing a familiar piece), and information about melodic register and *pathet* that shapes choices of *garapan* in the elaborating parts. Commercial recordings also serve as a source for emulation of particular individual styles. This type of information is often buried by pervasive problems of ensemble balance and recording quality that are further aggravated by the low quality of playback equipment available to most musicians. The *pesindhèn*'s voice can always be heard clearly and the *kendhang* is often clear, too, but other instruments such as *gendèr, gambang,* and *bonang* are only sporadically audible on most cassettes; the sound of the *rebab* is usually masked whenever the *pesindhèn* sings. Experienced musicians can apply their rich stock of knowledge to pull out details that are barely discernible in the relative obscurity of most commercial recordings, but beginners cannot hope to glean everything necessary from recordings. The lack of clarity almost guarantees variation in transmission. Few Javanese musicians have access to focused recordings of one or two instruments that enable much more precise emulation of a model. Such recordings might lead to the freezing of improvisation were they more readily available.

Nominal notation, the use of words to signify musical entities, whether individual sounds or larger patterns, has a longer history than written notation in Java. Drum syllables enable rapid communication about sound in the medium of sound using onomatopoetic combinations that are well-suited for mnemonic purposes. They are an important instructional device for dancers as well as *kendhang* players, enabling performers to memorize and reproduce patterns without actually playing

---

13. Bennett's paradigm for competence acquisition among rock musicians is one of spontaneous independent discoveries (1980: 181–82).

them on an instrument.[14] They also serve as a vital means of communication between these two groups when adjusting music to choreography, as we noted in chapter 2.

Other nominal types of notation are important, too. These include the names of patterns for *kendhang* and *gendèr* that serve as an efficient shorthand, as we have seen in the summary of my own learning experiences. One of the most interesting aspects of these patterns is the derivative nature of the names: drum patterns are named for the dance movements they accompany while most *gendèr* patterns are named for fragments of text *pesindhèn* sometimes sing to these patterns. Both deriations underline the systematic interconnectedness of Javanese performing arts. Further evidence of the extent of this associative network is to be found in the use of dance pattern names to describe puppet movements and the associated drumming in the shadow play.

Texts for vocal parts should be considered as a special form of notation that has importance, quite apart from any semantic content, as a means of encoding sounds to be vocalized. Texts may be combined with rudimentary notation representing the main pitches of the vocal line. The placement of ornaments is sometimes included, but the precise details of ornamentation are left to the singer's discretion within the narrow scope of traditional vocal idioms. When no pitch indications are included, the text serves as a frame of reference on which to hang one's memory of the melody. In performance this reference can be utilized as a means of remembering. Notebooks filled with texts may be used in performance without the stigma attached to other forms of notation. Texts can also be useful in the process of learning as a means of shaping one's perception and conceptualization of the melody. Djoko Sungkono, a musician who often accompanied *wayang* performances, told me that he had learned the instrumental parts to most of the *dhalang*'s songs with reference to the texts of these songs.

Conceptualizing one thing in terms of another is a form of mental notation, a way of making marks and consciously creating an associative network of memories, the new knowledge linked to older knowledge so that one evokes the other. When I asked musicians how they conceptualized *pathetan* when they played, they invariably mentioned the vocal line as a guide, even though the vocal line is rarely sung outside theatrical performances. In instrumental performances, musicians say that they hear the vocal part in their mind as they listen to the *rebab*. In other words, there is a chain of associations: vocal melody and text are mediated through the *rebab* melody to evoke the *gendèr, gambang,* or *suling* mel-

14. The Japanese *gagaku* repertoire is also learned in this manner, for example.

ody. As a conceptual model, the vocal line is superior to the closely related *rebab* melody because phrasing is clearly marked by pauses, while the *rebab* melody is continuous, and probably, too, because the sung text provides another associative framework. *Gendèr, gambang,* and *suling* parts for the longer *pathetan* consist of so many small patterns strung together that they become amorphous and difficult to remember for even the most accomplished musicians. They can only be recalled in relation to the melodic line. For the most difficult *pathetan* this line must be manifested—a mental image is insufficient, as I found on several occasions when highly competent musicians were incapable of performing the *gendèr, gambang,* and *suling* parts without the *rebab* or vocal as a reference. This would seem to indicate that mental representations of these pieces are too far removed from the *gendèr* or *gambang* parts and the surface details of these parts are too distracting to allow musicians to perform these pieces alone in a noninteractive environment.

Other referents exist for different types of knowledge. Sumarsam's concept of an inner melody abstracted from the melodic flow of the several parts of the *gamelan* provides such a model for knowing a piece in performance (1984b; see below). For other musicians the *balungan* itself serves as a frame of reference, but this in turn may be learned with reference to other frameworks such as drumming patterns (Mloyowidodo, personal communication), vocal melodies, or colotomic structure. The chain of association continues: drum patterns are sometimes learned and remembered in terms of choreography.

Prototypical pieces are nodes in the webs or networks of associations that a musician builds up. When a new piece is taught or perceived in terms of one already known, a new network is established or an old one strengthened. The connections may be very close or more loosely associative. A piece may be thought of as a simple transformation of another one or as a combination of the parts of several others. The historical relationship between these closely related pieces is often unknown and is in any case irrelevant to the process of acquisition. More loosely associated pieces may be connected in terms of mood or general melodic progression.

When Wasitodiningrat listed twelve pieces (two in each *pathet*) as a key to learning the *rebab,* he was guiding me toward such associations. He also spoke of the patterns used to play *pathetan* as a key to knowledge, containing the essence of idiomatic performance. Whether or not such claims are substantiated by others' experience, they imply the formulation of a matrix that organizes knowledge of basic practice and relationships within a musical system. They say much about how Wasitodiningrat conceives of performer competence and of Javanese *karawitan* as an integrated musical system in which one can apply the essential knowledge gained in one context to many other contexts, guided by the groupings established by the matrix of tuning and mode (Brinner 1995).

Such keys (*kunci*) to competence are central to Javanese conceptualizations of knowledge. A particular item or group of items is viewed as a prototype which contains the means of understanding a larger group of items (Anderson 1972: 45). The key may be conceived as "*ngèlmu*, esoteric knowledge with magical overtones; the keys to an older world of power and rivalry . . . Among *gamelan* players, this coveted know-how (together with some nerve) distinguishes the experienced musician from the others, those puzzled players who, when faced with a melodic impasse, *ngawur* awkwardly and meet a sort of musical dead-end" (Pemberton 1987: 27). Or it may be more pragmatic in nature. Sindoesawarno suggests, for instance, that once a singer has learned one melody for each of the eleven or thirteen *macapat* poetic meters[15] he (or she) is "on his way to becoming proficient" (1984: 398).

Melodic essence as a compact mental representation is invoked in explanations of the manner in which Javanese musicians hear and know a piece. Sumarsam's concept of inner melody (1984b) and Suhardi's *lagu* (Sutton 1979) are both elusive representations of the melodic flow of a piece that are not fully manifested in any one part but are present and accessible in the composite sound of the *gamelan*. Such conceptualizations are expressions of a lack of fixity that is balanced by a minimal amount of overall change in Javanese ways of music-making—Sutton's "dynamics of a steady state" (1982). The normal manner of transmitting musical knowledge through imitation involves capturing and reproducing the essence of patterned playing (*céngkok*) rather than the specific procedural knowledge of someone else's personal style. An essential characteristic of Javanese musical practice is the acceptance—indeed, the expectation—of reinterpretation or paraphrase, rather than note-perfect imitation or free improvisation.

This preference for paraphrase brings up a crucial limitation of most cognitive studies of memory in musical performance. Gruson (1988), Sloboda (1985, 1988), Pressing (1988), and others deal either with memorization of written music or with relatively free improvisation. But neither is relevant to the Javanese situation, which is situated squarely between these two possibilities: there is no fixed "text" to be memorized verbatim, yet the scope of a performer's freedom is not large, being re-

---

15. There is disagreement as to whether certain meters are *macapat* or belong to another category of sung poetry, hence the numbers eleven and thirteen.

stricted mainly to choice of pattern and realization of patterns from stocks of possibilities. Rarely are new patterns created or existing patterns performed in ways radically different from previous performances, but neither is everything frozen.

ACADEMIC INSTRUCTION

Faculty at the performing arts schools established by the Indonesian government in the 1950s and 1960s have developed rationalized, analytical approaches to imparting knowledge. Acting under Western influence and in response to the challenges of developing teaching methods to suit new learning contexts such as group instruction in classrooms, they have regulated the progression, pace, and means of learning. The standard curriculum includes a gradated repertoire of pieces in which associations between pieces are systematically exploited as students build on knowledge of earlier pieces through shared passages (Sukamso, personal communication). Students are encouraged to aspire to a well-rounded competence by being required to play all of the parts in the *gamelan*, although most students do have some specialization within this broad competence.

The contrast between the analytical approach fostered by the academy[16] and the traditional approach, which focuses on emulation unmediated by verbal instruction, was apparent in my studies with Harjito and Wasitodiningrat. As one of the first students to graduate from ASKI in Solo, Harjito has embraced the analytical approach, while Wasitodiningrat, despite his experience teaching at such institutions, has maintained much of the older methods of instruction. The newer approach is explicit and rule-oriented while the traditional one is largely intuitive. The role of notation is much broader within the academy (virtually all notation of elaborating parts originates in and is limited to such institutions), although earlier enthusiasm over the time-saving benefits of notation has been tempered in recent years by realization of the limitations of notation for this music (Supanggah, personal communication). One result of the differences between an evocative, unsystematic, traditional classification and the more recent rational approach to performance practice is that academically trained musicians often find it easier to extract a fragment and play it out of context. This difference is also evident in terminology: the traditional terms *lancar, tanggung, dados, wiled,* and *rangkep* for the different *irama* (performance tempi that are characterized by

16. The term is used loosely here to include both conservatories and academies.

particular density ratios between the faster-moving parts and the beat) are replaced by the ratios 1 : 1, 1 : 2, 1 : 4, 1 : 8, and 1 : 16, imparting a quasi-scientific legitimacy to practice, but the implied systematic simplicity actually obscures a complex set of relationships between the different *irama*. In fact, the rational outlook is sometimes more apparent in what teachers at the academy say than in what they do. For example, one of them can expound at length on how to construct an appropriate *gendèr* part for playing in the extended *irama rangkep* while his own playing does not correspond to this prescription (Kitsie Emerson, personal communication).

The teaching method adopted in the early days of KONSER (now SMKI) for the *gendèr* parts for *pathetan* offers an extreme example of alteration: these ametrical parts, usually performed by a single *gendèr* player together with *rebab*, *gambang*, and *suling*, were metricized and played in unison on thirteen *gendèr* (Harjito, personal communication). Clearly this was motivated by the desire to accommodate a large number of pupils (the thirty-nine in Harjito's class were divided into three shifts), but those students who went on to play *gendèr* in real performances had to relearn the *pathetan* in the rhythmically free manner in which they are supposed to be played.

Formulaic patterning is important to both methods of learning *gamelan*—it could hardly be otherwise given the pervasiveness of such patterning in the music. The task of discerning patterns and learning to select and manipulate them appropriately is largely left to the student in the traditional approach. In their efforts to rationalize, standardize, and simplify instructional materials teachers in the academy have taken a highly explicit approach to the formulaity of the elaborating parts in *gamelan*, publishing catalogs of patterns arranged in logical order according to mode and important pitches. Rhythmic aspects of the patterns are often simplified both because of the desire to abstract a standardized pattern and because of typographic limitations of Javanese notation. This simplification is most obvious in the notation of *gendèr* and *ciblon* patterns. Performance of the *ciblon* drumming patterns precisely as taught in the academy is immediately recognizable and is viewed with disdain outside the classroom. Fine drummers do indeed graduate from these schools, but essential aspects of their drumming are derived from listening to drummers beyond the school walls. The lack of finesse of this rigid and simplified formulaity is offset by explicit and detailed knowledge of the usage of drum patterns in the many different types of pieces and performance contexts which drummers encounter. Drummers who do not undergo this academic training often take a freer, more

intuitive approach, transferring patterns that they know from one context to another as needed.[17]

One of the biggest breaks with earlier methods of acquiring competence is the vastly expanded scope of the multiple competence required
of students: the curriculum includes special repertoires and practices formally restricted to the royal court, different regional styles of Central
Javanese *gamelan*, musical traditions from other parts of Indonesia (primarily Bali and Sunda), and frequent performances of new compositions
which depart from traditional musical practice in many ways. Other significant changes, which are not discussed here for lack of space, have
occurred in the relationships between teacher and student and in the
opportunities for practice and rehearsal, including repetition, fragmentation, and feedback. The intense and prolonged experience of learning
and performing in this artistic hothouse enables the best musicians to
master an impressively diverse competence, but there must be some
trade-off with quality and depth of knowledge. This emerges from the
mutual assessments of outsiders and academic musicians which I heard
in the early 1980s. Baldly stated, the academic musicians criticized other
musicians for their ignorance of proper performance practice, such as
the inappropriate use of modally specific melodic patterns, while the
nonacademic musicians commented on the lack of finesse and experience in the playing of academic musicians. Recently STSI has instituted
a program in which recognized nonacademic musicians are invited to
teach the more advanced students. This program should counter excessive formulaity.

DIACHRONIC CHANGES IN COMPETENCE

Academically trained musicians are not the only ones whose competence differs from earlier Javanese musical competence. The types of
competence attained by other musicians have also changed substantially
in the past generation. When complaining about the shortcomings of
younger musicians, older ones commonly cite aspects of repertoire and
performance practice. By the standards of the 1930s, a period seen by
some as the last great flowering of Javanese cultural activity and royal
support for the arts, there are gaping holes in the knowledge of most
musicians active today. But standards are a matter of perspective. Are

17. Before he studied at SMKI, Widiyanto did not know the special drum pattern for the
piece Ayak-ayakan Sanga and just used the common *kawilan* pattern, as many other drummers
do (personal communication).

pieces and practices now known only to a few musicians still an integral part of the competence, representing a standard against which all other musicians' knowledge of repertoire should be judged insufficient? Or are these part of a competence past, something which is no longer "natural," having outlived its context, usefulness, and interest?

Contemporary musicians appear to have mixed feelings about these questions. Efforts are being made at STSI to document, preserve, and revive obsolete aspects of the tradition that are in danger of being lost. The two Solonese courts have turned to the few remaining expert musicians who gained their competence in the 1930s for guidance in aspects of repertoire and performance practice. Yet the musicians who take part in the sporadic revivals of rarely performed pieces are also heavily involved in the *gamelan* music of today. The extent to which the interest in past practice will affect the general competence of these musicians is questionable. There are far more musicians who are unaware of revivals or of other aspects of the tradition that have changed or disappeared. A few of these changes are noted here in order to convey a sense of the ways in which individual domains of competence are changing.

Changes in repertoire are the most obvious. The many pieces that are rarely played and are disappearing from individual and collective memory are being displaced by numerous new compositions. The repertoire has also changed as a result of alterations or rearrangements of existing pieces. Vocal lines are added, colotomic structures are altered, and pieces are transposed to different modes and tuning systems. These types of change affect the singers most directly because the essence of the piece is unaltered and the instrumentalists can readily apply required transformational processes. A shift in emphasis from long instrumental pieces to shorter, vocally conceived pieces has continued throughout this century. Today the vocal-centered genre of *langgam* enjoys unprecedented popularity, displacing many other genres in performance. These pieces differ substantially in performance practice from most other *gamelan* pieces and do not have established traditions of *garapan*. There is also a high turnover in the *langgam* repertoire. It is doubtful that the Javanese repertoire was ever static, but the emergence and disappearance of pieces today is extremely rapid. When Widiyanto returned to Java after an absence of two years, he did not know the many new *langgam* that had entered shadow play performance in his absence. He had to hand over the drum to someone else when one of these was called for because he did not know when to cue stopping points and endings (personal communication).

Some musicians have attempted to revive or reintroduce older pieces which are no longer performed. It is worth comparing two such attempts, involving an old musician and a young one, for the contrasting motivations and implications for competence. An old musician who brings out a piece that he used to perform is attempting to keep his competence intact, to prevent his own knowledge from fading away, and to maintain some connection with the many members of his generation who are gone. He may also have a didactic aim: to make other musicians aware of the cultural heritage that they are losing. There is nothing experimental in such an attempt. By contrast, when a younger musician initiates performance of an old piece, he is trying to expand his competence by experimenting with his knowledge of repertoire, idiom, and performance frameworks. He is reaching back into a past that he never knew directly and is setting himself apart from other musicians of his generation who do not share his interests. Both of these musicians have encountered resistance and resentment from other musicians who are less interested in expanding their horizons than in enjoying performance.

Garapan, the ways in which musicians realize the essence of a piece, has certainly changed over the past few decades. While it is likely that *garapan* was subject to change in earlier times, too, the nature of that change may have been different. Martopangrawit made an important distinction between two types of change in *garapan*: certain kinds of alterations were within the scope of variation which he accepted and even expected—he claimed that his own way of playing the popular composition Gendhing Gambirsawit, for example, had changed over the years—while others were not acceptable, because he felt they showed a lack of understanding of *pathet*, of phrasing, or of some other aspect of the proper workings of *gamelan*. In particular, he deplored the failure of younger musicians to learn and maintain *pamijèn*, the special melodies which are mandatory for certain pieces and are not a predictable part of the pervasive formulaity of the music.[18]

Was Martopangrawit "right" in an absolute sense or in a relative one? The issue of authority is central to an evaluation of his assessments of younger musicians and indeed to an evaluation of criticisms based on violation of authenticity in any oral tradition. When one musician or group of musicians claims to know the right way to play a given piece, does that make all other interpretations wrong? The answer, for a member of the society, depends on perceptions of authority and feelings of allegiance. Prior to Indonesian independence the musicians of the royal courts were widely recognized as authorities—although not necessarily

18. These criticisms, which are implicit in sections of Martopangrawit's main theoretical work (1984), were a recurrent topic in my lessons.

by musicians at rival courts—and criticized other musicians, particularly villagers, for their ignorance of the fine points of the tradition. In recent decades, villagers' ignorance continues to be criticized but the role of authority has been claimed by musicians associated with the academy. These musicians are the most direct heirs to the courts, due in part to the presence of some of the most prominent former court musicians on the teaching staff, but the younger ones' claims to authority are not as widely accepted, perhaps because of a lack of respect for their competence and because of their willingness to tamper with traditional music in radical compositional experiments.

The issue of *pamijèn* highlights some of the problems surrounding authority in an oral tradition. If younger musicians do not learn these special melodies but play a more generally formulaic realization instead, *pamijèn* parts will disappear and will no longer form a part of Javanese musical competence. At what point will the renditions without *pamijèn* become correct? As the people who know the *pamijèn* parts die out, the existence of these parts may be forgotten. But if amnesia is not complete—if musicians know that once the pieces were played differently but no longer know how—are the non-*pamijèn* performances still incorrect? Will the pieces be less beautiful? If the answer to these questions is affirmative, then an unattainable standard of competence will have been established. Musicians will feel that they can never play as well as the old masters (cf. Wong 1991: 5).

Similar questions arise when enterprising young musicians attempt to expand their personal repertoires by learning rarely performed pieces from notated *balungan*. They re-create the pieces by analyzing the *balungan*, interpreting and elaborating on it by analogy to passages in other pieces which they know. Since nearly every piece contains some passages that cannot be deduced unambiguously from the *balungan* (even if these passages are not *pamijèn*), this autodidactic approach based on a partial written record must inevitably lead to changes in the way pieces are played, unless a more knowledgeable musician corrects the student or further reference is made to live performances or recordings.

The place of *garapan* in musicians' competence is also changing because many of the pieces which have been added to the repertoire in the last forty years do not fit traditional molds (see Becker 1980). In these pieces the vocal parts are usually the focus of composers and audience. The elaborating instrumental parts are unspecified, left to the initiative of the musicians, and the *rebab*'s role of melodic leadership is no longer relevant. Standards for *garapan* are unclear since composers have altered or discarded *pathet* and other aspects on which *garapan* is traditionally based. Should the trend of replacing long, complex instrumental compositions with shorter, simpler vocal ones continue, we can expect major changes in competence to result.

Musical competence is changing in other ways. Specializations associated with social groupings have shifted. Parts of the repertoires and practices that formerly characterized the localized competences of musicians at each of the royal courts are now forgotten while other parts are no longer restricted but have spread to the general public of musicians. Distinctions between the specialized court styles are further weakened by the considerable overlap in personnel between the *gamelan* groups of the two Solonese courts. Cassettes, radio broadcasts, and widespread mobility have also erased or reduced many regional differences. On the other hand, new localized competences have developed at educational institutions as a result of the intensive creative activity there and the emphasis on maintaining aspects of court competence that have not been adopted by the wider public.

Two examples should give some indication of the extent of change in competence. By the early 1980s the royal court in Surakarta no longer employed enough musicians to man the two ceremonial *gamelan sekatèn* which play in alternation throughout most of the day during a week-long celebration of Mohammed's birth. Students from STSI were brought in to fill the empty places and were ordered to memorize the entire repertoire by their director, Humardani. Surreptitious use of notation did not solve the students' problems because, as with so many other types of Javanese performance, the sequence of pieces was spontaneously decided by the leading musicians and the students had to scramble to identify the piece and find the notation. Fifty years earlier, there would have been no such problem: court musicians did not have to split their attention between as many different repertoires and styles as academy students now do, and they had ample opportunities to learn the traditional repertoire of hundreds of *gendhing* gradually by ear in performance rather than having to memorize large portions from notation for one special occasion. In addition to several rehearsals and performances each week at the court, musicians might perform as frequently as three or four times a week outside the court (Mloyowidodo, personal communication). While these pieces were the main repertoire for the court musicians fifty years ago, many of them are not part of the regular competence of today's academy students. Those old musicians who survive tend to see this trend only as a lessening of competence in the younger generation, but from the relatively neutral perspective of an outsider it seems that a shift has occurred. It would be an oversimplification to say that the old pieces have been replaced by new ones, but there does appear to be a trade-off between the traditional repertoire that was central to competence two generations ago and the many other genres, practices, and innovations the younger musicians have mastered.

The transfer of court practices to the academy has also involved substantial changes in interactive competence and in attitudes toward innovation and usage. These practices are seen as a heritage to be preserved and at the same time as source material for new compositions.[19] New compositions often depart sharply from all prior norms of performance. Academy students and faculty who have been involved in the creation and performance of concert pieces and accompaniment for dance and theater have developed an interactive competence which differs from that of other musicians. Older musicians and others who have trained traditionally do not have the preparation for the sudden shifts and juxtapositions of different regional styles or for the fragmentary use of pieces characteristic of the newer compositions emanating from STSI.[20]

I have emphasized the contrast between musicians at the academy and older court musicians because of the connections and the radical contrasts between these groups. Many changes of similar scope have occurred in *gamelan* performance by musicians outside the academy and are reflected in performers' competences. Some of the greatest differences between musicians inside and outside the academy involve the interactive implications of compositional innovation in the academy. We shall return to these innovations after discussing theoretical issues of musical interaction and norms of interaction in Javanese *gamelan*.

19. See, for example, comments by Hastanto, the current director of STSI, in Devereaux (1989).

20. See the discussion of *wayang padhat* at the end of chapter 9.

Part Two

Making Music

CHAPTER SEVEN

TOWARD A THEORY OF MUSICAL INTERACTION

The puzzle of Javanese *pathetan* performance first sparked my interest in musical interaction. Along with other American students I tried to learn several of these brief, unmetered pieces without knowing how they ought to sound. Our Javanese teacher taught us how to play the individual parts, but not how to fit them together to create a heterophonic texture beyond the realm of our experience, by a process that was obvious to him but not easily described. We would try to play together, but our only indication of success or failure was our more or less concerted arrival at the end of the piece. There was no common beat, no basic melody, no drummer to guide our efforts; in other words, the means of orientation and coordination basic to playing other kinds of *gamelan* pieces, means that also differed greatly from our Western training, were lacking. My fascination with this looseness of coordination and lack of familiar referents led to a year spent in Indonesia finding out how Javanese musicians played these pieces, what they listened for in each other's playing, and whether they really cared whether they reached the end of the piece together (Brinner 1985).

Similar mystifying experiences can be had easily enough in other musical traditions. A sensation of utter disorientation may send one grasping at wisps of melody, meter, harmony, or some other familiar aspect of sound on which to gain a footing and find one's bearings. These experiences in alien musical traditions bring home the miraculousness of successful concerted music-making in one's own, underscoring those aspects of musical orientation and coordination that are generally taken for granted once learned, just as the precariousness of perching on two wheels fades away for most bicycle riders. The most basic musical parameters are at issue here. In the course of ensemble performance we are constantly called upon to make swift and often unconscious judgments regarding musical time, deciding where the beat is or whose beat to follow in cases of discrepancies between different players. Did someone prolong a note within the context of a steady beat, or did he intend to retard the beat? Was that an intentional anticipation, an attempt to push the tempo, or a glitch best overlooked? Most musicians probably handle these questions without a thought, becoming fully conscious of them only if something begins to go awry. Similarly, intonation is continually monitored and modified in reaction to fellow musicians (as well as musical context), though not usually as the most pressing matter of business on the musician's mind. Sound quality, too, is regulated through minute but continual interaction of this sort, as musicians judge how loudly to play, and strive for blending or distinctiveness in tone color as the situation and aesthetic conventions warrant.

There are other instances of musical interaction, of course, which are more overt and may never cease to thrill or amaze. Listen to a Javanese *gamelan* of fifteen or more musicians slip through seemingly effortless transformations of one piece and then into another with only the most subtle of signals, or try to catch the tight ensemble of a Balinese *gamelan*, musicians interlocking faster than the eye can follow, or the mysterious meshing of parts in a West African ensemble that has given rise to a fair number of articles by outsiders concerned with pinning down beat and meter. In well-ordered realms of sound, musicians match wits and anticipate intentions, like North Indian soloists and drummers imitating each other while posing ever greater challenges, reaching breakneck speeds in precise coordination, or an Arab instrumentalist shading perfectly the beauty of a vocal melody. The stretched time of a Japanese *gagaku* orchestra breathing together, the spontaneous give-and-take of a small jazz ensemble, the magic of a string quartet playing "with one mind," or the concerted sound of a symphony orchestra matched with a soloist by a conductor who anticipates the soloist's shifting moods, dynamics, and tempi are just a few of the complex and beautiful ways that human faculties are challenged in musical interaction.

Interaction occurs in formal and informal performance, in rehearsal, and in other learning situations. Whenever two or more people engage in producing and manipulating sounds together, they affect each other by coordinating, directing, imitating, inspiring, or disrupting each other's performance. Overt leadership, the authority embodied in a conductor or divided among several musicians, is only the most obvious aspect of interaction; the many subtle workings of an ensemble, the ongoing microadjustments and negotiations of standards and authority necessary to coordination and blending, are less accessible but no less interesting. The conventions and dynamics of interaction are particularly worthy of study in those musical traditions in which interaction is typified either by shared leadership or by considerable individual freedom of response or improvisation. When both conditions exist, of course, the formative role of interaction is much greater. This is the case in musics as diverse as Javanese *gamelan*, American jazz or bluegrass, and numerous other traditions from Africa, the Middle East, and other parts of Asia.

CONSTELLATIONS OF ANALYTICAL CONCEPTS

To comprehend such a variety of interactions, we need a theoretical structure that is rich enough to capture the detail and mirror the complexity of interaction in specific musical contexts without losing a level of abstraction sufficient for comparison. We need common perspectives on a wide range of phenomena including types of roles and relationships, means of interchange, and the constraining or facilitating aspects of musical structure. Social dimensions and reflections of musical interaction cannot be ignored either, but a two-step approach will be taken here, with the clearly musical—sound-producing—aspects of interaction examined first in a normative light while social variables are held constant. The issues that arise when these variables are taken into consideration will be the focus of discussion in later chapters.

I propose four constellations of concepts for the analysis of interaction within and across stylistic and cultural boundaries. *Interactive network* comprises the roles assumed by performers and the relationships or links between them, *interactive system* refers to the means and meanings of communication and coordination, and *interactive sound structure* is a constellation of concepts associated with the constraints and possibilities inherent in the ways that sounds are put together. These three approaches seek answers to who, how, when, and where (in metaphorical tone-space), but attention must also be given to the "why" of interaction, the goals, rewards, pitfalls, and sanctions that may be subsumed under the rubric *interactive motivation*. It is imperative that interactive network, system, sound structure, and motivation be understood as overlapping views or perspectives, mutually illuminating rather than mutually exclusive; they are all necessary for a complete depiction and understanding of interaction. For instance, interactive network and interactive sound structure are both at issue when we ask whether conventions of timbre and texture isolate or unite distinct roles and ensemble sections. While some cultures and individuals devote more attention to the social process of music-making and others to the sound product with its internal logic, it is not possible to have one without the other: people making music together inevitably create structure, and all musical structures stem more or less directly from human agency. The approach advocated in this book balances these perspectives by dealing with abstractions of sound under the rubric of interactive sound structure and abstractions of human organization under interactive network.

INTERACTIVE NETWORK

Since musical interaction is a human activity, it is appropriate to turn first to the musicians themselves by considering the roles they assume or are assigned in the interactive network, the sets of relationships that prevail between them, and the musical domains within which they express themselves. Analysis of the interactive network in a given type of music involves questions of who controls or influences whom with regard to which aspects of musical activity. These questions may be asked at different levels of specificity: for a particular performance, for all the performances of a given group of musicians, for a type of ensemble, or for an entire tradition or repertoire.

A rudimentary typology of roles is implicit in most writing on musical interaction. Authors refer to the leader or leaders of an ensemble, perhaps indicating the domains they direct or control, and the musicians who follow their lead. Racy takes a step in this direction when he describes the "timbral demarcation of domains" (1988: 144) in the Arab *takht,* so does Shankar, who writes that the South Indian *pallavi* composition "is the soloist's territory, and it is sometimes dangerous territory for the accompanist" (1974: 115). But such distinctions are rare, despite the evidence that different nuances of leading, mediating, following, accompanying, and supporting are significant in many performance situations. My intent here is to examine and refine this typology, not to achieve a universal definition of musical leadership, for example, but to discover the dimensions of variation for such roles. In order to move gradually to this level of abstraction, I shall begin with brief sketches of a few contrasting examples.[1]

The conductor of a symphony orchestra, who holds a position of unchallenged musical authority, generally establishes the course of a

---

1. Each of these examples merits lengthier consideration, but this must be left to another book.

performance prior to rehearsals, choosing which repetitions to take and which segments to skip, if any, then communicating these verbally to the musicians in rehearsal. Since the path of each piece has already been mapped out with great precision in score by the composer, the conductor as leader is more concerned with interpreting the score and ensuring coordination, blending, and balancing of the huge orchestral forces at his or her command. Interpretation, the creative domain of the conductor, consists of making analytical decisions about the wealth of information conveyed in the score (such as what to bring out, at what tempo and dynamic level), conveying these decisions to orchestra members, and eliciting from them the playing which will make his or her conception a reality.

Leadership in a Javanese *gamelan* contrasts dramatically with the duties and prerogatives of symphonic conducting. Rather than residing unequivocally in the hands of one central conductor, it is shared among several musicians, each with his own domain of control and influence.[2] Compared with the symphonic repertoire there are far more decisions to be made regarding the overall course of the performance, because pieces are much less fixed in details and overall sequence and because programs are often assembled in the course of performance. These decisions, many of which are spontaneous, are communicated musically rather than verbally. At certain points one musician will have exclusive control while at other moments this control will pass to another musician by virtue of the instrument he plays and the structure of the music. Details of sound production by individual members of the ensemble are not as accessible to *gamelan* leaders as they are to a symphonic conductor. There is no score, but as we have seen in the preceding chapters, there is a rich web of orally transmitted knowledge regarding peculiarities of a particular piece, general idiomatic constraints and preferences for the individual parts, and, hopefully, consensus as to the *balungan*. The denser layers of the complex surface of the music are formed cumulatively from individual musicians' choices, made according to their competence and preferences. Melodic leaders can suggest particular choices through their own playing, but they do not dominate like a Western conductor, who can, for instance, ask an oboist to bring out a particular note. Coordination of these disparate layers and parts is actively controlled in most cases by the drummer. The blending, balancing, and accentuation so carefully manipulated by a Western conductor are left to the collective sensibility of the *gamelan* musicians: there are set conventions of volume for particular musical contexts, and awareness of these is fundamental

---

2. Some exceptions to this generalization will be noted in the next chapter.

to musical competence. In the course of playing a piece, several of these contexts arise and the shifts between them bring certain voices of the ensemble—human and instrumental—into the foreground while others recede, but the leaders and other musicians have no traditionally sanctioned means of accentuating particular parts or passages. It is only in recent years that dynamics have begun to be consciously worked out for specific effect in particular pieces (Widiyanto, personal communication).

Gamelan and orchestral leadership contrast in other ways as well. The drummer, who takes a large portion of the responsibility in a Javanese *gamelan*, sits in the middle of the orchestra, roughly equidistant from the other players. They can all hear him, but those in the front row have their backs to him. His cues are exclusively aural and completely integrated in the texture of the music; his leadership, like that of other leading members of the *gamelan*, is unobtrusive and largely unrecognized by the public—he takes no bow and receives no billing. Conductors, on the other hand, stand in full view of all members of the orchestra, convey their desires exclusively with visual cues that are extraneous to the musical product, and are accorded much attention by audience, management, publicists, and critics, clearly set above the other musicians in status. Finally, the conductor's post is not up for grabs but is generally given after much deliberation to an individual who has developed a special competence through extensive specialized training. Many Javanese musicians, on the other hand, are capable of assuming leading roles within a *gamelan*, thanks to their well-rounded competence, and often do so at a moment's notice, perhaps trading places between pieces, as we noted earlier.

The purpose of this comparison is not to demonstrate in some perverse fashion that *gamelan* and symphony orchestra are diametrically opposed, but to highlight some of the salient aspects of leadership that must be addressed in a theory of musical interaction. These include:

1. the *division of leadership responsibilities* among one or more performers in a constant or shifting arrangement;
2. *assignment* or *attainment* of leadership roles;
3. *explicitness* and *recognition* of leadership and *positioning* of these leaders for visual or aural effect (which may also indicate considerations of status);
4. the relative *spontaneity* or *rehearsed* nature of leadership, which in turn involves the time framework for leadership (which may be limited to the actual performance or include rehearsal and other nonperformative periods); and

5. the *domains* controlled and the *degree of control* or influence over aspects such as blend and balance, rhythmic coordination, or changes in tempo.

Other aspects are better discussed as part of the interactive system (e.g., the means of communication, musical, verbal, or visual, and its integration in the musical "fabric") or the interactive sound structure (e.g., questions relating to the overall progress of the piece, the degree to which it is prescribed in score or oral form, and the potential for alternative realizations of this prescription). This list is by no means exhaustive—the ways in which leaders inspire may be just as important but are much harder to pin down, as they are inherently more personal and less systematic—but it is a starting point.

Alongside the more or less explicit leaders in many interactive networks are musicians who play a mediating role. They relay or reinforce leaders' directives or cues either with their own explicit cues or by the act of responding appropriately to the leader and thus serving as an example for other musicians and validating their responses. These mediators may be recognized as subordinate or secondary leaders (such as the concertmaster and section leaders of an orchestra) or simply act as mediators on a provisional basis for less competent musicians who depend on them for help in following the lead.

Labeling one member of an ensemble "leader" implies that the others are "followers." Often enough this is true, but in many contexts this is an inappropriate term, since musicians may be musically or socially subordinate to a leader and interact with that leader without actually following. A possible alternative is the commonly invoked "accompanist," but this word carries connotations which are limiting or unfortunate. There may be many situations in which no term is needed at all, but when one is required "support" appears a likely candidate to contrast with "leader" or to distinguish those who are not in the sonic foreground at a given moment.[3] Analysis of supporting roles involves assessing how much room these roles allow for individual initiative and which domains are influenced or dictated by other performers. The drummer in a small North Indian ensemble *follows* the melodic "soloist's" lead in choices relating to the overall progression of a performance and *supports* the mel-

---

3. Racy notes that the male chorus which supported the male singer in the Egyptian *takht* ensemble was called *sannidah*, which literally means supporters or buttresses (1988: 139). Michael Tree, violist of the Guarneri Quartet, says that "any accompaniment figure that sounds like an accompaniment is already bound to hurt the group . . . A 'supportive' role perhaps, would be the more correct term . . . that has to enhance the lead voice . . . at that moment and even inspire it to go further or to play better" (Fink and Merriell 1985: 34).

ody by providing a metric underpinning as required by the soloist's choice of composition. Aside from this he is relatively free to fill this metric framework with rhythmic filigree that is complementary to the melody and not directly subordinate to it. In a vocal performance, the instrumentalist who shadows the vocalist's every melodic turn fills a role that is far more constricted and more clearly that of a follower throughout. There is no implication of a lesser degree of competence here, only a different sort.[4]

This Indian example provides an opportunity to make a further useful distinction among subordinate or nonleading roles: some types of support serve other performers as a *foundation*. I choose this word to convey the solidity of a frame of reference that is reliable because it is ongoing or regular and therefore predictable and absolute enough to anchor oneself in the shifting relativity that typifies much music-making. The North Indian drummer supplies orientation in the domain of time by repeating a drum pattern that demarcates a hierarchically articulated cyclical structure. A drone player fills another essential foundation role in this ensemble by providing orientation in the domain of pitch. Microinteraction and other nuances of performance rest on these foundation roles. Subtleties of intonation produced by a North Indian soloist take on special prominence and meaning as heard against the drone. Difficult performance situations may also be facilitated by an appropriate foundation: the extremely rapid interlocking of a Balinese *gamelan gong kebyar*, for example, takes place with reference to the steady beat provided by a musician playing the *kempli*, a small gong. Foundation roles make underlying musical order explicit. Players who fulfill these foundation roles may have little or no musical freedom and yet play vital roles as keepers of standards and arbiters of disagreement on time and pitch. As a result they may come under intense personal pressure from other musicians who find fault with the standards set.

In performance, roles may overlap or shift from one moment to the next, as a musician playing an accompanying or supporting role takes the lead momentarily by feeding pitches to a more foregrounded role. A player may also simultaneously fulfill different roles with respect to different musical domains, leading melodic aspects of the performance, for example, while following another player's rhythmic lead. Matters may be further complicated when a musician of lesser competence fills a leading role by virtue of the instrument that he or she is playing but a more competent musician who is playing a supporting instrument tries to override conventions and take the lead. Role differences may also be

---

4. See Wade (1984b) and the discussion below.

mainly a matter of perspective: musicians often have conflicting perceptions about their own importance, influence, or control within the ensemble. These overlapping identities do not dilute or detract from the usefulness of the basic distinctions suggested here, but underscore the need to delve into the interactive network and uncover all of the ways that musicians relate to one another in an ensemble.

Attainment of roles is a central aspect of an interactive network. Are the roles within an ensemble so flexibly defined that any player can assume leadership, or are they determined strictly by instrument? To what extent does general competence determine position within an ensemble? Is there an audition process, a system of seniority or progression "through the ranks"? Do players trade parts? Are leadership and support roles associated with status distinctions which may override considerations of training and experience, that is, competence? Clearly, the answers to and implications of these questions will differ for ensembles in which musicians play several or all of the parts as opposed to those in which specialized competences lead to specific parts. They will also differ depending on the interactive sound structure of the musical tradition: a tradition typified by freer structures, such as small-ensemble jazz, probably enables a greater flexibility of role taking, while one that is relatively fixed will tend to cement players into particular roles and relationships, unless complex mechanisms such as detailed orchestration are brought into play.

An interactive network is more than a set of roles. It is also defined by the relationships between members of an ensemble and the musical domains in which these relationships are played out. A musician leads, follows, mediates, or supports with respect to other musicians and to particular aspects of sound-shaping. To tackle this part of the interactive equation, we need to ask to whom a musician relates in a particular role and in which domain(s) this relationship is played out. By looking at relationships and domains, we shift our attention from defining an individual's "place" in the ensemble and move toward a view of the interactive network as a whole. Taking a concerto as an example, we would note that conductor and soloist have different, overlapping domains in which they exert some degree of control. Members of the orchestra will ordinarily submit to the leadership of the conductor, who may, in turn, be following or adapting to the soloist, thus acting as an intermediary rather than a more independent leader. But when a member of the orchestra has an obbligato part to play with the soloist, a new relationship that bypasses the conductor is created.

The structure of an interactive network derives from these roles, relationships, and domains, however transient or constant they may be. It is essential to capture the multiplicity of shifting and overlapping roles and relationships, to note what is relatively stable and when—to tie changes in the network to aspects of interactive sound structure, among other things. Ultimately this should lead to an understanding of how these networks form, how they mimic, influence, contradict, or augment patterns of social interaction, and how they limit or enable individual musicians and groups in the performance of particular musical styles and genres.

Identifying underlying principles and their implications for performers and performance is potentially both more revealing and more widely applicable across cultural boundaries than simply labeling roles or creating a complex and rigid typology of relationships with a specialized jargon. Here I am suggesting issues to think about and ways of thinking about them, not specific answers. The following chapters demonstrate some applications of these approaches.

Relationships between musicians can be characterized in terms of shades of influence, control, independence, support, and responsiveness. These characterizations should be linked to specific musical domains. The drummer who controls tempo in a Javanese *gamelan*, for example, influences melodic domains of action too, by favoring certain options over others. By playing one style of drumming, he causes other players to enter into interlocking relationships with each other to create a composite melody. Choice of a different drum and drumming style would cause these same musicians to adopt a heterophonic relationship in which they play simultaneous variants of a melody. But influence can also be asserted in a less dominant relationship, one of options rather than obligations. Other leadership roles in a *gamelan*, for example, are less "coercive" or deterministic: the player of the *rebab* is said to lead the melody, but the *pesindhèn*, who follows after in an overlapping, almost canonic relationship, may choose to ignore this lead and sing a compatible but dissimilar phrase.

Relationships in an interactive network are characterized not only by the amount of control or influence exerted, the domains affected, and the responsiveness of others but by *directionality*—the flow of influences and information. If decision making is hierarchically structured or delegated, for example, directives or influences flow from the top down, while responses flow from the bottom to the top. The person(s) at the top of the hierarchy may also monitor the music-making of those "beneath" in order to guide and correct where necessary. A cue may be aimed at one particular player, at the whole ensemble, or at just one section. We must also be alert to reciprocal relationships, since the links between musicians are often mutually constraining with constraints coming from the follower or supporter as much as from the leader. Given a relationship of some dominance in which musician A cues musician B to play certain things, B may have no direct control over A but can constrain A to give cues only at certain times.

A fundamental distinction must be made between intentional communication, in which one person signals to another, for instance, and ongoing or occasional listening and response to what the musician is doing even though he or she is not intending to communicate. The first relationship is causative—performer A initiates a sequence of musical events by doing something to which performer B responds—while the second is referential. Reliance on a drummer to maintain a rhythmic cycle exemplifies the latter: as long as both musicians are competent, one can rely on the other's drumming for its timekeeping function and listen consciously for other aspects, for the special intricacies, the unexpected and perhaps inspirational variations which exceed the drummer's foundational role. But that foundation is there, and should the nondrummer become disoriented momentarily, he or she can correct this by turning conscious attention to the basic time and cycle marking aspects of the drumming without awareness or any special effort on the part of the drummer. Nondirected or unintentional inspiration also occurs when something in one musician's performance sparks a response from another musician. Such a reception and transformation of ideas may occur without prior intention on the part of the first musician. A great musician participating in an ensemble of less competent players may spur the others on to higher levels of performance by his or her very presence, simply by finer quality of performance, without any intentional control or influence. Of course, this person may also cow the less able or experienced musicians into meek submission or inhibit them sufficiently to affect their playing adversely, once again by the mere fact of his or her presence.

When two or more performers operate in the same musical domain, the relationship between them is linked, at least in part, to the extent to which musical "material" is shared by them. Precise doubling of a melody requires an interactive relationship radically different from semi-independent heterophonic realizations of a melody, and this again differs from striving to complement the other's line, by adding what is missing, filling in the gaps, perhaps in an interlocking relationship. Interlocking is an extreme form of mutual dependence in which two or more performers bend their energies toward creating a composite melody or rhythm. From an interactive point of view, parts that are linked together and focused principally on harmonic blending stand in a relationship that shares common features with an interlocking relationship:

in both cases the two or more players are striving to create a composite and must match envelope (attack, sustain, release) and often timbre, too, in order to blend; but one relationship requires orientation to a composite simultaneity (a chord) and the other to a composite that unfolds consecutively in time.[5]

In musics built on heterophonically imitative shadowing and fore-shadowing of a featured musician by a subordinate musician, it is easy to make the superficial observation that the featured musician, often a singer, controls the performance, but closer inspection often reveals that many performance decisions devolve upon the "follower." The subordi-nate player may play an important "driving" role by setting up the solo-ist/focal role, anticipating the soloist's intentions, and perhaps correct-ing if the soloist errs. This sort of relationship is common in many musical cultures; a few geographically contiguous and perhaps distantly related examples may serve to illustrate the problem.

Accompanying the human voice with a melodic instrument in a closely imitative relationship while developing or exploring a modal structure is common to Arab and Indian traditions as well as many Cen-tral Asian musics. It is even found to a limited extent in Java although the modal structure is more rigidly laid out in a *pathetan* than in an Arab *mawwal* or an Indian *alap.* In each case the singer is recognized as the leader and the instrumentalist is charged with echoing the singer's me-lodic line: an Arab singer takes "the lead in exploring tonal areas of the *maqam* and in executing modulations to new *maqamat*" (Racy 1988: 145), and Indian singers of *khyal* "find means . . . to assert their position of soloist" (Wade 1984b: 29). But there is a tension latent in this hierarchi-cal structure which demands great skill of the instrumentalists, on one hand, and limits their means of gaining audience recognition, on the other, by placing them in the role of echo. This tension may be eased if the instrumentalist is given the opportunity to prepare the way for the singer. This is common in Arab musical practice where the instrumental-ist first improvises a *taqsim* and then goes on to echo or translate (*tarja-mah*, which literally means translation [Racy 1988: 145]) phrases of the following *layali* or *mawwal* improvised by the singer. In fact, Racy argues that instrumentalists have a clear responsibility to "warm up" the singer, and he interprets the entire progression of a classical Arab suite (*waslah*) as a buildup to the climactic vocal improvisations of the *dawr* (1988: 146 and 1983b: 399). But Arab musicians whom I interviewed in Israel complained that contemporary singers allow them an opportunity to improvise an instrumental *taqsim* too rarely.

5. Interlocking parts may include a "harmonic" simultaneous aspect, too, if they overlap.

When the leader is perceived to be less competent than the accompanying or supporting musician(s), the tension is likely to increase. A North Indian *sarangi* (bowed lute) player's relationship with the singer that he accompanies can be problematic: "If the vocalist is inexperienced, the *sarangiya* might suggest a musical idea to him. Most vocalists, however, do not accept this 'musical' advice, and it is not uncommon to hear a vocalist complain that the *sarangiya* attempted to anticipate him, and thus to mislead his own melodic development" (Neuman 1974: 170). Differences of competence also usurped interactive order in my study of the interactive network of Javanese *pathetan*. Although these pieces do not allow either the singer or *rebab* player much improvisatory elaboration in the domain of pitch, there is a fair amount of variation in timing and the quality of interaction hinges on the way in which the ensemble, led by singer and *rebab* player, arrive at each new focal pitch, as we shall see in the next chapter. When performing a *pathetan* together with a singer, most *rebab* players tend to follow well behind the singer, but some do precede and several said to me that they take the lead if the singer is inexperienced.

In these varied examples, the singer's conception of the "piece" is paramount and the instrumentalists are charged with supporting the singer's intentions even when anticipating them. The ability to second-guess implies either a simple musical system of very limited possibilities or a deep understanding and empathy, based on long personal association or on a highly systematic (and therefore predictable) way of making music. It is an ability that is probably utilized by all musicians; what varies is the degree to which they rely on it. In trying to explain this all-important capacity to anticipate the intentions of another musician, Michael Tree of the Guarneri Quartet fails to find a rational explanation: "There is an element, somehow, of telepathy or something extramusical going on" (quoted in Fink and Merriell 1985: 39). The smooth sailing of a Javanese *gamelan* through the most abstract, prolonged, and disorienting expansions of a composition with little overt guidance certainly appears to depend on this sort of sensitivity to the interactive network of fellow musicians.

Lapses of memory and plain lack of knowledge are potential dangers that an interactive network may help to avoid or ameliorate. Reminding one another of how the music goes is an essential aspect of interaction, particularly in musics performed without notation. Here the interactive network can serve as a safety net, stretched to catch musicians falling from their highwires and trapezes. This function is fulfilled on a regular basis by those playing foundation roles in the ensemble, but it may be performed on an ad hoc basis by various musicians when they direct prompts at a fellow musician who appears lost or unsure. When a Balinese *gamelan* performs long *lelambatan* pieces, the musician who plays *trompong* (a gong chime) leads the melody, with enough anticipatory ornamentation to remind other musicians of the melodic "path." But he himself can become confused and skip a phrase because of the length of these pieces and their internal repetitions. It is then up to the drummer to remind him of the correct place within the cycle by emphatically cuing colotomic markers. Hearing this, the *trompong* player should reorient himself and find his way back as smoothly as possible.[6]

To fully understand an interactive network, we need to go beyond analysis of individual roles and relationships to think about the structure within which these roles and relationships are "played out." We can talk about the focus of an ensemble, contrasting leaderless networks such as Feld describes for the Kaluli of Papua New Guinea (1986: 23) with those which have one leader, shifting leadership, or multiple leaders in different domains. Continuing along these lines, we can study hierarchy and other aspects of the division of labor and allocation of resources relative to the size of the ensemble, such as doubling and interactive redundancy in the network. If redundancy is fairly obvious, we need to discover possible aesthetic or social explanations for the presence of leaders in cases where they are not essential. These considerations lead to analysis of a network in terms of subordinate groupings or networks, perhaps overlapping, perhaps quasi-independent. The rhythm section of a jazz ensemble or the continuo players in a Baroque group exemplify networks within networks which have their own internal organization, priorities, functions, and means of communication. An understanding of the workings of these smaller units is a necessary stepping stone to achieving the full picture.

Thumbnail sketches of a string quartet, a North Indian chamber group, and an Arab *takht* are offered here as concrete illustrations for the characterization of particular interactive networks. These ensembles do not delineate a continuum and they are not equivalent, other than being similar in size and importance within the musical traditions of their respective cultures. Their value in the present discussion derives from the contrasts that point to some of the different ways that people organize their music-making.

The string quartet has crystallized as the chamber ensemble par excellence of Western art music, with a rich repertoire and an audience

6. This example was offered by I Wayan Dibia (personal communication), but I have since encountered similar instances in the course of my research in Bali.

wide enough to make ongoing professional ensembles of this sort viable, probably more viable than any other small ensemble in this particular musical tradition. The assignment of parts (as opposed to roles) depends on instrument. Only the two violinists can easily trade parts, and this is not common in professional ensembles. In most quartets the cellist cannot spontaneously switch parts with the violist. Each part is attained through extensive specialized training, although the players also share substantial areas of competence. Ideally, the level of competence should be roughly equal to ensure that each musician can match or complement whatever the others play. Leadership is traditionally vested in the position of first violin, with the second violin, viola, and cello cast in supporting roles. The very concept of "second fiddle" has entered the language signifying subordination or marginality. This is a superficial view, contradicted by the numerous passages in which the focus shifts to second violin, viola, or cello and by the fact that leadership responsibility is not necessarily linked to the domain of melody—an "accompanying" part often sets tempo and dynamics or initiates a phrase. Subnetworks within the ensemble are not fixed, but are formed and re-formed as domains and relationships between the four players shift according to compositional decisions conveyed in the score. At any moment one of the musicians may be driving and shaping the playing of the other three; the four may play as a single unit, split into pairs, or form some other combination as one or more players remain silent. Interactive relationships may be as varied as contrapuntal and chordal playing.

A North Indian *khyal* ensemble has a more hierarchical network of roles and relationships[7] with clear separation of domains. A soloist, who has control in the domain of melody and substantial influence in the domain of rhythm, is accompanied by a drummer, who may be fully as competent but is accorded a lower status, less recognition, and much less control over the progression of the performance. The drummer has some improvisatory freedom within the domain of rhythm but must supply whatever metrical foundation the soloist demands. Wade describes a shift of power in instrumental ensembles in the past few decades sparked by soloists who allow the drummer more opportunities to play featured solos within the performance and who engage in competitive interaction of a more or less egalitarian nature, and by drummers who demand this sort of recognition (1984b: 25–26). Far beneath these two musicians is the drone player, who supplies a foundation for the soloist's modal explorations and has no say in the performance at all, even the tuning of the drone instrument (*tambura*) being subject to the judgment

---

7. This description is based on Wade (1984b) and Neuman (1980).

of the soloist.[8] Performance and interaction in such an ensemble are predicated on a sharp bifurcation of competence between melodic soloist and drummer. Each must have a passive knowledge of many aspects of the other's art in order to interact, but the two players have no opportunity to actually cross over into the other's domain as the players in a string quartet do, although they do reach across the divide in imitative exchanges with particularly rhythmic melodic playing and particularly melodic drumming. The drone player is often a disciple of the soloist and gains competence in the course of performance as an actively involved listener. Another highly differentiated role in the *khyal* ensemble is that of the *sarangi* player. This musician, usually of lower social rank, must be able to echo the singer's line faithfully and fill the spaces between vocal phrases without overstepping the bounds of his domain as subordinate accompanist. "With the exception of a few singers . . . who treat the [*sarangi* player] as a partner in the ensemble, these vocalists find musical means in the course of a performance to assert their position of soloist" (Wade 1984b: 29).

The traditional *takht* ensemble of the Arab Middle East offers a contrasting interactive network. This ensemble consists of musicians who play melodic instruments—violin, *'ud* (lute), *qanun* (plucked zither), and *nay* (end-blown flute)—and a drummer or two, who play a *riqq* (frame drum) and *darabukkah* (goblet drum).[9] There is a clear division of domains between the melodic players and the drummers, paralleled by distinctions of competence. Beyond this, however, the assignment of roles within the ensemble is not preordained. The drummers form a subnetwork which provides a rhythmic foundation for the melody. It is fairly common for the second drummer to be an apprentice of the first (Taiseer Elias, personal communication) whose role is to maintain the meter while the more experienced drummer improvises complex patterns on this foundation. Through this interaction the second drummer attains competence, learning the basic patterns and ways of improvising on them.

The melodic instrumentalists in a *takht* are a more heterogeneous lot, each with his own specialized competence centered on the particular technique and idiom of his instrument. They improvise both simultaneously and consecutively upon composed melodies with ample opportunity for complex interaction. They also enter into reciprocal relation-

---

8. However, it is an honor to be asked to play the *tambura* (Wade, personal communication).

9. Racy writes about the *takht* as a thing of the past that disappeared in the 1920s (1988: 158), but it continues to function, if in somewhat altered form, alongside the larger orchestras which spread through the Arab world after World War I.

ships, taking turns playing improvised solos and maintaining drones or ostinati for each other (Racy 1988: 142).

The *takht* almost invariably performs with or includes a singer, who tends to hold a position superior to the rest of the ensemble due to the great importance placed on vocal music. The singer may subordinate the entire ensemble to his command, but some singers cross boundaries by playing an instrument, usually the *'ud*, and thus take a more integrated place in the network. The incorporation of singing occasions the type of heterophonic relationship described earlier in comparison with other singer-instrumentalist relationships.

INTERACTIVE SYSTEM

The interactive system consists of the means by which performers communicate, coordinate, and orient themselves. It includes a variety of acts—cues, responses, prompts, signals, and markers—which constitute a system because they are interdependent conventions intelligible to a group of people who use these conventions in a fairly consistent manner under recurring conditions.

A *cue* is perhaps the most obvious interactive device, a means of communicating between performers. The word has seen fairly indiscriminate use in the ethnomusicological literature. McLean proposed a simple typology in an analysis of Maori chant (1968), Gourlay refined and extended this definition (1972), and Ruth Stone has written extensively on the subject (1982). Here I am advocating a more restricted usage, defining cue as *a musical, verbal, visual, or kinetic act specifically produced for the purpose of initiating an interaction—that is, bringing about a change in the performance of others in the ensemble—that would not occur otherwise.* Intentionality, causality, and specificity are the key factors here: a cue is produced by one person to convey a message at a unique point in the course of a performance in order to request, suggest, or demand that other performers respond in some way. The concept is still broad enough to cover a range of meanings, because a cue can be an order, a stimulus, a reminder, or even a hint, but it is distinct from other communicative acts—signals and markers—that will be defined presently.

The essential aspects of a cue are its medium and its message. Performers make varied use of sight and sound: aural cues range from integral elements of musical expression to more extraneous sounds and even words, while visual means include facial expressions, stances, and movements of body parts, musical instruments, and other physical props. A performer may use several different means of cuing simultaneously or consecutively. A Javanese *dhalang*, for example, places a particular puppet in the middle of the screen to convey a break between scenes, taps on the puppet box in a certain way as a preparatory cue (a warning that he is about to sing), and then begins to sing, the initial pitch indicating a specific song that the musicians must accompany.

The positioning of performers is directly implicated in an analysis of interaction, as it limits or favors particular media and lines of communication, especially in relation to the acoustics of the performance space. A group of performers may be positioned to provide unobstructed lines of sight and equal audibility, or these avenues of communication may be partially or fully blocked. The structure of the interactive network comes into play, so to speak, in the placement of subgroupings of performers in proximity to enhance communication and cohesion, and to demarcate the subnetworks of the ensemble. A symphony orchestra exemplifies placement that favors visual cues from the conductor to the players and optimum audibility for the conductor in return, by positioning the musicians in a semicircle around the conductor. Considerations of sectional grouping and group hierarchy are also clearly manifested in this arrangement, which places section leaders at the heads of their cohorts, closest to the center of command. But this placement actually reverses the favored media of communication within a string section: section members sit behind their sectional leaders and may see the leader's bowing better than they hear it, while the leader hears well but cannot see the rest of the section at all.

The prominence and relative integration or isolation of this communication in the musical "text" are also important variables. The more distinct a cue is relative to the texture of the performance, the greater the audience's awareness of interaction. Conversely, music in which cues are fully integrated may convey an almost magical sense of effortless coordination. Some aural cues may be an integral part of a melodic or rhythmic line and are only made recognizable as cues through subtle musical devices, while others are not so subtle, extramusical sounds such as the Javanese *dhalang*'s tapping on the puppet box. The *dhalang*'s verbal cues are usually seamlessly incorporated in sung or spoken text, but in some performance contexts it is acceptable to directly address other performers in speech. These variables are all important for establishing the relative formality, cohesiveness, and explicitness of interaction.

The meaning of a cue rests on convention, prior agreement, and experience. Conventional cues are part of a common communicative repertoire or language. They may bear multiple meanings, but they should be readily identifiable for any competent player within a community. More specialized cues may be agreed upon in rehearsal or emerge from prior spontaneous communications, becoming part of an insider's language limited to as few as two performers. Such idiosyncratic cues can puzzle the most competent performer in the absence of sufficient rapport or mutual experience. Did the pianist nod her head at the violinist ("Let's bring out this passage"), the page turner ("Now! You idiot! Now!"), or the audience (demonstrating physical involvement in the music)?

The ambiguity that endangers idiosyncratic interaction frequently arises with more conventional cues that depend on context, timing, and directionality for their meaning. All parties to the communication must be aware of an ambiguous cue's range of meanings and the appropriate contextual factors that pare away irrelevant meanings, leaving a single, unambiguous message. The cuing player cannot expect a correct response if the cue is given at the wrong time or in an unclear context. As the case of the nodding pianist shows, directionality—the link between cue giver and recipient(s)—is also an essential aspect of the meaning of the cue, which may be clarified by direct eye contact but must otherwise be learned as a part of competence in ensemble performance.

A cue is given in order to evoke a reaction or *response* of some sort from other performers. The responder must note that a cue is being given, know that she is the one being cued, correctly interpret the message conveyed by the cue, select an appropriate response, and produce it with voice or instrument at the right time. Correct interpretation of a cue depends upon knowledge of all the possible messages conveyed, the contextual factors that narrow the meaning of a cue in any given instance, the desired response or range of responses, and the appropriate timing of the response. If the directionality of the cue is unclear or unfocused, someone must take the initiative, as Sugarman describes in her analysis of Prespa Albanian men's singing, where there is a general order of precedence for initiating and leading songs, but when a song ends it is not necessarily clear who will respond to this "cue" and initiate the next one (1988).

Considering both the timing and the predictability of a cue apprises us of the informational content of the message conveyed by the cue and offers a useful way of differentiating levels of interactive determinacy. Put simply, there are four possibilities (see fig. 11): a musician may (1) not know when a cue will be given or which cue to expect; (2) know that a specific cue is coming but not know when; (3) know when but not know what (which cue and, therefore, which response); or (4) know both what and when. The first situation places the highest demands on a musician's interactive skills, requiring a readiness to respond to a wide variety of cues at any moment, while the fourth demands the least, as the cue reaffirms a planned action rather than conveying new information. Interactive devices of the latter sort will be called "signals" to emphasize

CUE

TIMING	Indeterminate	Determinate
Indeterminate	Musicians do not know which cues to expect or when those cues might be given.	Musicians expect a particular cue but do not know when it will be given.
Determinate	Musicians expect a cue at a certain time but do not know which cue to expect.	Musicians expect a particular cue at a certain time.

Fig. 11. Cue predictability

this distinction.[10] In the second and third cases, the musicians who will need to respond to the cue are forewarned, knowing either that a specific cue, such as a command to stop playing, is coming or that at a specific time some directive (to repeat or go on, for example) will be forthcoming.

The time gap between cue and response is one of the most distinctive characteristics of particular types of interaction. This gap is often very brief and the response seemingly instantaneous. Such rapid response to cues, particularly unexpected ones, can generate great excitement for performers and audience. The gap between cue and response may also be flexible, allowing the responder(s) a greater degree of control. In a jazz ensemble, for example, when a soloist finishes improvising a chorus, another member of the ensemble is cued to take the next chorus, but this does not determine the precise onset of the next improvisation with relation to the ongoing harmonic and metric structure of the piece. The new soloist can begin to improvise in the last measure of the old chorus or wait to come in anywhere in the first few measures of the new one.

In other situations the gap is of longer duration and the cue is *preparatory*, giving advance warning that a response should be made at a particular moment. A preparatory cue may be only the first in a series of cues, as noted above for the Javanese *dhalang*'s song: the first cue sets up a general expectation, the second defines a more precise onset for the response. Since the duration of the gap, its relative flexibility, and its "placement" in musical time are all intimately linked to interactive sound structure, we shall return to this topic in the following section of this chapter.

A response that is not dictated by an intentional cue is likely to be

10. Gourlay subsumes this type of interaction under cue (1972), but I believe that the difference is significant enough to warrant a distinction.

RESPONSE	Obligatory	Optional
Unique	Musician(s) must produce one particular response.	Musician(s) may respond or not, but only one response is appropriate.
Multiple	Musician(s) must respond, but can choose response.	Musician(s) may respond or not. The response is not predetermined.

Fig. 12. Responding musicians' options

less bound by a conventional time gap. If a musician hears something inspiring (in whatever shape or form) from someone else in the ensemble, the response may be almost immediate—such as trying to match a particularly beautiful tone quality or dynamic[11]—or it may be considerably delayed as the musician mulls it over and waits for the appropriate moment to respond. In cyclical or strophic pieces the musician may wait until the next repeat: a musician in a Javanese *gamelan* may hear someone else play a special pattern and then match it in the next repetition of the cycle, or a jazz musician might take an idea from someone else's improvisation and transform it in the next chorus. Russell notes that in Kansas City jazz circles "to repeat another man's ideas was taboo. The great infighters of the jam sessions were adepts at taking another man's ideas, often his best ones, and turning them inside out, or using them as a basis for a new set of improvisations" (1971: 26).

The cue-giver's control can be measured in terms of the determinacy and predictability of cue and response, which may vary greatly. There are two major variables to consider here: a response may be obligatory or optional, and it may be precisely determined by the cue in a one-to-one relationship or selected from a pool of possibilities by the responder. Maximal control obtains when a cue obligates a particular response; control is minimal when the responder is not obliged to respond and has the option of choosing among several responses. Between these extremes, there are intermediate levels of control (see fig. 12).

Reciprocity is inherent to some responses because they also serve as cues to the original cue-giver or at least as constraining factors on the further actions of the original cue-giver. In other words, the responder may have some degree of control over the cue-giver if the latter must wait for the response before proceeding or if the manner of proceeding depends on the content of the response. Performer A may cue performer

11. See, for example, the interaction between drummer and singer which Wade notes in a North Indian performance of *khyal* (1984a: 72).

B to end the section, for instance, and A then may have to delay further action until B has responded.

The basic unit of interactive communication, a cue and response, is often elaborated through mediation or reinforcement, as one performer relays a cue to others (see fig. 13). The relayed cue, produced in response to an earlier cue from someone else, may "translate" the first cue into another medium (e.g., visual to aural) or add further information to make the message of the initial cue more specific or precise. Translation is particularly prevalent in performances involving extramusical elements such as theater, ritual, or dance. A visual or verbal cue from one of the nonmusician participants is received by a leading musician, who interprets the message and translates it into a new, musical cue.

The mediator may complete the original cue by clarifying the timing and coordinating a group response. The first cue sets up an expectation or warning, and the mediator cues the precise onset of the response. For example, the *ugal* (leading metallophone) player in a Balinese *gamelan gong kebyar* leads the musicians playing *gangsa* (metallophones on which rapid interlocking figuration is played) in responding to the drummer's cue. All the players have heard this cue, but the danger of slightly different response times is avoided by mediation: the *ugal* player "actualizes" or "specifies" the response with a visual cue, a hand gesture, timed to ensure perfect unison or precise interlocking of the *gangsa* section. When certain players consistently take the role of mediating cues given by others, hierarchies within the interactive network are established or strengthened, as in this Balinese case where the *ugal* player is one of the recognized leaders of the ensemble.

Cue reinforcement differs from mediation and is not as essential to the proper functioning of the ensemble. While a mediated cue augments the message of an initial cue, reinforcement merely involves reiteration of the message by other players. The "reinforcers" hear the cue and reproduce it, often in varied form due to idiomatic differences between instruments. Since they do this before the response to the cue is sounded, they may enhance interaction in a psychological sense by confirming the leader's message and the responding musicians' perception of that message (see fig. 13). When a Javanese *rebab* player plays a cue to switch to the *lik*, a section of a composition characterized by use of the high register, the cue is echoed by the *pesindhèn* and by players of *bonang* and *gambang* (and possibly *gendèr, suling,* and *siter*). Theoretically these reinforcements are not essential, but they validate the other players' reception of that cue and their anticipated responses and they also serve an acoustic function, spreading the leader's message to all corners of the ensemble since the sound of the *rebab* is relatively soft and does

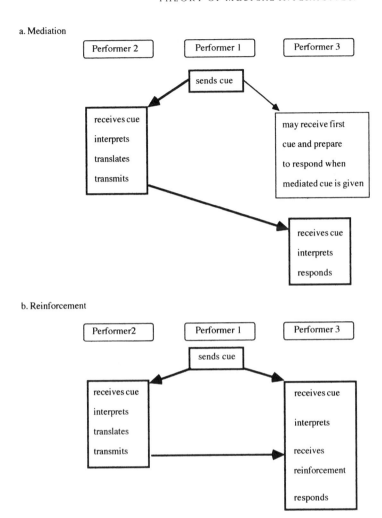

Fig. 13   Mediation vs. reinforcement

not always carry clearly in less than ideal performance circumstances. More important, these reinforcements are expected and if they did not occur, confusion might ensue, as this would, in effect, call the authority of the *rebab* player into question. This can happen when non-Javanese play *gamelan*, especially if they do not expect the cue because they have been told that it would come at another time.

Interactive systems also include and depend upon reminders and references that do not necessarily initiate a new sequence of actions but assist performers in establishing or maintaining their aural and conceptual orientation in performance. We can use the term *prompt* to distinguish those cues that are produced solely for the purpose of putting derailed musicians back on the tracks. Prompts are given in times of trouble while *signals,* defined above as predictable cues, are produced as reminders or warnings before disaster strikes. If a Javanese *rebab* player hears a singer straying from the correct melody, for instance, he can play a bit of the vocal line as a prompt. When the *lik* section of a Javanese piece occurs at preordained intervals, as it does in certain dance pieces, the *rebab* player's "cue" for the *lik* is actually a signal because it adds nothing new but reminds the players of the preordained path. Yet chaos might ensue if an expected signal were not given.

A *marker* is referential, like a signal; rather than evoking a direct response, it orients the performers with reference to pitch, rhythm, and position within the sequence of events. While a signal is given in advance, a marker literally "marks" an event as it occurs. Colotomic parts and cyclically recurring drum patterns are two obvious examples of markers which are thoroughly conventional and serve to ensure cohesion and congruent conceptions of "where" the performers are in the course of the performance. A conductor beating time serves a similar function, adding cues as necessary.

Markers can be continuous or intermittent, regularly recurring or unique, and they may vary in prominence and importance. In essence a colotomic pattern is a hierarchy of markers. A drone also offers a means of orientation and as such is an ongoing marker of tonal space. In addition to these conventional markers, a person may seize upon a moment or event within the musical flow as a point of orientation, as when a singer takes a starting pitch from a certain instrumental part. Many Balinese musicians remember long pieces with reference to those pitches in the basic melody (*pokok*) that coincide with colotomic markers (I Wayan Dibia and I Nyoman Sudarna, personal communication). The colotomic gongs are not only marking time and position within a hierarchically structured cycle, but also "marking" the pitches with which they coincide, making them more memorable and turning them into melodic markers. Markers can also facilitate coordination and obviate the need for an overt cue. By convention or prior agreement (nascent convention) a distinctive feature in the musical flow can be designated as the point at which some change is to be made in the manner of performance.

Reference and orientation to sounds produced by others in the ensemble are the most pervasive type of interaction, at least as essential to music-making as overt cues and responses. A competent performer may be perfectly capable of playing a piece unassisted, but when performing with other musicians he will monitor their playing, if only to check that the appropriate degree of synchronization is maintained. Standards of pitch, time, or dynamic must also be agreed upon and perhaps renegotiated in the course of performance as people try to resolve differences in their conceptions of these standards or as musical context requires modification. Psychological and social factors enter into these microadjustments when a performer who is completely sure of himself refuses to yield[12] or when people consistently defer to one person's standards because of his status, even though they do not agree with the tempo taken or possible deviations in pitch.

Many interactive relationships require a good deal more in the way of mutual reference and orientation. Interlocking is a particularly good example of this: the players must be constantly aware of where they "stand" in relation to their partners, and they are often aided by the presence of some regularly recurring marker or sets of markers which demarcate the temporal framework within which the interlocking parts mesh. Interlocking in various Indonesian musical traditions, for example, coexists with a cyclical colotomic framework marked by gongs and often some rhythmically simple melody that manifests the beat clearly. Other examples of orientation in time include the time line played on the *gankogui* bell in West African drumming ensembles or on the *clave* in many Latin American ensembles. In all of these instances players are probably referring to a conception of the composite, too, but the external reference sets a standard.

Orienting oneself by monitoring the overall flow and individual parts can extend to other domains and means, too. Synchronization and orientation are facilitated by reading from a score in a notated tradition, for example; they are also facilitated by the aural competence of an essentially oral tradition, where parts are fixed by tradition or stereotypically related to one another. In many Southeast Asian ensemble traditions, for instance, it is possible to predict the general drift of other parts from one's own and vice versa.

INTERACTIVE SOUND STRUCTURE

A network of performers creates music using an interactive system within interactive sound structures.[13] These structures affect interaction

12. E.g., Marika Kuzma, choral conductor at U. C. Berkeley, notes that students with perfect pitch are often the most intractable when a particular chord needs intonational adjustment, because they rely solely on their own sense of absolute pitch (personal communication).

13. I use "structure" in the general sense of "the aggregate of elements of an entity in their relationships to each other" (Webster's Ninth Collegiate Dictionary), not in senses current in linguistics and anthropology. I believe this is consonant with Giddens and Turner's usage when

by forming a frame of reference for performers and by determining when interaction can or should take place and in what form. When analyzing musical structure, there is a tendency, even among ethnomusicologists seeking analogies to social structure, to speak in abstractions removed from realms of human action. This may be understandable and even justifiable to a point, but it must not be forgotten that sound structures result from and, in turn, govern the ways in which people produce sound[14] through conventions of sequence (what sound or sound-making is to follow another) and compatibility (what sounds or ways of making sound go together simultaneously).

Musical "textures" are defined by the relationships between simultaneous strands of sound[15] and from any focus there might be within this structure. Textures are closely related to interactive networks: changes of texture are engendered by changes in the interactive network and vice versa. In the section on interactive networks, I discussed relationships in terms of roles and particularly in terms of degrees of control or influence between people. When looking at the same subject from the perspective of interactive sound structure, we can state these relationships in terms of the degree to which musical "material" is shared between parts or performers. A single strand sung or played in synchrony, for example, represents maximal sharing of material and, as an interactive sound structure, presents particular demands and opportunities for interaction, depending on variables such as standards of tonal blend and rhythmic coordination, the presence or absence of a regular beat, and the possibility or necessity of staggered breathing. Seen in interactive terms, the texture of Yemenite Jewish "organum" is similar to monophony, for all performers share a melody, but in the Yemenite case some of the performers start the melody a fifth above the others.

This points to the problematic natures of common labels for texture such as monophony, polyphony, homophony, and heterophony that are often difficult to define and apply even within one musical tradition. As tools for cross-cultural study they are nearly useless, yet they crop up repeatedly because they refer, however imprecisely, to sonic and human relationships that are of real formative importance in the making and perception of music. We can begin to refine our understanding of such relationships by noting the deficiencies of the labels that we use. In general usage, they derive principally from melodic distinctions; rhythmic

---

they write that "structure is both the medium and the outcome of the day-to-day conduct in which actors engage" (1987: 8).

14. Cf. John Blacking's "humanly organized sound" (1973: 3–31).

15. The term "strand" is used here to convey the ongoingness of most musical activity and to encompass not only melody but other types of sound sequences.

considerations are of secondary importance, and some common musical textures—melody and drone, melody and drumming, and percussive ensemble, to name a few—are not covered by these terms. On the other hand, heterophony and polyphony each carry a hefty bundle of connotations and can be applied to such widely differing musical textures that their utility is compromised.

Let us briefly traverse the spectrum of textures, continuing from the above example of maximally shared material. From this type of texture to some types of heterophony and overlapping (i.e., canonic) imitation is just a short step. Here, too, musicians perform a common part, but a multiple-stranded texture is produced by differences of timing, melodic nuances, instrumental techniques, and idioms. The catchall term "heterophony" is particularly problematic as it ignores the fundamental interactive differences between a number of distinct ways of making music. Are the parts rhythmically congruent or independent, overlapping, echoing? Do I play things at the same time as you or consistently later, or do I work around your melody? These different relationships may all occur in one piece or performance, but the distinctions are potentially meaningful and should not be glossed over with labels that are too broad.

A texture dubbed "polyphonic stratification" (see Hood 1971: 52) is widespread in Southeast Asia as a means of organizing ensemble music-making. It shares some of the characteristics just noted, such as different relationships of time lag between different parts, but differs significantly, highlighting the shortcomings of labels such as "polyphony" and "heterophony." A basic melodic conception guides and unites the musicians and may be manifested simultaneously (and "heterophonically") at various levels of abstraction or elaboration, yet some of these individual "realizations" of the basic melodic flow are so distinct that the term "polyphony" with its implications of independence seems appropriate.

Other multistranded textures are numerous and varied, but they are all based on the simultaneous production of fundamentally different musical ideas. Once again, my point is not to catalog but to indicate the dimensions of variation and some of the underlying principles. *Complementation* might be used to denote interactive structures in which musicians produce parts that combine to create an integrated aesthetic whole such as a harmony, a timbre, or a certain rhythmic density. This is a process controlled by composers in some traditions, but in music that is not rigidly prescribed, performers may join in by finding a "hole" in the "whole" and filling it. The Venda concept of singing along in harmony described by Blacking (1973: 85 and elsewhere) would appear to fit this model. So, too, would the ability of Balinese musicians to fit in a second, mainly offbeat, *sangsih* part to fill out the two-part interlocking composite implied by the basic *polos* part.[16] Javanese *gérong* (choral singers) slip easily into interlocking handclapping in certain sections of a performance by filling in all the divisions of the beat at a certain density. No prearrangement is necessary, because, as in the previous examples, there is a composite sound ideal that serves as an organizing structure for interaction.

Simultaneous structure is epitomized in European traditions by chordal harmony, produced by a confluence of parts. From an interactive point of view, these structures place strictures on intonation that have driven experimentation with different tuning systems over the centuries, culminating in equal temperament. To this day, however, singers and players of instruments with continuously variable pitch (particularly bowed strings) continue to diverge from the equal temperament enshrined in the piano and other instruments of fixed tuning. When no fixed-tuning instruments are used, musicians can tune each chord in ways that are not possible in equal temperament. When performing with equal-tempered instruments, on the other hand, singers and others must adjust their pitch at crucial points but can safely diverge at others in order to create the appropriate melodic and harmonic relations.

Processes of divergence and convergence are common to many types of multistranded texture. The reasons for converging at particular points will be discussed further in relation to consecutive structure. Here the important aspect to consider, from an interactive perspective, is the simultaneous structure toward which musicians converge. The Western example just noted concerns intonation governed by harmonic considerations. A similar example with radically different effect is to be found in the way Javanese musicians sing or play *rebab* in relation to the fixed tuning of a *gamelan*. The theorist Martopangrawit formulated this with respect to mode and *rebab* fingering positions: the most important pitches in the mode, fingered with the index or ring finger on the *rebab*, should coincide with the fixed tuning (which varies considerably from one *gamelan* to the next) while the other pitches, fingered with the middle and little fingers, might deviate from this tuning in accordance with the *rebab* player's own sense of intonation (personal communication). The Western example is driven by harmonic considerations, the Javanese by modal ones, but both involve interactive considerations of

16. Lisa Gold reports that in *gender wayang* lessons when she requested the *sangsih* part to go with a *polos* that she had already learned the teacher would proceed to play the *polos* and say "go ahead, play the *sangsih*" (personal communication).

pitch modification for convergence with and divergence from other performers in the ensemble.

Other examples of convergence derive from timbral considerations. Both Gage Averill and Tim Rice report on singers aiming to produce a physical effect with the confluence of their voices in certain simultaneous structures. Rice, writing about Bulgarian singing, says that women aim to "make the intervals ring like bells" (1988: 55). Averill has analyzed the sonority that barbershop quartets aim for when they "ring" certain chords and has found striking spectral (i.e., timbral) enrichment compared with other chords in the same song (1990). The resolution of dissonance to consonance that drives Western contrapuntal thinking is another example of divergence and convergence, based on the relative tension of intervals. It is easy enough to hear dissonance and its resolution in a choral performance, for example, as a type of human interaction with harmonious blend as the goal, not just metaphorically but in terms of the physical sensation of dissonance and consonance.

Focus is also a distinguishing trait of simultaneous sound structures. It can be a single strand, several strands, or even an unsounded musical conception that is manifested through a variety of musical representations.[17] In *concertante* pieces and many accompanied songs in the Western tradition, for example, simultaneous structure is set up to project the focal part on the backdrop of other parts. A similar characterization could perhaps be made of the relationship between master drummer and ensemble in a West African ensemble. But the focal part need not be the leader's part, since leaders may direct the ensemble from less foregrounded roles within the texture or may not contribute directly to it at all. Focus is a subjective quality open to dispute and multiple interpretations. The idea I wish to convey here is that listeners and musicians frequently think of some aspect of the overall sound as predominant and that this colors the conception of texture and interaction.

If texture is the common term for the simultaneous aspects of interactive sound structure, then form is perhaps the closest cognate for consecutive structure, the unfolding of music through time. There are many different culturally specific ways of conceptualizing and realizing such structures. Movement through physical space is a common metaphor, and with it comes the possibility of "mapping" the progression, naming "signposts" along the way, and perhaps talking about forks in the road, points at which paths of related pieces diverge or converge (Brinner

---

17. Examples include a basic theme or drum pattern festooned in garlands of elaboration or a latent melodic conception such as Sumarsam's inner melody (1984b).

1985: 173–75). Leaders are responsible for driving the ensemble along these paths, choosing between different options and advocating or enabling a particular realization or interpretation of the abstract or not fully actualized music-in-potential. Even seemingly egalitarian or leaderless ensembles must rely on someone to decide "which way to go." While Racy characterizes the heterophonic music-making of the Arab *takht*, for example, as "spontaneously producing individualized musical interpretations" (1988: 144) in an essentially leaderless way, it is clear from his analysis of a *tahmila* that leadership devolves upon various members of the ensemble who alternate as soloists and in the process determine the progression of the call-and-response sections of the piece.

The really important issue here, the one that is perhaps hardest to approach and pin down in a single tradition, let alone cross-culturally, is the nature of the piece as it exists in musicians' minds. However important the process of performance might be, there must be some potential structure or outline of possibilities that musicians share. The question of notation is peripheral here, affecting only the relative fixity and perhaps the detail of the conception. Nattiez's position that "in musics of the oral tradition, the musical product is merged with the act of performing, and there is no longer a material prototype for the 'work'" (1991: 73) is perhaps true in the most restricted sense, but a common cognitive structure can be just as concrete for performers as a written score and subject to interpretation, too, so "materiality" is immaterial, so to speak. A musical composition can be a reasonably robust cultural artifact without the benefit of notation and can require interpretation just as a notated composition does in order to produce an audible musical result.

In order to understand the consecutive aspects of interactive sound structure, it is useful to define two aspects, sequence and progression. *Sequence* is the latent order of events at whatever level one chooses— phrase, section, piece, medley, or performance occasion. *Progression* is the manner in which musicians proceed through a sequence, realizing its potential in actual performance by making choices among the possible ways of playing the sequence.

Sequence is a conceptual model, fixed in memory or in writing as a blueprint for performance. Certain aspects of performance may be specified in great detail while others exist as options or clusters of options. The score of a symphony is such a blueprint, in which the composer has determined aspects such as pitch, rhythm, and timbre in terms of who plays what when, leaving some latitude for dynamics, relative emphasis, tempi, repeats, and the placement of the work within a larger concert program. Progression through this sequence is controlled largely by the conductor insofar as he or she succeeds in interacting with members of the orchestra and elicits from them a sonic product to match his or her conception; the last variable, program sequence, may be decided by someone else. By contrast, a large Javanese composition is much less fixed in most aspects and it requires several leading musicians to make many decisions about the basic sequence of the piece in a given performance, but the piece's place in a larger sequence of pieces, a "concert program," is fairly well determined by its modal and formal attributes.

The sequence of a piece or other musical artifact, whether taken from a score, elicited as a "map" from performers, or deduced from transcriptions and observations of multiple performances, enables us to pinpoint the location of particular types of interaction and to analyze the prescriptive power of form in this area. We need to discover whether the sequence depends on a relatively fixed interactive network or on shifting focus between different interactive networks. The interactive system is also implicated here, because the conceptual model of sequence is essential as a means of orientation for the performers; crucial points may be articulated by signals and markers to aid performers.

Determinacy and *linkage* of progression through a sequence are pertinent variables for an assessment of the relative fluidity or fixity of interactive sound structure. These variables raise the same issues that were addressed above in connection with interactive network and system, but here they are seen from a different perspective. A well-defined sequence is largely predetermined while a more loosely defined sequence is created in performance as a result of decisions made by the performers (and perhaps by external agents, as well). This gross differentiation must be refined for individual musical traditions in order to obtain a contrastive measure of interactive causality.

The progress of an ensemble through a sequence may be tightly or loosely linked in terms of temporal coordination. Loosely linked parts coincide approximately without being locked together in one particular temporal relationship. This is typical of some Javanese genres that will be analyzed in later chapters and of interaction in congregational chanting in Jewish and Japanese Buddhist traditions, for example. Within a segment of the overall sequence of prayer the congregants chant the same melody, each at his or her own pace, but overall progression from one segment to the next may be more closely coordinated, creating a concerted beginning for each section. Intentional noncoordination, planned avoidance of simultaneity, typifies some Japanese music, such as *kumiuta* and *tegotomono* songs with *koto* or *shamisen* accompaniment in which the vocal and instrumental versions of the melody are similar in pitch but differ radically in rhythm and rarely coincide. Unmetered Baroque recitative is one European example in which distinct parts are loosely coordinated; this setup has its own interactive problems and potentials as continuo players attempt to assess, match, or prod the singer's phrases without the benefit of a steady beat or a clear cuing system.[18]

In a consecutive interactive sound structure with more explicit interactive conventions musician A may lead and B follow or respond but the interval, or time gap, between lead and response is flexible. Such loosely coordinated consecutive musical structure is illustrated well in the generic prelude (*netori*) and coda (*tomede*) that precede and follow each piece in a Japanese *gagaku* performance. The *tomede* is characterized by a well-defined sequence of final interactions among the musicians, but the progression through this sequence is very loosely defined because there is no beat and the timing of individual elements within the *tomede* sequence can vary significantly. Similar temporal looseness of interaction can also occur in a metered context, as I shall demonstrate later with Javanese *palaran*. For the moment, it is sufficient to note that when such temporally loose progression takes place in a metrical framework, individual actions are coordinated with this framework but the time gap between acts, between cue and response, is not predetermined.

Innumerable cases of tight musical coordination in a wide variety of traditions contrast with these examples of loosely defined simultaneity. The Western orchestral ideal, for example, is based on full synchronization, and this holds for most chamber music, too. But one should not be too quick to label an entire tradition "tightly coordinated" without checking the tolerances of conceptually simultaneous performance. A subtle range of simultaneity may actually be tolerated and even valued. For example, in some jazz styles it is acceptable to play off the beat by an unquantifiable amount (as opposed to executing precise counter-rhythms against the beat) but this is probably a function of tempo, being more acceptable and noticeable at slow speeds than in fast playing.

Elements of the interactive system (cues, responses, signals, and markers) create and articulate structure, but they also occur within structure, at some points and not at others, and are dependent·on that structure for their meaning. The connection between interaction and structure may be as simple as prearranged markers ("When we reach point X, we should play in such and such a manner until we reach point Y") or considerably more complex. The different degrees of determinacy in a cue-response interaction (shown in fig. 14) illustrate both the phenomenon of linkage discussed above and some of the ways in which

---

18. Elizabeth LeGuinn has written an unpublished paper on some basic aspects of interaction in this context.

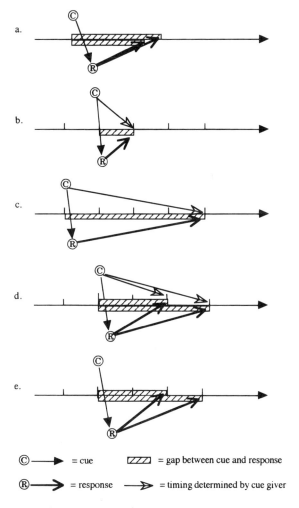

$\textcircled{C} \longrightarrow$ = cue $\boxed{/\!/\!/\!/}$ = gap between cue and response

$\textcircled{R} \longrightarrow$ = response $\longrightarrow\!\!\!>$ = timing determined by cue giver

Fig. 14   Degrees of determinacy in the cue-response gap

cue and response can be contingent on musical structure. This figure demonstrates in a simplified manner how responses may be timed to fit the musical structure. Similar constraints on the timing of cues have been omitted for the sake of clarity. Figure 14a shows interaction in a music without regular pulse: the cue-giver cannot determine the timing of the response precisely, and therefore only one arrow emanates from the symbol ©; there is no arrow pointing toward the time line to indicate the moment of response. The other examples occur in rhythmically regular music, and the short vertical ticks on the time line indicate recurrent events within the structure such as beats, downbeats of measures, or beginnings of rhythmic cycles. The cue may tell a musician to respond immediately (fig. 14b), after a set amount of time (e.g., after four beats/ ticks [fig. 14c]), or at any of several possible times (fig. 14d). The cue may also leave the response time to the discretion of the responding musicians, who will still need to coordinate their response with the underlying structure of the music (fig. 14e).

These examples also show how interaction can affect structure: responses determine the further progression of the music, and the timing of these responses depends on interaction between the musicians. The Arab *tahmila* and Japanese *netori* are good examples of large-scale musical structures shaped by interaction: each performance is the cumulative effect of give-and-take by the musicians as they progress through a loosely determined compositional sequence. On a larger scale still, the entire program of a Javanese *gamelan* performance is determined by the choices made by leading musicians.

This discussion of interactive sound structure has focused on music alone, but the same considerations apply to interaction in performances that involve additional elements such as dance or ritual. The structures of such contexts may become more complex as musical structures are subsumed in ritual or theatrical structures of a larger scale. Structural flexibility is often necessary in such situations to ensure coordination of disparate activities. The sequence of events may be fixed, but the progression through that sequence is often subject to variation and music is adapted to these needs, as we shall see in later chapters.

INTERACTIVE MOTIVATION: ETHICS AND AESTHETICS

What motivates people to interact musically in particular ways in a given situation? It is doubtful whether the overt and hidden goals, the rewards or incentives to interact in certain ways, and the penalties or sanctions for failure to do so, in short, the ethics and aesthetics of interaction, are ever fully knowable, but attempts to discover these aspects of interaction can and should be made, whether one starts with broad cultural and social "truths" or a patchwork piecing together of anecdote and observation. A partial list of common goals might proceed from the pragmatics of keeping things together to the aesthetic fulfillment derived from a perfect blending. There is generally some concern with correctness, ensuring that everything fits together and is balanced properly; this may be heightened by the demands of ritual rightness for religious ceremonies. The excitement of spontaneous exchanges is certainly common to many traditions as is the expectation that musicians will collectively exceed their individual potentials. Any study of interaction, though it be focused on network, system, or structure, concerns these and possibly other motivations, because musical interaction is not a mechanical system but a way of human being.

Motivation may be the aspect of interaction least susceptible of systematization, not just for the rescarcher, who constantly runs the risk of essentializing ("the Javanese do X" or "the English do Y"), but for the makers and bearers of tradition, for the people who create conventions and norms by favoring one attempt or solution over another and by repeating certain decisions and actions but not others. Among all the normative behavior that keeps a society from disintegrating there is bound to be non-normative thinking and action; if the prejudices common to many societies are to be believed, this is more likely with deviant musicians than with many other occupational groups.

Most reports on interactive motivation in ethnomusicological literature make broad statements, reducing complex psychological machinations to simple stories. When scholars do investigate individual motives, perceptions, and reactions, they may have difficulty writing about something so personal and private; again, there is a tendency to generalize. Perhaps the best we can hope for is an evocation of the tension between those individual motivations which the researcher is privileged to discover and the broad strictures and preferences of the social groups within which these individuals live. In any event, a longer list of questions and a more global approach to musical interaction in future research could change the situation radically. In the following pages I have brought together a few examples of work that has been done in this area and indicate some connections that may be drawn.

By asking how interaction is evaluated in a given society or culture, we can begin to formulate goals which may not be readily accessible through direct questioning. Answers may be couched in terms of sound ideals such as fullness, tight coordination, blend, or diversity, or human qualities revealed through sound like compatibility, support, challenge, or mutual inspiration. To a certain extent this parallels a distinction between culturally and socially prescribed goals, with cultural prescription concerning aesthetic effect and social prescription entailing consideration of status, roles, and codes of behavior, the ethics of music-making both inside and outside the performance event.

Interactive goals conceptualized in terms of sound ideals cover a wide range. Feld tells us, for example, that the "Kaluli prefer sounds to be dense, compact, without breaks, pauses, or silences. When two people sing together, the subtleties of the shifting length of overlap (or with a

leader and group, the nuances of the alternations) are the locus of aesthetic play and tension" (1986: 23). Balinese musicians strive, among
other things, for interlocking so smooth that the individual parts blend
into a single composite. In the modern *kebyar* style they also achieve
instantaneous shifts through overt interaction in response to dramatic
cues. On the other hand, Javanese musicians traditionally favor harmonious ensemble achieved through subtle interaction, with many gradual
transitions and some temporal leeway in the coincidence of many parts.
That both Balinese and Javanese musicians can invoke the concept of
communal cooperation or harmony (*rukun, gotong royong*) as an interactive model for music shows how careful one must be in connecting
musical ideals with social ones as Keeler (1975), Sutton (1979), and Suyenaga (1984) do. There is in fact a harmoniousness, a communal aspect
to these two traditions that contrasts sharply with the individual prominence favored by the conventional interactive networks and structures
of Hindustani music, for example, but there are nuances to this spirit of
cooperation that require fine-grained description if we are to contrast
Javanese and Balinese interaction.

Attainment of a particular physical or mental state is another type of
interactive goal that is basically aesthetic in nature. The "ringing" sonority mentioned above in connection with Bulgarian singing and barbershop quartets exemplifies achievement of a physical sensation as a measure of successful interaction.[19] Arab instrumentalists' goal of inducing
saltanah (a deep immersion in the mode) in a singer through an intensi-
fying sequence of modal statements exemplifies mental state as goal
(Racy 1988: 146). This avenue of exploration leads, of course, to a consideration of interaction between musicians, dancers, and trancers, an
area pioneered by Rouget (1985).

Blending and distinctiveness are contrasting aesthetic goals that may
express ideals of sound and of human interaction. The potential for
blend or distinctiveness can be assessed by evaluating the instrumentation of an ensemble, in terms of variety of instrument types, timbres and
playing techniques, and the relative preponderance of independent and
interdependent roles in the interactive network, looking for relationships such as doubling and interlocking that generally require close synchronization. Thus, Racy links his argument that the Arab *takht* is characterized by individuality and compatibility to the heterophony typical
of this ensemble and to the instrumentation, which consists of plucked

19. Commenting on Averill's (1990) paper, Mark Forry noted that Yugoslav men speak of
vocal sonorities causing their hair to stand on end.

strings of differing timbre (*'ud* and *qanun*) played in different registers and contrasting sustained sounds (violin and an end-blown flute) also differentiated by register, all of these instruments being well matched in volume with each other and with the frame drum that completes the ensemble (1988: 142–43). He also notes that these ideals are "violated, restricted or simply modified" in modern Arab orchestras with their large string sections and emphasis on uniformity of unison or octave playing (1988: 158). In the contrasting Balinese and Javanese examples cited earlier there is a notable difference between the sections of a Balinese *gamelan gong kebyar,* which demand perfect unity among members in order to play precise unison or interlocking parts, and the somewhat looser Javanese *gamelan,* in which most instrument types are played by a single person, thus requiring less uniformity and giving more scope to individuality. This contrast is directly linked to musical content: the Balinese need for precise interlocking by groups of musicians severely limits the possibilities for improvisation, whereas the looser coordinative requirements of a Javanese *gamelan* allow improvisation, however limited, by most members of the ensemble.

Competition is a basic human behavior which is expressed musically in many ways, highlighted, condoned, or suppressed by interactive networks and structures and codes of interactive behavior. Competitive interaction involves challenges, rankings, excitement, and tests of competence sometimes similar to other competitive events. In its baldest form the goal may be a simple matter of endurance, as Nattiez describes for the Inuit *katajjaq,* in which two women "repeat a brief motif at staggered intervals, until one of the women is forced to stop, having either run out of breath or tripped over her own tongue" (1991: 56). Wade points to competition and challenge as primary motives in Hindustani performance, citing two examples: *larant,* in which the *tabla* player attempts to match the *sitar* or *sarod* player's rhythm as closely as possible in simultaneous performance, and *sawal-jawab,* in which the *tabla* player repeats the rhythm just played on the *sitar* or *sarod* (1984b: 26). A South Indian vocalist can challenge and even attack a violinist by singing a *pallavi,* a complex composition which the violinist must repeat precisely: "Every accompanist should have a vast knowledge of the form, so that he can face any situation. Otherwise, a *pallavi* can be used as a weapon against his reputation and dignity" (Shankar 1974: 115).

The cutting contests in which jazz musicians have matched wits and improvisational skills have played a formative role in the development of new styles. Ross Russell sums up a chapter devoted to Kansas City jam sessions thus:

> Over the years the jam session . . . brought about the interchange of ideas
> among local and visiting musicians, set high standards for performance, sub-
> jected them to the pressure of head to head competition, and put the final
> touch of confidence on talent ready for greater achievement. It also served to
> bring unknown talents to the public eye and to the attention of band leaders.
> (1971: 30.)

Participation in such a jam session tested and augmented a musician's
competence. Victory delivered a direct reward of enhanced status with
the possibility of better employment and new creative associations.

We need to ask not only how musicians are expected to interact in
performance but what is in it for the individual musician. Taking a look
at the symphony orchestra, and leaving aside for the moment the aesthetic developments that have spurred the growth of this type of ensemble in Western Europe and later in other parts of the world, one
must wonder at the rise and continued existence of an institution in
which highly talented and trained individuals subject themselves to the
direction of conductors, authoritative by calling and sometimes tyranni-
cal, too, to the financial control of management, and to the potentially
deadening repetition of repertoire in concert after concert. Beyond the
financial stability, what is it that brings a musician to choose this career
over solo or chamber music opportunities? How is it, for example, that
a Western composer has a mandate to use the instruments, and therefore
the musicians, as he or she sees fit, so that it is not at all beyond the
realm of plausibility to keep one of these highly trained and talented
individuals on stage to play a few notes or phrases, while another group
of musicians is called upon to play repetitive figuration seemingly for
hours on end?

Particular interactions may be motivated by the need to stave off disaster caused by miscommunication or lapse of memory. Michael Tree
describes a Guarneri mishap:

> In the middle of the rather fast movement there comes a *fermata* bar, rather
> suddenly, and then I always expect that the attack after the *fermata* will come
> in very quickly—almost like a singer taking a quick breath and coming right
> in. But Arnold [first violinist] didn't do that, and I almost fell off my chair,
> because I had committed myself. And so, of course, I immediately had to
> backtrack. (quoted in Fink and Merriell 1985: 44.)

Unfortunately he does not tell us how he backtracked. The ways in
which a skilled musician copes with such mishaps are intimately related
to the tolerances of the interactive system and should be a prime area
of research.

Interactive responses to forgetting may take a number of shapes: a musician may feel lost and project or signal this, asking for help by means of visual signs or a drop in volume and assuredness of performance; or a musician may feel that someone else is performing his or her part wrong and strive to get that person's attention and set that person back on the right track, again by visual or sonic means. A whole ensemble may begin to come apart at the seams if several musicians are uncertain at the same moment. Knowledge and self-assurance must then be brought into play by at least one musician, or preferably a nucleus of musicians who are sure of themselves, to keep the music going. These musicians need not fulfill leading roles in the normal interactive network, but they must be playing parts that enable them to reassert fundamental frameworks—melodic, temporal, or otherwise—and remind others of the proper course to follow.

Interaction may break down when musicians do not agree on the sequence or progression of events. If such problems cannot be solved by reference to authority vested in a member of the ensemble, an appeal must be made to some other person, to artifact (a score, a recording), or to memories of past performances. A guiding artifact may be the piece as it is known or conceived with standard performances as a reference, or it may be a particular notated version to which performers are responding in their own ways while endeavoring to make music together. Some of the complexities this multitude of possibilities can engender arose in a clash I witnessed at a rehearsal one evening in Java. The musician who was hired to teach and lead the group wrote notation for a piece on the blackboard. He was challenged by a foreign student of *gamelan*, who said that she had the piece differently from her teacher, Martopangrawit. The leader deferred to her because Martopangrawit was his teacher, too (and perhaps also because he was taken aback by her behavior), and substituted the student's version of the piece for the one he knew well. His own authority, which had been unquestioned in the group, was suddenly called into question by someone of lesser competence who invoked a greater authority who was not even present.

Other challenges can occur within an ensemble. They may spur the musicians on to greater heights, or they may cause more or less serious deterioration of the performance and the ensemble. A clash between individual goals or individual and group goals is potentially problematic, but may bring to the surface aspects of interaction that would otherwise remain hidden from outside view. With the spread of heavily amplified popular musics during the past few decades, soundmen have attained significant power over the balance and overall dynamic intensity of musical performances. A soundman must negotiate the conflicting demands of musicians who want to be heard at or above the level of others in the band. Depending on his ability and desire to stand up to band members' conflicting demands, he may achieve a position of authority as final arbiter, shaping a gestalt that none of the band members can directly control.

Excitement may be one of the more widespread goals of musical interaction. Cumulative loudness is just one way, perhaps the coarsest, of generating excitement. Excitement is also linked with spontaneity, which may derive from a string quartet negotiating a challenging score or an orchestra and soloist well matched in a concerto performance. Aleatoric freshness has been sought by Lutoslawski and other contemporary Western composers who set up unusual interactive networks by writing scores with repetitions for individual musicians cued loosely enough to other parts to guarantee irreproducible results.

Spontaneity in ensemble performance goes hand in hand with the foregrounding of improvisation and interaction, since improvised ensemble musics must rely heavily on interaction for charting a sequence or progression through an established sequence. Jon Higgins connected the indeterminacy of Bharata Natyam dance—which keeps accompanying musicians on their toes—with the goal of spontaneity when he wrote that the dancer "may omit or repeat or otherwise lengthen or shorten. These are the options of a dancer who refuses to tie herself to an inflexible plan, knowing that her greatest moments as an artist spring from the freedom to make spontaneous choices" (1973: 181).

A final pair of contrasting dance genres is presented here to bring out other aspects of spontaneity as an interactive goal. The point of comparison is the link between choreographic flexibility and performer interaction, not the equivalence of these dances. The Javanese *gambyong* dance offers an example in which an important kind of spontaneity has largely been abandoned but not forgotten. This type of dance is structured in such a way that the drummer changes his pattern at the end of each cycle, alerting the dancer to perform the matching movement pattern during the next cycle. After the fixed initial patterns the sequence of patterns is flexible so long as an alternation between standing and moving patterns is observed. However, many musicians claim that dancers have become so accustomed to fixed choreographies that they are no longer capable of following the drummer.

Several types of solo male Balinese dance, on the other hand, allow the dancer a great deal of flexibility in choreography, which is reflected in the drumming, since the drummer must echo the dancer's every move. As the *gamelan* plays a short repetitive melody, the dancer can cue an *angsel,* a rhythmic break, at any moment.[20] For the dancer an *angsel* requires relatively little movement, but the drummer must increase the intensity of his playing dramatically. A dancer who wishes to best a drummer can keep an *angsel* going virtually indefinitely with little effort while he wears the drummer out. This is not the primary goal of the dance by any means, but it is a potential of the interactive network, system, and structure that has been exploited more than once for reasons of personal rivalry (Dibia, personal communication).

Interactive motivation may be positive or negative in nature, a goal to be achieved or failure to be averted, but it is bound to be a factor at some level in any ensemble performance. In the most precisely rehearsed performance there is still a certain flexibility or lack of predictability, as the outcome depends on the interaction of the players. Often there is more to interaction than that: the adding together and blending or matching of contributions from multiple sources may result in something greater than the sum of the parts. A unique excitement can be generated in ensemble performance as players negotiate the dangers of high speed and wide-ranging excursions of various sorts, stretching the net of referential well-being without falling through the holes.

20. See Tenzer (1991: 50), for example.

CHAPTER EIGHT

MUSICAL INTERACTION IN
JAVANESE *GAMELAN*

The flexibility of Javanese *gamelan* performance makes interaction fundamental to this tradition. Performance decisions ranging from the choice of pieces to be played to many aspects of the way in which these pieces will be performed can be spontaneous because the core competence includes extensive knowledge of interactive networks, systems, and structures. An essential part of the Javanese music-making experience is missing in those rare performances that are completely predetermined—cues turn to signals, and the sense of spontaneity is lost; but even then the plan is often altered in performance, either because one of the musicians forgets and gives a cue leading to an alternate route or because of external pressures such as the time restrictions of radio broadcasting or recording.

Neither the spontaneity nor the systematicness of this interaction is fully conveyed in writings on Javanese music. Most statements are normative and apply only to pieces known as *gendhing* and to the context of *klenèngan*, not dance or theater performances. Contradictions in these writings are a pale reflection of the variety of actual practice: nearly every aspect of interaction depends on context, and interactive priorities are shuffled from one musical genre to the next. This variety is greater still when one considers individual musicians' preferences, strengths, and weaknesses and the interpersonal dynamics of performance.

To convey the basis of this interaction and the extent and nature of variation, I have selected a few contrasting musical structures and performance contexts. Thus, I begin with an analysis of interaction in *klenèngan* in three genres that differ significantly with regard to interactive network, system, and structure, and then proceed to briefer discussions of interaction in other contexts and the interpersonal aspects of music-making.[1] The three contrasting genres are defined by formal distinctions and performance practice: a *gendhing* is metered, has a well-defined, symmetrical, and cyclical structure, and is played by the full *gamelan;* a *palaran,* played by a large subset of the *gamelan,* has a far less regular strophic structure; a *pathetan* is a short, noncyclical piece played by a small nucleus of musicians. The degree of coordination between musicians differs for each genre and is reflected in the sense of ensemble. In *gendhing* and most other *gamelan* genres a uniform metrical framework preordains simultaneous arrival for all parts (except the relatively free *pesindhèn* and *suling*) at important structural points that occur with great regularity and are clearly articulated by colotomic instruments.[2] *Palaran* occupy a median position between the almost amorphous flexibility of *pathetan* and the relative rigidity of *gendhing:* instrumental and vocal parts are synchronized over a metrical underpinning, but large-scale links are loose. No rigid temporal framework binds the performers in *pathetan:* since there is no common beat and the individual parts are not fixed to begin with, they can mesh with each other in loose synchronization in an infinite number of ways.

In performance, one *gendhing* is likely to be followed directly by others which are based on shorter cycles but are not necessarily shorter in performance time; other types of pieces may follow these. A *pathetan* may precede this medley and almost always concludes it; several *palaran* may be inserted toward the end. A series of such medleys constitutes a *klenèngan,* a music-making occasion which may be linked to some celebration or other event, but has its own logic of progression (Brinner 1989/90).[3]

GENDHING

The term *gendhing* can denote (1) *gamelan* music in general, (2) any *gamelan* composition, (3) only those compositions that are regularly structured, or (4) in the most narrow sense, a subset of the last category. The term is used here in the third sense to include pieces with cycles of 8 to 256

1. Limitations of space preclude discussion of regional variation.

2. Judith Becker (1979) discusses the correlation between number of coincident parts and relative structural significance.

3. Sutton discusses the range of contexts for such music-making (using the Yogyanese term *uyon-uyon* [1982: 22–23]).

Instrument	Number of players
rebab, gendèr, gambang, gendèr panerus, celempung, suling	6
bonang, bonang panerus, slenthem	3
kendhang	1–2
gong, kempul, kenong, kethuk, kempyang	2–4†
saron demung, saron barung, saron peking	3–8*
pesindhèn	1–5*
gérong	2–5*
TOTAL	18–33

† Depending on whether musicians play more than one instrument each.
* Total occasionally exceeds this normal range.

Fig.15. Composition of a full *gamelan*

beats in length. *Gendhing* constitute the vast majority of pieces in the *gamelan* repertoire—approximately nine hundred are notated in Mloyo-widodo's three-volume collection of the Solonese repertoire (1977)—and the bulk of any performance. A large *gendhing*, consisting of two sections, each with a melody cast in one or more long cycles of 64, 128, or 256 beats, may easily last fifteen or twenty minutes.

Interactive Network

The constitution of a Javanese *gamelan* is variable: the number of musicians in a full *gamelan* may range from fewer than twenty to more than thirty (see fig. 15). This variation in size is mainly a function of the number of singers, female and male, and the number of musicians playing *saron*. These are the only parts that are doubled (*saron* and male chorus) or duplicated (female soloists generally sing in alternation). Smaller *gamelan* ensembles, such as *gamelan gadhon* (featuring the softer instruments) and *cokèkan* (featuring plucked zithers), have considerably fewer instruments and instrumentalists may double as singers. The following analysis refers to the full *gamelan*, in its many variations, but applies in most respects to smaller ensembles, too.

There are many facets to the interactive network of a *gamelan*, even within the restricted formal context of *gendhing*. This has engendered a variety of relatively brief and simplistic descriptions that are couched chiefly in terms of groups (i.e., subnetworks) defined by musical function or domain and roles distinguished mainly in terms of leaders and supporters, with occasional reference to requisite levels of competence. Figure 16 illustrates the main conflicts and congruencies between groupings noted by Martopangrawit (1984: 12), Sumarsam (1984a: 112),

Martopangrawit	Time/Irama		Melody/Lagu		
Sindoesawarno	Rhythm		Skeletal	Flowering	
Sumarsam	Structure	Time	Abstraction	Mediation	Elaboration
Wasitodiningrat front		*kendhang* 1		*bonang* **3**	*rebab* **4** *gendèr* 4
middle	*gong* *kenong*		*slenthem* **2** *demung*		*gambang* 4 *celempung* *suling*
back	*kempul* *kethuk* *kempyang*		*saron barung*	*bonang pan.* *saron pan.*	*gendèr pan.*

KEY

Numbers 1 to 4 indicate Surakarta court ranking according to Mloyowidodo; all unnumbered instruments are of the lowest rank

pan. = panerus

Single underline = instruments of the soft ensemble

Double underline = instruments of the loud ensemble

No underline = instruments common to loud and soft ensembles

Fig. 16. Functional divisions of a Central Javanese *gamelan*

Wasitodiningrat (Hood 1984: 92–93), Sindoesawarno (1987: 315, 318), and Mloyowidodo (personal communication).[4]

Musicians and scholars divide the *gamelan* on the basis of three distinctions: distinctions between time-keeping instruments and melodic parts (including voice); distinctions between levels of abstraction and elaboration of the melodic line; or distinctions between two dynamic levels which are linked to performance practice, repertoire, and context. In essence these are distinctions of domain. They are all valid, representing particular viewpoints within Javanese culture and reflecting different facets of the complex reality of *gamelan,* but they are difficult to combine in a single model.

The contrast between soft and loud groups is a common functional division of the *gamelan* that is linked to specific performance contexts and practices. The loud *gendhing soran* are played without the instruments of the soft-sounding group, *palaran* are played without the loud group, and many *gendhing* may be performed in such a way that the louder parts come to the fore in some sections and recede to the background in oth-

4. Kartomi compares Javanese classifications, including some of those cited here, but does not distinguish between the relative musical importance of the instruments and the status of the people who play them (1990: 84–107).

ers (instruments not included in either category are played with both groups). This division has important implications for interaction, as it groups performers in particular relationships.

Martopangrawit, Sindoesawarno, and Sumarsam offer related, but increasingly more complex, divisions of the *gamelan* (hardly surprising, since all three were associated with the same educational institutions). The basic distinction is between *irama* and *lagu*, the realms of time and melody. Sindoesawarno adds a basic distinctive feature of simultaneous sound structure, contrasting "flowering" (i.e., elaborating) and skeletal melodic groups. Sumarsam takes this further and distinguishes between those elaborating parts that are distinct from the skeletal melody and those that mediate between these two groups. He also distinguishes between drums, which regulate progression through time, and gongs, which demarcate musical structure by marking off progression through time. He is the only one to include singers (as part of the elaboration group, not shown in fig. 16), but the other authors cited here would certainly maintain that singers are an integral part of the *gamelan*.

The front row–back row distinction that was discussed in earlier chapters is sometimes refined by the addition of a middle category. I have selected Wasitodiningrat's version of this classification because it is available in print (excerpted from an interview conducted by Hardja Susilo [Hood 1984: 92–93]) and is corroborated in most respects by an incomplete list published by Sindoesawarno (1984: 398). In this hierarchical model, instrument placement correlates with levels of elaboration or abstraction and degrees of competence.

Delegation of responsibility within the network of musicians is mentioned in virtually every source dealing with *gamelan*. Terms such as *kewajiban* (obligation) and *bertanggung jawab* (to be responsible) also surfaced frequently in my conversations with musicians. Responsibility links a musician, by virtue of the instrument he or she plays, to a particular domain and conveys authority over that domain. In the models represented here this is reflected by distinguishing leader and supporter roles.

It is instructive to look at some Javanese definitions of musical leadership and support. Soekanto (also a colleague of Martopangrawit and Sindoesawarno) defines the role of the leader (*pamurba*) as "he who has power, who has authority, who leads (*anuntun*) . . . the leader of *irama* is the *kendhang* . . . who has authority or who leads and arranges [regulates] the *irama* of the music-making" (Soekanto 1966: 4, my translation) and contrasts this with *pamangku*:

> *Pamangku* . . . means here: the one who receives, who follows (*tutwuri*), who accompanies (*ngetutake*). *Slenthem*, *saron demung*, *saron barung* and *saron panerus* (*pe-*

king) are the ones whose responsibility in the performance of *gendhing* is to become the *pamangku lagu*, meaning the ones who follow the playing of the *bonang barung* . . . the *kethuk* is the one which in the performance of *gendhing* has the responsibility of being the *pamangku irama*, meaning the *kethuk* player always just follows the *irama* of the *gendhing* . . . If the *irama* of the *kendhang* asks/ invites (*ngajak* [N.B., not commands]) for *seseg*, the *kethuk* player must follow in speeding up; contrariwise, if the *irama* of the *kendhang* asks to slow down the *kethuk* player must then follow in slowing down. (Soekanto 1966:4, my trans- lation.)

Martopangrawit expands on this distinction:

> The supervisor of *irama* (*pamurba irama*) is the player with the authority to set the *irama*. Such is the case with the supervisor of *lagu*, also. The *rebab*— i.e., the *rebab* player—has the authority to make decisions, and can also be called the leader. The *rebab* player determines the course of the melody. All decisions relating to *irama*, such as speeding up, slowing down, and changing from one irama to another, are under the absolute leadership of the *kendhang* player. As to choosing the *gendhing*, choosing whether to play in the *sléndro* or *pélog* tunings, or deciding whether or not to move to the higher register (*ngelik*), the *rebab* player is in charge . . .
>
> The upholding instruments are those that carry out a task to enable the supervisor's ideas to reach fruition. For example, the supervisor of *irama* may wish to change from one level of *irama* to another, and the instruments that uphold the *irama*—like soldiers—must not deviate. They should not set their own tempi, for not only will their efforts be in vain, but they will disrupt the flow of the *gendhing*. The case is similar with the supporters of *lagu*, also. If the supervisor of *lagu* determines the *gendhing* in the *buka* of, say, Ladrang Moncer, but after the *gong* the *gender* player proceeds to play Ladrang Wilujeng—thus, disobeying the supervisor of *lagu*—the result will be a breakdown of the *gend- ing*. (1984: 15.)

Among the many noteworthy aspects of this passage, the most perti- nent at present is that Martopangrawit explicitly raises the prospect of interactive failure in the first pages of a major treatise on *gamelan* theory and practice, in recognition of the importance of interaction in Javanese music-making. It is also telling that he defines the supporter's role as enabling the leader's ideas to reach fruition, implying that there is a unity of conception based on undeviating obedience by the supporting players. By contrast, Soekanto has the leader asking or inviting the oth- ers to follow him. Martopangrawit's idiosyncratic ideas about leadership were expressed in his own playing, which was extremely dynamic and aggressive by Javanese standards, and in comments he made to me about particular younger musicians being "good at following," the highest praise I heard him accord anyone.

Wasitodiningrat and Mloyowidodo report more detailed hierarchies based on considerations of competence. It is worth returning to Mloyo-widodo's rationale for the Solonese court ranking of musicians[5] because competence is linked to interactive concerns. The ranking is actually more complex than shown in figure 16, because different types of drums are distinguished. The small *ketipung*, technically the least demanding drum and one of the easiest instruments in the *gamelan*, is assigned to the head musician because he can subtly direct changes of tempo through this instrument.[6] The large *kendhang gendhing* is played by the second in command, who interprets the commands of the head.[7] These two drum-mers are ranked at the top because they must know the repertoire inti-mately in terms of the appropriate sequence of events for each piece and the proper progression through that sequence, a progression that is effected largely through changes of tempo guided by the drummers. The *rebab* player, who actually chooses which pieces to play and guides the melodic instruments, is ranked beneath the *slenthem* and *bonang* play-ers because they must be more competent than him: they must know more of the repertoire so that they can respond to any introductory cue that the *rebab* might play. The *rebab* player can know a smaller portion of the repertoire because he will only choose pieces that he knows. The *bonang* and *slenthem* players, who together lead and determine the precise details of the *balungan*, have no such luxury and must be prepared at a moment's notice to play whatever the *rebab* dictates. The *gendèr*, though technically more difficult than *kendhang, bonang,* or *slenthem*, is ranked lower still because it offers a musician no direct authority over the course of the piece. Furthermore, as noted in chapter 4, Martopangrawit and Mloyowidodo both claimed that a *gendèr* player could play a piece adequately in a fairly formulaic way, wending his or her way from one cadential pitch to the next without knowing or remembering the precise details of the *balungan*.

The importance of functional domains in this ranking is demon-strated in the transferal of leadership roles to functionally equivalent instruments in the ceremonial *gamelan sekatèn*. In this unusual ensemble of

5. This was discussed in chapter 4 and was corroborated in almost all respects by Marto-pangrawit.

6. Remember that this rationale for ranking applies only to the Solonese court, where musicians were generally constrained to playing the instruments commensurate with their rank. There is much greater freedom elsewhere and even in the courts today.

7. It is interesting that the reverse relationship was prescribed in Yogyakarta (Hood 1988: 189).

enormous instruments (the smallest metallophone in *gamelan sekatèn* is equal in size to the largest metallophone of a regular *gamelan*) there is no *rebab* or *kendhang* and leadership is shared between the large gong chime (*bonang*), played by two musicians, and the largest metallophone (*demung*). Each *gendhing* is preceded by a long ametrical solo played on the higher row of the gong chime. According to Mloyowidodo (personal communication) the musician who plays the *kendhang* in the regular *gamelan* plays the lower row of gongs in *gamelan sekatèn* and cues the other musicians to emphasize a cadential pitch in the melodic solo: "He's the one who produces the cadential cue (*salahan*)." The regular *rebab* player sits at the *demung*, where he retains the leadership role of choosing the *gendhing* that follows the introduction. The *gendèr* player faces him at the other *demung*, maintaining his role of reinforcing the beat. The fundamental assumption here seems to be that *interactive competence is primary:* the best person to lead the *gamelan sekatèn* to each cadential pitch (*sèlèh*) is the regular drummer, the best person to choose the piece to be played is the one who does it most often for the regular *gamelan* (the *rebab* player), and stability of tempo is assured by pairing the *rebab* player with the *gendèr* player, who plays the most important filling-in role in the regular *gamelan*.

While the sources surveyed here agree that temporal and melodic leadership is divided between *kendhang* and *rebab*, respectively, in reality interactive decision making is considerably more complicated. Most of the evidence that I will present to support this contention is drawn from observation of actual practice, but written sources give a few indications of complications. Poerbapangrawit writes that "the relative pace of this melody is determined by either the *kendhang*-player or the *bonang*-player" (1984: 417), and Kunst says that the *kendhang* "leads—be it according to hints given by the *rebab*" (1949: 212). This is echoed in the *Pakem Wirama*, which states that tempo changes should be initiated by *rebab* or *bonang* and maintained by *kendhang* because the *kendhang* player may not be familiar with the *gendhing* being played (Hood 1988: 203–4). Here we see inequality in competence due to differing specializations or levels of experience taken as a basis for analyzing interaction, just as it serves as a rationale for the Solonese court ranking described above (though with a different conclusion). Wasitodiningrat has also said on several occasions that the *rebab* player can indicate a change of *irama* to the drummer, and he taught me as a *rebab* player to reinforce certain of his drumming cues to the rest of the *gamelan*.

Kunst suggests hearing the rich texture of *gamelan* in terms of five functional groups—cantus firmus, colotomic, countermelody, paraphrasing, agogic—without actually noting which instruments fit in each

(1949: 247), perhaps realizing that some instruments can be made to fulfill one function or another, depending on performance context and the performance practice determined by context. Although problematic in other respects, his classification is closer to the reality of shifting networks than the more static and rigid Javanese models because of this overlap of functions. At one point he writes: "Although, as we said before, the orchestral leader usually plays the *kendhang*, yet it may also happen *that he prefers the rebab*" (1949: 223, my emphasis). This suggests a hierarchy of nested or overlapping domains rather than a clean split between melody and rhythm.

Rebab leadership is one of the more puzzling aspects of *gamelan* interaction because the sound tends to get buried in the texture of the full ensemble. The instrument is not much of a match for a full *gamelan* unless performance conditions are optimal, yet this diminutive spike fiddle is consistently designated as the melodic leader. Only Sukamso has questioned this leadership in print (1992: 58–59), claiming that the ideal of *rebab* leadership is often contradicted in fact. Soekanto, for example, tries to explain the importance of the *rebab* through metaphors and etymologies: "The word *yatmaka* [soul] is from the word *yatma* [soul], which means *nyawa* [soul, spirit, life]. The *lagu* or *wiletan* [melody, embellished melody] of the *rebab* is the jewel of music-making (*tatabuhan*), so much so that it can be likened to the soul or spirit of the music-making of *gendhing*" (1966: 4, my translation). Kunst notes that "Javanese mysticism compares the *rebab* with breathing, and the *kendhang* with the heart-beat" (1949: 223, fn. 2). Thus, the power of the *rebab* is to be seen as emanating from within.

There are two pragmatic answers to this puzzle of inaudible leadership. First, the sound balance has changed since melodic leadership was assigned to the *rebab*: in the past the *rebab* player did not have to compete with electric amplification of the singers' voices, with the louder *ciblon* drumming style that has become increasingly popular, or with the greater volume of the larger and more numerous bronze instruments that constitute the "standard" modern *gamelan*. Second, the sound of the *rebab* can be made to carry when needed. The *rebab*'s complex timbre and the continuity of a *rebab* melody—it is the only completely continuous melodic line, since the vocal and *suling* melodies are broken with frequent pauses and the other parts are percussive—afford it an acoustic presence greater than its basic dynamic level warrants.[8] There are also stratagems to make the *rebab* melody heard. Some of the most important cues in-

---

8. The sustained sound of the *gendèr* and *gendèr panerus* can be continuous, too, but it blends in where the *rebab*'s more complex timbre stands out.

volve a dramatic glide to the upper register which cuts through the texture of the *gamelan*. A player can also place accents between beats when fewer of the loud percussive instruments are struck. Martopangrawit praised his grandfather for his use of *kosokan tunggakan*, an emphatic syncopated type of bowing, to highlight the *balungan* and make himself heard (personal communication).

The *rebab* player guides the melody mostly by hints and subtle anticipations, not feeding it note by note like the *bonang* player. Sutton writes that

> one of the most notable tendencies is for the *rebab* part to hint at a tone of hierarchical weight, such as *gatra* finalis, but to move toward a subsequent tone rather than to confirm what it has suggested . . . Similar flexibility is observable throughout and contributes to a steady state aesthetic by avoiding the cumulative action of progressing toward convergence with each *gatra* final. Some tones are stressed, others only hinted at. The *rebab* part may seem at times to be aiming for convergence with a *gatra* final only to change course, as if losing interest before completion and becoming enraptured by another. (1982: 183.)

This is because the *rebab* directive is realized by other musicians on other instruments: the *rebab* player has shown the way and is free to lead on to the next segment, which I take as highly directional and progressive, propelling one's attention forward even as other musicians work out the implications of the *rebab* player's earlier direction. One can also understand this in terms of Wasitodiningrat's teaching that the *rebab* player can choose at any moment whether to lead the *balungan*, prompt the singers, or play his own melody (personal communication).

Leadership roles associated with other parts are more limited for a variety of reasons. After the *rebab*, the *bonang* is the instrument most commonly cited for melodic leadership, and, as noted above, it may also be involved in rhythmic leadership. In loud-style pieces it is the undisputed melodic leader, but it is clearly subordinate to *rebab* and *kendhang* at other times, serving as a subsidiary leader of a subnetwork of metallophones playing the *balungan*. This is partly due to *bonang* playing techniques. While *mipil* is suited to leading because the player anticipates the *balungan*, taking pairs of notes and repeating them two or four times with some stylization (see fig. 10), the other *bonang* techniques are too abstract, often providing insufficient information about the melodic path.

There has been some debate over the extent of *gendèr* leadership in the many pieces classed as *gendhing gendèr*. The introduction (*buka*) to a *gendhing gendèr* is played on the *gendèr*, but once the introduction is over, it is not clear whether the *gendèr* player should have any more authority in these pieces than in others. In the nineteenth-century *Serat Sastrami-ruda*, we again find yet another instance of differences and deficiencies in competence being cited as the basis for a particular interactive network: "Although *gendhing gender* certainly don't use the *rebab* when played in *wayang*, since *gender* players nowadays rarely know *gendhing gender* they are led by the *rebab* player" (Kusumadilaga 1981: 49, my translation). The *gendèr* plays a number of essential roles, to be described shortly, but it is not well suited to leading the full ensemble because *gendèr* melodies are only loosely related to melodies played on other instruments and because the sound of the *gendèr*, characterized by soft attack and long sustain, permeates the texture of the *gamelan* but does not cut through it.

Singers are featured but never really lead the *gamelan* in the performance of a *gendhing*. This is perhaps due in part to a subtle status differentiation between instrumentalists and male singers and to a less subtle status differentiation between instrumentalists and female singers that is linked to gender. As for other instrumentalists, the colotomic parts and skeletal melody are too slow to enable the players to exert control over the long haul, but there are certain moments when the gong player takes the initiative and a strong *demung* player can certainly lead in fast, loud sections. The importance of the *demung* player increases dramatically in *wayang*, as we shall see in the next chapter.

Mediation and reinforcement, which are aspects of an interactive system, become roles, too, when they are matched frequently and consistently with particular instruments or players, as they are in *gamelan*. Rather than taking the initiative in determining the sequence or progression of the performance, these musicians ensure that communication takes place within the ensemble. When the *rebab* indicates that the melody should ascend to the high register (*ngelik*), other musicians, particularly the *gambang* and *bonang* players and the *pesindhèn*, follow along and in so doing reinforce the direction taken by the *rebab*. One can also view this sort of interaction as enrichment: the *rebab* and *gendèr* players together define the sense of *pathet* (mode) through their choices of patterns and their ways of surrounding important pitches and getting from one point to the next. The *gendèr* player reinforces the modal interpretation of the *rebab* and may even lead, depending on the relative seniority and experience of the two players. Similarly, the *gendèr* player reinforces and sometimes mediates in the domain of rhythm. It is possible to do this on other instruments, but the *gendèr* is most frequently cited as a referent. As a result it is the heart of smaller *gamelan* ensembles (*gamelan gadhon* and *cokèkan*), where it assumes greater responsibility for establishing and stabilizing *irama*.

Because of the integrated nature of *gamelan*, any part can offer some reference to musicians playing other parts. But some parts are more central than others and offer more of a foundation. The colotomic instruments offer a musician orientation within the cyclical structure of a *gendhing* while the *slenthem* or *saron* players assert the *balungan*, providing a solid reference for the freer-flowing parts. The musicians who play foundation parts and provide reference to others have a responsibility to follow the leaders not only for their own sake but for those who may be relying on them. Gong and *kenong* players, for example, must have a strong sense of form and *kendhang* cues. Similarly, the *slenthem* player should be one of the more knowledgeable players, not just knowing more pieces but also having an unerring feel for *irama* and *kendhang* cues and the connections between the *slenthem* part and the parts played on *gendèr* and *bonang*. A knowledgeable *slenthem* player frees the *bonang* player from the responsibility of leading the *balungan* too closely and allows him greater interpretive flexibility.

As this last point shows, musicians who follow also put constraints on those who lead. One musician said that when he leads a *gamelan* and considers playing a difficult piece at a *klenèngan*, he "looks around" first to see if those seated at the most demanding instruments are capable of doing the piece justice. Constraints on leadership are also recognized in a passage from the *Pakem Wirama* that states that the drummer should watch the *gendèr, gambang, bonang, bonang panerus,* and *demung imbal* (interlocking) to see that the *irama* is comfortable (Hood 1988: 203). At each level of *irama* the drummer must be sure that the fast parts are proceeding at a speed which is neither impossibly fast nor so slow that they drag, causing musicians to double their own speed (i.e., shift *irama*). Certain court dances break this convention: the correct tempo is so fast that the *gambang* player can no longer play normal patterns, but rather than switch to a lower ratio he must alternate hands or play syncopations which imply a steady flow that is physically impossible to maintain with regular *gambang* patterns.

Some of the relationships noted here constitute subnetworks. The *kendhang* and *rebab* stand in special relationship to one another, as do the *rebab* and *gendèr*. When explaining a particular choice of melodic pattern for the *gendèr*, musicians often link it to the *rebab* melody and to the *pesindhèn's* vocal. The *gambang* player follows the *rebab's* lead closely in moving between upper, middle, and lower registers, but also may listen to the *gendèr* for choice of pattern and modal definition. Players of other elaborating parts (*panerusan*) such as the *suling, celempung,* and *gendèr panerus* have much in common, responding similarly (though with idiomatic differences) to the leaders' cues. Vocal parts, especially the female lines, are closely related to the *rebab* melody much of the time. Since a *pesindhèn*

a. *Lancaran*

beat	o o o o o o o o
kethuk	x x x x x x x x
kempul	x x x
kenong	x x x x
gong	x
composite	t . t N t P t N t P t N t P t N
	G

b. *Ladrang*, last phrase (*salahan*)

beat	o o o o o o o o
kempyang	x x x x
kethuk	x x x x
kempul	x
kenong	x
gong	x
composite	p t ptPtp t p N
	G

KEY

x = stroke   p = *kempyang*   t = *kethuk*   P = *kempul*   N = *kenong*   G = *gong*

Fig. 17 Interlocking colotomic parts

mainly sings out of phase, starting and ending each phrase later than the *rebab*, she can easily follow the *rebab*.

The male chorus, *gérong*, is a special subnetwork unto itself. These men have less individual freedom than most of the instrumentalists because they must sing in unison. Although they sing precomposed parts, there is substantial variation in these melodies so it is necessary to follow the lead of one singer. This group also fills the very different role of providing interlocking handclapping. As noted earlier, there is sufficient mutual sensitivity to allow them to switch easily between these two relationships.

The musicians who play colotomic instruments share similar concerns and form a unit that produces mutually related parts: the more frequently played instruments subdivide units of time demarcated by the less frequently played ones. In some dense colotomic structures played at high speed one can hear the *kenong* interlocking with the *kempul* and the *kethuk* interlocking with their composite (fig. 17a, a pattern that lasts about four seconds), or the *kethuk* interlocking with the *kempyang* (fig. 17b, also lasting about four seconds). The close links between these parts are recognized in the common practice of assigning *kempul* and gong to a single musician; *kethuk* and *kempyang* are also often played by a single musician, who may play *kenong* as well. As a group the colotomic players follow the drummer closely and create an ongoing temporal frame of reference for the rest of the ensemble.

The *bonang*, *slenthem*, and *saron* players form a subnetwork focused on the skeletal melody and its most directly linked elaborations. Within this grouping other relationships form, binding players in a mutual process of music-making, principally through interlocking between the two *bonang*, between two *saron* of the same size, or between *saron demung* and *slenthem*. Examples of this interlocking will be examined presently.

These subnetworks are determined by common performance goals and methods and by core players who offer focus and leadership. The parts played on *bonang*, *slenthem*, and *saron* are more closely related to one another than the parts played by the *panerusan* group, in which each member plays a unique instrument with a unique idiom. At the other extreme, the colotomic group of players are locked in the most rigid performance sequence and mainly alternate rather than play simultaneously. Other affinities and groupings do exist, but for present purposes this depiction should suffice. The fact that there are other ways of "slicing the cake" should simply be taken as an indication that the interactive network of Javanese *gamelan* is too complex to be contained in a single definition because relationships shift with context and sound structure.

While the positioning of *gamelan* instruments and performers varies considerably depending on the performance area and the number of instruments, certain aspects are faithfully maintained even in cramped quarters. The most important of these is an orthogonal layout in which all instruments are parallel or perpendicular to each other and to the front of the performance area (see Sutton 1982: 30). Instruments tuned to the *pélog* scale are placed at right angles to *sléndro* instruments of the same type so most of the the musicians in the ensemble are facing the same direction at any given moment. The elaborating instruments are generally placed toward the front, the skeletal melody parts in the middle, and the colotomic parts in the back. The softer instruments are usually grouped in one area while the louder ones are in another. *Saron* players who interlock with each other are seated in proximity as are the *bonang* players. The *rebab* player generally sits in the middle of the front row with his back to the *gamelan* and the resonator of his instrument facing forward projecting toward the audience and away from the *gamelan*. This is a symbolically important position, but it does not help overcome the acoustic obstacles that make it difficult for some to hear the *rebab*. The drummer, on the other hand, is situated efficiently in the center of the ensemble, where he is as equidistant as possible from the far-flung members of the ensemble.

Interactive System

One of the most noteworthy aspects of these arrangements is that they do not favor visual communication between the lead musicians or between these musicians and the others. Some musicians actually face away from the others, the *rebab* player's back is turned to most of the ensemble, and the drummer is only partially visible. This does not matter, because *gamelan* musicians rely almost exclusively on sonic cues. Aside from performances that include important visual components such

as dance or shadow play, visual cuing is only used for corrective purposes. One occasionally sees surreptitious hand gestures to indicate a
significant upcoming pitch or colotomic instrument or drum stroke (but
these visual prompts only work if the person in need of a prompt happens to look at the one offering it). Sindoesawarno, a leading educator,
writes that these prompts should be given "unobtrusively in movements
that do not disturb the atmosphere but are clear enough to be understood" (1987: 346).

Nonetheless, musicians can and do use their eyes on occasion. *Saron*
players are generally seated in such a way that they can see the *slenthem*
player's mallet and get an indication of the next pitch if they are uncertain. I have observed this to occur when the *balungan* is so extended that
a pitch is played only once every twelve seconds or so. The *slenthem*
player can actually ensure unanimity in this part by holding his mallet
for all to see over the pitch that he is about to play. Even leading musicians may refer to this in confusing passages (Paimin, personal communication). When musicians interlock on a single metallophone, seated
on either side, some visual coordination becomes essential to avoid
collisions.

But most cues and markers are conveyed through sounds that are integral to the musical "text." As part of the process of acquiring competence, musicians must attune their ears and minds to the many subtle
cues which are woven into the ongoing flow of the leading parts. It is
simplest to illustrate the wide variety of explicit cues used in the performance of *gendhing* in the examples of interactive sound structure below.
At this point it will suffice to note that cues can vary in length and
complexity from a single sound, such as the low-pitched drum stroke
that cues the gong, to a long and involved pattern, such as the drum
pattern that cues the *gamelan* to end a piece or the melodic introduction
to a *gendhing* played on the *rebab, gendèr,* or *bonang* that identifies the piece
for the other musicians and sets the basic mood and tempo. Most cues
affect all members of the *gamelan* directly or indirectly. For example, a
cue from the *rebab* to move to a high-register section of the piece directly
affects all melodic parts. It may not call for any changes in the colotomic
parts, which continue to mark the cycle, or the drumming, which continues to regulate tempo and coordination with a set drum pattern, but
the drummer and colotomic players need to notice this change in the
sequence in order to maintain their orientation.

Cues and responses are precisely tied to specific points in the sound
structure of *gendhing*, regulated not only by the metrical organization but
by larger cyclical and melodic considerations. Thus, the time gap be-

tween cue and response is well defined and does not vary at the player's discretion. This is one of the most important aspects of interaction in *gendhing*, one which distinguishes it from *palaran* and *pathetan*.

Some cues, melodic ones in particular, are echoed or reinforced by a number of players. Again, the *rebab's* signal to move to the high register is a good example because it is picked up by *bonang, gambang,* and *pesindhèn* and literally "resounds" throughout the *gamelan,* spread by their agency to all corners. There is also an aesthetic side to this seeming redundancy, for each echo is produced in a different instrumental (or vocal) idiom and enriches the original utterance.[9]

The colotomic parts are markers par excellence since they articulate points in the structure of the piece and serve as a reference for every other part in the *gamelan.* Musical thinking is oriented first and foremost toward the gong as final goal and demarcator of the largest cycle, the *gongan.* By extension, this type of thinking is applied to subdivisions of the *gongan,* the phrases (usually two or four in number) which are marked by terminating *kenong* strokes and together constitute a full *gongan.* Other markers offer different types of reference: the *kethuk* is particularly important as it delineates the *middle* of smaller units and serves as a marker for the *pesindhèn,* who generally begins to sing her phrases after a stroke on the *kethuk.*

The interactive system also involves the intricate relationship of interlocking parts. The two gong chimes, *bonang* and *bonang panerus,* exemplify this, with a well-defined leader-follower relationship. In the technique called *imbal* the *bonang* player repeats a pair of notes leading to the beat and the *bonang panerus* player fills in the "spaces" in time and pitch (fig. 18). In each mode there are a standard pair of pitches and several alternate pairs to which the *bonang* player can switch in order to respond to registral or modal aspects of the main melodic flow of the piece.[10] The *bonang panerus* player follows the lead of the *bonang,* playing whichever pair of pitches interlocks with the *bonang* pair. The order in which the two pitches are played may be altered at any moment by either of the players without relation to the other. Two or four beats of *imbal* are usually followed by a *sekaran,* a "flower" pattern leading to the principal pitch in the *balungan.* Reaching the point labeled X in figure 18, the *bonang* player can continue to play *imbal* or begin a *sekaran.* Depending on the *sekaran* chosen by the *bonang* player, the *bonang panerus* player may

9. See Sumarsam (1984a: 107, 111) and Susilo (1987: 7) for the views of two Javanese performer/scholars on the aesthetics of "redundant" ornamentation.

10. See Sutton (1993: 102) for a tabulation of common practice.

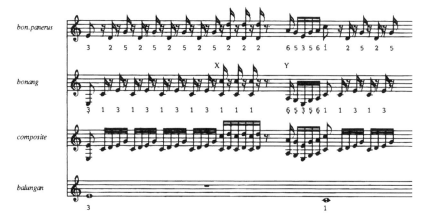

Fig. 18 Interlocking *bonang* relationships

continue to interlock, try to match the *bonang* pattern, or continue play-ing his offbeat pattern, although it no longer interlocks. Thus, the *bonang* player clearly leads, but the *bonang panerus* player sometimes has several options for response. If the *bonang* player repeats a pitch in octaves, the *panerus* player can easily respond by filling in with the upper neighbor played in octaves offbeat, but if the *bonang* plays a melodic pattern (such as that shown at point Y in fig. 18) the *panerus* player's response is less predictable: if the *bonang* pattern is a common one or the *panerus* player is familiar with the *bonang* player's style, he can match it; otherwise he may play a different *sekaran* leading to the same goal tone or go back to playing a pitch or a pair of pitches on the offbeat. These options are shown in figure 19.

This example illustrates a number of important features of Javanese musical interaction. It shows how a subnetwork functions both in accor-dance with the dynamics of its own internal system and structure and in relation to the larger network within which it is embedded, responding to some events (manifestation of beat, for example) and leading to oth-ers (such as the goal tone, which is in turn referential). It shows that while leader and follower can refer to the same external events, the leader may add more information and reinforce the referential frame-work: both players in this example refer to rhythm and pitch informa-tion gleaned from the rest of the *gamelan*, but the *bonang* player's part contains additional reference points for the *bonang panerus* player. Fur-thermore, the interlocking *bonang imbal* is an important stabilizer of the

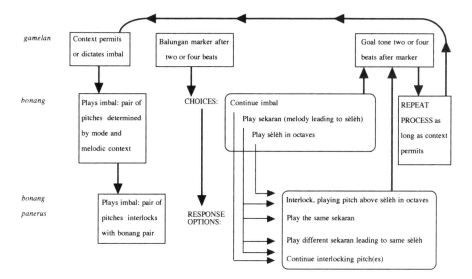

Fig. 19 Interactive decisions in an interlocking network

tempo and can serve as a rhythmic reference for other musicians. The example also demonstrates the difference between cues that demand a particular response and cues that give the responding musician several options.

This description may appear complex enough, but there are additional options. The rhythm of *imbal* is fairly regular, but the *sekaran* can be played off the beat in ways that are difficult to describe or notate. The *bonang* player can switch to a different pair of *imbal* tones at any time or throw in *sekaran*-like scraps of melody at other points than those I have indicated. *Bonang imbal* can be a highly personalized and improvisatory medium, particularly when played at the highest level of *irama*, known as *rangkep*, in which the basic beat is stretched to the utmost and the elaborating parts are fastest. In such situations the interlocking is extremely rapid but the sense of melodic progression becomes tenuous because the sequence of goal tones is so elongated. The *bonang* players depend on other members of the *gamelan* more than ever for orientation and affirmation of the beat and melody. When studying *bonang* from Mloyowidodo, known for his *bonang* playing, I requested that he demonstrate how to play *imbal* in *irama rangkep*. He declined, saying that he could not do so without the support of several other musicians for orientation and that if the whole *gamelan* were playing, then *"bisa hidup sendiri"* ([it/his playing] would come alive of its own accord). He also said that he needed a live situation so that he could respond spontaneously to his surroundings, imitating *sekaran* played on other instruments or even nonmusical sounds surrounding the performance such as the clinking of tea glasses on trays.

Interlocking interaction is also common for pairs of metallophone players. Depending on context the interlocking parts might be played on small, medium, or large *saron* (i.e., *peking, saron barung,* or *demung*) or even on *demung* and *slenthem*. Space does not permit as full an analysis of the interactive systems in these relationships as I have given for *bonang imbal,* but a few points should be made. There are two basic types of interaction, both of which involve an onbeat part and an offbeat part: (1) melodically complementary interlocking is produced when one player plays neighbor tones to the pitches chosen by the other player; (2) an echoing type of interlocking is produced when one musician imitates the other by striking the same pitch a half beat or quarter beat later resulting in repetition of each pitch. In either case, one player leads and the other follows, but the leader is not as dominant as the *bonang* player is in relation to the *bonang panerus*. Both types of interlocking demand split-second reactions from the player who follows: on several occasions I have witnessed a musician straining to echo another, trying to guess which pitch would be hit next (the derivation of these parts from the *balungan* is not fully predictable). The second point to be made is that when this interlocking involves the *slenthem,* this important foundational instrument suddenly shifts from playing fairly consistently on the beat to playing consistently off the beat. I have not noticed Javanese musicians struggling with this loss of a basic referent, but non-Javanese students of *gamelan* usually find this a truly wrenching experience the first few times, as it deprives them of one of the most important means of orientation.

Other types of imitation can emerge spontaneously in performance, momentarily linking musicians in relationships that are not sustained. Just as Mloyowidodo imitates patterns from other instruments when he plays *bonang,* the *suling* player can pick up a melody played on *gambang* or sung by the *pesindhèn*. Sumarsam gives an example of a common cross-rhythm that can be played in certain spots in a wide variety of pieces by drummer and *gendèr* and notes that "these moments of imitation increase the atmosphere of excitement in irama rangkep" (1975: 164); this pattern can also be imitated by the *bonang* players. Such imitative interaction is not systematic in any sense, depending solely on the initiative, taste, and talent of the musicians, but it is enabled by the systematic nature of the elaborating parts and the pervasiveness of certain melodic phrases.

Interactive Sound Structure

The simultaneously sounding parts of a *gamelan* are related in a stratified texture characterized by a clear hierarchy of rhythmic densities that correlates roughly with register, the faster parts tending to be higher in register than the slower ones. With few exceptions the rhythmic densities of the parts stand in fixed binary ratios to one another (2:1, 4:1, 8:1, etc.). This hierarchical system, ensconced in the idioms of the individual parts and in their mutual fit, ensures constant orientation to *irama* for all musicians. Furthermore, the melodic parts can generally be conceived as heterophonic representations of some shared melody manifested according to various idiomatic preferences and constraints. This leads to a high degree of independence around a unifying core: "One concept . . . may be manifest in many variant forms without necessarily becoming something else and without being inconsistent with the essential unity underlying the multiplicity" (Sutton 1982: 290). I have already alluded to the importance of this from an interactive standpoint in the discussion of interactive network: the simultaneous sound structure not only provides rhythmic orientation but also is referential in the complex domain of pitch with regard to general restrictions of mode and specific information about the path of the melody. Competent players can derive their parts from others thanks to their knowledge of the relationships between parts. Thus, simultaneous sound structure manifests the relationships of the interactive network.

Consecutive sound structure in *gendhing* is based on a few well-defined types of colotomically articulated cycles and on a general sequence of sections that is particularized for individual *gendhing* but still loose enough to allow for different progressions in the performances of a given piece. Only pieces that have been linked to a fixed choreography follow a fully preordained sequence. For all others the sequence is defined in performance through interaction among the musicians.

Every *gendhing* has a *buka*, a melodic introduction that identifies the piece modally and melodically to varying degrees. Some introductions are linked unambiguously to a single *gendhing* while others are common to several. A few are so widely used that they can be regarded as generic, conveying little information about the upcoming piece other than its tuning and mode. This essentially interactive goal of alerting other musicians to the identity of the piece is in fact one of the main purposes of the introduction: "During this introduction the players have an opportunity of getting into the atmosphere of the piece to be played and ensure proper 'teamwork'" (Kunst 1949: 311). Starting a piece with a solo melody that is joined at some point by the regularizing beat of a drum and then by the full ensemble is an elegant and serviceable solution to the problem of getting a large number of musicians going together, particularly when the selection of repertoire is spontaneous and is not communicated verbally. This practice is common to many other ensemble traditions, especially in Southeast Asia.

The *buka* itself can last about fifteen seconds, which ought to allow time for other musicians to identify the piece to be played, but many *gendhing* introductions start off in similar fashion and the particular piece is not identifiable until the last few notes. When I asked Harjito, for example, how musicians could tell whether Gendhing Gendu was required or Gendhing Lokananta, since they have the same *buka*, he answered that the identity of the piece would become clear four beats *after* the main section of the piece began, where the melodies of the two pieces diverge, and that the *rebab* player would show which path to take.[11] Mloyowidodo was less sanguine about the capability of musicians to interact properly in such a situation nowadays, recounting how he incurred the wrath of other musicians when he played *rebab* and led them through the seldom-played Gendhing Agul-Agul, which has the same introduction and first phrase as the more familiar Gendhing Kagok Laras. He said that only the drummer knew what he was doing. The *kenong* player failed to follow their combined lead and continued to mark sixteen-beat phrases as in Kagok Laras rather than the sixty-four-beat phrases of Agul-Agul.

The *kendhang* player joins the melodic soloist for the last four or eight beats of the introduction. His pattern may indicate to the other musicians whether the piece has a short cycle, such as a *ketawang* or *ladrang*, or a longer one. He also stabilizes the beat if the soloist has not already done so or changes it if he feels that it is too fast or too slow. In other words some of the leadership responsibilities are transferred at this point from *rebab* to *kendhang*. According to the *Pakem Wirama*, the soloist should set the appropriate tempo for a *gendhing* and not wait for the *kendhang* to regulate it (Hood 1988: 203), but many musicians play the initial part of a long introduction in a rhythm irregular enough to obscure a sense of beat rather than establish one.

From this point on there are many possibilities, which depend on (1) the colotomic form, which is strongly associated with certain performance practices and methods of progressing through a sequence, (2)

---

11. There are more extreme cases such as Gendhing Prihatin and Gendhing Semukirang which do not differ until the last phrase of the first *gongan*, over a minute into the piece; they share a *buka* with several other pieces.

characteristics associated with other methods of classifying *gendhing*, (3) the particular form of the piece and any special details of sequence, and (4) the cumulative choices of the leading musicians. It would require many pages to begin to enumerate all of the possibilities and follow them to their different conclusions.[12] It will suffice here to survey the interactive requirements and possibilities associated with one piece, Gendhing Gambirsawit. Later comparison with *palaran* and *pathetan* structures will further clarify the relationship between interactive processes and the sound structure of *gendhing*.

Gambirsawit, like several hundred other *gendhing*, consists of two main sections: a *mérong* and an *inggah*. The *mérong* is based on a sixty-four-beat cycle and is usually played several times. The *lik*, a related melody based on the same colotomic structure and performed mainly in the high register, is usually inserted once between repetitions of the *mérong*. The transition from *mérong* to *inggah* is accomplished within the *mérong* cycle. The *inggah* is then played several times and may be interrupted for vocal solos (*andegan*).[13]

Leadership within the interactive network devolves mainly upon *rebab* and *kendhang*, who communicate the decisions that determine the sequence of the piece and many aspects of the progression through this sequence. However, roles shift according to the interactive structure and other performers take on more limited leadership at several points, which will be examined in detail presently. The *rebab* player selects the piece, communicating his selection through the *buka*. In the course of the *mérong* he usually decides when to switch to the *lik*. His control of this transition may be usurped if the *gérong* sings the choral melody associated with a particular choreography, for then the onset of the *lik* is predetermined. The *rebab* may even cue the transition from *mérong* to *inggah*, but this must be mediated by *kendhang*. Some other *gendhing* have a transitional section (*umpak inggah*) which is cued by the *rebab* melody; only after this change in melody does the drummer take over control of the transition.

The *kendhang* player, for his part, controls both major shifts and small fluctuations in tempo from the moment that he joins the *rebab* player's *buka* until the end of the piece. The major shifts lead from one *irama* to another and, in some instances, serve in turn as cues to proceed to the next section or to conclude the piece. The drummer's leadership extends

12. Vetter (1986) has abbreviated descriptions of all the performance sequences and progressions played at the royal court in Yogyakarta during the course of an entire year!

13. As in many other *gendhing*, the *inggah* of Gambirsawit can be replaced with other pieces. Since this takes place by prior arrangement, this complication will not be considered here.

beyond the domain of temporal organization because his choice of *irama* and drumming style, particularly in the *inggah*, determines salient aspects of other musicians' performance. Sparse drumming in *irama* 2 calls for more subdued playing while florid elaborating patterns and livelier playing are invoked by a rapid and complex drumming style played on the *kendhang ciblon*, principally in *irama* 3 and 4. In the latter case, the drummer also causes a change in the interactive network: the two *bonang* players enter into an interlocking relationship (*imbal*, see fig. 19), and the male singers also clap hands in interlocking rhythms in those phrases which have no vocal part.

At certain moments the interactive network shifts. In the last few beats of a *mérong* cycle it is customary to stretch the beat, slowing to such an extent that there may actually be a brief pause before the gong is struck.[14] The normal tempo is resumed as soon as the gong is struck, without a gradual acceleration to parallel the retard. This distortion and resumption of the beat are achieved by a subtle interaction in which the *gendèr* and *kendhang* usually take leading roles: the *kendhang* initiates the retard while the *gendèr* is primarily responsible for reestablishing the beat after the gong or *kenong* sounds.

As the musicians approach the final gong of the piece, a similar interaction takes place (as we noted in chap. 2). The last beat leading up to the final gong is greatly stretched, and timing is determined by a network of musicians. The drummer sets this process in motion as he retards the beat during the last phrase, but control is transferred to the *pesindhèn* and gong player during the last beat. The *pesindhèn* stretches out her final melisma while everyone pauses. This silence has a ragged beginning because the musicians playing in the faster strata of the ensemble pause later than those who play at the slower paces. When the gong player decides to strike, after an interval of time that is constrained but not precisely defined by convention, he cues the rest of the *gamelan* to play the last note of the piece and the *pesindhèn* to finish her melisma (see fig. 20). The musicians usually strike the final note nearly but not precisely together because there is no clear referent for synchronization: the drummer has already ceased playing, and the gong itself has a slowly building attack that lacks the precise onset of a drum stroke or a stroke on one of the smaller colotomic gongs.

In the first and second phrases of the *inggah* the drummer has the option of cuing an *andegan*, bringing the entire *gamelan* to a halt in mid-cycle. The cue—a special drum pattern, usually played with a significant

14. In the longest cycles, four times longer than the *mérong* of Gambirsawit, a similar retard may also occur before the phrase-marking stroke of the *kenong*.

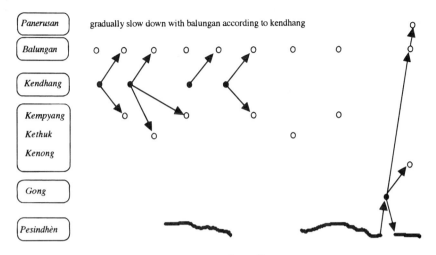

Fig. 20 Final gong: interaction at the end of a *gendhing*

retard of the beat—sets in motion a complex chain of events: the musicians slow down and pause just before playing their cadential note,
which they withhold until after the *pesindhèn* sings a melisma and the
gérong sing the first half of a stylized call. The *pesindhèn* then sings her last
note and the *gérong* sing the other half of their call. When all are silent,
the *gendèr* player prompts the *pesindhèn* with the first pitch or two of her
solo. The *pesindhèn* may ignore this and sing a different solo than the one
initiated by the *gendèr*, who then has no choice but to go along with
her, prompting key pitches in the rhythmically free vocal solo (Paimin,
personal communication). At a predetermined point the drummer enters, reestablishing the tempo and beat that were interrupted at the *andegan*. He is joined by the *gendèr* player, who reinforces the beat and its
principal subdivisions before the rest of the *gamelan* resumes playing.

The consecutive sound structure of a *gendhing* constrains interaction
by limiting the choices and timing of interaction. The cycle on which a
piece is based can be contracted or expanded through *irama* changes and
even interrupted at select points for vocal solos, but it cannot be trun-
cated or otherwise mutilated. Transitions to *lik* and *inggab*, changes of
irama, and other transformations can only be initiated at certain points
in the form. The *rebab* cue for the *lik* of Gambirsawit is only meaningful
if given about four beats before the gong of the *mérong;* the *kendhang* cue
to stop for an *andegan* is expected at two particular moments in the *inggab*.
The choice of *irama* and drumming style is likewise constrained. It would
be highly unusual (though not completely unheard of) to play the *kend-*

bang ciblon with its complex, rapid patterns during the *mérong*. Such drumming is suited to the *inggah* of Gambirsawit. Interlocking handclapping is likewise restricted by simultaneous and consecutive structure: the *gérong* only perform this while the *kendhang ciblon* is being played and only in that part of the cycle which does not have a choral melody.

The interactive orientation of the *gamelan* changes in most *inggah* sections, because the *balungan* is so sparse and extended that a note is hit only once every six seconds in *irama* 3 or once every nine or ten seconds in *irama* 4, while the fastest elaborating parts are moving along at thirty-two or sixty-four times this speed. As the sound structure is extended and made more abstract, the importance of explicitly marking frames of reference or referential points in the course of the piece increases. The *balungan* is no longer a melody in itself but a series of goal tones (*sèlèh*) which function as markers in the realm of pitch and time: the formulaic melodies played on the elaborating instruments generally lead to each of these pitches (sometimes to a modally appropriate substitute) and cadence precisely on each *balungan* pitch.

Underlying the ability to operate in such conditions is the sense of time that Javanese musicians develop, a sense which allows them to estimate long spans of musical time with great precision. This alone is not enough, however, for it is also necessary to interact with fellow musicians to assure synchronization at all levels, from the maintenance of a common pulse to agreement on location within the sequence of the piece. Drumming exemplifies this well: in faster *irama* and shorter cycles, a single through-composed drum pattern is equivalent to one gong cycle in length. The *kendhang ciblon* parts played in *irama* 3 and 4, on the other hand, are pieced together from shorter formulae to fill in the cyclical form and are linked to specific points in the colotomic structure in accordance with the dance patterns that they originally accompanied.[15] A good drummer knows "where" he is in the cycle at any time, but it certainly does not hurt to have individual *balungan* pitches and *kethuk, kenong*, and gong marking off the structure. For less competent musicians or for those situations in which confusion arises, these markers become essential. Musical conception in *irama* 4 is so protracted and surface detail so dense that it is extremely difficult to play alone at this speed and level of abstraction. Some musicians declined to record *gendèr, rebab, bonang*, or *kendhang* alone for me, and those who did agree inevitably had trouble at some point, either eliding or interpolating material because they had no external frame of reference and their internal sense of orientation was strained to the limit while performing at top speed.

---

15. Some are notated in Sumarsam (1987).

Difficulties of performance in an extended sound structure may also beset those who are playing the slow-moving parts such as the *balungan* and the colotomic parts. These musicians can orient themselves melodically and temporally to the patterns of the *gendèr* or the *bonang*, because they lead to a cadence on each *balungan* note. The constant interlocking handclapping and the interlocking *bonang* playing also serve to strengthen the temporal matrix that spans the interval between one *balungan* note and the next. To ensure the proper playing of the gong, which might be struck after a stretch of three to six minutes, the drummer plays a cue just before the gong stroke. The most straightforward version of this cue, also used in other contexts such as *palaran* and *pathetan*, is a single low stroke on the big *kendhang*. There appears to be a connection by acoustic association between cue and response: the drummer evokes the rich, low sound of the big gong with the lowest, most resonant boom available on his drums. This cue is so effective that the drummer can use it—prepared by a characteristic series of damped strokes on the *kendhang ciblon*—to ask the gong player to momentarily abandon his colotomic function and emphasize one of the cadence points in the middle of the cycle with a stroke on a smaller *gong suwukan*.

There are other problems of orientation which depend on an interactive solution. When playing a relatively abstract *inggah* section, it is not hard to lose one's place in consecutive occurrences of a particular pitch progression. In Gendhing Gambirsawit, for instance, the first phrase ends with the progression from pitch 2 to 1 and the second phrase begins with a repeat of this progression. The same sequence occurs from the end of the second phrase through the beginning of the third phrase. There are two potential sources of confusion here: one may forget within the sequence 2121 whether the first 2 or the second 2 has just passed; or one might conflate the two occurrences of 2121, moving from the end of the first phrase directly to the beginning of the third phrase, eliding the entire second phrase. This kind of mistake is particularly easy to commit when playing a highly repetitive ornamental part on instruments such as *celempung*, *gendèr panerus*, or *bonang*, but it is possible for anyone to err in this manner. Clues from other musicians set this straight, and the player who senses that he is lost can generally maintain a steady flow of sound while fishing around aurally for a scrap of terra firma on which to rest his next cadence.[16] A musician who does

16. However, I recently witnessed one rehearsal of a less common piece in which the *gendèr* player actually had to stop and look at the *slenthem* player, who was also confused and hesitant, probably because the *rebab* had just repeated a phrase for the second time when only one repeat was called for.

not know that he is lost will probably discover this at the next *balungan* pitch when his cadential melody does not coincide with any other. When playing alone, there is no such reference, of course, and some musicians whom I recorded solo asked that someone play *balungan* or some other part for this reason.

A *gendhing* is generally performed within a larger framework. Musical interaction actually begins before the *buka* when one of the leading musicians calls the *gamelan* to order with a cue: a light tapping on the *kendhang*, a brief *bonang* melody, a brief *rebab* formula called *culikan* (literally, a cook's taste of a dish), which tests the tuning, or a *grambyangan*, a pattern that roams up and down the *gendèr* in loosely synchronized octaves. The melodic fragment played on *rebab*, *gendèr*, or *bonang* not only cues the other musicians to listen for the *buka* but also identifies the tuning system and mode by emphasizing key pitches and serves to get the player "in the mode." After the tuning test the *buka* may be played directly or the *rebab* player may start a *pathetan*, a more expansive discursion on the mode. If he does not then proceed to the *buka*, one of the singers (usually a man) will sing a *bawa*, an independent song whose last phrase leads into the *gendhing*, substituting for the *buka*.

When a *gendhing* is brought to a close, it is often linked directly to successive pieces to form a medley. The drummer does this by maintaining the tempo as he plays the ending pattern rather than slowing down. Just before the final gong he plays a pattern that introduces the next piece, usually in *ladrang* or *ketawang* form. While the drummer determines the form of the ensuing piece, it is up to the *rebab* player to determine which *ladrang* or *ketawang* to play. The drummer may also lead to pieces in the less colotomically regular *ayak-ayakan* or *srepegan* forms. More often than not the drummer also cues one or more *palaran* in the middle of the *ayak-ayakan* or *srepegan*. The *rebab* player will almost always initiate a *pathetan* at the end of the sequence or if one of the pieces in the middle is brought to a full close.

PALARAN

Song is the focus of *palaran*,[17] a *gamelan* genre of relatively recent but obscure origin that consists of ametrical vocal melodies fitted loosely to metrical instrumental settings. While far less numerous than *gendhing*, *palaran* are very popular. They are performed in every *klenèngan* and provide an important vehicle for dialogue in several theatrical genres, particularly *wayang wong*, *Langen Driya*, and *Langen Mandra Wanara* (Vetter

17. The Yogyanese equivalent of *palaran* is *rambangan*.

1984). Despite this wide usage and popularity, *palaran* have not been accorded much attention in writings on Javanese music.[18] The overall sequence of a *palaran* is determined by the vocal melody and is strophic rather than cyclical. The progression through this sequence is loosely defined, being determined by complex interaction between the singer and several key members of the *gamelan*.

Interactive Network

Palaran require a solo singer, male or female, a *kendhang*, the colotomic instruments, and all the soft elaborating instruments except the *rebab*. The *bonang* are silent, and the *saron* and *slenthem* are played sporadically if at all. The *gérong* contribute interlocking handclapping and often insert short melodies between solo phrases. Since *palaran* are played in conjunction with other pieces, the positioning of instruments and performers is the same as for *gendhing* and does not reflect the interactive requirements of this genre.

Leadership is apportioned in a fairly unusual manner, compared with other *gamelan* contexts. It depends on a core group consisting of singer, drummer, and *kenong* player. The drummer initiates the *palaran* and sets the *irama* (there are two possibilities, and he can switch from one to the other at certain points), regulates the tempo within that *irama*, and cues the ends of phrases. At the end of a poetic verse he determines whether to continue playing *palaran*, to go on to another piece such as *srepegan* or *sampak*, or to stop. The singer usually decides which *palaran* to sing, within constraints of appropriateness and sequence (some *palaran* may be linked together while others may not), and sets the pace, except at phrase ends, when control reverts to the drummer.

The *kenong* player determines which pitch is to serve as the tonal center at any given moment, on the basis of his knowledge of the vocal line. The sequence of these focal pitches is fairly fixed, but the *kenong* player decides when to proceed to the next pitch in the sequence. Thus, he may act in several roles: as a mediator, interpreting the singer's pacing of the melody for the other musicians, as one who lays a foundation by marking temporal units and referential pitches, or even as a leader when he anticipates the singer by setting up pitches before the singer has begun to head toward them. The choice of role depends on the relative competence of the singer and *kenong* player and also on each performer's willingness to take the initiative. The *kempul* player may also be involved in this to a lesser degree, either following the *kenong* player or deciding

---

18. A brief report by Santosa (1979) including some transcriptions of vocal parts is one exception.

on his own when to switch to a different pitch. If he switches before the *kenong*, he forces the *kenong* to follow on the next beat. Some musicians also attribute a guiding role to the *gambang* player, who plays a variant of the vocal melody in heterophonic relation to the singer; to the extent that he anticipates the singer and the singer responds to this, the *gambang* player could be said to guide the vocal part.

The players of the other elaborating parts follow the lead of these core musicians. All except the *suling* player repeat static patterns that are connected by transitional patterns and bound by metrical and melodic frameworks. The metrical framework is articulated by *kenong, kethuk, kempul*, and an occasional *gong*, while the melodic framework is established by *kenong* and *kempul*. There is copious reference and redundancy of foundation in *palaran*, since the *kenong* and *kempul* both give pitch orientation to the singer and elaborating instruments and these pitches are reiterated and emphasized on the elaborating instruments. This interactive network is altered significantly for theatrical use when the singing is done by actors on the stage rather than singers in the *gamelan*.

Interactive System

In most ways *palaran* offers a more flexible interactive environment than *gendhing*. The singer is almost completely free, while others have some flexibility but are bound by aspects of the sound structure to work with metrical units of a certain length. The drumming is very loosely prescribed, and the drummer really only needs four cues: one to initiate a *palaran*, another to cue a phrase ending, a third to change *irama*, and a fourth to move on to another piece. There is considerable variation in the phrase-ending cue, which may begin four beats or six beats before the end of the phrase at the drummer's discretion. The singer leads by means of his or her pacing of the melodic line and placement of syllables, without any explicit cues. The *kenong* and *kempul* players' pitch choices may be considered a cue rather than a marker or a signal because they are making definite something that is flexible by deciding that the time has come to move on to the next tonal plateau.

The interactive system of *palaran* is characterized by a mixture of flexible and semiflexible response time. Responses to drum and *kenong* cues are timed to fit within the metrical framework of interactive sound structure, but there is some looseness since the metrical units are short and some players may respond before others. Estimation is an essential aspect of this interaction, as the drummer, *kenong*, and *kempul* players try to predict the duration of each segment of a vocal phrase. This skill, which depends on extensive knowledge of performance frameworks and procedures as well as aesthetic sensibilities and familiarity with fellow musicians' performance styles, is of far greater importance in *palaran* and *pathetan* than it is in *gendhing*.

Interactive Sound Structure

The sonic texture of *palaran* is unlike anything else in the *gamelan* repertoire: it is static yet in constant motion; tonally and rhythmically it is both fragmented and focused. The vocal melody is highlighted against an instrumental background in which the main pitch of the vocal melody is reiterated on *kempul* and *kenong* and circled by elaborating patterns that converge on this pitch every two or four beats. The shifting, kaleidoscopic nature of this texture derives from the indeterminate duration of tonal centers: musicians do not necessarily shift from one tonal center to the next at the same time. This contrasts with *gendhing*, in which melodic divergence between parts is greater and spans longer stretches of time, but convergence is far more regular and the sense of melodic flow more closely coordinated. Most elaborating patterns played in *gendhing* are built on directional melodies that flow from one goal pitch (*sèlèh*) to the next (usually every fourth beat) in the space of five to eight seconds. In *palaran*, musicians (other than the aforementioned *gambang* and *suling*) repeat and vary much shorter fragments that circle around one *sèlèh* and last about one or two seconds. Only when shifting from one tonal center to the next are the melodies more directional, and these, too, are usually brief. The regular pace, rapid reiteration of tonal center, and repetitiveness of ornamental patterns contrast strongly with the sustained melodic motion and irregular rhythm of the vocal line.

The consecutive sound structure of a *palaran* derives from the combination of two completely unrelated sources, which may explain the flexibility of a form that seems to border on amorphousness. The vocal line is based on a traditional melody associated with one of the eleven to thirteen different *macapat* meters. Each meter is defined by the number of lines in a stanza, the number of syllables in each line, and the final vowel of each line; in most meters both syllable count and final vowel differ from one line to the next. *Macapat* melodies are rhythmically free and, when used for recitation of poetic texts, barely ornamented. When adapted to *palaran* performance, the melodies are sung in a more ornate manner but remain basically free in rhythmic organization: some singers relate directly to the beat, creating a sense of syncopation, while others are more independent rhythmically. Singers select texts from a large body of written and oral verse. Some texts, such as certain verses of the Wedatama poem by Prince Mangkunegara IV or selections from the *Langen Driya* dance operas by R. M. H. Tandakusuma, are especially common.

	a. Fast *irama*		b. Slow *irama*			
beat		o	o		o	o	o	o
kethuk	x	x			x		x	
kenong		x	x			x		x
kempul			x					x

Fig. 21 Basic colotomic structure of *palaran*

The other source for *palaran* sound structure is the *gamelan* genre *srepegan*, which is defined by a specific type of *balungan* and colotomic pattern. The basic colotomic pattern of *srepegan* is adopted unchanged for *palaran*, but the *balungan* is not, which accounts in part for the rootless, floating effect of this kind of piece (*pathetan* are the only other *gamelan* pieces without a *balungan*). The colotomic structure of *palaran* is dense (see fig. 21; patterns A and B are the basic colotomic units in fast and slow *irama*, respectively). The *kempul* provides the primary metrical referent marking the end of each elaborating pattern. The internal structure of these units is never violated—there is no half unit, for example—but higher-level grouping into phrases is much more fluid, depending on the singer's pacing and on the drummer's response to that pacing. Certain *palaran* contain additional structural elements: brief transitional melodies that are sung by the *gérong* or played on *saron* and lead to the pitch center of the next vocal phrase.

The interactive possibilities and constraints of *palaran* are captured in three diagrams.[19] Figure 22 represents the sequence of cues and responses that initiate a *palaran*. The drummer's initial cue evokes different responses, all timed to begin when the gong marks the end of the current cycle. After the gong the drummer maintains the tempo or cues a shift to a slower *irama* (resulting in colotomic pattern A or B of fig. 21). The singer then begins to sing the first line of a *macapat* stanza. The *kenong* and *kempul* players sound the tonal center of each segment of this line. The tonal center may shift once or twice within the line or not at all depending on the melody, which is fixed by oral tradition in its large outline. The many arrows in the right half of the diagram represent the complex system of reference and reinforcement in the domains of pitch and rhythm; this portion of the diagram actually overlays the central portion.

The musicians maintain a static texture focused on each tonal center

19. Time flows from left to right, and vertical alignment indicates simultaneity. These diagrams have been simplified slightly for legibility; the greater melodic scope of the *gambang* part has not been represented, for instance.

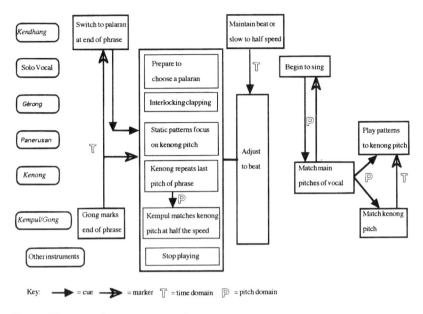

Key: ➤ = cue   ⇒ = marker   𝕋 = time domain   ℙ = pitch domain

Fig. 22 Transition from *srepegan* to *palaran*

and shifting in response to the vocal, *kenong*, and *kempul* until the end of the phrase approaches. Here the drummer's knowledge of the particular *palaran* and his sense of estimation are called into play. As he hears the singer nearing the end of the phrase, he cues the other players to switch from static patterns to cadential ones, timed to coincide with the end of the phrase (fig. 23). He must fit his cue to the colotomic structure, beginning it immediately after a *kempul* stroke, and he must allow the singer enough time to finish the phrase in approximate synchrony with the instrumentalists' responses. The drummer's pattern ends with a cue to the *gong*, which he can play on the large *kendhang*. This is the same as the pattern described earlier for *gendhing*, but here it is a cue rather than a signal because the microform of *palaran* is unpredictable. The gong player then responds in accordance with the ongoing metrical framework of *kethuk*, *kenong*, and *kempul*. In some meters the end of each phrase is marked by gong while in others only a few phrases are so marked, the others ending with a *kempul* stroke.[20] The final gong or *kempul* stroke marks the end of the phrase, freeing the musicians to embark on the next phrase or the transitional *gérong* or *saron* melody leading to that phrase.

20. Since *gong* and *kempul* are often played by the same musician, it is a simple matter to turn from one to the other. They may be hung on the same rack or on two parallel racks with the player seated in between.

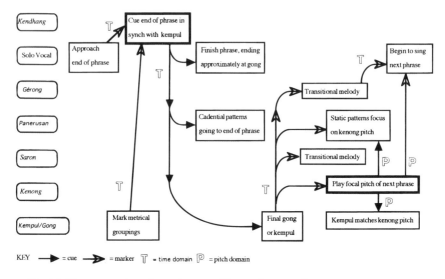

Fig. 23 Cuing to end a *palaran* phrase and begin the next phrase

The *palaran* continues in this manner following a set sequence of phrases. If the initial *irama* is slow, the drummer may accelerate to the faster *irama* for the last phrase or two. In any case, as the end of the last phrase approaches he must direct the musicians to play another stanza (with the same cue used to initiate *palaran*) or give the opening cue for some other piece, usually *srepegan*, which flows seamlessly out of *palaran* because of their shared colotomic framework. The sequence of events, the network, and the cues, markers, and responses that come into play when the drummer decides to end the *palaran* and return to *srepegan* are represented in figure 24. If he cues a second *palaran*, a new singer often takes over and decides whether to sing another verse of the same *palaran* or a different meter, tune, and text, essentially repeating the process depicted in figure 22.

In sum, a *palaran* is characterized by a fairly loose progression in metrically defined chunks through a fixed sequence. A few concrete examples are offered here to complement this abstract depiction of *palaran* interaction. Drawn from a comparative analysis of several performances of Palaran Pangkur, they demonstrate that the main outline and even many of the details of this commonly performed piece are stable, varying little from one performance to the next, but the precise confluence of parts and the length of phrases vary considerably. The *kempul, kenong,* and vocal parts of the first phrase of one performance are notated in figure 25 (beginning after a transition from a previous *palaran*). The pro-

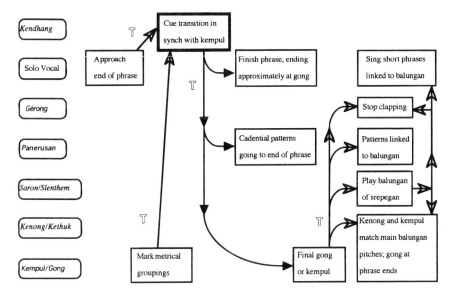

Fig. 24   Returning to *srepegan* from *palaran*

gression of goal tones marked by *kenong* outlines the path of the vocal phrase and is reinforced by the *kempul* (6 is substituted at the beginning, since there is no *kempul* tuned to pitch 2).[21] The *kenong* player anticipates by several beats the singer's ascent to pitch 5 at the end of her half-phrase while the *kempul* player follows the vocal more closely. Such clashes between *kenong* and *kempul* are potentially confusing for other musicians who must match their elaborating parts to one or the other. The *kendhang* part, omitted here for lack of space, begins with three variations on a pattern that lasts two *kempul* beats. The relatively sparse drumming includes enough syncopated strokes to subdivide the beat and control it subtly. When the singer begins the last segment of the phrase, the drummer is in mid-pattern and must wait until the next *kempul* stroke to begin his phrase-ending cue, which contrasts with the preceding patterns in volume and in rhythm: the strokes are louder and unsyncopated.

Five versions of the first two phrases of Palaran Pangkur (fig. 26) illustrate the scope of variation in pacing, choice of pitches, and interaction between the *kenong* and *kempul* players. Some incongruencies between gong and *kenong* pitches result from the availability of gongs in a particular *gamelan*, but other pitch choices are probably deliberate and reveal

21. A full set of *kenong* ranges from 2 to high 2 and *kempul* ranges from 3 to high 2, but this high 2 only suits a vocal part sung in the high register.

Lokananta Recording ACD131, ca. 60 *kenong* strokes per minute

V			2 2		22 2 1 123 2 123 5					23 22		1		2		6̣1		6̣
			x x		xx x x				'		x x								
N	2	2	2	2	5	5	5	5	5	5	6	6	6	6	6	6
P		6		6		6		5		5		6		6			
G															◯

KEY
V = vocal   x = syllable onset   N = *kenong*   P = *kempul*   G = gong

Fig. 25 Palaran Pangkur Sléndro Sanga, first phrase

KGD069*
N   6 6 6 6 6 6 5 5 5 5 6 6 6 6 6 6 6 6 6 6 6 6 6 6 5 5 5 5 5 5
P/G   6   6   6   5   5   6   ② 6   6   6   6   6   5   5   ①

ACD131
N   2 2 2 2 5 5 5 5 5 5 6 6 6 6 6 6 6 6 6 6 6 6 6 6 6 6 5 5 5 5 5
P/G   6   6   6   5   5   6   6   ⑥ 6   6   6   6   6   6   5   5   ②

KS3
N   2 2 2 2 2 2 2 2 5 5 5 5 5 5 2 6 2 2 2 2 2 2 2 2 2 2 5 5 5 5 5 5
P/G   6   6   6   6   6   6   6   ② 6   6   6   6   6   5   5   5   ②

ACD144
N   2 2 2 2 2 2 2 2 2 2 6 6 6 6 6 6 6 2 2 2 2 2 2 2 2 2 2 5 5 5 5 6 i̇
P/G   6   6   6   6   6   6   6   6   ⑥ 6   6   6   6   6   6   5   5   ⑤

KGD018
N   2 2 2 2 2 2 2 2 5 5 5 5 6 6 6 6 6 6 6 6 6 2 2 2 2 2 2 2 5 5 5 5 5 5 5
P/G   6   6   6   6   6   6   6   6   ⑥ 6   6   6   6   6   6   5   5   5   ②

N = *kenong*   P/G = *kempul/gong* (*gong* is represented by ◯)   * Recording numbers are listed in the discography.

Fig. 26 Comparison of colotomic parts in recordings of Palaran Pangkur

differing conceptions of the tonal progression of the piece. Several dis-
agreements between players such as that noted for ACD131 are also
evident. The second phrase of recording ACD144 is noteworthy because the *kenong* player leads to the opening pitch of the third phrase
with the progression 5 6 i̇; this anticipation is probably the reason for
gong 1 at the same point in recording KGD069. The general sonority
of the gong creates a sense of finality for this phrase while the actual
pitch leads inexorably to the next phrase, which is centered on i̇.

```
ACD131*
V              56  i  i  i      i  5 i 6  5     '    i2   6   56 i
               xx     x x      x  x                 xx
N      i  i  i  i  i  i  5  5  5  5  5  5  i  i  i  i
P/G       i        i        i        5        5        5        i        ()


KS3
V              56  i  ii    i 5 i6  5      '    i2      6i65   6 i
               xx    xx  x x                    xx
N      i  i  i  i  i  i  i  i  5  5  5  5  i  i  i  i
P/G       i        i        i        5        5        i        i        ()
```

KEY

V = vocal   x = syllable onset   ' = breath   N = *kenong*   P/G = *kempul*/gong (() = gong)
* Recording numbers are listed in the discography.

Fig. 27 Palaran Pangkur Sléndro Sanga, third phrase

Two versions of the third phrase, transcribed in greater detail in figure 27, show that despite identical overall duration these versions differ in the pacing of the vocal melody and the relationship between voice and colotomic instruments. In the first recording the *kenong* player anticipates the vocal move to 5 in the middle of the phrase and the *kempul* follows the *kenong* precisely. In the second the *kempul* player follows the vocal closely and seems to be cuing or prompting the *kenong* player, who lags considerably.

The *gendèr* player did not wait for guidance in the second performance but changed his patterns at the same moment as the *kempul*. This *gendèr* part (fig. 28) offers an excellent example of the sort of figuration that a good musician produces to ornament a tonal center while maintaining readiness to respond to cues immediately—in this case from the voice, since the *kenong* player did not fulfill his role as mediator. As the singer soars up to í, the *gendèr* player, I. M. Harjito, repeats a melodic pattern with his left hand (revolving around 1), while his right hand plays a static pattern that is generic for the mode of *sléndro sanga* and can fit various left-hand melodies. Harjito's avoidance of the main pitch on the beat is a typical method of creating a lively fullness of sound without actually going anywhere.[22] At the point marked "a" Harjito moves to 5, the next goal tone, with a minimal alteration of his left-hand melody.

22. I did not have a chance to discuss this performance with the musicians involved, because I left Java immediately afterward, but I had learned this particular *palaran* from Harjito and have since had occasion to discuss such interaction with other musicians.

gendèr										a		b		c		d
rh	5 2̣ 6 2̇ 5 2̣ 6 2̇ 5 2̣ 6 2̇ 5 2̣ 6 2̇ 5 2̣ 6 2̇ 5 2̣ 6 2̇ 5 2̣ 6 2̇ 56·6·6·65
lh	·1216121·1216121· 216121· 216121· 21612165616561·56123·3·32126·15
kenong	1̇	1̇	1̇	1̇	1̇	1̇	1̇	5	5
kempul	1̇		1̇		1̇		5		5
vocal			5 6	1̇	1̇ 1̇	1̇	5	1̇ 6	5

gendèr		e		f			g			
rh	2̇ 1̇ 2̇ 5 2̇ 1̇ 2̇ 5		5		65 · · ·61 ·6·6·65
lh	6123·3·3·32 ·321·61561·56165165 · 656 5 6 1 321
kenong		5		5	1̇	1̇	1̇	1̇
kempul				1̇		1̇
gong								2
vocal		1̇2̇			6 1̇ 6 5		6	1̇

source: KS3, Gendèr: I. M. Harjito;

rh = right hand; lh = left hand

Right hand part is indistinct from f to g.

Fig. 28 Gendèran from the third phrase of Palaran Pangkur

He does not commit himself fully with this move, since he plays it half a beat late and moves away again, but since the singer also moves to 5 at the same moment, he proceeds to land on 5 again at letter "b" in synchrony with the kempul move to 5. The transition is not complete, though: he plays an octave run in the left hand which leads up to a high 5 at letter "c" and then descends to a more emphatic cadence at letter "d," coinciding with both kenong and kempul and finally altering the static right-hand figure to emphasize pitch 5 in a different way.

At this point the singer has finished her move to 5 and pauses. Since it is not the gendèr player's role to lead to the next focal pitch, Harjito marks time with another ascent to the high 5 at letter "e," which allows him to move rapidly to 1 the moment that he hears the singer do so (letter "f"; some of the right hand pitches are omitted here because they are not clear on the tape). When the drummer begins the phrase-ending cue, Harjito responds with a full cadence to 1 by moving to low 5 at "g" and then emphatically back to 1, ending with a descent to the bottom of the gendèr range. Thus, we see how a masterful musician can maneuver skillfully in this kaleidoscopic wash of sound, by hinting at a cadence but not completing it until the appropriate moment, by hanging on a pivotal pitch while being prepared to move to the next focal pitch instantaneously, and by responding gracefully to the drummer's gong cue and playing a full cadential pattern to end the phrase with finality.

PATHETAN

A *pathetan* is an ametrical piece, performed by a small subset of the *gamelan*, that has strong modal associations (*pathetan* can be translated roughly as doing the mode) and is relatively brief, rarely lasting longer than three minutes and often as little as thirty seconds. The repertoire is small: there are four to six different *pathetan* in each of the six main *pathet*. The performance of *pathetan* varies with context (see Brinner 1989/90). In *klenèngan* they are played routinely after most *gendhing* and before solo songs (*bawa*) to contextualize the *gendhing* and *bawa* within a mode and to articulate the overall sequence of the *klenèngan*. In *wayang* they convey a calm mood and articulate the dramatic structure. In dance performances *pathetan* accompany dancers as they enter and exit or pause between sections.

Interactive Sound Structure

Pathetan are the only *gamelan* pieces that have no common pulse and thus no *irama* or set rhythmic relationships between the simultaneously sounding parts.[23] Like *palaran* they lack *balungan*, but they also lack colotomic structure. They are not cyclical and not usually repeatable, unlike strophic *palaran* or cyclical *gendhing*. Thus, all of the structural frames of reference common to other *gamelan* genres are lacking except melody.

The melodies of *pathetan* are characterized by a stereotypical construction of tonally restricted phrases. Most phrases are tonally stable, centered on a single pitch which is chanted by the singer and repeated by the *rebab* player, minimally ornamented with neighboring tones. While the *balungan* of a *gendhing* offers a regularly paced succession of goal tones as a melodic referent toward which musicians can aim their melodies, most phrases in a *pathetan* are extended tonal plateaus linked by brief transitions which favor a loosely coordinated convergence of parts. The crucial points for coordination are the transitions between one tonal center and the next, which occur both within and between phrases. As in *palaran* the individual parts are constructed mainly of short modules centered on a goal tone. These are repeated and varied as necessary until the musician feels that it is time to proceed to the next goal tone via a transitional melody that is not repeatable.

One further aspect of *pathetan* sound structure is crucial for interaction: the melodic interrelatedness of *pathetan*. The *pathetan* within each mode are closely related, sharing several phrases at least (Brinner 1985:

---

23. I begin this discussion with sound structure rather than interactive network or system for narrative reasons. There is no hierarchical significance to the order of presentation.

165–225, 429–46). Several *pathetan* exist in short and long versions that require the musicians to listen carefully to the leader for cues to guide them along a common path. These relationships are both potential sources of confusion and opportunities for choices that have interactive ramifications. Some of the more unusual or more complexly related *pathetan* are confusing because of diverging and converging melodic paths, and partial rather than full sharing of sections. Musicians may confuse one *pathetan* with another, particularly in instrumental performance, in which the continuous *rebab* line provides a hazier guide than a singer's clearly segmented phrases. But even this somewhat hazy guide is better than none. The *gendèr*, *gambang*, and *suling* parts to these *pathetan* are largely formulaic and are sometimes so amorphous because of meandering melody and stereotypical filigree that the main melodic thread of the vocal or *rebab* line is absolutely essential for accurate performance. Several times I encountered this problem with fully competent musicians who set out to record the *gambang* or *gendèr* part to one of the more difficult *pathetan* at my request only to stop in the middle and ask me to play the *rebab* melody so that they would have a reference, something with which they could interact and orient themselves.

A *pathetan*, then, can be characterized as a loosely regulated progression through a well-defined sequence. There may be one or more turning points in this sequence where the leader must choose between two or more possible paths, but the possibilities for shaping the sequence are far more limited than in *gendhing*. On the other hand, the progression through the sequence is highly variable, since the simultaneities in a given performance as well as the precise sequence and progression all result from the musicians' collective efforts and interaction.

Interactive Network

The network for *pathetan* performance is determined by context: in *klenèngan* four musicians play *rebab*, *gendèr*, *gambang*, and *suling*;[24] in *wayang kulit* or *wayang wong* the network also includes a *dhalang*, who sings, two or three musicians, who play *gong*, *kenong*, and *kempul*, and another, who uses the *kendhang* for cuing the gongs. For certain court dances the vocal line is chanted by a chorus and only *rebab*, *gendèr*, and *gambang* are played. Since *pathetan* are always incorporated in larger performance sequences, the interactive requirements of this genre do not affect the positioning of instruments and musicians. Visual communication is unusual and often impossible: although *rebab*, *gendèr*, and *gambang* often are grouped to-

24. *Suling* may be omitted if an instrument or performer is lacking.

gether as part of the soft group within the full *gamelan,* the players of these instruments are unlikely to be facing each other and the *suling* player may be seated at quite a distance.

Many of the musical channels of communication that characterize the full *gamelan* and apply to the performance of *gendhing* do not apply to *pathetan* performance because of the size and nature of the ensemble and because of the loose musical structure. Most of the subnetworks that exist within a full *gamelan* are irrelevant: there are no interlocking relationships or fixed rhythmic ratios between parts, nor are there groupings based on similarities of construction or idiom because the core instruments are so distinctive. Because of the reduced ensemble and loose structure, the leading melodic role, filled by *rebab* or *dhalang,* takes on an important referential role as well.

A major characteristic of the principal relationships in the *pathetan* network is the order in which members of the ensemble begin and end each phrase in their loosely coordinated progress through the piece. This order of precedence is not a rule but, rather, a common conception that shapes performer expectations and evaluations. In *klenèngan* the *rebab* player leads, playing first and determining which *pathetan* is to be played. The *gendèr* is the next to start, followed by the *gambang* and finally the *suling.* This order should prevail throughout the *pathetan* as the *rebab* continues to lead, initiating all transitions and each new *sèlèh.*

Most musicians, aware of the exceptions that occur in practice, spoke to me of differing degrees of freedom and constraint for each part with reference to the *rebab* or to the ensemble as a whole. The most important constraint is that the *gendèr* follow the *rebab:* this link is the strongest in the network and the one my teachers spoke of most often and in greatest detail. It is these players who will quickly take control of the music at the beginning of the *pathetan* if the *dhalang* is a weak singer or knows the *pathetan* poorly (DR).[25] A *gendèr* player can push the leader forward if the pace is too slow, but such a performance is generally felt to be unsatisfactory. It is the *gendèr* player's responsibility not only to stay behind the

25. I base the following statements on comments by a number of musicians including Darsono (DR), I. M. Harjito (IMH), Djoko Sungkono (DS), Suhardi (SH), Martopangrawit, Mloyowidodo, the late *dhalang* Soetrisno, and B. Subono (SB), who is both a *dhalang* and a musician. I have attributed statements directly in the text with the initials shown here in parentheses and so dispense with the notation "personal communication." The recordings of *pathetan* which I made at specially convened sessions provide most of the material for my analysis, supplemented by performances recorded or observed at the Mangkunegaran palace and elsewhere. Several of these musicians listened to recordings selected from these sources and offered general comments and detailed criticisms that have guided my analysis.

leading musician but to know how much to lag in order to allow sufficient time to respond without becoming confused, especially when performing *pathetan* that can branch off in several directions (SH).

The *gambang* player is not as restricted as the *gendèr* player, but neither
is he as free as the *suling*. His chief responsibility is to follow behind the
rebab without lagging too far behind. Musicians agree that the *gambang*
is less influential than the *gendèr* and the relationship with the *rebab* is
usually not as close as that between *rebab* and *gendèr*, although one musician interviewed felt that these three parts share equal responsibility for
the quality of the performance (DS). Another said that he must defer to
the *gendèr* (SH), but DS said that the *gambang* may precede the *gendèr*
on occasion.

The *suling* player is the least influential: he cannot affect the course
of the *pathetan*, although he can prompt by pointing ahead to approaching *sèlèh* and changes of register (DR). He is free to arrive at a *sèlèh*
before the other musicians as long as he pauses between phrases to allow
the *rebab* to lead to the next phrase (IMH; DS). If he rushes too far ahead
or plays very short phrases, he creates the undesirable impression that
he is leaving his companions far behind (DS).

Leadership in *pathetan* is highly constrained by the need to listen to
and wait for the players who follow. The *rebab* has absolute control only
over the beginning of a *pathetan* (SH). When one musician said that it
sounds very bad if the *rebab* falls behind the *gendèr* or the *gendèr* gets ahead
of the *rebab* (DS), he implied that there is a normative pacing and phrasing for *pathetan* since the *rebab* player could only fall behind (as opposed
to the *gendèr* getting ahead) as judged against some such standard. The
rebab player should not proceed through the *pathetan* so slowly that the
others push ahead or so quickly that they are left behind. This constraint
is strongest with regard to the *gendèr* and weakest for the *suling*, but interdependence extends beyond dyadic relationships. If, for instance, the
gendèr sèlèh comes too long after the *rebab sèlèh*, this is not only bad in itself
but also creates problems for the *gambang* player (DS).

Opinions differ more regarding the order of precedence in vocal performances, evidence of the rivalry between musician and *dhalang* that we
shall explore further in chapter 10. While everyone agrees that the *dhalang* enjoys a special position within the ensemble, a *dhalang* tends to
declare the primacy of the vocal part while musicians attribute greater
importance to the instruments. Each *dhalang* with whom I spoke stated
the order of precedence as vocal-*gendèr*-*gambang*-*suling*, with *rebab* a subordinate who trails the vocal. Soetrisno and Subono went so far as to state
that the *rebab* is unimportant because it simply doubles the vocal melody.
This is countered by some musicians who feel that the *rebab* player's

responsibilities are at least equal to those of the *dhalang*, that the *dhalang* is just another member of the ensemble. Ideally the *dhalang* listens to the instrumentalists and is as dependent on them as they are on him. Musicians frequently criticize a *dhalang* for rushing ahead without regard for the instrumentalists. Several specifically stated that it is the *dhalang*'s responsibility to know the patterns of the instruments, especially the *gendèr*, so that the musicians can aid him and so that he does not rush them unduly. According to Martopangrawit, the *dhalang* always followed the *rebab* player's lead in colonial times; a court *dhalang* was lower in rank than the *rebab* player and only asked (*minta*) for a particular *pathetan* after which the *rebab* player took the lead, but now the *dhalang* no longer follows the *rebab* because he feels his own power or authority (*kekuasaan*). Martopangrawit felt that the current supremacy of the *dhalang* upsets the unity of the ensemble and ruins the *wayang* performance, which should ideally be a cooperative effort. Suhardi noted that in broadcasts of *wayang* from Surakarta in the 1960s there was extremely close coordination among the musicians, but often a *dhalang* performing with these musicians would not listen to them and would get so far ahead that the musicians were forced to skip several phrases in order to adjust to the *dhalang*.

Most musicians, especially younger ones, hold a more moderate view of the comparative importance of *rebab* and voice. They acknowledge that musicians may have enjoyed greater prominence in the past but feel that nowadays the *dhalang* should lead most of the time, the *rebab* leading only occasionally. Many feel that the result is unpleasant if the *dhalang* does not lead. The *rebab* is sometimes forced forward in vocal performances because it would sound bad to extend the previous phrase any longer,[26] but it is really undesirable for the *rebab* to leave the *dhalang* behind (SH) and the *gendèr* player should follow the vocal, not the *rebab*, if there is a difference of opinion (IHM).

Several musicians stress that the degree to which a *dhalang* leads depends to some extent on his competence. Djoko Sungkono, who frequently plays *rebab* in *wayang* performances, says that he gauges whether to follow or lead by the experience and ability of the *dhalang*. He suggests that the *rebab* follow the vocal most of the time, preceding it chiefly in the transitional passages. According to Harjito the *gendèr* player can push the *dhalang* forward with his playing if he is more competent than the *dhalang*. Darsono says that the *rebab* should not lead the melody (*murba lagu*)[27] in a vocal performance, but if the *dhalang* does not sing *pathetan* well the *rebab* player may lead by consistently playing ahead of

---

26. The importance of the integrity of each part will be discussed below.
27. Cf. Martopangrawit's use of this term in the full *gamelan* discussed in chapter 7.

the *dhalang* more loudly and with greater emphasis; however, such behavior is very conspicuous. The reverse may also occur: it is rare to find
a knowledgeable *rebab* player in the villages, so the musician playing
rebab in a village *wayang* usually just floats along on the stream of the
dhalang's melody (DR). Because of this, a *rebab* player may appear not to
know the *pathetan* if he lags behind the *dhalang* consistently (DS). Here
we see that mutual assessments and potential impressions add another
layer to the basic "system" of interaction in *pathetan*.

Within the larger network of *wayang* performances the *gong, kempul,
kenong,* and *kendhang* constitute a subnetwork that supports the vocal line
by marking the end of certain phrases, reinforcing the *dhalang's* last utterance of the *sèlèh*. Thus, the various gongs fulfill the articulative part of
their regular colotomic function by demarcating the phrasing of a *pathetan* but without the regularity of a hierarchically subdivided cyclical
structure. For a given phrase, *kempul* and gong are mutually exclusive, the
player choosing one or the other depending on the mode, pitch, and
melodic register of the melody (opinions differ as to which gongs may
be used) while the *kenong* doubles these strokes. These instruments also
serve an important referential function by reinforcing the *dhalang's* orientation to the mode and tuning—one *dhalang* complained that *kempul*
players are often *kuminter* (too clever) and take such great liberties that
they disturb him rather than supporting him (SB).

The overriding consideration in this subnetwork is matching the vocal pitch while timing is not codified; in other words, priorities are re-
versed relative to *gendhing* performance. Both Martopangrawit and Mloyowidodo insisted that timing is a matter of *rasa* (feeling) and cannot be
taught—no two musicians would strike the gong or *kempul* at precisely
the same moment in *pathetan*. In practice, the connection between vocalist and gongs is usually mediated by the *kendhang* player, who constrains
the timing. He also helps the *gendèr* player to establish a regular beat and
control the tempo in the instrumental sections known as *umpak gendèr*
that occur toward the end of a few *pathetan*.

Interactive System

To make sense of *pathetan* interaction, it is useful to distinguish cues according to medium, signification, and context. Most cues are sounded;
visual cues are limited to puppet or dancer position. All aural cues are
integral to a musical line except the *dhalang's* tapping on the puppet box
and some *kendhang* strokes which function principally as cues.

The most powerful cues define the path of the *pathetan*. The initial
cue is particularly significant because it initiates a complex sequence
of events and places heavy demands on the other members of the en-

semble. These musicians must recognize that a *pathetan* rather than some other type of piece is to be played, they must identify the *pathetan* by its starting pitch and contextual information (see Brinner 1989/90), and they must begin to play in accordance with the accepted order of entry of the parts. The situation is particularly demanding because of the brief response time: while the introduction to a *gendhing* may last fifteen seconds or more, musicians should respond to the initial cue for a *pathetan* within one or two seconds. In *klenèngan* it is relatively simple to realize that a *pathetan* is called for (though the *buka* of some *gendhing* sound surprisingly similar to the opening of certain *pathetan*), but in *wayang* a *dhalang* can also cue other types of songs. The distinction is chiefly contextual: at a given point in the drama only one type of song is appropriate. On several occasions I have witnessed a *rebab* player misinterpret the situation and join in, only to discover as the melody took an unexpected turn that the piece is not a *pathetan* but a *sendhon*, which does not involve *rebab*.

Path-defining cues can also occur in the middle of a *pathetan*. In *pathet pélog barang*, for example, the longer Pathetan Wantah diverges from the more commonly performed Pathetan Jugag in the third phrase. As the end of the second phrase approaches, the musicians must listen more carefully to the *rebab* or *dhalang* to know which path to take. The cue in this case is subtle: the *rebab* melody for the third phrase of Pathetan Jugag goes from pitch 3 to 2, while in Pathetan Wantah the 3 is repeated (see fig. 29). The rest of the phrase is quite different, but by the time it is played the musicians should already have taken an irrevocable turn down one path or the other. Thus, the musicians must react on the basis of a single pitch, sensing whether pitch 3 is transitional, leaning toward 2, or the stable beginning of a tonal plateau. This is complicated by the fact that the previous phrase is composed of repetitions of pitch 2 alternating with 3. Thus, when the *rebab* player moves on to the third phrase, he must make clear to the others that he has done so and is not merely ornamenting the end of the second phrase with another alternation between 2 and 3.[28]

A second type of cue is a pitch prompt directed at the *dhalang* to aid his intonation and remind him of the next bend in the melody. An experienced *dhalang* with a good memory and sense of pitch does not need these prompts, but they are present nonetheless and have helped more than one less competent singer. Pitch prompts come from the *rebab* (fig. 30) and, less often, from the *gendèr*. *Gong*, *kempul*, and *kenong* tones

---

28. Similarly, a single crucial pitch distinguishes Pathetan Lasem and Kagok Lasem in *pélog nem* or the long and short versions of Pathetan Ngelik in *pélog lima*.

	Phrase 2			Phrase 3			

Jugag   7̄ 6̄ 7̄ 2̄   2̄ 2̄   2̄ 3 2̄ 3̄   2̄3 7̄ 2̄   7̄67 7̄

Wantah   7̄ 6̄ 7̄ 2̄   2̄ 2̄   2̄ 3 2̄ 3̄   3̄   3̄5 3̄

ˉ = up bow   ˋ = down bow

Fig. 29 Diverging *pathetan* in *pélog barang*

dhalang   35 6   3 5   3 2   '   2 3 5

                                                           ®

rebab   2̄   3̄5   3̄53̄ 2̄3   2̄ 2̄ 2̄ 2̄ 3 2̄ 2 3̄5 5̄   2̄ 3̄5 5̄

                                              p

' = pause at end of phrase; p = prompt; ® = response

This passage appears in most *pathetan* in *pathet sléndro nem*.

Fig. 30 Pitch prompt

serve a related function: as pitch markers they provide a reference for feedback on intonation and mode by emphasizing the principal pitch of certain phrases. Several performers stressed that this is necessary because the *gendèr* may not be audible enough for the *dhalang* in performance.

Other types of cues occur in the course of a *pathetan* to facilitate coordination of the parts by initiating a transition to a new goal tone (*sèlèh*), signifying arrival at a *sèlèh* and terminating a *sèlèh*. The musicians are not necessarily helpless without these cues, nor do they remain idle while waiting for a cue; rather, the cues serve to guide and remind the musicians and to validate the pacing of the individual parts. All three types can be as subtle as a single change of pitch or emphasis; some cues, however, involve major changes of register.

Cues that initiate a transition in the responding parts may not be transitional in the cuing part itself. In the third phrase of Pathetan Sanga Wantah, for example, a lengthy transition to pitch 2 played on the *gendèr*, *gambang*, and *suling* is cued by a single sustained pitch 2 in the vocal or a slightly more ornate module in the *rebab* part (fig. 31a).[29] Neither of

29. In these *pathetan* excerpts the vertical alignment of the parts indicates very rough synchrony that could vary greatly in performance. The parts never proceed in the lockstep that typographic representation implies.

a. Pathetan Sléndro Sanga Wantah, transition from second to third phrase

dhalang	1 6 1	'	2		'	

$$\begin{array}{ll} & \text{s} \qquad\qquad ©/\text{s} \\ \textit{rebab} \quad & \overline{1\ 2}\ \ 1\ \ \ \overline{2}\ \ \overline{12}\ \ 1\ \ 2 \qquad 2 \qquad 2\ 6\dot{1}\ 2 \end{array}$$

```
                        s      ©/S
gendèr   · 6 i 5 · 6 i 5 i 6 i 5 3 · 3 5 3 · 3 2 5 3 5 2
          1 1 1 165 ·  53561 1 161 ·561656165615 3 2 · 1 2
                                · s  ®                        S
gambang  11523162121 5 5 1 5 1 5556123536 6536153656565562
                         s  ®                                  S
suling      i6i '  6 2 i6i  '   5 6 5 2  2  6i 6i653 65 3532
                  s          ®                                S
```

b. Pathetan Sléndro Manyura Jugag, transition from first to second phrase

dhalang	1 6 1	'	3 5 3 23 2	

```
              s             ©        S
rebab    i  2 12  i    3   3   32  161 2 2
              s         ©              S
gendèr   6 5 6 i ·6· 6 i 6 5 6 i · 6 i 6 2 i 2 6
          · 1 · 1 ·65 63 · 1 · · 6 1 2 612 2 532
                          s  ®              S
gambang  11523162121·62121·3366263·3321352·665361536562
                      s  ®                        S
suling      i6i ' 6 2 i6i  '  3  3  3 32352  6 6 6 i 6535 32
                  s         ®                            S
```

s = last sounding of *sèlèh*; S = first cadence on new *sèlèh*; © = cue; ® = response; ' = pause
$\overline{3}\ \ \overline{3}$ = up and down bow for *rebab*. Vertical alignment indicates approximate simultaneity.

Fig. 31 Cues that initiate transitions

these cues can be considered transitional in itself because they simply sound the new *sèlèh*, but both initiate transitions in the other parts. On the other hand, the second phrase of Pathetan Manyura Jugag begins with a transition to pitch 2 in all parts, and the cue itself is therefore part of the transition (fig. 31b). Cues to initiate a *sèlèh* directly occur in phrases based on a reiterated or sustained pitch and are so straightforward that they need little explanation. The leading performer simply sounds the *sèlèh*, and the other players follow suit. Cues that terminate a phrase generally occur in phrases based on a reiterated pitch and consist of alternating this central pitch with its upper neighbor on the *rebab* or with its lower neighbor on the last syllable of the vocal phrase. This last syllable is also a cue to the colotomic instruments, generally mediated by the drummer, who plays one low stroke on the large *kendhang* just as he cues the gong in a *gendhing* (see fig. 32).

Pathetan Sléndro Sanga Wantah, end of fourth phrase

dhalang	5	5	5	3 5	'

© s

rebab	5̄	5̄	5̄ 6̄	5̄

© s

gendèr	6 5 · 5 6 5 · 5 6 · 5 6 5

2 ·16̣ 5̣ 2 ·16̣ 5̣ 2 6 · 1 5̣

® s

gambang	2235365 2261̇536565

® S

suling	6 2̇ 3̇2̇ 3̇ 2̇ 1̇6̇1̇ ' 1̇6 5 ' 5̇3̇5̇

® s

kendhang	m
kempul	5

®

s = last sounding of sèlèh; S = first cadence on new sèlèh; © = cue; ® = response; ' = pause; m = mediated cue
3̄ 3̱ = up and down bow for rebab. Vertical alignment indicates approximate simultaneity.

Fig. 32   Cue to end a phrase

Most of the cues discussed thus far are directed by the *rebab* player or the *dhalang* at the whole ensemble. Only the drum cue to the colotomic players and the pitch prompts for the *dhalang* are more limited in directionality. Responses to general cues differ according to instrumental idiom, but they are all linked intimately with the cues that evoke them. Each musician knows according to context and cue whether to bring a static pattern to a cadence, shift to a transition, or move from a transition to a static pattern.

The most intense and complex type of interaction in *pathetan* involves a bidirectional exchange in which the second musician's response then cues the first musician. This pattern (notated © > ® = © > ® in the examples) is most common in interaction between *rebab* and *gendèr*. In figure 33a the *rebab* player moves from the end of one phrase (pitch 6̣) via a transitional melody to pitch 1, the *sèlèh* of the next phrase. As he moves away from 6̣, he cues the *gendèr* player (and the others) to begin their transitions. When he reaches pitch 1 with an emphatic down-bow (©2; often preceded by an ascending glide), he cues the others to reach pitch 1. He then sustains this pitch, extending the down-bow until the *gendèr* cadence (®2/©3; pitch 1 in the right hand followed by 1̣ in the left hand). He then responds to this (®3) by repeating pitch 1 in accelerating alternation of bow strokes, culminating in a cadential formula that includes the upper neighbor, pitch 2. Such involved patterns of interaction can occur several times in the brief course of a *pathetan*

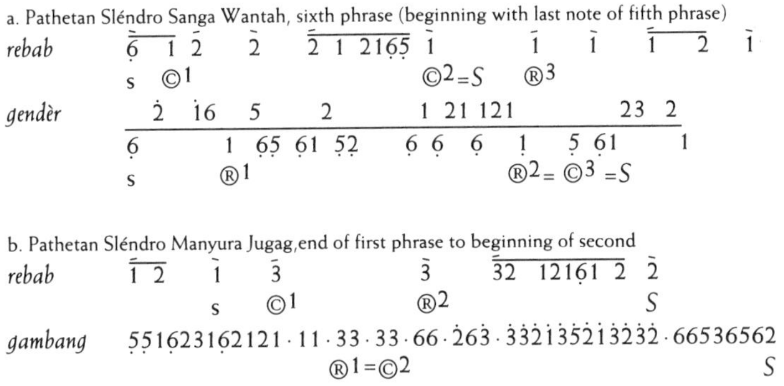

a. Pathetan Sléndro Sanga Wantah, sixth phrase (beginning with last note of fifth phrase)

b. Pathetan Sléndro Manyura Jugag, end of first phrase to beginning of second

s = last sounding of *sèlèh;* S = first cadence on new *sèlèh;* Ⓒ = cue; Ⓡ = response; ' = pause

$\overline{3}$ $\overline{3}$ = up and down bow for *rebab.* Vertical alignment indicates approximate simultaneity.

Fig. 33   Responses that function as cues

and are the mark of a cohesive performance in which the leader also follows. However, this interaction may fail to take place if the musicians do not or cannot make the effort to coordinate, as we shall see in chapter 10.

While this pattern of interaction is most consistently observed in the *rebab* and *gendèr* parts, it can also occur between other members of the ensemble. For example, Darsono explained the way in which a *rebab* player should work with a *dhalang* in terms of such bidirectional interaction: the *rebab* player waits for a vocal phrase to end, then slides (*mbesut*) to the pitch of the next phrase, initiating a transition while the *dhalang* pauses; when the *dhalang* begins to sing that phrase, the *rebab* adapts his version of the melody to the pace at which the vocal phrase draws to a close. This pattern is then repeated for the next phrase. A similar type of interaction between *rebab* and *gambang* (fig. 33b) should probably be considered more as an ideal than as common practice—Wasitodiningrat taught me to listen for the *gambang* when playing this particular transition on the *rebab* as a means of orienting myself and ensuring that the ensemble was more or less together; however, a *rebab* player is not as bound by this interaction as he is by similar exchanges with the *gendèr* player or *dhalang.*

Because there is no temporal matrix for *pathetan,* the time gap between cue and response is inherently flexible and only loosely definable. This is one of the most striking contrasts with *gendhing* and *palaran.* Drum cues for gongs at phrase endings only define a range of timing, not a precise moment at which the gong players must respond. The gap between drum stroke and gong stroke is usually about two or three seconds, whereas without a drum cue the gong players would have more freedom of play. Likewise, the © > ® = © > ® pattern (fig. 33a) places an ill-defined limit on the time lapse: the *gendèr* should reach the *sèlèh* before the *rebab* player has to change bow, that is, within four or five seconds of the *rebab*'s first sounding of the *sèlèh*.

A substantial portion of the interaction in *pathetan* takes place without cues, on the basis of a performer's ability to estimate the time it will take other players to finish a section or arrive at a *sèlèh* and on the ability to manipulate one's own part idiomatically to adapt to this estimate. In other words, the musician must know how to fill time skillfully and must estimate how much time needs to be filled so that he does not end up killing time and appearing to wait. *Gendèr* and *gambang* players work with estimations of the time it will take the *dhalang* or *rebab* player to get to the next *sèlèh* and knowledge of the time that it takes them to perform their own transitions. This is crucial because most transition patterns are not easy to shorten or lengthen and should not be repeated, yet the musician must avoid arriving too early or too late.[30] *Palaran* makes similar requirements but within a metrical frame of reference.

The adaptive strategies of abbreviation and extension that performers must master in order to coordinate with other members of the ensemble are integral to the interactive system and sound structure of *pathetan*. Limitations and possibilities vary with the idiom (Brinner 1985: 226–325). A *dhalang* is loosely bound by the number of syllables in a text phrase, but pauses between phrases and certain phrases that are sung to a single vocable (*kombangan*) allow the *dhalang* to wait for the musicians (Probohardjono 1984: 441). This flexibility in the vocal part is important, as it affords the instrumentalists the time necessary to play transitions from one pitch to the next and to complete phrases that are generally somewhat longer than the vocal phrases. Numerous musicians told me that a performance in which the singer pauses only briefly is unsatisfactory. Several pointed out that such a performance is problematic for the instrumentalists and said that unusually extended vocal phrases can also be disorienting for the instrumentalists. Unlike the *dhalang*, the *rebab* player cannot pause between phrases but can extend them. Transitional phrases are very difficult to alter, but repeated pitch phrases are easily modified within fairly wide limits: the *rebab* player can adapt

---

30. While I cannot vouch for Javanese musicians' inner sensations on this point, I know from my own experience that embarking on a transition too early and realizing it in midstream is rather like a cartoon character running off the edge of a cliff, seeing nothing below, and then backpedaling frantically before the inevitable crash.

```
sèlèh:    2                          1
gendèr
a.        2              235   3    i
          2        6  1        2  1
b.        2        2  3  5     3  2   i
          2   6  1                1
c.        2              235  3      i
          2   6   6  6  1       2  1
d.        2        235  3      3  23        i
          2   6  1        216  1   2   1
```

Fig. 34   Options for extending a *gendèr* cadence on pitch 1 in *sléndro nem pathetan*

to the pace of the other musicians by changing the duration of bow strokes or by adding another pair of reiterations of the pitch (so as to end on a down-bow).

The *gendèr* player can call on a large stock of adaptive methods to adjust to the vagaries of the vocal or *rebab* lead. For example, Harjito taught me a number of options for a problematic spot in Pathetan Sléndro Nem where the vocal and *rebab* melodies hover on pitch 2 and then move down to cadence on 1 briefly before returning to 2. It is particularly important that the *gendèr* player not precede the leader at this point. If the leader's pacing is fast this presents no problem, but if it is slow the *gendèr* player must resort to one of several options for extending the melody on 2 before moving to 1, including: pausing before beginning the module 61235321 (fig. 34a), changing the speed of this module (fig. 34b), repeating part of it (fig. 34c), or adding another module (fig. 34d). According to Harjito, the last possibility is the least acceptable because the *gendèr* player should have anticipated the pacing of the *rebab* or vocal and used one of the first three methods to maintain the appropriate coordination and pacing.

After this interaction, the *rebab* or vocal can hang on pitch 1 or move very quickly to 2, requiring the *gendèr* player to adapt once again. If, for instance, the leading player touches only briefly on pitch 1, then the *gendèr* can play the simple part notated in figure 35a. But if the leader sustains pitch 1, then the *gendèr* part must be extended by pausing (fig. 35b), by adding a module that reiterates the cadence on pitch 1 (fig. 35c), by expanding this module (fig. 35d), or by combining these options (fig. 35e).

The *gambang* and *suling* idioms offer a different type of flexibility which enables the musicians to adjust their parts by cadencing several times on a pitch without necessarily imparting the sense of finality associated with a *rebab* or *gendèr* cadence. A cadential pattern in the *gambang*

```
sèlèh:    1                    2
gendèr
a.        i̇              2̇
          1        232
b.        i̇                    2̇
          1              232
c.        i̇                    2̇
          1      ṣ6111    232
d.        i̇              2̇ i̇ 3 2̇i̇      2̇
          1      ṣ6111                    232
e.        i̇                    2̇
          1      ṣ6111    23232
```

Fig. 35 Options for extending a gendèr cadence on pitch 2 in sléndro nem pathetan

idiom can be made to sound less final if it is played rapidly, without pause or retardation; only with the proper accentuation and pauses does such a module really signify arrival at the sèlèh. Likewise, the suling player usually pauses when he is really finished playing patterns to a sèlèh. Before this he may play two or three patterns cadencing on the same pitch. Both suling and gambang idioms allow several repetitions of a pitch at the beginning of a phrase as another delaying tactic. Pivotal modules that can be played either as a reiteration of the sèlèh or as the beginning of a transition provide an additional means of flexibility, particularly in the gambang idiom.

Interactive Motivation

The overriding consideration in this manipulation of modules is to maintain the integrity of one's own part. When time is lacking and a musician needs to catch up to the others, a strategy of playing short modules is preferable to omitting essential pitches or modules. When a musician is forced to wait, the integrity of his or her part should be maintained by avoiding undue pauses or inappropriate changes in speed. Suhardi, in particular, emphasized that the gendèr player should add patterns rather than disrupt the accelerating rhythmic pattern that characterizes many phrases.

The motivation to maintain the integrity of each part is as important a constraint on pathetan as the order of precedence. It applies not only to each performer with regard to his or her part but also to the leading player, whose decisions affect that part. Several musicians told me that the dhalang should take idiomatic instrumental limitations into account and pause long enough between phrases to allow the musicians to play transitions in their entirety. But he should not prolong phrases to the point where *rebab* bowing becomes too extended or too many repetitions of a module are required in the *gendèr* or *gambang* part, as these modules are not infinitely repeatable (DS); if he sings too slowly, "the *gendèr* dies" (SH). The *dhalang* should wait until the *gendèr* player has finished a transition before he begins a new phrase (IMH). Sungkono criticized one recording, even though he approved of the close coordination between *rebab* and *gendèr*, because the *rebab* sounded rushed rather than calm. He had the opposite criticism of another recording, in which the *gambang* part was good but cooperation with others was poor, and noted that he might have had the same problem because of the *dhalang's* protracted style of singing.

The players' obligation to maintain the melodic interest and independence of their parts entails playing melodies that do not consist solely of mechanically repeated holding patterns. A *sèlèh* should be prolonged skillfully so that the player does not appear to be waiting for the next cue (DS). Suhardi criticized a performance in which the *gendèr* player seemed hesitant, as if he feared getting ahead of the *rebab*. The *gambang* part, for instance, should not be so melodically restricted that it consists of little more than the *sèlèh* and an auxiliary tone. Wasitodiningrat often emphasizes the importance of playing an independent *gambang* part and criticizes the average player for following the *gendèr* and *rebab* parts too closely. Such opinions confirm the need for diversity which Sutton (1982) and Suyenaga (1984) have noted for full *gamelan* in performance of *gendhing*.

Given the loose structure and flexible relationship between the parts of the ensemble typical of *pathetan*, the question arises as to just how tightly musicians should coordinate with each other and how closely they should approach simultaneity when converging on each goal tone. This was neatly answered by Djoko Sungkono with the paradoxical statement that the musicians "are not together but must be together." He compared the process to people walking to a movie theater following different paths but all arriving in time for the show. Suhardi expressed this as a set of flexible relationships: when the *rebab* reaches point X, the *gendèr* player should arrive approximately at point Y.

Simultaneous arrival at a *sèlèh*, called *tumbuk sèlèh* (Widiyanto), is an ideal that is not easily achieved. Widiyanto and Darsono both explained that it is rare for a group of experienced musicians to *tumbuk sèlèh* the first few times that they play *pathetan* together—this can be achieved only by learning each other's habits and stylistic predilections. Other musicians supported this ideal: Djoko Sungkono valued a high degree of coordination, and Suhardi repeatedly praised performances that were *kompak* (meaning compact, but also to work together harmoniously). He criticized one recording I played for him, saying that it was "not so good; all the musicians are professionals, but [the ensemble] is not tight enough."

Further investigation shows that this ideal of simultaneity in *pathetan* performance is relative: absolute simultaneity should be approached but not attained. Performances in which the *gendèr* or *gambang* player actually plays exactly together with the *rebab* or vocal were criticized. Suhardi specifically stated that exact simultaneity is undesirable. He praised the *gendèr* player in one recording by saying that the musician knew how much to lag behind the *rebab*. Djoko Sungkono also specified that tightness of ensemble did not mean precise rhythmic synchronization.

Some musicians summed up the key to *pathetan* performance with the Indonesian expression *menyesuaikan diri* (to adapt oneself to something external). The implication is that one must fit in with the other members of the group by adapting the pacing and content of one's own part to the idiosyncrasies of their performance while maintaining a certain degree of rhythmic and melodic independence. The word *cocog* (suited, fitting) is also used to express this ideal of performance behavior. The concept of being *cocog*, of behaving in an appropriate manner, is central to Javanese culture and social behavior in general (cf. Suyenaga 1984: 100). Several musicians said that the goal of the performer is to play *serasa dengan yang lain* (with the same feeling as the others), and Darsono also said that there should be *adu rasa* (compatibility).

The extent of this interdependence is demonstrated by the difficulty encountered when a musician attempts to record all the parts of a *pathetan* by overdubbing:[31] the two parts that can provide the best melodic referent are the vocal and the *rebab*, but they are dependent on the *gendèr* and the *gambang* for rhythmic shape. I discovered this while working with Wasitodiningrat on a multitrack recording of *pathetan* for his American students. He was not satisfied with the results. When I related this to Harjito, Harjito said that he had had a similar experience. More recently, Widiyanto solved this problem by recording the *gendèr* as a basic referent for timing and intonation, recording the vocal track with this support, and then rerecording the *gendèr* so that it followed rather than led the vocal (personal communication).

Two performances of Pathetan Sléndro Sanga Wantah will serve here as examples of the variation that is acceptable in the performance of a single musical entity. As with every *pathetan*, the degree to which the parts should be coordinated with one another fluctuates in the course of Pathetan Sanga Wantah. During some phrases it is unnecessary for the

---

31. Cf. Simha Arom's method for studying African music (1991).

Phrase #	Sèlèh	Coordination
A	2	staggered entrance, *rebab* or voice followed by others in turn
B	1	closely synchronized; *gendèr* response can serve as cue to *rebab*
C	2	closely synchronized; *gendèr* response can serve as cue to *rebab*
D	5	loose beginning; cue at end which serves as rendezvous
E	6̣	loose with rendezvous at end; *gendèr* cadence cues leader (voice or *rebab*) to continue
F	1	close, *gendèr* response serves as cue to *rebab*
G	2	loose
	5̣	loose, *rebab* and vocal can finish before others; *gambang* and *gendèr* often coordinate last pitch

Fig. 36. Fluctating degrees of coordination in Pathetan Sléndro Sanga Wantah

musicians to synchronize closely, but they should converge at other points, which can serve as rendezvous in case the players fall too far out of synchronization (as in fig. 33b). Martopangrawit talked about the *gendèr* and *gambang* parts having "places to wait."

The guidance I received from my teachers and gleaned from hearing numerous performances of this *pathetan* is synthesized in figure 36. The beginning of this *pathetan* consists of a brief transitional passage leading to pitch 2 that may be omitted from the *gambang* part but is always played on *rebab* and *gendèr*, with the *gendèr* transition timed so as to arrive at the *sèlèh* shortly after the *rebab*. The *rebab* player then proceeds to reiterate the *sèlèh* in a typical © > ® = © > ® pattern. Similar patterns of interaction between *rebab* and *gendèr* occur at the initiation of the *sèlèh* in the second and third phrases. The fourth phrase differs from the preceding phrases because the beginning is less clearly marked. The fifth phrase is the most complex melodically, moving through a number of focal pitches. Coordination is relatively loose here, although the *rebab* should be the first to begin and the first to arrive at the final goal tone, low 6. This pitch serves as a rendezvous where the leader waits for the others before embarking on the more tightly coordinated sixth phrase. Once again the initiation of the *sèlèh* involves a © > ® = © > ® pattern. The final phrase, like the fifth, flows through several focal pitches and coordination is somewhat looser, although the *rebab* should still precede the other instruments.

A common type of interaction, conducted without overt cues, occurs at the end of every *pathetan*. The *rebab* and vocal parts may end well before the others, but the *gambang* and *suling* players often delay their last note until the *gendèr* reaches his or her last note. While such coordination is extremely common, a few players consider it unnecessary, exemplifying the coexistence of conflicting conceptual models that lead musicians to perform differently and evaluate performances differently.

The performance transcribed in figure 37 illustrates the norms of interaction which I elicited from musicians. It is not a "perfect" performance inasmuch as the individual parts are not ideal examples of idiomatic manipulation of melodic modules, but it is a cohesive performance in which the musicians worked well together.[32] The leadership of the *rebab* player is clear and unchallenged throughout the *pathetan*, and the other players' responses are also properly timed: the *gambang* and *suling* players generally follow the *gendèr*, and no one lags too far behind. The interactive aspects of this performance are emphasized in figure 38, a line graph in which static passages are marked — — — — and transitional ones >>>>, respectively. The cadential *rebab* figures which feature alternation of the main pitch with its upper neighbor are indicated by a caret, and cue-response patterns are marked with ©, ®, and arrows. These arrows also clarify the sequence of events, which might otherwise appear to be simultaneous due to typographic condensation. Phrases are indicated by letters placed above the graph, directly below the Arabic numerals that mark elapsed time in seconds. The most significant points of interaction, highlighted by shaded rectangles placed below the graph, include the beginning of the *pathetan*, the two arrivals at pitch 1 at the beginning of the second and sixth phrases, and the transition to pitch 2 at the beginning of the third phrase.

Many other performances fall within the loosely defined limits of acceptable interaction for this *pathetan*. For instance, a somewhat different pattern of interaction emerges in the performance represented in figure 39. The most important © > ® = © > ® patterns are observed, although the *gendèr* player follows the *rebab* almost too closely throughout much of the performance and rushes to the finish, preceding the *rebab* cues in the last phrase. Variations in the temporal placement of *gambang* and *suling* cadences and phrases are particularly common, as these parts are less constrained than *rebab* and *gendèr*.

The influence that particular individuals can have on the shaping of a *pathetan* as they interact musically and socially will be discussed in chapter 10. Before addressing interpersonal aspects of *gamelan* perfor-

---

32. The performers' anonymity is preserved here by substituting letters for names because some of the following analysis rests on evaluation of the temperament and social interaction of individual musicians. None of my comments are intended to disparage the ability of any of these musicians—all are competent and some are truly outstanding. However, the capacity or desire to interact with other musicians is not directly related to other aspects of musical competence.

Recording:SU5-B6, 1983. Personnel: *Rebab* (Rb) = C, *Gendèr* (Gd) = Q, *Gambang* (Gb) = A, *Suling* (Sl) = E

```
Sec 48. . . . . .49. . . . . .50. . . . . .51. . . . . .52. . . . . .53. . . . . .54. . . . . .55. . . . . .56. . . . . .57. . . . . .58. . . . . .59. . . . . .60. . . . . .61. . . . . .62. . . . . .63. . . . . .64
Rb        6      6 6 1 6       ╯1 2            2   2 2 2    3 32  ⌄ 1 2          ╯ 1                        1  11   1 2 1     2          1       2
Gd     6      1 6 2      16      5          2            1      2    1 2    1         1            123  21    1 23   2  235     6  5  1  65
         356                1     65   5  61   5 2     6     5    6      6    5 6      1     65  56         56          1     5                  1 5
Gb    5 1 6            65  5  1  6  2      5  5  1  6  2  1  2  3  1  6  2  1  2  1  65  6  32  5  6  3  2  5  3  21  65  5  6  1  5  2  3  1  6  2  1    65  5  6  1  2  3    2  5  6  3
Su                                     652        2           16  '     3235   2⌃  '      6 ╯1653  65 ⌃⌃321  '     662  1⌄'6  5⌄⌃321 1⌄   '        1  2  3

Sec 64. . . . . .65. . . . . .66. . . . . .67. . . . . .68. . . . . .69. . . . . .70. . . . . .71. . . . . .72. . . . . .73. . . . . .74. . . . . .75. . . . . .76. . . . . .77. . . . . .78. . . . . .79. . . . . .80
Rb       3  2   ⌄         ⌄        ╯ 1                      216 3   5   5       23                      5
Gd          2          356                    1       5      3     2              3 5          2    1                            2
         61                      16              1             65     3     5    32 2       5   235                                  5
Gb          2  16   2  3  2   16  2  3  1    65   5     32  2  3  5  3   6 1 5   3    6     5    6    5     5     5    6    5    6          5  6     5
Su       3       3   3  2  1   '        3⌄  5   2⌃   3     1  2  '     6 ⌃      6 ⌃      612      ⌃  '    6  165365  65  6532165   '        5  5̸     5            '
```

KEY

sec = time in seconds, rb = *rebab*, gd = *gendèr*, gb = *gambang*, su = *suling*

⌄ = brief sounding of pitch below, ⌃ = brief sounding of pitch above, 3̆ 3̄ = *rebab* upbow and down bow,

╯ = ascending glide, ╮ = descending glide, 5̸ in the *suling* part represents a lowered 5, ✗ in the *gendèr* part indicates a damped note, ' = pause in the *suling part*

The vertical alignment of parts represents approximate simultaneity, but typographic limitations preclude precise representation of rhythm particularly in the *gambang* part.

Fig. 37 Pathetan Sléndro Sanga Wantah

recording: SU5-B6 *Rebab* (Rb) = C, *Gendèr* (Gd) = Q, *Gambang* (Gb) = A, *Suling* (Sl) = E

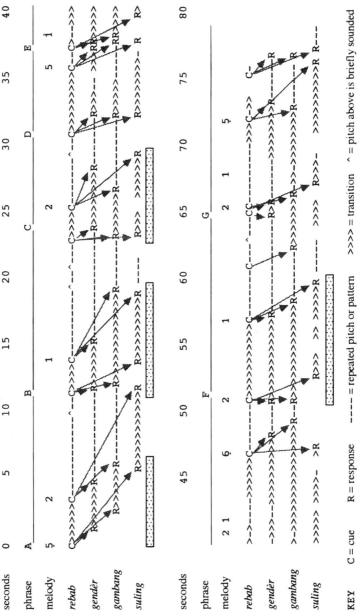

KEY   C = cue   R = response   ---- = repeated pitch or pattern   >>>> = transition   ^ = pitch above is briefly sounded

Fig. 38   Pathetan Sanga Wantah—interaction chart l

recording: SU2A10; *Rebab* (Rb) = D, *Gendèr* (Gd) = F, *Gambang* (Gb) = H, *Suling* (Sl) = G

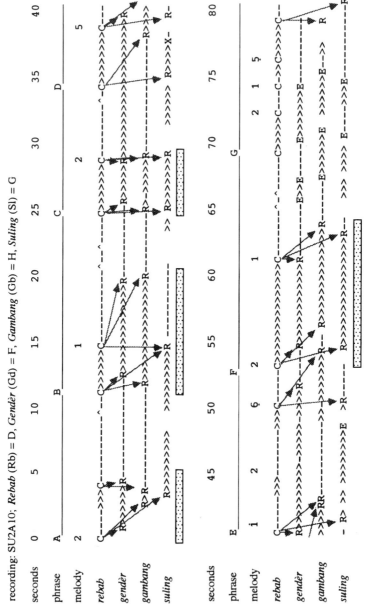

KEY   C = cue   R = response   ---- = repeated pitch or pattern   >>>> = transition   ^ = pitch above is briefly sounded

Fig. 39 Pathetan Sanga Wantah—interaction chart II

mance, a brief look at some other Javanese performance genres will provide an opportunity to consider some of the ways in which interactive networks and systems are complicated by the participation of nonmusical performers and by the demands of coordinating music with other events.

CHAPTER NINE

INTERACTION IN JAVANESE
MULTIMEDIA PRODUCTIONS

G*amelan* music is a central aspect of any performance of Javanese *wayang kulit*(shadow play), whether as quiet background for narration, as a vehicle for lively battle scenes, or as nondramatic entertainment before, during, and after the play. Since much of this music must be coordinated with puppet movement and speech produced by a *dhalang* who is external to the *gamelan* network, working with different interactive system, structures, and motivation, *wayang* affords an opportunity to extend our discussion to multimedia performance, in which complexity increases and the distribution and mediation of control is altered.

A *wayang* performance is largely spontaneous: the overall scheme is well defined, but the details are infinitely variable and a single story may be presented in very different ways. Because of this spontaneity, performer interaction is the essence of *wayang*, as rapid-fire cues and responses fly between *dhalang* and musicians. A discussion of the chief interactive differences relative to other *gamelan* performance contexts is offered here in lieu of the book-length treatment that *wayang* interaction merits.

Interactive Network

The interactive network is more ramified and yet less diffuse in *wayang kulit* than in *klenèngan* because it is centered on a single person, the *dhalang*,[1] who enters into particularly close performance relationships with

---

1. See van Groenendael (1982) and Keeler (1987) for lengthy discussions of *dhalangs*.

certain members of the ensemble. The *dhalang* is almost always male, often musically competent, and generally regarded as spiritually potent. He controls most aspects of the performance, including the selection of musical pieces and the way that they are performed, but he relies on leading musicians to relay his wishes to the rest of the group, to enact them, and to regulate the moment-by-moment unfolding of the music. He is constrained, in turn, by the ability and readiness of the musicians to follow his cues and by conventional structures, dramatic and musical, that determine when he can bring a puppet onto the screen, for instance, or when he can call for softer music as background for his narration.

The *gamelan*, which is arrayed behind the *dhalang* on the same platform, has expanded in this century from a small set, consisting mainly of the softer instruments and limited to one tuning, to the full *sléndro/pélog* ensemble commonly heard in *klenèngan* and dance performances.[2] Ideally a *dhalang* is accompanied by a steady group of musicians who are familiar with his style, including the standard practices, defined regionally or otherwise, that connect him with a school or tradition and his personal preferences and methods of communication (idiosyncrasies that tend to be emphasized in the search for fame in today's climate of intense competition). Yet often enough a *dhalang* must perform with a group of strange musicians because he is invited to perform away from his home area or for some other reason. In such cases the *dhalang* will try to bring a handful of musicians who have worked with him to play key parts in the *gamelan*. There appears to be fairly broad consensus regarding the most crucial roles, and this reveals common conceptualizations of the roles, relationships, and priorities of the interactive network.

The *gendèr* and *kendhang* players are the most crucial to the success of the *dhalang* and the *wayang* performance as a whole (cf. van Groenendael 1982: 156). The *gendèr* player fills several key roles, accompanying all of the *dhalang's sulukan* (songs that include *pathetan*, *sendhon*, and *ada-ada*), playing the introductions to many of the *gendhing* that the *dhalang* cues, and providing a nearly continuous improvisation (*grimingan*) when the other musicians are silent. The intimacy of this relationship is reflected in the positioning of the *gendèr* closest to the *dhalang* and frequently, too, by close familial ties: a *dhalang* is often accompanied by a female relative.

A *wayang* drummer must be constantly alert to every nuance of the *dhalang's* speech, puppet manipulation, and rhythmic tapping on the *kotak*, the puppet box placed to the *dhalang's* left. Besides regulating the pace and flow of the music as he would in other contexts, he must trans-

---

2. Wasitodiningrat dates the adoption of *bonang* and other loud instruments to the 1930s and attributes it to the influence of *wayang wong* (personal communication).

late the *dhalang*'s cues into drum strokes and sonically enhance the puppets' movements. Conversely, the *dhalang* is dependent on the patterns
of the *kendhang* to bring his puppet movements to life and to guide the
gamelan, keeping it on a steady course while he creates a battle scene,
starting and stopping the music at a moment's notice, and so on. In the
best of circumstances, this symbiotic relationship is based on extensive
familiarity with each other's style—the *dhalang*'s way of manipulating
the puppets and the drummer's playing preferences—but the basic patterns of movement and sound are sufficiently conventional to enable a
dhalang and a drummer who are strangers to work together to create an
adequate, if not exemplary, performance.

The *rebab* player should also know the *dhalang*'s style well, although
he exercises less control in *wayang* than in *klenèngan*. Like the musicians
who play *gendèr* and *kendhang*, he leads at times, mediating between *dhalang* and *gamelan*, but he is less frequently involved in this mediation than
either of them. In some village performances a *rebab* is lacking or played
only during *pathetan* and soft sections of pieces by a musician who otherwise plays one of the louder instruments such as *saron* or even *kendhang*.

The gong player is also considered a core musician. The *Serat Sastramiruda*, a nineteenth-century manuscript, offers a brief interactive explanation of this musician's importance that is still echoed today: he needs to
respond appropriately to the *gendèr* and *saron* (i.e., the *balungan*) in battle
music and to the *kendhang* for changes of speed and for endings (Kusumadilaga 1981: 48). The importance of proper timing of strokes on *kempul* and gong (usually played by the same musician) during battle music
is also cited: these strokes occur on every beat, and their timing can
make or break a performance. The referential role of the gong player as
demarcator of the largest musical units is essential not only for the musicians but for the *dhalang*, too, who must maintain his orientation to the
musical framework in order to time his puppet movements and his cues
properly. Familiarity with the *dhalang*'s singing style is desirable because
the gong player articulates vocal cadences and provides tonal orientation in *pathetan* and other songs, as we saw in the previous chapter.

Some performers also include the *demung* player in the core group
because he can lead the other *balungan* players, particularly in loud, fast
passages. The *slenthem*, which is the leading *balungan* instrument in *klenèngan*, is less effective because it lacks the *demung*'s volume and incisive
attack. Because the *demung* is a recent addition to the *wayang gamelan*, it
is not mentioned in the *Serat Sastramiruda* among the essential instruments
for *wayang* and it is omitted even from recent prescriptive writings
(e.g., Probohardjono 1954: 4; Nojowirongko [1954]: 61; Darsomartono
1978a: 2 or 1978b: 20). The *bonang*, added at the same time as the *demung*,

is still not considered a mainstay of the *wayang* ensemble, despite the fact that it is a leading instrument of the standard *gamelan*, because its mediating role in *wayang* is relatively limited. I have witnessed crucial *demung* leadership in some unconventional passages that other leading musicians were powerless to influence: the drummer could not indicate pitch, the *gendèr* and *rebab* players were not playing in these sections because they were too loud and fast, and the *bonang* player was playing an abstraction of the melody that did not convey enough melodic information. We have here a fine example of reinforcement: the drummer alone cannot bring about the quick changes required in loud pieces, but if one *demung* player is attuned to him, the others can follow. The need for a cutting sound and leadership in rapid *balungan* has increased in recent years due to the adoption of the full *gamelan* as the norm for *wayang* and the proliferation of flashy new melodies and performance practices.

Singers are often a part of the core group, too, as the performance of newly composed, vocal-centered pieces has become more common in the middle act of a *wayang*. Such pieces are ignored in the highly conservative pedagogical literature so it is not surprising that singers are not mentioned as part of the core group, but if a *dhalang* is to call for one of these new pieces, usually his own composition, he must have singers who know the parts.

In most cases these contingency plans are not necessary because a typical *dhalang* performs with the same musicians night after night (over 80 percent of performances according to van Groenendael 1982), establishing a common base of communication and expectations that obviates the need for explicit rehearsal (a comparative rarity for most musicians). But the interactive responsibilities that form the rationale for the core ensemble hold true even in the most cohesive group.

In contrast with *klenèngan*, line of sight is an important consideration for the positioning of leading musicians in a *wayang* performance. The *kendhang*, *gendèr*, and *rebab* players need not be able to see each other, but they must have a good view of the *dhalang* and the screen and so can usually be found in approximately the same places: the *gendèr* directly behind the *dhalang*, the *kendhang* just behind the *gendèr*, and the *rebab* to one side of the *gendèr* (fig. 40). The positioning of other instruments and musicians varies widely. Visual communication can be important for the two musicians who play interlocking parts (*imbal*) on *saron* when they face each other over a single instrument (fig. 40b), but they may play side by side on separate instruments (fig. 40c). The three arrangements shown in figure 40 are taken from pedagogical texts that ignore the common expansion of the *gamelan* to include both *sléndro* and *pélog* instruments and a full complement of *bonang*, singers, gongs, and *saron*. They show the gong rack at the back, although it is usually placed to one side to give spectators a better view of the screen, and they also include the *kecèr*, cymbals that were used in the past to amplify the puppet movements but are now rarely heard.[3] Nonetheless, they reflect some of the constants and variables in instrument placement, particularly the central positioning of the lead musicians and the frequent necessity of placing some musicians facing away from the others due to lack of space. Nojowirongko, for example, notes that in some cases the instruments may be placed to the side so that a large number of spectators can see the *dhalang*, but the *gendèr, rebab,* and *kendhang* must remain behind the *dhalang* because they are the ones who receive his cues ([1954]: 62). Spatial constraints can become particularly pressing when a full *gamelan* is used, as Probohardjono recognizes when he says that a small *gamelan* is really sufficient for *wayang* and that one should approximate his layout *if space allows* (1954: 4). Since there is no lack of space in court performances, the aesthetic requirements of instrument placement in parallel positions facing the screen can be realized (Nojowirongko [1954]: 62).

Interactive System

Much of the interactive system of *wayang* is codified and transmitted through pamphlets such as Probohardjono 1984 (pp. 496–502) and schools of *padhalangan* (the *dhalang's* art); summaries are even available in English (Heins 1970; Lysloff 1990: 56–64; Sumarsam 1984a; Van Ness and Prawirohardjo 1980: 56–59). A *dhalang* cues through percussive patterns (*dhodhogan*), vocal techniques (*wangsalan, kombangan, buka celuk,* and other musical uses of the voice), and puppet position or motion. *Dhodhogan* are rhythmic patterns tapped with a hand- or foot-held mallet (*cempala*) on the puppet box or on the bronze plates (*keprak*) hanging on the side of the box. They are used to start and stop pieces, to cue changes of speed and volume and transitions to new pieces. Though standardized in principle, these patterns vary according to personal stylistic preferences. Some *dhodhogan* require considerable musical skill on the part of the *dhalang*, as they must be timed precisely to the music in order to communicate properly. This is particularly crucial for those *dhodhogan* that interlock with drum patterns. Musicians must know the meaning of these patterns and, moreover, be able to distinguish significant cues from other uses of the *cempala* such as articulating dialogues, creating an air of intensity and excitement, or enhancing the puppets' motion. In the heat of battle, there is little difference between a cue to accelerate or finish a

---

3. I saw *kecèr* being played only in one self-consciously traditional performance commissioned by a group of Japanese *wayang* connoisseurs.

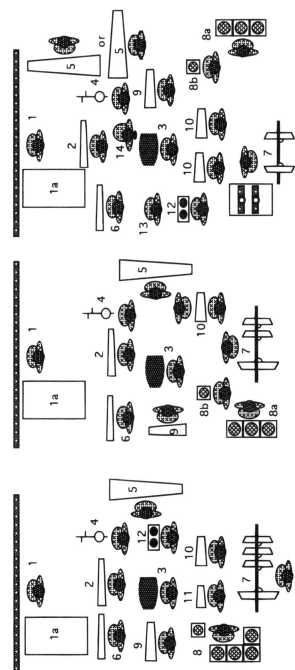

a. Probohardjono 1954:6

b. Nojowirongko [1954]: 61

c. based on Darsomartono 1978a:2 and 1978b:20

KEY 1 = *dhalang* and screen 1a = puppet box 2 = *gendèr* 3 = *kendhang* 4 = *gambang* 6 = *gendèr panerus* 7 = *gong &kempul*

8a = *kenong* 8b = *kethuk* 9 = *slenthem* 10 = *saron* 11 = *saron panerus* 12 = *kecèr* 13 = *suling* 14 = *pesindhèn*

Fig. 40 Three prescriptions for *wayang kulit* setup

piece and the sound effects that accompany blows delivered by one puppet to another. These nuances are among the most problematic aspects
of *gamelan* performance for foreign students who have difficulty filtering
significant codes from the sound stream in which they are embedded.

Significant information is also embedded in *wangsalan*, the verbal
riddles or allusions to composition titles that are used to cue longer
gendhing. A *dhalang* works these into his narration or dialogue as an
oblique means of requesting a particular piece.[4] For example, he might
end a spoken section of the performance with the words *lir sabdaning
kukila* (like the voice of a bird), which refers to the piece Ladrang Kandha Manyura (*kandha* = speech or voice, *manyura* = peacock's call),
marking this phrase as a cue by saying it with rising intonation and following it with a single tap on the puppet box. The *dhalang's* verbal cue
sets up the interaction, and his tap *completes* the cue by marking a more
precise timing for the onset of the piece (cf. Lysloff 1990: 56–64). One
of the melodic leaders then interprets and relays this command to the
rest of the *gamelan* in musical terms by playing the introduction of the
intended piece.

Some *wangsalan* consist of clear synonyms or actually incorporate part
of the title unaltered while others are fairly obscure. This aspect of interactive competence is particularly important for players of the leading
melodic instruments and is stressed in writings on *wayang* performance
practice: "Therefore a musician really needs to know and memorize all
of the *dhalang's wangsalan* and those who really have to know the *dhalang's
wangsalan* are 1) the *rebab* and 2) the *gendèr* because the two of them are
the ones who can start a *gendhing*, while the others just follow along"
(Djakoeb and Wignyaroemeksa 1913: 109). Knowledge of *wangsalan*
was one of the domains in which prospective teachers were tested when
the faculty of the newly formed performing arts conservatory in Surakarta was being selected in the early 1950s (Wasitodiningrat, personal
communication).

A *dhalang* can also cue a piece melodically by singing the first note of
a song (*sulukan*) or a vocal substitute for the instrumental introduction
to a *gendhing*. To interpret a *sulukan* cue correctly, the musicians must
determine (1) that the *dhalang* is singing a *sulukan* rather than speaking
in a particularly sonorous and pitched voice, as he does for certain char-

---

4. Benedict Anderson has noted that such oblique cues can also flow from the *pesindhèn* to
the *dhalang*: "When the *pesindhèn* . . . at a wayang performance wishes to rest and to warn the
puppeteer . . . to take over, she weaves the words *ron ing mlinjo* (leaves of the mlinjo tree) into
her song. Since these leaves are also known as *so* and the Javanese verb for rest is *ngaso*, the
connection is at once felt, and to the mystification of the uninitiated, the dhalang immediately
takes over the burden of her singing" (1990: 129).

acters; (2) which type of *sulukan*—*pathetan, sendhon,* or *ada-ada*—is being performed, on the basis of the dramatic situation and the presence or absence of agitated tapping on the box or *keprak;* and (3) which song is being performed, on the basis of the initial pitch and the dramatic/musical context. For example, if the *dhalang* begins to sing a high 6 in the first portion of a performance, the *suluk* must be in the first *pathet* (*slèndro nem;* see "Interactive Structure" below). If the *dhalang* is not tapping on the box or *keprak,* then the song is not an *ada-ada,* but a *sendhon* or *pathetan,* specifically Sendhon Pananggalan, Pathetan Kedhu, or Pathetan Lasem depending on dramatic context. Sendhon Pananggalan is appropriate for expressing confusion or anxiety, primarily during the first audience scene when the king is confronted with a problem; Pathetan Kedhu is appropriate at a later point in the same act, after the army overcomes natural obstacles; Pathetan Lasem is appropriate for a refined king from a foreign land. It is particularly important that the *rebab* player interpret the context quickly in order to know whether to pick up his instrument, because he plays only in *pathetan,* not in *sendhon.* Thus, the *dhalang's* active knowledge of performance practice must be matched by a fairly complex passive understanding of *sulukan* usage on the part of the leading musicians.

This example emphasizes the potential ambiguity of a cue. Many of the cues in *wayang* are ambiguous or context-sensitive. The precise meaning of a cue is defined with reference to the context in which it is given such as the overall structure of the play or the structure of a particular piece. Contextual information should filter out conflicting meanings to leave a single unambiguous message.

A *kombangan,* a syllable or phrase chanted on a single pitch, can lead musicians to the high-register *lik* section of a piece, to another piece, such as an *ayak-ayakan* after a *sampak,* or to a return to full volume after soft playing. Once again we encounter the issue of interactive competence: according to an anonymous *kraton* manuscript on *wayang* cues, "The *udhar*(full volume) was always cued with *kumbangan* but since many *dhalang* did not *nggendhingi* [roughly, know about music] it became acceptable to just tap the *kothak*" (Anonymous 1982: 11). This reference to earlier practice may indicate the turn of the century or earlier, since Martopangrawit, who transliterated this manuscript, attributed it to the years 1929–36.[5]

A wide variety of subtle and not so subtle uses of puppets facilitates interaction. The *kayon,* a special "tree of life" puppet, is placed in the

---

5. The derogatory attitude toward the general competence of *dhalangs* is typical of Martopangrawit's views and may be his own addition. I have not seen the original.

middle of the screen to demarcate scenes; its angle marks progress through the dramatic structure and therefore indicates musical mode as well (see the discussion of interactive sound structure below). Certain puppets move to characteristic rhythms when they enter or exit: as soon as the drummer sees the *dhalang* pick up one of these puppets, he prepares to alter his drumming at the next appropriate moment in the musical structure. By taking a puppet out of the box and putting it on the side of the box before moving it to the screen, the *dhalang* gives another "setup" cue to the drummer, alerting him that this is the last puppet to be brought on for that scene so he should be ready for the *dhalang*'s cue to direct most of the musicians to stop playing so that the narration can be heard (Anonymous 1982: 10).

The leading musicians fulfill double roles in relation to the *dhalang*. When they respond directly to some cues, by accompanying a song or by emphasizing puppet movement through special drum patterns, these musicians are in a closed relationship that does not involve the rest of the *gamelan*. At other times they serve as mediators between *dhalang* and *gamelan* by interpreting the *dhalang*'s cues and translating them into musical cues. Even when the *dhalang*'s cue itself is musical, the translation is more integral to the flow of the music because it is incorporated into the ongoing play of the *kendhang*, *rebab*, or *gendèr*.

These mediated relationships are important ways of ensuring concerted responses by the ensemble and removing some of the burden of coordination from the *dhalang*. Responsibility for the precise timing of each response is delegated to one musician. There is little ambiguity in the directionality of the *dhalang*'s cues. Most of the cues tapped on the box or bronze plates are directed at the drummer while vocal cues, whether spoken or sung, are directed at the melodic leaders. The *rebab*, *gendèr*, and *bonang* players need to know the division of the *wayang* repertoire into *gendhing rebab*, *gendhing gendèr*, and *gendhing bonang* so that when the *dhalang* cues a piece, the player of the appropriate instrument will perform the introduction. For the other musicians these mediated cues are relatively simple to follow: if they do not understand a *wangsalan*, they have five or ten seconds to identify the piece from the introductory melody before they have to join in.

The drummer's leadership of the *gamelan* is far more complex and prominent than the melodic players'. This complexity is due largely to the fluent mix of cues with sound effects and ongoing drum patterns that have no interactive significance and to the rapid response times required. Almost all the faster pieces are introduced by the drummer following a brief rhythmic cue from the *dhalang*. The drummer regulates the tempo and *irama* as well as the volume of the ensemble and the slow or fast endings of pieces in accordance with cues from the *dhalang*. He shepherds the ensemble by playing just behind or ahead of the beat as necessary. In general, *wayang* drumming is characterized by a subtle flexibility of rhythm by which the drummer makes the beat and tempo clear without actually playing precisely on the beat. Anticipation of the *dhalang*'s probable course of action and timing is an essential interactive skill for the leading musicians. The drummer, in particular, must anticipate puppet movement in order to emphasize important moves effectively.

Within the multilayered world of a *wayang* performance, orientation is of the utmost importance. The soft *grimingan* that the *gendèr* player improvises while the *dhalang* is talking serves as an ongoing set of markers, reiterating the tuning and mode as a frame of reference for the *dhalang* when he breaks into song. The importance of this tonal reference is underlined repeatedly in writings on *wayang*: the *dhalang* must concentrate on many things at once (deciding on story line, narrating, moving puppets, cuing musicians, and singing), and he must switch rapidly from one activity to another so he risks starting a song on the wrong pitch, a potential disaster—as we saw in the Prelude—since the initial pitch is an essential characteristic of the cue to the other musicians. The wide variation in tuning among ensembles increases the danger of disorientation; even a musically competent *dhalang* needs reminders of the tuning of an unfamiliar *gamelan*. Characteristic modal patterns serve to orient both the *dhalang* and the other musicians to the overall structure of the play.

Orientation is also a concern during the *dhalang*'s songs (we have already seen how various gongs provide orientation in *pathetan*) and his narration over soft accompaniment (*sirep*). The *balungan*, usually an important line of reference, is missing during a *sirep* so the *dhalang* has to refer to the colotomy, the drumming, and the relatively complex melodies of *rebab* and *gendèr* for timing and tuning his cue to the other musicians to return to full volume. Furthermore, he must orient himself to this while reciting a scene-setting narration.

It is to be expected that cues will be missed or misinterpreted in such a complex and unrehearsed production. In their introductory book on *wayang*, Van Ness and Prawirohardjo talk about the relative rarity of such slipups and the tension and subsequent release surrounding successful interpretations of cues: "It is precisely this kind of momentary tension and its release when everyone does the right thing, and many other moments like it that constitute a great deal of enjoyment that the

Javanese derive from participating in a *wayang kulit* performance" (1980: 59). They also say that a *dhalang* should never speak directly to the musicians (1980: 57), but this does occasionally happen when indirect means of communication fail: "If, in the middle of a gendhing . . . the dhalang's hands are both at work and he is unable to give a clear signal, or the signal is not heard by the musicians, then the dhalang often will utter the words, 'wau ta' [meaning roughly, what I just said!] as a request to the musicians to play softly (sirep), stop, and so forth" (Probohardjono 1984: 499). In one instance of interactive failure I actually saw a *dhalang* turn around and tell the *rebab* player the name of a *gendhing* after the musician did not respond to the conventional oblique verbal reference.

Interactive Sound Structure

The largest sound structure in *wayang* is the fixed sequence of three *pathet* (a term that signifies both dramatic act and musical mode) in *sléndro* or *pélog* that forms the overarching framework for the eight or nine hours of every traditional *wayang* performance. The same sequence of musical modes governs the selection of *gendhing* in a *klenèngan*, but in *wayang* it is a more precisely defined trajectory (see A. Becker 1979). The music of the *gamelan* serves a dramatic purpose by defining every major juncture along the way and so articulating the structure of the play.

This structure is important for the orientation that it provides, which ensures successful interaction between *dhalang* and musicians by lending ambiguous cues specific meanings. For example, the *dhalang's* rhythmic cue for *srepegan*, a musical piece played to accompany action of moderate intensity, calls for the same colotomic structure in each *pathet* but an entirely different melody. The appropriate choice depends on the musicians' attention to the course of the performance: they must know what the current *pathet* is even if the *dhalang* has been talking for the past half hour and the musicians have been relaxing, smoking, and eating. A more detailed orientation to the progress of the play is necessary in order to distinguish between particular *sulukan* because musicians must also take mood, scene, and characters into account.

Within the *pathet* structure many smaller sound structures are performed. These consist of the *gendèr* player's loosely shaped *grimingan* and many well-defined entities—pieces with names, beginnings, endings, and relatively rigid forms. The *gendèr* player creates free-flowing *grimingan* by weaving together patterns from *sulukan* and *gendhing* in order to maintain a sense of *pathet* and to reflect and enhance the atmosphere that the *dhalang* creates with his voice and puppet manipulation. The *dhalang* can actually ask for a tense *ada-ada* accompaniment while he speaks by tapping rapidly as he would when singing an *ada-ada* (Anonymous 1982:10). Although *grimingan* is ostensibly solo music-making, a subtle but beautiful interaction takes place when the gong, *kempul,* and *kenong* players respond to cadential patterns played on the *gendèr,* particularly those patterns drawn from the ends of *sulukan.* The drummer can inter-ject himself into this interaction by cuing the gongs with a single low stroke on the *kendhang,* as he does in the performance of *pathetan* and other *sulukan.*

Almost all of the independent pieces played in *wayang* fall into three large categories, *sulukan, gendhing lampahan,* and *gendhing.*[6] The contrast be-tween *klenèngan* and *wayang* has already been discussed with regard to the interactive structure of *pathetan.* The other types of *sulukan, sendhon* and *ada-ada,* are usually restricted to *wayang* and constrain performers much as *pathetan* do. These pieces are not cyclical, and most may be abbreviated or extended by following the *dhalang's* vocal melody.

Gendhing and *gendhing lampahan* provide radically different frameworks for interaction. The colotomic cycles of *gendhing* are long and unalterable (see chap. 7), constraining the *dhalang's* pacing of puppet movements, narration, and intermittent singing. This provides a measure of predict-ability to the musicians: cues to change speed, change volume, or finish the piece can only be initiated and responses given at well-defined points within the cycle. The timing of cues and responses for initiating a *sirep,* a reduction in volume that allows the *dhalang* to narrate, is shown in figure 41 with respect to the thirty-two-beat cycle of a *ladrang.* During one repetition of the piece the *dhalang* cues the drummer just before the sixteenth beat (C1) to prepare for a *sirep.* The drummer mediates this cue (M1), and the other musicians respond (R1) by accelerating and shifting to a faster *irama.* As the musicians approach the eighth beat of the next cycle, the *dhalang* gives another cue (C2), mediated immedi-ately by the drummer (M2). The musicians respond (R2) by slowing down, and most of them stop playing at the eighth beat, leaving the *rebab, gendèr, kendhang,* and colotomic players to continue the piece softly at a slower *irama.*

Gendhing lampahan, a category that includes *ayak-ayakan, srepegan,* and *sampak,* are relatively short and provide the *dhalang* with a much more flexible musical accompaniment that can be stretched, compressed, and otherwise altered to suit the action. Interaction is less predictable, and musicians must be ready to respond to the *dhalang* at any moment.

While relatively few *gendhing* are played in a given *wayang,* these

6. A few pieces which feature the *pesindhèn* do not fit these categories.

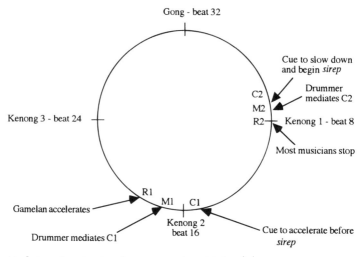

Fig. 41   Interactive structure in *wayang*: cuing *sirep* in a *ladrang*

pieces place the heaviest burden on musicians' competence because they must be ready to play any one of several hundred *gendhing* from memory at a moment's notice. By contrast, *gendhing lampahan* are played far more frequently in *wayang* but they are much shorter than *gendhing* and far fewer in number.

There is a striking contrast between the drumming for these two classes of compositions. For *gendhing* a drummer plays fixed patterns, with minor flexibility, that are congruent in length with the colotomic structure of the piece. For *gendhing lampahan* he improvises on loosely defined patterns and mixes these with sound effects. During battle scenes, which are accompanied by *srepegan* and *sampak*, the drummer may leave the *gamelan* on "automatic pilot" once he has established the appropriate tempo, and turn his attention to the puppet action, anticipating and responding to puppets striking one another, being hit by arrows, falling, and rushing on and off the screen. An experienced drummer can enhance the effect of these motions immeasurably by setting them up with a few choice strokes, ending with a loud stroke or cluster of strokes timed perfectly to the puppets' motion and to the crashing of the *dhalang's keprak* (the overlapping bronze plates hung on the side of the puppet box). These bursts are timed to fit the musical structure in the large sense—they usually come at the end of a phrase—but they generally fall a fraction of a beat after the gong. The ability of the other musicians to hold their tempo steady against emphatic "out-of-time" rhythms is a crucial aspect of interactive competence.

Interactive Motivation

The intricate cross-references and multiple strands of melody that contribute to the beauty and interest of *gamelan* performance are less important to the success of a *wayang* performance than the instantaneous, concerted responses to cues from the *dhalang* and drummer that must match puppet action. Since many of the musical shifts are far more abrupt than in *klenèngan*, the value of close coordination is much higher. Standards of synchronization in *klenèngan* are loose by comparison.

A *dhalang* is seen not only as a performer but as a spiritually powerful person who is a potential mediator between members of the audience and other forces. As such, he is in a realm apart from the musicians. There seems to be some consensus that the musicians are responsible for supporting the *dhalang*. There is a fair amount of controversy over the precise balance of power, as we shall see in the next chapter, but it is highly unlikely that a musician would attempt to upstage the *dhalang* or could succeed if he tried. In terms of entertainment, the spotlight of audience attention falls clearly on the *dhalang*, though he can, and usually does, turn this light briefly on the *pesindhèn* at certain moments.

WAYANG WONG

The theatrical form *wayang wong panggung*, performed by actor/dancers on a proscenium stage, is connected to *wayang kulit* by a web of cross-influences. The interactive network is significantly larger because it includes actors with minds of their own rather than puppets subservient to the will of a *dhalang*.[7] The actors take on some of the roles and responsibilities of the *wayang kulit dhalang*: group improvisation of dialogue replaces the *dhalang*'s solo improvisation, for example. Actors take turns responding to one another sequentially in speech and in song (Susilo 1984, 1987) unlike most *gamelan* interaction, in which all parties are performing and interacting simultaneously.

A *dhalang* narrates and directs the musical aspects of a *wayang wong* performance. Since he must regulate and coordinate the actors' danced entrances, exits, and battles, he must have a greater knowledge of dance than is necessary for *wayang kulit*. On the other hand, verbal skills are less important. The spiritual associations of shadow play *dhalang*s are completely lacking in *wayang wong*.

The positioning of performers in *wayang wong* is a direct extension of *wayang kulit* practice: the actors face off from left and right sides of the

---

7. Since Hardja Susilo has discussed interaction in *wayang wong* extensively (1984, 1987), I limit my comments to a comparison with *wayang kulit*.

stage similar to the puppets on the screen, although they do make some use of the depth of the stage. The *dhalang* sits facing them in the middle of the *gamelan*, which is arrayed facing the stage, much as it would face the screen in *wayang kulit*, and the leading musicians sit in the center, near the *dhalang*. Thus, the *dhalang* maintains a visual link with the actors and physical proximity with the musicians who mediate his cues.

There are a few important additions to the interactive system of *wayang kulit*. There is greater use of vocal introductions to *gendhing* and *palaran;* these are often sung by actors rather than by the *dhalang*, which means that sometimes the musicians bypass the *dhalang* and turn their attention toward the actors. When such vocal introductions are used by the *dhalang*, they "can take the place of a narrative cue, rhythmic signal, or instrumental introduction; their use is therefore an efficient device by which a dhalang can eliminate some of these steps to increase dramatic effect" (Susilo 1984: 134). Susilo also talks about some of the challenges presented by other types of cues:

> Performed in isolation and at an appropriate place and time, *kombangan* may signal the musicians to proceed to another piece, to *udhar* (return to previous dynamic levels and instrumentation), *malik* (switch to the other tuning system), go to *ngelik* (the portion of a composition that exploits the upper register), or to *ompak* (a coda). They may also be used merely to add vocal texture to the piece. For a novice musician, the challenge is to distinguish one type of kombangan from another. (1984: 133–34.)

and with regard to *dhodhogan:*

> The different rhythmic patterns may sound continuously, with one pattern for one purpose followed by another pattern for another purpose without a clearly discernible break. For a novice musician, the challenge of performing music in a theatre context is obvious—he must learn to discriminate between these rhythmic patterns according to what they are meant to convey [and to whom]—distinctions that are in many cases more subjective than acoustic. (1984: 130.)

The interpretive skills required by this interactive system are similar to those needed to understand and follow drumming in both *wayang kulit* and *wayang wong:* musicians must distinguish between outright cues, ongoing patterns that regulate tempo and filler, and "sound effects" played in response to puppet movements.

The interactive sound structures of *wayang wong*, though similar to those of *wayang kulit*, are more condensed in several ways. The pace of the performance is quicker and the overall structure more compact and less rigid. A performance does not last more than four hours and may

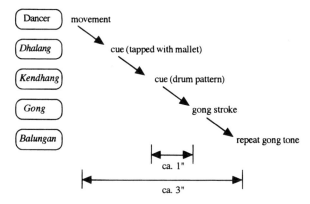

Fig. 42 Typical *wayang wong* interaction chain

be finished in as little as two. The *pathet* sequence is not only greatly condensed but loosely interpreted, and there is a preference for brevity in individual pieces as well. It is unusual to play any of the longer *gendhing* or *sulukan* in a *wayang wong* performance. More important, from the standpoint of interaction, is the common practice of further abbreviating these short pieces (Susilo 1984: 141–42). The practice of spontaneously altering the structure of a piece to accommodate particular dance moves is an excellent example of the interactive complexities of *wayang wong*. Figure 42 diagrams Susilo's prose description (1984: 143) of a typical interaction.

Palaran is an interactive sound structure that is not much used in *wayang kulit* but that figures prominently in *wayang wong* and other, less common dramatic forms as a vehicle for dramatic dialogue. Two actors improvise an interchange subject to the constraints of melody and poetic meter associated with this form (Susilo 1987: 6). These constraints overlay the already complex musical interaction discussed in the analysis of *palaran* in chapter 7.

WAYANG PADHAT

The intensification evident in *wayang wong* is greater by far in *wayang padhat*, an experimental variant on the traditional shadow play developed over the past two decades at STSI (Brinner 1992). Performances of *wayang padhat* may last as little as half an hour by making iconic use of fragments of most of the elements of traditional *wayang kulit*. In addition to their use of fragmentation, the creators of *wayang padhat* depart from tradition by utilizing a much larger repertoire drawn from a variety of regionally distinct traditions and styles. This eclecticism serves expressive goals, but it also has important implications for competence and interaction. Performers must exceed traditional competence to master a range of pieces that are beyond the experience of most musicians. They must also forgo most of the spontaneity of a traditional performance and rehearse intensively because the traditional interactive system is overloaded to the point that it can no longer function unaided in shaping the performance. As the repertoire is enlarged, cues become more ambiguous because they refer to a greater number of pieces. Through rehearsal these cues tend to become mnemonic signals that serve to remind performers of prearranged actions rather than to communicate new information.

The interactive network is also altered in intriguing ways. The *dhalang* delegates some of his singing responsibilities to the musicians, many of whom are also competent *dhalangs*. When he has the *pesindhèn* or one of the male musicians continue singing a *sulukan* he has started, the *dhalang* is able to create a greater density of performance and experience by talking over the *sulukan*. When he shares his vocal production with other members of the ensemble, he also gains a multiplicity of voice qualities to reflect a larger array of emotions and characters.

While these innovations are not focused on interaction per se, they drastically alter the network and sound structures of the Central Javanese tradition and affect the interactive system, too, pushing it beyond its capacity for spontaneous expression. As a result, rehearsal, which is a logical extension of the formalized education instituted in STSI and other performing arts schools, has grown greatly in importance. This development is observable to a lesser degree outside STSI as *wayang* groups begin to rehearse more because the use of special compositions or performance techniques exceeds traditional competences and interactive abilities.

CHAPTER TEN

INDIVIDUALS MAKING MUSIC TOGETHER

Cultural autonomy and uniformity have been assumed thus far in my presentation of Javanese musical interaction. I have ignored social constraints on performance and differences between individuals for simplicity's sake, writing about performers who are equally competent and are motivated only by musical or theatrical concerns, not personal or social ones. These artificial conditions rarely, if ever, obtain in actual performance. As individuals making music together, we notice, exhibit, and often exploit our different abilities and degrees of knowledge. As humans being musical together, we can rarely ignore the personalities of other members of the ensemble because, among other things, personalities are directly linked to issues of authority concerning the right or the power to influence or command the musical conduct of the ensemble and its individual members. We shall turn first to social issues and then to the juncture of competence and interaction.

SOCIAL AND MUSICAL INTERACTION

Acknowledgment of the central role that individual psyches and social patterns play in musical interaction does not imply social determination of musical interaction. The connections among social, psychological, and musical patterns are varied, and music-making is more than a dim reflection of social structure: it may be a parallel—rather than purely derivative—expression of some of the same concerns that structure social interaction, but it may also offer a different way of being and acting together, even serving as a catalyst for social change or an outlet for psychological needs that are not satisfied in other types of human interaction. While musical interaction is likely to be strongly influenced by or related to other social interaction, and may be conceived in terms of everyday exchanges or institutionalized social roles, it is highly specialized and likely to differ from any other type of social interaction because of the medium of exchange—sound—which is culturally structured and constrained. Musical interaction is not merely an exchange between two or more active participants, but a joint creation of a sound product to be received and judged by an audience (not necessarily human or completely passive) in ways that other exchanges usually are not. This aesthetic attention to interactive process and product involves a far greater control of the technique and details of interaction than is generally possible in other realms of social activity.

Ethnomusicologists have devoted considerable attention to structural resemblances and parallels between social and musical organization, including musical analogs of social interaction such as hierarchical interactive networks or specific musical roles that are conceived in terms of social hierarchies or roles and vice versa. But we hear only rarely about another fundamentally different relationship between social interaction and musical interaction. This arises from the mixing of social and musical issues that is probably unavoidable in any music-making situation: personal rivalry, intimate friendship, kinship, deference toward social superiors, and professional and organizational obligations may all directly affect musical processes and products.

The interactive structures of music differ from other interactive structures most significantly with respect to time. A far more precise orientation is required as musicians create, agree upon, and submit to highly detailed temporal frameworks. When other forms of interaction such as theater, dance, marching formations, and martial arts are precisely coordinated in time, music is often the means of regulating this interaction. Musical interaction is further distinguished by the large number of named interactive structures—musical compositions or genres—which are consciously rehearsed and extensively reiterated and re-created within a performance and from one performance to the next. Only the most formal social interchanges begin to approach this degree of definition, explicitness, and repetition.

Explicitness also distinguishes musical interactive systems from other communicative systems. Musical cuing, prompting, signaling, and marking are generally more systematically and unambiguously defined than most other types of communication. Unresolved ambiguities in communication would lead rapidly to chaos. In a study of interaction between orchestra members and conductors, for instance, Faulkner has found that ambiguity of a conductor's expressive signs lowers a player's sense of control over performance and reduces his or her ability to forecast or adjust to what colleagues will perform (1973: 150). Discussing unpredictable, inconsistent, or conflicting directives, he adds that "inadequately defined cues and cognitions not only lack authoritativeness, they are themselves generators or causes of subsequent conduct such as open disrespect, sullenness, . . . making and taking of role distance" (1973: 151). In this case, musical interaction influences social behavior, which affects further musical interaction.

Musical interactive networks with their constituent roles and relationships tend to differ from other networks with respect to differences in quality (levels of competence) and differences in kind (specialization). Differences in competence between novices, professionals, and intermediate levels are of much greater importance in music than in general social interaction; these differences are recognized and often accommodated in the structure of interactive networks. Few forms of concerted human action are built on such precisely regulated interaction among people with different specializations. Communicative skills and means can differ substantially from one musical specialization to another, requiring passive knowledge of relevant aspects of others' specialization in addition to active mastery of one's own.

Despite these differences musical and social interaction overlap significantly. From an analytic perspective there are basic similarities in the channeling of expectations and actions. Consider, for instance, the sociological view that "macrostructures and collective orientations circumscribe what actors do in concrete situations."[1] Restated, this describes a fundamental relationship among the forces that shape music-making: musical macrostructures (such as prescribed ensembles and roles, predetermined aspects of musical structure, and performance contexts) and collective orientations (such as shared musical knowledge and goals) circumscribe what musicians do in performance. Rather than repeating this exercise by transforming other sociological propositions, we can turn directly to some of the conceptual tools developed by sociologists to evaluate their usefulness for ethnomusicological purposes.[2]

One of the main ways in which people channel expectations in social interactions is by taking roles—patterns of behavior and status in rela-

---

1. Jonathan Turner summarizes Goffman's affinity to Durkheim in these words (1988: 91).

2. The following discussion is based mainly on Turner's survey and synthesis of leading sociological theories of interaction (1988).

tion to others—and by anticipating and interpreting others' actions and stances in terms of roles. While these roles can be complexly defined and consciously manipulated, creating great variety, a relatively small number of roles probably suffice for most people. Such stereotypical thinking is particularly apt in music, since many roles are clearly marked by the instrument or part that a person plays and negotiable aspects are often limited. In some situations, however, jockeying for position is an essential part of the music-making process, occurring prior to performance in the claiming or assigning of parts and during performance as musicians vie for leadership or defer to others. Musicians also take roles as innovators, defenders of tradition, figures of authority, and so on, that extend well beyond performance but impinge upon it.

Authority is of central importance in musical interaction. Deriving from ensemble role, superior competence (real or perceived), greater experience, seniority, higher social standing, assertiveness, or a combination of these and other factors, it creates a focus within an ensemble and a means of initiating and maintaining concerted action. When it is tested or contested by other musicians, the results are likely to be audible, although perhaps in subtle ways.[3]

Recognition of authority or claims to authority within an ensemble sets up unequal relationships, a subject of major concern to sociologists who study the formation, maintenance, and subversion of social inequalities. Domination, readily apparent in the treatment of music and musicians by the privileged in many societies, also occurs among musicians. From a macrocosmic perspective we ought to ask whether particular musical roles and associated values strengthen the hand of the musician in the superior position and whether musical relationships engender social ones: does the power that derives from a prominent role in an ensemble lend the role-holder enhanced status outside of music-making situations?

Framing and staging are further sociological concepts, particularly associated with the work of Erving Goffman, that are relevant to the study of musical interaction: "Framing denotes the process of cognitively delimiting the range of acceptable behaviors in a situation. And staging denotes the use of physical props, the division of space, and the relative positioning of actors" (Turner 1988: 108). We frame interactions with opening and closing rituals that delimit appropriate roles, actions, and reactions. The reader should have little trouble identifying framing aspects of musical performances in Western concert halls. In Javanese

---

3. See Faulkner's discussion of orchestral musicians' attitudes toward conductors (1973) and my discussion of *pathetan*, below.

klenèngan, where applause and other overt opening and closing markers are uncommon, a *pathetan* is one of the framing devices used to mark the border between musical and nonmusical activity (Brinner 1989/90), thereby marking points of transition from one set of interactive norms to another. Similarly, "staging" channels expectations and actions. The use of space, including the positioning of musicians and instruments (props capable of manipulation for many communicative purposes) with respect to each other and to the audience, is well worth comparing to the use of space in other interactions within the same society in order to read the meaning of this staging, particularly regarding hierarchical relationships.

Some sociologists, particularly Harold Garfinkel and other ethnomethodologists, have emphasized the importance of creating "facticity," a sense of shared reality (Turner 1988: 49–51, 95–97). The presumption of shared worlds and some form of intersubjectivity necessary for social interaction is crucial for musical interaction. Discrepancies between musicians' conceptions of musical reality are immediately manifested in problems of timing (beat, tempo), intonation, or harmony (in the broad sense of appropriate concurrent soundings). While language and gestures are used in an attempt to convey a sense of facticity and persuade others in social interaction, in musical interaction a definition of common ground, beginning with standards of pitch and beat, is often provided by leading and foundational roles. Musical realities may differ in more subtle ways, too, and it is the resolution of such differences that is most interesting as different personalities, roles, and assertive or persuasive gestures are revealed.

Sense of self, a central concept in sociology and psychology, is a fundamental aspect of musical interchange that may be foregrounded in virtuoso display or blatant leadership over subordinate musicians, but is no less essential, if less accessible, in the shaping of a musician's most minute decisions regarding timing, volume, and timbre. This is one of the most important yet neglected aspects of interaction not only among musicians but between musician and researcher. Which persona is the musician projecting in an interview? Is he or she offering a straightforward assessment, exaggerating, or playing down capabilities and achievements? A researcher whose own self can hardly be removed from the picture must try to answer these questions by observing a musician in action, by matching deeds with words, and by eliciting different perspectives within a group of musicians.

Self is a broader concept than status, which it encompasses. It is influenced by social order but is subject to contextual and perceptual variation. In the temporal wash of music in process, there are often no ob-

jective absolutes, no unquestionable authorities or immutable points of
reference. Aspects of time, pitch, volume, and timbre are all relative,
subject to the production, perception, and negotiation of participating musicians and modulated by each individual's sense of self: self-
assurance and self-worth relative to the other players present. This gives
rise to a drama played out in myriad ways with results that vary from
homogeneous blend to insistent independence. Value is variously placed
on competitive interplay, clear-cut hierarchy, or "selfless" bending and
blending, to name a few contrasting choices that have overt aesthetic
and social dimensions. Here more than anywhere else it may be difficult
to filter out the "nonmusical." In many situations other senses of self such
as professional pride, economic competitiveness, and personal dislikes
affect musicians' judgments and performance.[4]

Synthesizing the work of other social scientists, Turner stresses a distinction that has great potential for ethnomusicological analysis of musical interaction: a person has a core self that is transsituational, carried
from one context to another unaltered, and a transitory self consisting
of perceptions that shift with context (Turner 1988: 61). Turner's formulation can be improved by recognizing that the core self changes, too,
over the long term, being formed and transformed throughout a person's
life as he or she passes through different stages of competence acquisition and social roles and relationships. The following hypothetical example, a composite based on my observations of musicians from various
parts of the world, illustrates both short-term shifts in transitory self and
long-term changes in an evolving core self.

Musician A, who is young and still has a lot to learn, is aware of his
shortcomings and is deferential to more experienced musicians almost
to the point of hesitancy, although his confidence increases noticeably
when he plays the pieces he already knows well. When problems arise
in performance, he is not sure enough to serve as an anchor for other
musicians searching for a melodic or rhythmic point of reference. As he
gains more experience and increases in competence and self-confidence,
his core self changes. His playing is no longer hesitant. There are new
context-dependent variations in his transitory self: while he still is deferential to older, more famous musicians, in their absence he displays his
musical mastery and asserts himself as a leader. He no longer defers to
those older musicians whom he considers less competent. He begins to
become known as a teacher, too, and in this capacity projects a different

---

4. Feld, for example, writes explicitly about Kaluli men's interest in the picture that he
painted of some kinds of Western musicianship as means for sexual encounter (1982: 232).

sense of self, emphasizing traditional pieces, practices, and values—despite the innovative performances in which he takes part as a practicing musician—because that fits his conception of a teacher's role. At a later stage in life, when most of the musicians who were his seniors have died or retired, his core self changes yet again as he moves into a role of respected authority. His knowledge is vast, and he no longer feels that other musicians have anything to teach him. To those younger musicians who seem genuinely interested he relates as a benign and generous teacher, but toward other students he is enigmatic. Many musicians see him as a crotchety old man, an opinionated relic of the past who nevertheless casts a long shadow over performance practice because of his acid criticisms and his unparalleled knowledge.

While I have emphasized the interaction between participating musicians, relationships to nonmusicians such as patrons and other audience members often influence music-making. There may also be significant internalized interaction with mental images of musicians who are not present: with teachers and role models, with dead or absent composers, with past masters and past performances. These may all crowd into a musician's consciousness and perhaps be projected into the auditors' consciousness as well.

A musician may shift rapidly between several transitory selves, even projecting conflicting images to different people simultaneously. The principal variables affecting this transitory self include the degree of familiarity with other musicians present, awareness and assessment of the relative competence, confidence, and authority of those musicians, and a sense of one's own competence relative to the musical task at hand, including the performance context, type of piece, instrument, and role to be played. Transitory self is also affected by the degree to which a musician depends on other performers and, conversely, is able and willing to support them.

Awareness and mutual dependence and support form the interactive web of ensemble playing, modifying the generic patterns of interaction in a musical system. We can rotate this constellation and rephrase it to say that musical interaction in a given situation will depend on the relative degrees of competence of the players and their mutual awareness and interdependence. Each of these three aspects is assessable only in relative terms, yet that hardly lessens the utility of distinguishing among the three and bringing them together to analyze the dynamics of a particular performance, the ways in which roles and patterns of interaction inherent to a given piece, ensemble, genre, or style are modified by a unique combination of social and musical personalities.

SOCIAL DIMENSIONS OF JAVANESE
MUSICAL INTERACTION

Links between the patterning of Javanese society and *gamelan* have been noted on numerous occasions by Javanese and non-Javanese. Musical hierarchies have been likened to social ones, and, conversely, the interactive network of *gamelan* has even been proposed by Indonesian nationalists as a model for a harmonious society "where each member has the duty to perform a particular task" (Pemberton 1987: 24). Analysts have also traced specific aspects of Javanese social behavior and cultural preferences in musical interaction, including preferences for smoothness, indirection, consensus, and the avoidance of confrontation (Keeler 1975, 1987; Suyenaga 1984). In general, these writers take an idealized, macrocosmic view of *gamelan*. Javanese writers, in particular, tend to mix descriptive and prescriptive elements. We get little sense of what happens at the microcosmic level of actual musical interaction, of the extent to which these prescriptions are fulfilled, or of the consequences of conflicting musical and social hierarchies. Pemberton has noted that the musicians themselves are missing from these idealized images (1987: 24, fn. 16). In the following pages, links between Javanese social and musical interaction are reevaluated with particular attention to the microcosmic. Keeler's work (1987) is the main reference here because, as a thoughtful synthesis of his own research and work by others, it is the most comprehensive analysis of Javanese social interaction available. Many of Keeler's main points are corroborated in the work of the Javanese anthropologist Koentjaraningrat (1985).

Music-making in Central Java is a communal activity. The performance ethic has been aptly compared with the fundamental social concepts of *rukun* (meaning compatibility or cooperation) and *gotong royong* (meaning mutual cooperation, working together in harmony; Keeler 1975; Sutton 1979; Suyenaga 1984: 97–99). Implicit in these terms is the assumption that differences of opinion and conflicting intentions are settled communally with a minimum of friction. Preferably consensus is attained through indirect mediation and through established nonverbal modes of behavior rather than by open discussion and argument or by explicit dictates from a higher authority.

As in many other areas of Javanese life, individual prominence in a *gamelan* is neither the norm nor the ideal. Traditional opportunities for solo musical performance are virtually nonexistent, and displays of soloistic virtuosity within a group performance are relatively rare and are not highly valued or rewarded by other performers or by the audience. Explicit competition between individual musicians is not usually seen as an aesthetic focus—when I described competitive patterns of Hindustani musical interaction reported by Neuman and Wade, Javanese musicians said that they never interact in a similar manner—but this deserves further attention. One *gamelan* teacher has written: "The playing of a *gamelan* group must be smooth and harmonious. The situation must be avoided in which one person tries to show off his expertise to the disadvantage of others, for then the playing will not be harmonious. It must be remembered that *gamelan* playing is a collective activity" (Gitosaprodjo 1984: 384). But competition does occur, of course, or Gitosaprodjo would not find it necessary to admonish students on this matter. Susilo briefly discusses competition in the performance of *palaran* in *wayang wong* (1987: 6), and Pemberton writes about the possibilities for conflict in the ceremonial *gamelan sekatèn*, noting that interactive structure and network enable musicians to subvert one another if they choose. The *bonang* introduction to a piece

is generic and simply sounds the prescribed melodic line of the mode . . . immediately following this "introduction" any one of a number of compositions in the mode may appear. The actual choice of the specific composition lies in the hands of the first demung . . . and therein lies the fun. Since the bonang player must lead the chosen piece, the demung player chooses carefully, either to expose the bonang "master" with an obscure composition, or to hand him a lightweight piece (knowing full well that sooner or later positions will switch). Built in to this scene is the enticing possibility of subverting the "master," musically. (Pemberton 1987: 25.)

Overt competitiveness was remarkably absent within the groups I observed, although there may have been hidden rivalries. Competitiveness does occur between groups in the *gamelan* contests that have been established over the past few decades.

Smoothness is a cultural and social ideal in Central Java. Traditionally, abrupt transitions have been avoided, particularly in the spheres of influence of the royal courts. Keeler writes, for example, that in *wayang* "there should be no sudden or unmotivated jumps in excitement" (1987: 193–94), and Poerbapangrawit says that in *gamelan* performance "even if the *irama* is to leap, or is to be cut off, the process must not be jerky. The emotional quality must still be even" (1984: 424). Smoothness is inextricably bound up with the practice of *gamelan*, which many see as a means of developing refinement.[5] Ideally a Javanese person strives to maintain equilibrium verbally, physically, and emotionally. The impor-

5. See Hatch (1979) for a discussion of the implications of the term *karawitan*, which commonly denotes *gamelan* music and also bears the connotation of refinement or elegance.

tance of balance in social interaction has been noted by Sutton (1982: 15–21), who finds the same goal in musicians' choices of patterns: "In keeping with the steady state ethos, one strives for balance and smoothness in fit and in flow through time" (1982: 291).

The ideal of smoothness encourages particular modes of behavior in social and musical interaction. Conflict is generally avoided through heightened sensitivity to the nuances of others' actions and through consensual decisions, mediated authority, and deference. An encounter between strangers, for example, is the occasion for elaborate mutual assessment as each party attempts to determine the level of speech required by Javanese language and social etiquette. Smoothness does not mean uniformity: in a group situation a person may speak in a familiar, jocular way to his juniors, switch to a formal, restrained tone and vocabulary when speaking to a person of higher status, and then switch again to an intermediate linguistic register more distant than the first, but not as reserved and formal as the second.

Unless the commanding party enjoys unequivocal social superiority, commands or directives are socially problematic and so are often cushioned and couched as requests. The interactive system of *gamelan* provides the musical means for bypassing the social awkwardness of situations which arise from conflicts between social and musical roles. Most decisions are communicated through musical conventions, thereby avoiding the social complications of verbal commands that might arise in a leadership hierarchy that is not congruent with social relations. Vetter notes that repetition allows musicians to correct their playing while avoiding "the socially awkward interaction of discussing a problem" (1986: 195). Musical commands may be more direct than verbal ones. However, when describing such interaction, there is a tendency to call it "asking" or "inviting" (*ngajak*) rather than "commanding":

> Whenever the leader wants to invite the other players to do something together, he gives an appropriate hint, *sasmita*, on the instrument he is playing. (Sindoesawarno 1987: 345.)

> If the *irama* of the *kendhang* asks/invites (*ngajak*) for *seseg*, the *kethuk* player must follow in speeding up; contrariwise, if the *irama* of the *kendhang* asks to slow down the *kethuk* player must then follow in slowing down, and so forth. (Soekanto 1966: 4.)

Although a *kendhang* or *rebab* cue can be direct, conveying unquestionable authority, this directness is dissimulated in these authors' verbal descriptions.

Is this social awkwardness the reason for developing such a complex system of musical interaction? Or do the same basic motives (or deep structures) underlie the subtle cues and indirectness of social interaction? In the absence of historical records pertaining to musical interaction it is unlikely that these questions can be answered. We can note, however, that both musical interaction and social interaction in neighboring Balinese and Sundanese cultures are considerably more direct. Comparative work on neighboring traditions should shed further light on the relationship between musical and social interaction.

Indirection and mediation are common ways of handling interpersonal relations in Central Javanese society. Many types of social interaction, particularly those involving transactions and requests, are embellished by circumlocutions and the use of intermediaries. It is not difficult to find parallels to these preferences in musical interaction, although it is important to note one crucial difference. The pace of interaction is often far more rapid in music than in social contexts. When a swift change is required, musicians can dispense with indirectness and mediation without negative social consequences.

The preference for mediated authority rather than direct control is well expressed in a sociopolitical metaphor for *gamelan* leadership quoted by Jaap Kunst:

> According to a Javanese conception the *rebab* may be called the *raja*, and the *kendhang* the *patih* (prime minister) of the *gamelan* community (the *gong*, which subdivides the composition according to fixed laws, may be called the *jaksa* (here = judge)); in other words, according to this view the *rebab* is admittedly the principal instrument, but it has delegated the real work, i.e., the leading of the orchestral society, to the *kendhang*, which, as it were, translates the former's instructions into a form easily understood by the community, whilst the *gong* sees to it that all melodic phrases are equitably allowed the same length. (1949: 223.)[6]

Javanese concepts of inner power and the exercise of that power are implicit in this metaphor. A truly powerful person does not need to display his or her power overtly; its very presence is often enough to overcome enemies and obstacles. This line of reasoning can easily be extended to *wayang kulit*, in which delegation and mediation of authority are more explicit, the *dhalang* controlling the *gamelan* through an array of musical intermediaries. Keeler links dissembled control to spiritual

---

6. Pemberton notes that this formulation was "still in circulation among some older *gamelan* musicians in Solo in the 1970's" (1987: 23, fn. 13) but later protests that "behind the facade of functional order that a *gamelan* orchestra presents to nonmusicians, however, the spirited play within this know-how distinguishes all *gamelan* players, no matter how bad they are, from their ascribed roles as musical clerks in a model bureaucracy" (1987: 27).

power: "The dhalang's dissembled control over his players at once obscures and makes more mysterious his place at the center of the performance as the single authority in control of its execution" (1987: 182). It is clear to everyone that the *dhalang* is in control, yet his leadership is communicated indirectly, mediated by leading musicians.

When Javanese *gamelan* is played in a refined manner, leadership is rarely overt. The head of a palace *gamelan* does not lead ostentatiously but may play relatively simple and unobtrusive patterns on the smallest drum (see chap. 8), or he may even "lead" without playing (Brown and Toth 1971). A *rebab* player's lead permeates the *gamelan* subtly yet thoroughly. A drummer can also lead in subtle ways, although the means for strong assertions are certainly at hand. It was highly instructive to observe the ways in which Widiyanto led the *gamelan* group at the University of California, Berkeley, in the late 1980s. By drumming softly and subtly, he trained the musicians to listen carefully to nuances that other teachers might have avoided with American students. This practice left its mark not only on the musical interaction, which improved significantly, but also on the social interaction: attentiveness and a subdued, reflective atmosphere replaced the chatting and joking that previously had followed each piece. Even when playing as energetic a piece as a *sampak*, Widiyanto and other musicians of a similar mind prefer to "shepherd" the beat by playing slightly before or after it, as necessary, rather than coinciding with it precisely (as we noted in chapter 9). When appropriate, this carefully concealed control can be replaced in an instant with forceful drumming.

Contrasting musical conceptions, personal styles, and competence were all at issue in one particularly dramatic display of differing approaches to performance that I witnessed at a *gamelan* rehearsal in Solo. While accompanying a dancer, the regular leader of the group was drumming in a refined manner appropriate to klenèngan. A dance drummer arrived and replaced him in the middle of the piece, switching immediately to an explosive style that nearly sent the drum flying across the room. The two drummers played functionally similar patterns, but one blended subtly with the rest of the ensemble, as is appropriate in the context of klenèngan, while the other dominated assertively, as is more appropriate for dance. This is not just an issue of taste, personality, or conception but of competence: a drummer who specializes in dance drumming has a different way with the instrument, a different volume and timbre to the strokes, though the klenèngan drummer might know and use all of the same patterns of strokes.

Among the many things that have been written about Javanese concepts of power (Anderson 1972; Ricklefs 1974; Keeler 1987), the aspect most pertinent to understanding musicians' responses to leadership is the tension between an attraction to powerful centers and a reluctance to submit to domination. A person can derive power by association with a more powerful person. This is sometimes offered as an explanation of musicians' readiness to serve in the court *gamelan:* the spiritual rewards derived from association with the most powerful centers of traditional Javanese culture are far more important than the monetary compensation, which has dwindled to almost nothing in recent years.

At the same time, most musicians maintain substantial independence, which is often ensured, ironically, by multiple allegiances. Keeler argues that Javanese society exhibits "a tendency to distribute kinds of authority among several different persons . . . there seems a pervasive impulse to limit the nature and intensity of any single bond. By recognizing authority in a variety of distinct figures, people limit the degree of authority they acknowledge in—and the degree of dependency they feel upon—any one of them" (1987: 107). This is true of the basic interactive network of a *gamelan* in which multiple centers of power are institutionalized by division of leadership responsibilities among several people. Musicians' attributions of knowledge to several sources rather than a single teacher (noted in chap. 6) also manifest a tension between independence and lineal association.

Differences of opinion and musical conception are fostered by the variability inherent in an oral tradition that has developed and changed for centuries over a large area. In most circumstances the players of the elaborating instruments enjoy considerable freedom within individual spheres of action which limit external influence (Suyenaga 1984). Sutton notes that "so long as the players appear through their playing to have internalized the basic principles of the music system, the group leader will not normally impose his own personal preferences on others" (1982: 26). Thus, he links the nature of an interactive relationship to the appearance of competence, to the leader's *perception* of the other musicians' knowledge and ability. He emphasizes the interactive nature of this variation: "A skillful musician adjusts his or her part as fluctuation in the other variable parts is perceived. The search is not a lonely quest but one made in the company of others and in response to them" (1982: 291).

A normally enculturated Javanese musician develops personal preferences and constructs an understanding of appropriate variation through the experience of hearing numerous renditions of a piece. Musicians develop different, sometimes conflicting, interactive ideals. As I noted in an earlier chapter, coordination between *gendèr, gambang,* and *suling* at the end of a *pathetan* is extremely common, but some musicians do not consider it mandatory. Because of the aesthetic and social ideal of smooth-ness, musicians will generally adapt to one another and iron out these differences in performance, unless there are serious incongruities in the organization of the ensemble.

Some groups are molded by a single musician with a strong personal-ity and musical opinions. Such a leader takes a more active and intrusive role in determining what members of the *gamelan* play. This is usually met with an outward deference and submission that may mask inner opposition and conflict. In one such instance, an old musician, recog-nized as an authority on traditional practices and pieces no longer gen-erally known, had been invited to coach a group for a broadcast concert. In one piece he wanted the *bonang* to be played in a slow, simple style (*mipil lomba*) that is diametrically opposed to the rapid interlocking style (*imbal*) now common for such pieces. The *bonang* player did as he was told but expressed his resentment when we spoke later. The playing technique was part of his competence, but the application of it in this context was not and he did not find it aesthetically appealing. Yet there was no socially sanctioned way for him to resist the authority of the older musician.

What do we mean by "authority"? The term can imply expertise and proficiency, but also command and domination. Perhaps the most telling gloss is mastery, which, like authority, denotes both a relationship to people and a relationship to knowledge. The link between these two meanings (serendipitously comprehended in a single English word) en-capsulates one of the most important connections between competence and interaction.

Recognized authority is credit in the bank. Having attained a certain level of competence, one is free to break rules, experiment, deviate from the norms. The validating power of perceived competence is evident in Susilo's observation that particularly weak examples of improvised inter-action between two *wayang wong* actors were acceptable "because they technically do not violate the above set of constraints and perhaps *more importantly were performed by master artists.* However, a similar performance by novices would probably be considered unacceptable, i.e., a mistake" (1987: 9, emphasis mine). The audience judges a performance by the performers' reputations—their perceived competence—in addition to what actually transpires in performance. Of course, in some circum-stances novices are judged much more leniently than master artists, but there are certainly many examples of this phenomenon in other cultures: one must learn to play "by the book" and be judged competent before one has the license to do things differently.

Authority should also be understood in terms of obligations and responsibilities to others. The message underlying much of the guidance I received from my teachers was that musicians who are in a position to lead—by virtue of the instrument they are playing—ought to do so. A *gendèr* player needs an especially strong sense of *irama* to play in a *gamelan gadhon* (a small subset of the full *gamelan*) in order to assist or replace the *kendhang* and take responsibility for the steadiness of the tempo and smoothness of transitions from one *irama* to another (Harjito, personal communication). A *rebab* player has a responsibility to the singers: his playing should indicate the appropriate melodies to the *pesindhèn* or *gérong*, particularly if they are unsure of their parts (Wasitodiningrat, personal communication). These and other assessments of interactive responsibilities are often couched in terms of averting mishaps; they imply social obligations of creating or maintaining order.

Keeler evaluates the spiritual potency of a Javanese village headman in terms of his ability to fulfill a variety of obligations to the people of the village: "If the headman's potency was sufficiently great, there would be no contests of will: people would submit voluntarily to his benevolent guidance. If there is discord, this reflects poorly on the headman's potency, which is proved insufficient to assure harmony" (Keeler 1987: 87). To the extent that this holds true in the realm of *gamelan*, a less than satisfactory performance reflects poorly on the authority of the leading musicians.[7] But there is a crucial difference between social interaction in a village and a *gamelan*. Keeler talks about the problematic nature of status differences in village society and the attendant maneuvering which tend to work against too much submission to anyone's authority. These problems appear to be muted within a musical situation because musicians' status and independence tend not to be threatened to the same degree by submission to the leading musicians' conceptions of a piece. They are shielded by the prescribed roles of the instruments they play, and since many have the ability and opportunity to take on other roles on other occasions they enjoy greater flexibility than in a nonmusical context: there is a good chance of taking a leading role on another occasion. One cannot move from village to village or switch social roles with similar ease.

The ideals of noncoercive and dissimulated authority that Keeler has observed in village interaction surface in *gamelan* performance in musicians' tendency to lead subtly, to play their own parts with conviction but without too many overt concessions to other musicians who may be having difficulties. There appears to be a belief that the aura of

---

7. Such an assessment certainly might be made in other cultures but perhaps not with the overtones of spiritual mastery implicit in the Javanese case.

this knowledge should carry the others through. Blatant corrections or prompts are avoided; they would contradict the smoothness that should pervade performance. I have observed Javanese musicians teaching Americans with contrasting approaches to guidance: while some call out pitches or correct in other overt ways, others simply continue to play their own part, on *kendhang, rebab, gendèr,* or whatever, in the apparent conviction that their authority will carry the piece and that those who are having trouble will catch on sooner or later as knowledge of the piece flows from teacher to student through the act of performance, not through stopping, correcting, and starting over again or through verbal instruction. It is certainly more difficult for most American students to adapt to this more subtle approach, but it can produce good results in the long run, forcing students to rely on their own ears and analytical powers to gain their bearings and figure out what they should be doing on the basis of what others are playing.

A master musician, one who clearly stands out in competence within an ensemble, can inspire and instill confidence by the very fact of his or her presence and, of course, by the authority of a performance that serves as a reliable reference for the lesser musicians. Even at the highest levels of competence one can find disparities within an ensemble and the concomitant need to rely on one or more musicians who have greater general competence or specific knowledge for the piece or situation at hand. We shall return to this aspect of authority presently.

When roles within an ensemble are associated with particular instruments, as they are in Javanese *gamelan,* the social interaction that occurs in the matching of musicians and instruments determines the possibilities for ensuing musical interaction. The matching process is likely to be most significant when musicians can play many parts within an ensemble, as most Javanese musicians can thanks to the prevalence of well-rounded competence. In *gamelan* groups that do not have a fixed disposition of parts or roles the process of deciding who is to play what may be worked through anew at every meeting. Even in groups with fixed assignments musicians often move from one instrument to another, depending on who is present.

Ostensibly the assignment or taking of parts in a *gamelan* should match the relative competence and status of the musicians. Poerbatjaraka, a prominent Javanese literary scholar and musician from Surakarta, describes a division of labor and authority according to kinship status: "When I play gamelan with my two younger brothers, I play *rebab,* one of my brothers plays *gendèr,* and the other plays *kendhang.* The *rebab* is tuned by one of these two, not by me. Only after the *rebab* is tuned and [bowed to check the tuning] is it given to me. This is according to good, traditional, Javanese etiquette" (1987: 268). But matters are not always so simple, due to other aspects of Javanese etiquette such as hesitancy to be too forward. Deference to age or other status-enhancing qualities can cause extensive maneuvering rather than a straightforward matching of musicians and instruments. Often the best musician will not go directly to the *rebab* because this would be too overtly assertive. Rather, he sits down instead at a relatively unimportant instrument such as a *saron* and waits to be invited by his fellow musicians to move to the *rebab*. If a younger or less experienced musician is already seated at the *rebab*, a lengthy exchange may develop in which the "junior" musician feels compelled to offer the instrument to the "senior" musician. The latter often declines for the first piece, forcing the lesser musician to "sweat it out" (Harjito, personal communication). In his excellent discussion of the nonverbal communal determination of ensemble positions in the Yogyakarta palace *gamelan* Vetter notes the converse of the behavior just described: "Less experienced musicians arriving early and seeing the higher status and technically more demanding instruments unclaimed will remain on the periphery of the *gamelan* waiting for better players to arrive in order to avoid a situation such as that just described" (1986: 191–92).

These processes were played out at a *klenèngan* which I sponsored in 1983 that included a number of older, well-known musicians and a group of young instructors and students from ASKI. The older musicians were picked up by car and so arrived together. They proceeded to go through a largely nonverbal shuffle of seat and instrument selection that placed most of them at the instruments they played best, though each would have been capable of playing most of the other parts. The younger musicians arrived very late and thus were not forced to play any of the leading parts. There were no apparent conflicts or difficulties since no one was placed in a socially untenable position.

A court rehearsal that I witnessed recently exemplifies some of the ways in which social status and musical standing impinge upon role taking. Since the regular drummer had not yet arrived, the *rebab* player, who was the official leader, asked a younger musician, who was sitting with the singers, to play *kendhang*. The latter claimed ignorance, although he is in fact a capable drummer, and suggested his younger brother, who had made the mistake of stepping out of the room for a moment. At this point the nobleman in charge of performance activities entered the room and ordered the older brother to play *kendhang*. The command was conveyed in a most direct manner that could only come from someone of high status speaking to a person of greatly inferior standing. It was motivated by a nonmusical sense of self completely incommensurate with relative musical competence in this case, since the young musician was far more competent than the person giving the command. Yet the musician who was commanded to drum still managed to evade the job by remaining seated with the singers and getting his younger brother to do it when he returned to the room. The common hesitancy to take a leading role was exacerbated in this case by the sequence of pieces that was to be played: a rarely performed dance suite. Although the drummer only needed to play simple, standard patterns, he had to set some unusual tempi and follow a precise progression to fit the vocal text.

Role taking is affected by framing, by contextual knowledge of possible conduct. Musicians' freedom to switch roles is a function of the formality of a performance context. Harjito noted that a *klenèngan* to celebrate the birth of a baby is more relaxed than one for a wedding so that, at the former, musicians can switch around (personal communication). Perceptions of the relative competence of other musicians in an ensemble also frame interaction and role taking. Authority and competence are relative to the competence of others present: a person may play a front row instrument in one *gamelan* and a middle or back row instrument in another depending on his relative standing within the ensemble. For example, at the broadcasts at KONSER which I attended in 1983 Mloyowidodo invariably played the *bonang* by virtue of being one of the two most venerable and competent musicians present and a recognized authority on repertoire and *bonang*. According to Mloyowidodo, the man who played *slenthem* in these broadcasts was a good *bonang* player in his own right but was happy to play *slenthem* for Mloyowidodo at these broadcasts. This assessment bolsters the storyteller's prestige, of course, but it also reflects the fact that the musicians playing subordinate parts are often capable of playing more demanding roles in the ensemble. Some may choose to play subordinate roles in order to give other musicians a chance to gain experience or because they feel insecure relative to other musicians and want to avoid embarrassment. Conversely, Vetter reports that better players did not attend some rehearsals in the Yogyanese palace, forcing others into parts that they were not competent to play (1986: 193).

INTERACTION IN *PATHETAN* PERFORMANCE

Pathetan provide an apt vehicle for demonstrating the influence of personal and interpersonal factors on interactive processes and musical product because the ensemble is small and therefore easier to observe in detail than the full *gamelan*. In addition, the quality of interaction is readily apparent due to the temporal flexibility of this genre, which requires constant adjustment to one's fellow musicians. Interaction in *pathetan* performance is profoundly influenced by the relative status, age, and perceived ability as well as the personalities and tastes of the performers and by how well they know one another. This is observable in normal performance, but I found it helpful to intensify the effects of these factors by organizing recording sessions devoted solely to *pathetan*, selecting particular combinations of musicians and asking them to play certain *pathetan* several times, trading instruments each time, in order to isolate roles constructed by individuals from those associated with particular instruments. Since I could not possibly read the thoughts of each musician in the course of a performance or expect a candid group analysis after a *pathetan* had been played—most of these musicians did not feel free to express opinions of the performance in front of the others—I relied on extensive discussions of the recordings with individual musicians, including some who had participated in the recorded performances and some who had not.[8]

These recordings clearly showed that a person's power to influence the outcome of a performance may be enhanced or limited depending on the instrument played. An overly assertive player can cause far more trouble on *gendèr* than on *gambang* because the defining relationship obtains between *rebab* and *gendèr*, with the *rebab* establishing the melody and the *gendèr* emphasizing the focal pitches. The *gambang* contributes to both of these efforts but is primary in neither so anticipation of the melody or an extremely delayed cadence is not as jarring on *gambang* as on *gendèr*. This is truer still for *suling*.

With the addition of a singer the interaction in *pathetan* performance changes in nature, partly because the ensemble is larger but mainly because there are two potential leaders, the singer and the *rebab* player. When the singer is a *dhalang* of *wayang kulit*, the interpersonal aspects of interaction may become entwined in the tensions inherent in a genre in which one person, the *dhalang*, holds a privileged position over the others, controlling a large array of performers and performance elements. The latent conflict over power, prestige, wealth, and recognition is manifest in musicians' disparaging comments on the musical competence of *dhalang*s.

When these tensions arose in the *pathetan* recording sessions, they were played out in various ways. In one case the *rebab* player, who was a colleague of the *dhalang* and of similar status, worked cohesively with him. The *gendèr* player, who was clearly superior in musical competence,

8. See chapter 6 in Brinner (1985) for transcriptions and more detailed analysis.

age, and status, disagreed with their conception of the *pathetan* and tried to force his own pacing at several points, with poor results. In a different session, a *rebab* player was paired with a *dhalang* whom he did not know and chose to play it safe by lagging behind the vocal throughout. This was probably the best choice under the circumstances, since the *dhalang* in question had an unusually expansive conception of *pathetan*, drawing out phrases far longer than the norm. Had the *rebab* player insisted on his own, faster pace, he would have created conflict for the other musicians, who would have had to decide which leader to follow. An incompetent singer might have lost such a contest, but given the apparent competence of the *dhalang* in this case, the *rebab* player probably would not have succeeded in pulling the other musicians with him. Here we see that the sense of self that a performer projects is a potent force in interaction, but its strength is augmented or diminished by the characteristics of stereotyped roles within the ensemble. It is also clear that familiarity with fellow musicians enhances coordination because shared experience creates facticity, providing a basis for understanding other musicians' decisions and anticipating their subsequent moves. The cohesiveness gained through such familiarity can even compensate for weaknesses in individual parts: the performance discussed in chapter 7 (fig. 38) was judged superior to others in which the individual parts were more finely crafted but coordination was weaker.

Because patterns of deference to elders are deeply ingrained in Javanese society, the age differences within an ensemble may significantly affect performance. If younger musicians play the less important instruments, *gambang* and *suling*, while older ones play *rebab* and *gendèr*, then patterns of social interaction are congruent with the patterns of musical interaction implicit in the hierarchy of the *pathetan* interactive network. However, if musical roles are not congruent with social hierarchy, a problematic and potentially uncomfortable or unsatisfying situation arises because social and musical priorities conflict. The younger musician should lead because he is playing the leading instrument, yet it is impolite to precede and dictate to the older musician. If the younger musician has sufficient confidence and the older musician is willing to take the role associated with a subordinate instrument, the performance can succeed. Otherwise, the older musician may push from an inappropriate position, creating an audibly unpleasant performance, or a sort of stasis may evolve in which the younger musician tries to follow rather than lead the older musician, who, in turn, is waiting for the younger musician to set the pace and play the usual cues. Such a situation undermines the cuing system and may wreak havoc on the performance.

Status differences can affect the coordination of an ensemble in ways similar to age differences. In Central Java a musician's status among other musicians appears to derive more from other musicians' perceptions of his competence or ability than from his standing in general society. The latter comes into play mainly in cases of extreme disparity and is far more noticeable among the oldest musicians, who reached adulthood when the feudalistic patterns of the royal courts still dominated Javanese social intercourse. Since status is otherwise based largely on musical competence and older musicians tend to be more knowledgeable than younger ones, younger musicians have double reason to defer to their elders. Of course, an older player who is not particularly well known for his technical ability or knowledge generally does not pose a threat as a figure of authority to a younger musician who is clearly more competent.

A revealing conflict developed in one performance when a younger *rebab* player who took an interest in my research agenda tried to hold a slow pace throughout a *pathetan* despite the extremely rapid *gendèr* playing of his former teacher. Musicians who heard the recording found it unsatisfactory; the consensus was that the younger musician should have submitted to the *gendèr* player because of the latter's greater authority and ability. The younger musician had predicted before the recording that he would win in a contest of will because the *rebab* player has the right to lead and he had the self-assurance to exercise that right, but he told me afterward that he was uncomfortable. As a fully competent musician approaching middle age, he did in fact emanate mastery and self-assurance in most situations, yet he was also extremely well mannered and deferred to older musicians out of politeness, even when they were clearly less skilled and knowledgeable than he. In other words, his core self was characterized by confidence based on musical mastery, but the transitory self varied in the degree to which he projected this confidence and mastery and in the degree to which he depended on the people present in the ensemble. In this case he tried to adopt a transitory self that did not fit the situation, creating both internal and external conflict. Another configuration of musicians indicated that the problem in this performance was due not to the *gendèr* player's age but to his status and to the sense of self that he projected: when another older musician played *gendèr* and the young musician again played *rebab*, his strategy worked and he felt quite at ease. He was not overawed, and the *gendèr* player, although playing rapidly, did not have the musical authority, or possibly the temerity, to push ahead of him repeatedly. A common pattern of mutual deference emerged: respect for age was balanced by respect for competence and the traditional role of the *rebab* player.

The younger musician's experience in these two performances highlights the differences in character between the two older players. While the first one fought the younger musician and won, the second one was flexible and willing to adapt to the *rebab*. When these two older men played *rebab* and *gendèr* in yet a third configuration, the results were unsatisfactory again because the flexible player, who was clearly of a lesser caliber, appeared to be overawed by the more assertive *rebab* player and did not enter into a mutually binding relationship with him. He was unnerved enough to begin a transitional pattern several times (such patterns are usually not repeatable). On listening to a recording of this performance, another musician commented that this *gendèr* player seemed to be fearful of preceding the *rebab*.

When an assertive player plays a leading part, his leadership is unambiguous; even when he plays a supporting *gendèr* or *gambang* part, he can dominate a performance (although the *gambang* can dominate only if all the other players acquiesce). In contrast, a shy, deferential musician usually submits to the leader and if he happens to be playing the lead, he may do so subtly without appearing to lead, or he may be shaken by a more assertive musician who is playing a supporting part. These contrasting situations were evident in another session, when two competent musicians who are diametrically opposed in personality and behavior took turns playing *rebab*. The first was an unusually assertive person by Javanese standards. He clearly felt that he was in charge of the session, helping to select and invite the musicians and dominating the discussion between pieces. When he played *rebab*, he did not loosen his control of the performance at any point. Even when he played *gambang* in another performance, he asserted himself musically. The other *rebab* player was younger and extremely quiet and modest, even by Javanese standards. He led without leading and would have been overrun by the *gendèr* and *gambang* players had they not been respectful of the position of the *rebab* within the ensemble and of this musician's skill on the instrument. Returning to Java nine years later, I found that this young man had developed into a far more confident and extroverted musician; he was still deferential to musicians who were older or higher in status but without being intimidated or obsequious.

Whatever the historical relationship of social and musical patterns of interaction—a chicken and egg question—smoother results are likely when hierarchies or other types of relationship coincide as they do in Poerbatjaraka's example of matching musical and family hierarchies and in some of the *pathetan* performances cited here. This is not a trivial conclusion: while we would probably not expect the converse to be true—that musical performance is enhanced by reversing social

roles and relationships—we might expect music-making to be impervi-
ous to social relations, yet in this case it clearly is not. This conclusion
is grounds for further exploration of different types of social and musical
relationships in order to improve our understanding of why certain combinations tend to work while others may be problematic. Specifically
we need to examine different types of social disparities to discover
which are most likely to have an effect on music-making and which are
more neutral.

The problems engendered by a musical hierarchy that does not
match age and status hierarchies are not limited to *pathetan* performance.
At a court *gamelan* broadcast I observed a particularly striking conflict
when the leading melodic instruments, *rebab* and *bonang*, were played by
young radio station musicians while old palace musicians played other
instruments, including the *slenthem*, which carries the *balungan* and should
follow the melodic lead of the *bonang* and *rebab*. There were many mistakes in this performance, some of them due to the old *slenthem* player,
who refused to follow the lead of the younger musicians and played a
different version of the piece. One musician who was not taking part
complained to me that the court musicians were "too fanatic" about "notation." They were not actually reading notation—the commentator
meant their own version—but his word selection implies authority and
fixity. The performance was seriously affected by conflicting constraints,
which hampered the creation of a sense of facticity: the young musicians
from the radio station did not defer to the older musicians, and the older
musicians did not respect the authority inherent in the roles played by
the younger musicians, implying that they did not regard these younger
musicians as sufficiently competent. It is significant that the older musicians did not feel compelled to follow, because the constraint to follow
authority is deeply ingrained in this tradition. In this same performance,
for example, the radio announcer listed the program in the wrong order,
which upset the musicians deeply, causing a great deal of grumbling,
but no one corrected the announcer and the *rebab* player followed the
announced order rather than the planned one despite the ensuing violation of norms of program sequence.

This particular struggle for musical power has another facet, the clash
between a conservative court tradition—and its associated competence—and the more eclectic approach of the radio musicians. In the
worldview of many court-affiliated Javanese there is a persistent differentiation between the "inside" and an "outside" which begins just beyond
the palace walls. In this case the inside/outside conflict may well have
been exacerbated by the fact that the concert took place within the
palace walls. It is important, too, to keep in mind that my primary infor-

mant on this occasion was a leading member of the radio station group who was some thirty or forty years younger than many of the palace musicians. Linking authority to role rather than age was important for maintaining his own sense of self in performance situations where he played leading roles among musicians who were older and sometimes wiser.

Conclusion

CHAPTER ELEVEN

MUSICAL COMPETENCE AND INTERACTION

Issues of competence and interaction are intertwined in the example that concluded the previous chapter, as they have been at many points in the course of this book. Competence encompasses interaction. Yet viewed from another angle, competence is one of the elements brought into play in interaction. The connections between these complementary aspects of musicianship and music-making can be expressed in the following three propositions:

1. interactive procedures and frameworks constitute central domains of competence for any ensemble performer;
2. interaction validates, enriches, and alters competence;
3. through successful interaction musicians can exceed the limits and overcome the lapses of individual competence, supporting and spurring each other on.

The first proposition has been amply documented in the preceding chapters. We have seen that the precise and extensive knowledge of interactive matters acquired by musicians is part of an ordered body of knowledge, a competence. Knowledge of context frames the performance and thus defines appropriate conduct and musical choices; knowledge regarding ensemble, including roles and relationships, constitutes the interactive network; knowledge of repertoire provides interactive structures; and knowledge of interactive procedures, including cues, responses, and other forms of musical communication, provides a musician with ways of working with others. Thus, interactive competence is a multifaceted structure linking many domains of competence, far more than the simplistic "stock of musical experiences" posited by Schutz (1976: 168) or the "stocks of knowledge" inserted by Turner in his modeling of social interaction (1988: 105, 114, 158).

Competence is validated, enriched, and altered in interaction because our social and musical interactions are largely the playing out of expectations that rest on prior experience. As these expectations are fulfilled or contradicted, present experience is added to prior experience. While interacting with others, musicians test, revise, and augment elements of their competences, including the declarative knowledge that frames conduct and the procedural knowledge utilized in the course of interaction. Augmentation of knowledge has been noted by Faulkner, who asserts that "part of the sum total of recognized musical knowledge is generated in ongoing organizational action" (1973: 156), while the centrality and changeability of framing are acknowledged in Bennett's remark that "perhaps the most crucial feature of any [rock] group is that the definitions and interpretations which comprise its collective knowledge are impelled by and shaped through interactional events" (1980: 6).

Competence is constructed from a mass of objective achievements cloaked in subjective personal and interpersonal assessments and representations. Musicians are likely to have a sense of how well they have mastered different aspects of competence relative to personal goals and to the norms and maximal achievements in their musical community. They also assess each other's capabilities based upon personal contact, perceived accomplishments, communal ranking, and so on. Audience evaluation may also play an important role in the shaping of a musician's sense of self. This perception of self is conveyed—masked, exaggerated, or otherwise altered—in presentation of the self to others with humility, self-assurance, bluster, and so forth. A performer may have a quasi-absolute sense that he or she is a competent musician, but the level or adequacy of this competence in comparison with that of other musicians in a given situation is transitory and open to redefinition or calibration, depending on the relative assertiveness and competitiveness of the people engaged in interaction as well as judgments of their relative skill. Another musician may even affect one's playing by the mere fact of his or her presence. When I suggested this possibility to several Javanese musicians, they agreed with unexpected vehemence. At a later date, one of them unwittingly proved the point when he failed on three successive attempts to play the introduction to a piece that I had heard him play flawlessly on other occasions. He was intimidated by the presence of a higher authority, Mloyowidodo, who is now widely regarded as the most knowledgeable musician in Solo.

The ascription of authority—whether institutionalized, informally recognized, or spontaneously developed anew at each performance—is one of the more important defining characteristics of an ensemble tradition, bringing together considerations of competence and interaction. Musical authority is a matter of competence both proven and perceived; it can be projected by or upon a musician. If members of an ensemble believe that one of their fellows knows "the music" better, they may be tempted or forced to rely upon or defer to him or her. However subtle this attitude may be when a performance flows smoothly, it will come to the fore in tenuous situations when musicians struggle to create, maintain, or repair a shared musical reality—facticity. As they seek to reach agreement on matters such as beat, intonation, or progression through a compositional sequence, to whom do they turn for guidance or confirmation?

This dependence is taken a step further when musicians follow a leader's errors. For example, at a recent rehearsal at the Mangkunegaran palace Mloyowidodo was playing *bonang*, leading the long composition Gendhing Rambu from memory while the other musicians used notation from his anthology of *gendhing*. When he skipped eight beats in the melody, the others followed him with little show of disruption, suspending their own notation-based reality to maintain facticity with their leader!

A sense of facticity engenders mutual trust, a quality whose importance for successful interaction has been noted by a few authors (Faulkner 1973: 149, 155; Lysloff 1990: 55). In American *gamelan* groups, I have noticed that a single strong *balungan* player can instill in an entire section of musicians the confidence necessary to overcome split-second hesitations over identification and interpretation of cues, hesitations that might otherwise ruin a performance. The psychological distress ensuing from a lack of trust is captured in Gerald Moore's argument for long-term associations between singers and their accompanists, which he contrasts with a singer's last-minute rehearsal with an unfamiliar accompanist: "The singer's lack of confidence in—and ever-growing hatred for—his colleague at the keyboard does not help matters . . . To the conscientious artist it is a comfort to have with him a companion who knows his repertoire and has rehearsed constantly with him" (1950: 100). At issue here is the dependency of interaction on a highly localized type of framing: individualized knowledge of other musicians' playing styles, with all the quirks, the strengths, and the weaknesses of their competences and the ways that they tend to interact. Bennett emphasizes such localized knowledge for rock musicians: "The formation of any rock enterprise is the initiation of a new and unique way of knowing how to make music together. That way of knowing is based on the amalgamated resources of its individual members" (1980: 18).

It is not only the interactive aspects of competence that affect interaction: discrepancies in other domains can hinder interaction. Regional variations and generational differences in the content of particular domains—items known only by older or younger performers, or known in conflicting versions by groups on either side of some demographic divide—may seriously hamper music-making, as we saw in the example of the court *gamelan* radio broadcast at the end of chapter 10. Repertoire and ways of performing inevitably change, and these changes are not accepted and absorbed at the same rate by all musicians. Different attitudes and rates of acceptance often, though not necessarily, correlate with different age groups. Generational differences are more insidious than regional ones, because they occur within a community. Yet they preclude a sense of shared reality and thus call into question the unity of that community and the continuity of its tradition.

Disparate levels of competence reach an extreme in ensembles of non-Javanese students led by Javanese musicians. Less competent musicians derive essential psychological reassurance from the teacher. When a sufficiently large number of players lack conviction and a sense of self-assuredness, difficult passages can turn into disasters. For example, Widiyanto taught the *gamelan* group at the University of California, Berkeley, to slow down considerably and pause before the gong stroke at the end of each cycle of a *gendhing*, then to resume the original tempo immediately after the gong was sounded. An interesting learning process of sensitization to the required behavior was followed by increasingly successful execution of this fairly difficult interaction, which depends on a general consensus for stretching and resuming the beat and on specific actions by *kendhang, gendèr,* and gong players. But at some point an exaggerated sense of retard began to appear, seemingly from nowhere. Each person hesitated slightly for fear of playing the last note of the cycle before the gong player entered. These minute hesitations snowballed into ludicrously long pauses after which it was extremely difficult to reestablish a sense of a common beat. It finally became necessary to explicitly halt this overcompensation or "hypercorrection" in order to resensitize everyone to the limits of appropriate timing, instilling an essential sense of confidence in individual and group competence to perform this task.

Together musicians can exceed their individual capabilities, supporting and spurring one another on. They can also fall miserably short of the mark if interaction fails to bring forth a shared sonic reality due to differences of opinion, personality conflicts, or other sources of incompatibility. Surpassing individual potential through group interaction has inspirational, physical, and cognitive dimensions. In ensemble performance one musician can inspire another to respond to his or her musical ideas and this second performer may, in turn, suggest other ideas in a musical exchange that can be highly rewarding for all involved, expanding musicians' competence while affording intense pleasure. The extent to which such exchanges are openly recognized, encouraged, and formalized varies, as we saw in chapter 7.

The physical dimensions are relatively straightforward. The blending of a violin section does not simply increase the volume of a single violin but differs qualitatively. The same can be said for choral and solo singing. Ensemble performance enables more musical lines to sound simultaneously, and it allows greater independence among those parts. Dividing a melodic or rhythmic part into two interlocking parts allows musicians to achieve a speed and precision of articulation beyond the reach of a single human being.

The cognitive dimension is more pertinent to the present discussion of competence and interaction. When too much knowledge accumulates, one person can no longer assimilate and retain everything: the burden of communal memory must be divided. Similarly, there are probably rough limits on the array of sound-producing skills that an individual can maintain. Such limits on knowledge and skills are often recognized formally in specialized competences associated with specific repertoires, contexts, and instruments or roles, the type of specialization most pertinent here. Individuals master separate pieces of a puzzle, and through interaction their complementary competences mesh to create a performance that is beyond the capabilities of each participant. The symphony orchestra is one of many manifestations of this phenomenon. More extreme cases are to be found in multimedia performances such as Balinese and Javanese dance and *wayang*, Japanese Noh and Kabuki, and the like: the specializations of actors, dancers, and puppeteers are clearly distinct, but successful interaction depends on the specialists' intimate knowledge of substantial portions of each other's specializations.

Where role switching is possible, interactive requirements and responsibilities often favor the development of multiple competence.

> For [Balinese] dancers, it is essential to know the music very intimately. They should understand not only the feeling, but also the sequence and structure of music that is used to accompany them. Likewise as a musician, one should understand the structure of the choreography, the phrasing of the movement,

in order to underline and reinforce certain gestures within it. (I Wayan Dibia in Vitale 1990: 17.)

Complementation and overlap of competences may also extend to ritual officiants:

> Among the Ga of Ghana cantors, drummers, horn-blowers and all others who contribute to musical interaction on ritual occasions are made a part of the priestly group . . . Because of this they are also expected to be familiar with the repertoire of songs, drumming and dancing and of course the technical skills required in performance so that they can interact with priests, mediums, and the ritual assembly. On the same basis some knowledge of the music and dance of the religious group is expected of the other members of the priestly band since they may now and then assume brief leadership of a dance event, and in the case of mediums, also act as the central focus of performances of possession dancers. (Nketia 1989: 121.)

Comparable examples of interaction based on the overlap of complementary specializations are likely to be found in many other types of music.

Musicians can also share the burden of memory through an informal division of knowledge within a specialization. Balinese *trompong* (gong chime) players who lead a *gamelan* in the performance of *lelambatan* at temple ceremonies may each know only four or five of these long, abstract compositions well enough to lead the *gamelan*, but when one has exhausted his repertoire another takes over and the group can continue to play. The other musicians can usually play a larger repertoire than individual *trompong* players, so long as each *trompong* player knows his piece well enough to show the others the way (I Wayan Saplug, personal communication). In such cases the overlapping but distinctive memories of individual "memory specialists," who know specific items better than anyone else, are the focal points of communal memory.

As musicians propel themselves like acrobats through sonic "space," they hold guide wires and stretch a safety net for each other. They provide orientation and reminders for one another to ensure that they will meet in midair or maintain their balance on the wire, to stave off asynchrony or serious lapses of memory, and to keep one another from falling to the net. Musicians who play drones, harmonic accompaniments, or colotomic parts may provide more constant references and take fewer risks, but virtually no one stands with both feet firmly on the ground throughout a performance. Moments of uncertainty and conflict almost inevitably arise, requiring reestablishment of facticity.

Ideally the dynamics of ensemble interaction sustain and reinforce a musician's conception and performance of a piece. In primarily oral ensemble traditions this is especially important because of the burden of memory, which is considerable even when it is shared among members of the ensemble. While notation alone is certainly not sufficient to ensure a perfect performance—and can in itself be the source of extensive disagreement—it does provide a concrete common referent that is external to human memory and more stable in time than transitory perceptions.[1]

When the parts in an ensemble are closely related melodically, as they are in Javanese *gamelan*, musicians hear parallels and reminders in the other parts. In other types of music, composite conceptions— whether harmonic or rhythmic—can serve a similar purpose: hearing the other parts, a musician finds the "spaces" which he or she is supposed to be filling. Transformational knowledge enables a musician to translate something played in one part into an idiomatic equivalent. This is one of the most basic and essential skills of a Javanese *gamelan* musician. On the basis of informal observation and experience with a large number of Westerners and Javanese, it seems that Westerners learning an ensemble part are often bothered by other parts at first, needing to shut them out. Javanese, on the other hand, are usually aided by other *gamelan* instruments when learning a new piece because of this transformational knowledge, which they use to make analogies to pieces they already know and to derive one part from another, simultaneously sounding one. It is an exhilarating experience for a non-Javanese to reach the point where it is possible to sit down with a group of musicians without notation and join in playing a piece that one has never played before in this particular way, on this particular instrument, or perhaps at all. This does not lead to superlative performances, but the process can be thrilling as you stretch your senses to pull every shred of orientation, every hint of melodic guidance, from the many enveloping acoustic strands, exploiting all the pertinent aspects of competence to situate yourself and play appropriately for the part and the piece, and straining your memory to grasp it all so that the next time round the cycle you can go back and correct, continuing to build on knowledge already accumulated.

Javanese musicians commonly use a number of terms to describe this process of floating along on the river of *gamelan*.[2] Susilo distinguishes on an aesthetic basis between *"ngawur* (lit. to blunder), denoting an out-of-style or irrelevant improvisation," and *"ngambang* (lit. floating) [which]

1. Notation may give rise to other complications such as the accidental elisions in sight-reading studied by Sloboda (1985: 250).

2. See, e.g., Sumarsam (1975) or Suyenaga (1984).

can refer to musical improvisation by players who do not have a clear idea of where the music is going . . . occasionally *ngambang* is tolerated, but never *ngawur*" (1987: 9). In other words, the musician who is temporarily lost should not play something inappropriate (*ngawur*), but should float along by maintaining idiomatic density and patterning without contradicting the flow of the rest of the *gamelan*. Sutton speaks to this when he mentions a technique of *celempung* playing called *kacang asin* (salt peanuts!) which "allows a musician to play for a gendhing he has never heard, for it neither anticipates nor coincides with the balungan. Instead it provides constant orientation with respect to pathet" (1982: 179). Widiyanto demonstrated for me how to play *celempung* in such a way as never to hit the *sèlèh*, the goal tone, while keeping a steady flow of sound with minimal effort (which can be useful after hours of playing).

The process of being reminded in performance replicates the learning process but is probably far more efficient—ideally almost instantaneous—since associative processes are recalling or reconnecting items already stored in memory rather than storing new items and making new connections. The flexibility of the more complex parts in *gamelan* is important because it affords a musician the space to forget and drift momentarily without destroying the piece: the safety net is elastic. Within the loose temporal framework of a *pathetan*, for example, the musicians have time to remember and remind one another of the path with prompts and overt cues. This dependence is best expressed, perhaps, in the words with which one musician excused his difficulties in playing a piece alone: "Kalau enggak ada temannya, jalannya sering ménggok," which translates loosely as "Without companions one's path often strays."

The centrality of mutual dependence and collective re-creation to the traditional Javanese *gamelan* experience is underlined by its absence in the innovative *wayang padhat* discussed in chapter 9 (and in Brinner 1992). In this form the traditional system of interaction is bypassed and the safety net has gaping holes in it, because events are so condensed and changes are so rapid that traditional interaction is no longer possible. Spontaneity is abandoned in favor of prearranged and thoroughly rehearsed sequences of events. The general competence imparted by oral tradition is inadequate and must be supplanted by specific knowledge of the details of a particular performance.

The most convincing testimony to the workability of the Javanese safety net of ensemble interaction that I have observed occurred at a *klenèngan* at a private house in Solo in the summer of 1983. Martopangrawit played *rebab* and Mloyowidodo played *slenthem*, along with other fine musicians. At the end of one *gendhing*, the drummer did not bring the *inggah* section to a final halt but signaled a continuation to a *ladrang*, a common enough practice. This put the ball in Martopangrawit's court, since a drummer can indicate the form of the ensuing piece (in this case a *ladrang*) but cannot cue melodically to determine a particular piece. This choice must be made clear in the first phrases of the *ladrang* by the *rebab* or *bonang* player. The other musicians play along, hoping to identify the piece as quickly as possible, because when pieces are joined together in this manner, there is no *buka*, no solo introduction during which members of the ensemble can sit passively and listen for identifying characteristics. In this case all of the musicians except Mloyowidodo were mystified by Martopangrawit's choice for rather longer than usual. There were looks of discomfort and whispered exchanges while Martopangrawit and Mloyowidodo plowed on. The drummer and colotomic players were probably not as troubled as some of the others, because they knew that the piece was a *ladrang* and so could repeat the pattern appropriate to that form while waiting for the smoke to clear. The *balungan* players could watch the mallet of the *slenthem* player and try to hit the same pitches. The players of the elaborating parts had the hardest time as they floated along, groping for familiar landmarks while keeping their parts going, but it all worked out in the end as the musicians began to identify the piece and find their place in it.

The difficulty was occasioned by Martopangrawit's translation of a *pélog* piece (Ladrang Tirtakencana) to *sléndro*, which is an uncommon transformation both for this specific piece and in general: tuning transformations usually go in the other direction, from *sléndro* to *pélog*. The eventual success of the performance was due to the coordinated cooperation between two old buddies playing core instruments, to the fact that the form of the piece had been established and so could be maintained by drummer and colotomic players, who are less concerned with details of melody, and to the competence of the other musicians, who were able to keep on floating (*ngambang*) until they derived sufficient information from *rebab* and *slenthem* to find some solid ground.

This anecdote emphasizes the importance of the *rebab* for melodic guidance in pieces which, for one reason or another, are unfamiliar or problematic. It also demonstrates the resilience of the interactive network (enough essential roles were filled to keep the piece going), the importance of the interactive system and framework (other players were able to pick out melodic clues with reference to the *ladrang* framework) and what might be called mechanisms of harmless—and sometimes ingenious—procrastination. Furthermore, it highlights the importance of mutual familiarity: the two musicians who knew what they were doing all along and held the performance together had shared a lifetime of music-making. Last, but not least, it is evidence of the effect of confidence and authority projected by a leading musician. Although I have no direct comparison for this particular incident, I doubt that a lesser *rebab* player would have taken such a risk or played it out so firmly to such a successful conclusion in the face of such confusion.

QUESTIONS FOR THE FUTURE

Where do we go from here? I hope that the theoretical concepts and frameworks developed in this book will inspire others to take a similarly integrative approach, to look at the totality of musical thought and practice in a community—however large or small—in terms of cognitive and interpersonal challenges, potentials, and accomplishments. This approach highlights the relative significance of different aspects of a musical tradition and offers a way to evaluate change and to connect practice with theory. It also offers a sociologically informed view of interactive relations that is not shaped solely by political or economic assumptions or by a narrow concern with status. Rather than a sociology of music focusing on social issues, we then have a socially aware ethnomusicology, focused on music-making and music made, yet cognizant of the web of interpersonal relations in which music-makers are entangled. I believe that meaningful comparisons can be made on the basis of such integrative understandings of musical competence and interaction in particular communities. The brief examples I have drawn from other cultures to complement the Central Javanese material indicate some of the possibilities for further work.

Developments in the field of cognitive musicology are crucial to this endeavor. We do not yet have a clear idea of the nature of mental representations of music formed by musicians or the role that these representations play in knowing and making music. Besides mental "soundings"—remembered or imagined internal auditions—there are certainly other important representations such as kinetic and kinesthetic patterns of fingers and voice, visual images of symbolic representations, mnemonics, and associative knowledge of words, movements, and other "extramusical" phenomena. Must these representations be shared by individuals, or is it possible for musicians holding fundamentally different conceptions of a piece to perform satisfactorily together? Are certain types of representation favored in teaching and others favored in theory or in practical discussion? Are private representations different in essence from those expressed publicly? We come here to fundamental problems of levels of analysis (see Slobin 1992) and the representativeness of representation: having gained access to private representations (our own or others'), how do we relate these to representations that are common (recurring, though perhaps not sanctioned, explicit, or conventional) and public (consensual or prescribed)?

These questions lead back to a consideration of authority and norms, both implicit and explicit, and then to a reconsideration of the concept "tradition." The latter is so overworked that it has been used sparingly in this book, often replaced by circumlocutions such as "music-making community" and "musical culture" that are scarcely less problematic. Since we cannot replace it altogether, we should continue to think of more consistent ways of defining it. To the extent that a musical tradition resides in the minds of the bearers of that tradition, we can define it in terms of performer competence and interaction as an aggregate of musical knowledge, skills, and ways of making music that are "bundled" together by a group of musicians, enabling them to interact within their community, however that might be constituted.[3]

The approaches of cognitive science may help us to better understand the link between a tradition and its bearers. We have seen the overlap of social and musical interactive competences. What of connections with other cultural competences? Is there something about a Javanese way of being—some perceptual skills or conceptual habits—outside the specific realm of music that enables Javanese musicians to do what they do? Without advocating a "patterns of culture" holism, we should still be able to ask whether some musical competences are so tied to other forms of cultural knowledge and ways of being as to preclude outsiders from ever really attaining "full" competence. This outsider/insider dichotomy that continues to trouble ethnomusicologists and anthropologists—if in ever-changing theoretical garb—must boil down to a difference in experience and the knowledge derived therefrom, unless we subscribe to a narrowly hereditary (in-group genetic) basis for cultural competence. Is the unattainability of some insider competences just a question of length of exposure or of enculturation that must occur by a certain age or at a certain stage in a person's development? Perhaps an outsider who has developed a social and musical sense of self in one community can replicate enculturation in another only by transcending that sense of self.

Today these questions can be answered provisionally, if at all, by

---

3. I leave open the question of how many years must pass before some bundle of musical practice is recognized as a tradition.

looking for parallels between social and musical interaction such as those sketched here or links between competence in music and other cultural domains. They may never be answered with finality, but they can motivate deeper study of the ways in which people know and make music.

Appendix

GENDHING LUNGKÈH

This excerpt is transcribed from the recording session described in "Two Performances." While the notes of the *balungan* are evenly spaced in the transcription, the tempo actually slows from an initial 120 *balungan* beats per minute to about 30 beats per minute by the end of the third system. As the duration of the *balungan* beat expands, there is more time for the other musicians to fill. The *gambang* player does so at a rate of 8 notes per beat (played in parallel octaves) while the *gendèr* player fills in at a basic rate of 4 to 1, subdividing this further on occasion. The *suling* part is the least accurately represented in this transcription because it is the most florid and rhythmically irregular. The gong is played once in this excerpt, indicated by an oval surrounding the first pitch of the *balungan*. The parts do not coincide precisely at this point because the beat leading up to the gong was stretched.

Key

rb = *rebab*

gd = *gendèr*

gb = *gambang*

kd = *kendhang*

su = *suling*

ps = *pesindhèn*

Kendhang strokes

B = dah, a low, resonant stroke on the large head of the drum
P = dung, a higher, resonant stroke on the large head of the drum
o = tong, a high stroke on the rim of the small head
1 = ket, a soft tapping (damped stroke) on the large head

Ornaments in *rebab, suling,* and *vocal*
^ indicates that the pitch above was briefly sounded
˘ indicates that the pitch below was briefly sounded

Appendix Beginning of a performance of Gendhing Lungkēh Recording KS13; May 15, 1993

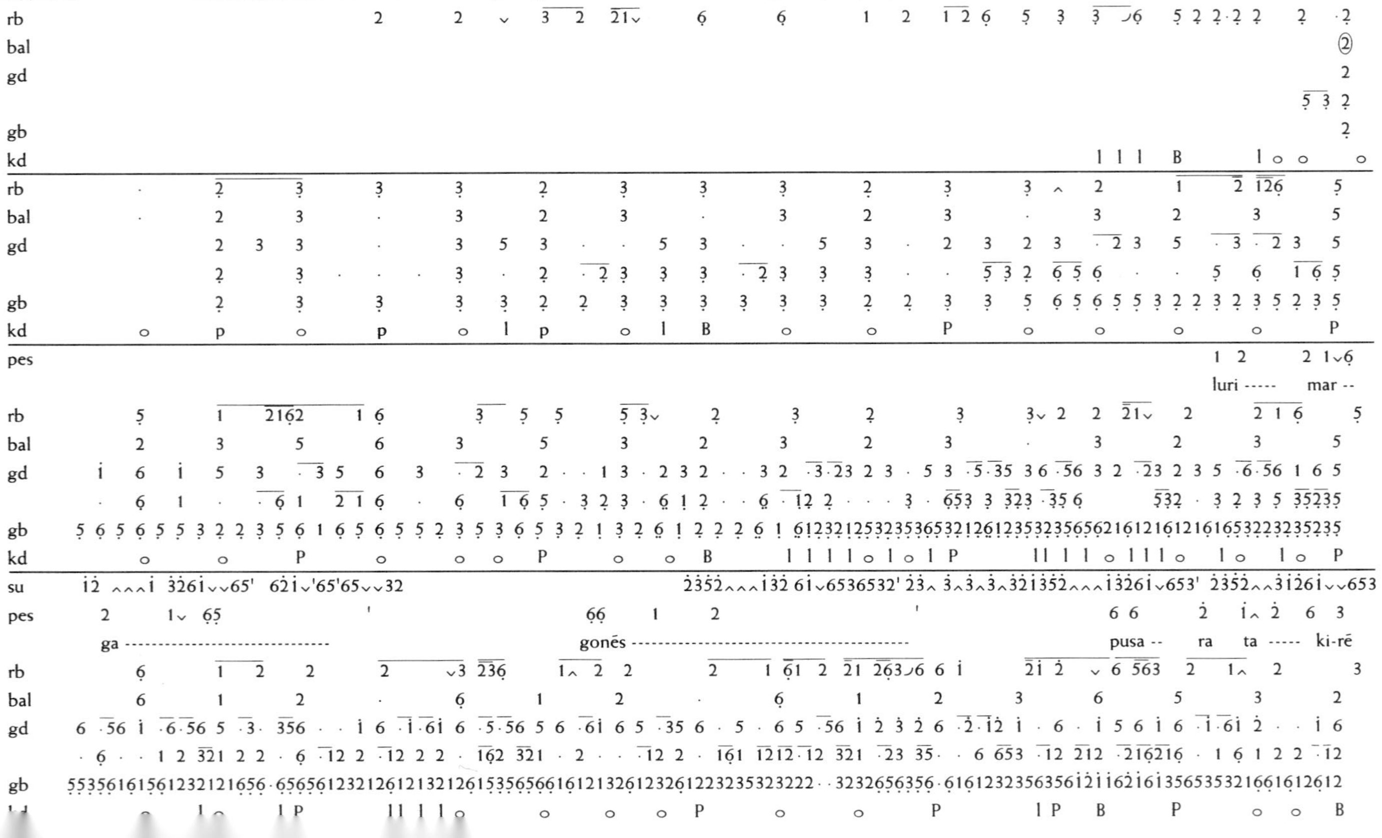

GLOSSARY

BALINESE TERMS

angsel	Rhythmic break in a cyclical structure.
gangsa	Metallophone with cylindrical resonators.
kebyar	Dominant style of Balinese music developed in the 1920s.
kendang	Drum.
kotekan	Interlocking parts.
lelambatan	Long ceremonial compositions.
polos	The more basic of a pair of interlocking parts; complemented by a *sangsih*.
sangsih	The part which interlocks with the *polos*.
trompong	Melodic set of ten gongs suspended horizontally in a single line. A lead instrument.
ugal	Leading metallophone; also refers to the musician who plays this instrument.

JAVANESE TERMS

ada-ada	Subgenre of *sulukan*: a type of song expressing tension; performed in *wayang* by a *dhalang* accompanied on *gendèr, gong, kempul,* and *kenong*.
andhegan	Temporary break in a *gendhing*; the musicians stop while a singer sings a solo.
balungan	Basic melody of a *gendhing* or the form of this melody as played on *saron* or *slenthem*.
bonang	Set of ten, twelve, or fourteen small gongs suspended horizontally in two rows and played melodically.
bonang panerus	Small *bonang*, pitched one octave higher.
celempung	Large plucked zither strung with pairs of metal strings.

325

cempala	Wooden mallet used by a *dhalang* to strike the *kotak* and *keprak*.
céngkok	Melodic or rhythmic formula.
ciblon	Medium-sized barrel drum played in an ornate manner; the section of a piece in which this drum is played.
demung	Largest *saron*.
dhalang	Puppeteer in *wayang kulit*; narrator and music director in *wayang wong*.
dhodhogan	Rhythmic patterns played on *kotak* and *keprak*.
gadhon	Small *gamelan* consisting of the elaborating instruments, singers, and minimal *balungan* and colotomy.
gambang	Multioctave xylophone played with two padded mallets.
garap	Realization of the essence of a piece by a singer or instrumentalist in accordance with modal frameworks, idiomatic processes, and specific characteristics of the piece.
gatra	A four-beat unit that is the smallest unit of organization of most metrical *gamelan* music in Central Java.
gendèr	Metallophone with twelve to fourteen thin keys suspended over cylindrical resonators and struck with two padded mallets.
gendèr panerus	Small *gendèr*, pitched one octave higher.
gendhing	A composition; in a more restricted sense *gendhing* refers to long, multisectional pieces.
gérong	Male chorus in regular *gamelan*; mixed chorus in certain court dances.
gongan	A cyclical unit of music marked by a gong stroke.
gong suwukan	Large suspended gong played to mark the end of a cycle in short pieces or as a means of accentuation in some longer pieces.
imbal	Interlocking play.
inggah	Second large section of a *gendhing*.
irama	Set of temporal relationships deriving from the speed of the beat and the ratio of the faster-moving parts to the beat (2 : 1, 4 : 1, 8 : 1, etc.)
kempul	Medium-sized hanging gong played colotomically. A *gamelan* usually contains at least three differently pitched *kempul* for each tuning system.
kendhang	Two-headed barrel drum.
kenong	Horizontally suspended gong played colotomically. A *gamelan* usually contains one *kenong* for each pitch in the sléndro and pélog tuning systems.
kenongan	A phrase that is marked at the end by a *kenong* stroke. Usually there are two or four *kenongan* in a *gongan*.
keplok	Interlocking handclapping.
keprak	Set of bronze concussion plates hung from the *kotak* and struck rhythmically with a *cempala* by the *dhalang* for cuing and emphasis.
kethuk	Small horizontally suspended gong played colotomically.
ketipung	Smallest drum in the *gamelan*.
klenèngan	Performance of *gamelan* without theater or dance.
kombangan	Vocable sung by a *dhalang* in *sulukan* or *gendhing*.

kotak	Wooden box in which shadow puppets are stored; placed next to the *dhalang*, it also serves as an instrument when struck with a *cempala*.
lagu	Melody.
laras	Tuning system.
mérong	First large section of a *gendhing*.
minggah	*Inggah* or the act of going to the *inggah* section of a *gendhing*.
palaran	*Gamelan* genre featuring rhythmically free solo voice with metrical instrumental playing.
panerusan	Collective term for the instruments of the *gamelan* used to elaborate the basic melody.
pathet	Mode (approximately); major segment of a play.
pathetan	Subgenre of *sulukan*: a type of song expressing calm and defining a mode (*pathet*); performed in *wayang* by a *dhalang* accompanied on *rebab, gendèr, gambang, suling, gong, kempul,* and *kenong*. Performed instrumentally in *klenèngan* on *rebab, gendèr, gambang,* and *suling* as prelude or postlude to *gendhing*.
peking	Smallest *saron*.
pélog	Seven-toned tuning system.
pesindhèn	Female singer in a *gamelan*.
rebab	Bowed spike fiddle with two strings.
sampak	Short, rapidly performed *gamelan* genre used primarily to accompany battle scenes.
saron	Metallophone with six, seven, or nine keys resting on a resonating trough and struck with a hard mallet; ranges in size from the large *demung* through the *saron barung* to the small *peking*.
sasmita	Cue given by the *dhalang* to the *gamelan*.
sèlèh	Goal tone toward which melody leads.
sendhon	Subgenre of *sulukan*: a type of song expressing sadness or confusion; performed in *wayang* by a *dhalang* accompanied on *gendèr, gambang, suling, gong, kempul,* and *kenong*.
senggakan	Stylized cries performed by the *gérong*.
sekatèn	A type of ceremonial court *gamelan* consisting of unusually large instruments and played mainly to mark the birth of the Prophet Mohammed.
sirep	Softer section in which most instruments of the *gamelan* are silent; followed by *udhar*, a return to full volume.
siter	Plucked zither strung with pairs of metal strings.
sléndro	Five-toned tuning system.
slenthem	Metallophone with six or seven large keys suspended over cylindrical resonators and struck with a padded mallet.
srepegan	Short, rapidly performed *gamelan* genre used primarily to accompany movement and battle.
suling	End-blown bamboo flute.
sulukan	Songs sung by a *dhalang* in *wayang kulit, wayang wong,* and dance; see *pathetan, sendhon,* and *ada-ada*.
suwuk	The ending section of a piece; the act of ending a piece.

udhar   The entire *gamelan* resumes performance at full volume after a *sirep*.
wayang   Generic term for theater; also means puppet.
wayang kulit   Shadow play with water buffalo hide puppets.
wayang padhat Condensed form of *wayang kulit* developed at STSI in the 1970s.
wayang wong   Theatrical genre similar in conventions to *wayang kulit* but using human actors.

Bibliography

ADLER, THOMAS
1979   "The Acquisition of a Traditional Competence: Folk-Musical and Folk-Cultural Learning among Bluegrass Banjo Players." Ann Arbor: University Microfilms.

ANDERSON, BENEDICT. R. O'G.
1965   *Mythology and the Tolerance of the Javanese.* Ithaca: Modern Indonesian Project, Cornell University.
1972   "The Idea of Power in Javanese Culture." In Holt, Claire, ed., *Culture and Politics in Indonesia,* pp. 1–70. Ithaca: Cornell University Press.
1990   *Language and Power: Exploring Political Cultures in Indonesia.* Ithaca: Cornell University Press.

ANDERSON, J. R.
1982   "Acquisition of Cognitive Skill." *Psychological Review* 89: 369–406.

ANONYMOUS
1861   *Winner's Perfect Guide for the Guitar, In which the Instructions are so clearly and simply treated, as to make it unnecessary to require a teacher. For Practice, more than 150 Operatic and Popular Airs are added, Forming a Complete Collection of the Best Melodies of the Day.* Boston: Oliver Ditson & Co.
1982   *Cathetan Kawruh Pedhalangan.* Typescript transliteration from Javanese script by R. Ng. Martopangrawit. From Radyapustaka, ca. 1929–35. Surakarta.

AROM, SIMHA
1991   *African Polyphony and Polyrhythm.* Cambridge: Cambridge University Press.

329

ASTONO, SIGIT
1990   *Pengenalan Terhadap Cengkok Cengkok Siteran.* Surakarta: STSI.

AVERILL, GAGE
1990   "Four Parts, No Waiting: The Ideal of Male Camaraderie in Barbershop
        Harmony." Paper delivered at the AMS/SEM/SMT annual conference,
        1990, Oakland, CA.

BAILY, JOHN
1988   "Anthropological and Psychological Approaches to the Study of Music
        Theory and Musical Cognition." *Yearbook for Traditional Music* 20/1: 114–24.

BECKER, ALTON
1979   "Text-Building, Epistemology, and Aesthetics in Javanese Shadow The-
        ater." In Becker, Alton, and Aram Yengoyan, eds., *The Imagination of Reality:
        Essays in Southeast Asian Coherence Systems,* pp. 211–43. Norwood, NJ: Ablex
        Books.

BECKER, ALTON, AND JUDITH BECKER
1979   "A Grammar of the Genre Srepegan." *Journal of Musical Theory* 24/1: 1–43.

BECKER, JUDITH
1979   "Time and Tune in Java." In Becker, Alton, and Aram Yengoyan, eds., *The
        Imagination of Reality: Essays in Southeast Asian Coherence Systems,* pp. 197–210.
        Norwood, NJ: Ablex Books.
1980   *Traditional Music in Modern Java.* Honolulu: University of Hawaii Press.
1981   "A Southeast Asian Musical Process: Thai *Thaw* and Javanese *Irama.*" *Ethno-
        musicology* 24/3: 453–64.

BECKER, JUDITH, AND ALAN FEINSTEIN, EDS.
1984   *Karawitan: Source Readings in Javanese Gamelan and Vocal Music.* Vol. 1. Ann
        Arbor: Center for South and Southeast Asian Studies, University of
        Michigan.
1987   *Karawitan: Source Readings in Javanese Gamelan and Vocal Music.* Vol. 2. Ann
        Arbor: Center for South and Southeast Asian Studies, University of
        Michigan.

BENNETT, H. STITH
1980   *On Becoming a Rock Musician.* Amherst: University of Massachusetts Press.

BLACKING, JOHN
1970   "Tonal Organization in the Music of Two Venda Initiation Schools." *Ethno-
        musicology* 14/1: 1–56.
1971a   "Deep and Surface Structures in Venda Music." *Yearbook of the International
        Folk Music Council* 3: 91–108.
1971b   "Towards a Theory of Musical Competence." In DeJager, E. J., ed., *Man:
        Anthropological Essays Presented to O. F. Raum,* pp. 19–34. Cape Town: C.
        Struik.
1973   *How Musical Is Man?* Seattle: University of Washington Press.

BLUM, DAVID
1986   *The Art of Quartet Playing: The Guarneri Quartet in Conversation with David Blum.*
        Ithaca: Cornell University Press.

BOURDIEU, PIERRE
1977   *Outline of a Theory of Practice.* Trans. Richard Nice. Cambridge Studies in Social Anthropology 16. Cambridge: Cambridge University Press.

BRINNER, BENJAMIN
1985   "Competence and Interaction in the Performance of Central Javanese *Pathetan.*" Ann Arbor: University Microfilms.
1989/90 "At the Border of Sound and Silence: The Use and Function of Pathetan in Javanese Gamelan." *Asian Music* 21/1: 1–34.
1992   "Performer Interaction in a New Form of Javanese Wayang." In Foley, Kathy, ed., *Essays on Southeast Asian Performing Arts: Local Manifestations and Cross-Cultural Implications*, pp. 96–114. Berkeley: Centers for South and Southeast Asia Studies, University of California.
1993   "Freedom and Formulaity in the *Suling* Playing of Bapak Tarnopangrawit." *Asian Music* 24/2: 1–38.
1995   "Cultural Matrices and the Shaping of Innovation in Central Javanese Performing Arts." *Ethnomusicology* (forthcoming).

BROWN, ROBERT E., AND ANDREW TOTH
1971   *Javanese Court Gamelan from the Pura Paku Alaman, Yogyakarta.* Liner notes. New York: Nonesuch Records.

BRUNER, EDWARD
1986   "Experience and Its Expressions." In Turner, Victor W., and Edward M. Bruner, eds., *The Anthropology of Experience*, pp. 4–32. Urbana: University of Illinois Press.

CHERNOFF, JOHN MILLER
1979   *African Rhythm and African Sensibility.* Chicago: University of Chicago Press.

CLIFFORD, JAMES
1988   *The Predicament of Culture: Twentieth-Century Ethnography, Literature, and Art.* Cambridge, MA: Harvard University Press.

CLIFFORD, JAMES, AND GEORGE MARCUS, EDS.
1986   *Writing Culture: The Poetics and Politics of Ethnography.* Berkeley: University of California Press.

DARSOMARTONO, S.
1978a   *Dodogan ing salebeting Gending² Wayangan Ringgit Purwa Wacucal.* Surakarta: Yayasan PDMN.
1978b   *Tuntunan Pakeliran.* Sala [Surakarta]: PDMN.

DASILVA, FABIO, ANTHONY BLASI, AND DAVID DEES
1984   *The Sociology of Music.* Notre Dame, IN: University of Notre Dame Press.

DAVIDSON, LYLE, AND BRUCE TORFF
1992   "Situated Cognition in Music." *World of Music* 34/3: 120–39.

DAVIS, MARTHA ELLEN
1987   "'Native Bi-Musicality': Case Studies from the Caribbean." *Pacific Review of Ethnomusicology* 4: 39–56.

DEA, ALEXANDER
1980   *Bawa: A Javanese Solo Vocal Music.* Ann Arbor: University Microfilms.

DEVEREAUX, KENT
1989   "Interview: 'It's Not Official Till the Gong Is Hung'; Dr. Sri Hastanto, S.
         Kar." *Balungan* 4/1: 7–18.

DJAKOEB AND WIGNYAROEMEKSA
1913   *Layang Anyumurupaké Pratikelé Bab Sinau Nabuh Sarta Panggawéné Gamelan.*
         [Dutch title: *Over de Gamelan.*] Batavia: Drukkerij Papyrus.

DJEDJE, JACQUELINE COGDELL
1986   "Change and Differentiation: The Adoption of Black American Gospel
         Music in the Catholic Church." *Ethnomusicology* 30/2: 223–52.

DOWLING, W. JAY, AND DANE HARWOOD
1986   *Music Cognition.* Orlando: Academic Press.

EISENSTADT, S. N.
1964   "Social Change, Differentiation and Evolution." *American Sociological Review*
         29/3: 376–86.

ELIAS, TAISEER
1990/91 "Problems Facing the Arab Musician or Student of Western Classical Mu-
         sic." *Music in Time,* pp. 29–36. Jerusalem: Rubin Academy of Music and
         Dance.

FAULKNER, R. R.
1973   "Orchestra Interaction: Some Features of Communication and Authority
         in an Artistic Organization." *Sociological Quarterly* 14: 147–57.

FELD, STEVEN
1974   "Linguistic Models in Ethnomusicology." *Ethnomusicology* 18/2: 179–217.
1982   *Sound and Sentiment.* Philadelphia: University of Pennsylvania Press.
1984   "Sound Structure as Social Structure." *Ethnomusicology* 28/3: 383–409.
1986   "Orality and Consciousness." In Tokumaru, Yoshihito, and Osamu Yama-
         guti, eds., *The Oral and the Literate in Music.* Tokyo: Academia Music.

FINK, I., AND C. MERRIELL WITH THE GUARNERI STRING QUARTET
1985   *String Quartet Playing.* Neptune City, NJ: Paganiniana Publications.

FORREST, WAYNE
1980   "Concepts of Melodic Pattern in Contemporary Solonese Gamelan
         Music." *Asian Music* 11/2: 53–127.

GABRIELSSON, ALF
1988   "Timing in Music Performance and Its Relations to Music Experience." In
         Sloboda, John, ed., *Generative Processes in Music: The Psychology of Performance,
         Improvisation, and Composition,* pp. 27–51. Oxford Science Publications. Ox-
         ford: Clarendon Press.

GARDNER, HOWARD
1984   "The Development of Competence in Culturally Defined Domains." In

Shweder, Richard A., and Robert A. Levine, eds., *Culture Theory*, pp. 257–75. Cambridge: Cambridge University Press.

1987   *The Mind's New Science: A History of the Cognitive Revolution*. 2d ed. with a new epilogue. New York: Basic Books.

GEERTZ, CLIFFORD
1973   *Interpretation of Cultures*. New York: Basic Books.
1983   *Local Knowledge*. New York: Basic Books.

GIDDENS, ANTHONY, AND JONATHAN TURNER, EDS.
1987   *Social Theory Today*. Stanford: Stanford University Press.

GILES, RAY
1974   "*Ombak* in the Style of Javanese Gongs." *Selected Reports in Ethnomusicology* 2/1: 158–65.

GITOSAPRODJO, SULEIMAN
1984   "Ichtisar Teori Karawitan dan Teknik Menabuh gamelan." [Summary of the Theory of Karawitan and Technique of Playing the *Gamelan*.] Trans. Judith Becker. In Becker, Judith, and Alan Feinstein, eds., *Karawitan*, vol. 1, pp. 336–87.

GJERDINGEN, ROBERT O.
1988   *A Classic Turn of Phrase: Music and the Psychology of Convention*. Philadelphia: University of Pennsylvania Press.

GOURLAY, K. A.
1972   "The Practice of Cueing among the Karimojong of Noth-east Uganda." *Ethnomusicology* 16/2: 240–47.

GRUSON, LINDA M.
1988   "Rehearsal Skill and Musical Competence: Does Practice Make Perfect?" In Sloboda, John, ed., *Generative Processes in Music: The Psychology of Performance, Improvisation, and Composition*, pp. 91–112. Oxford Science Publications. Oxford: Clarendon Press.

HARNISH, DAVID D.
1991   "Music at the Lingsar Temple Festival: The Encapsulation of Meaning in the Balinese/Sasak Interface in Lombok, Indonesia." Ann Arbor: University Microfilms.

HARWOOD, DANE
1987   "Interpretive Activity: A Response to Rice's 'Toward the Remodeling of Ethnomusicology.'" *Ethnomusicology* 31/3: 503–10.

HASTANTO, SRI
1990   "Pathêt I: Pathêt di dalam Laras Pélog pada Karawitan Jawa Tengah." *Seni Pertunjukan Indonesia. Jurnal Masyarakat Musikologi Indonesia* 1/1: 155–87.

HATCH, MARTIN
1979   "Towards a More Open Approach to the History of Javanese Music." *Indonesia* 27: 129–54.
1986   "Social Change and the Functions of Music in Java." In Frisbie, Charlotte

J., ed., *Explorations in Ethnomusicology: Essays in Honor of David P. McAllester.* Detroit Monographs in Musicology. Detroit Information Coordinators.

HAYES-ROTH, BARBARA
1977   "Evolution of Cognitive Structures and Processes," *Psychological Review* 84/3: 260–78.

HEINS, ERNST
1970   "Cueing the Gamelan in Javanese Wayang Kulit." *Indonesia* 9: 101–27.

HIGGINS, JON
1973   "The Music of Bharata Natyam." Ann Arbor: University Microfilms.

HOOD, MANTLE
1954   *The Nuclear Theme as a Determinant of Patet in Javanese Music.* Groningen: J. B. Wolters. Reprinted by Da Capo Press, 1977.
1960   "The Challenge of Bi-Musicality." *Ethnomusicology* 4: 55–59.
1966   "Slendro and Pelog Redefined." *Selected Reports in Ethnomusicology* 1/1: 28–48.
1971   *The Ethnomusicologist.* New York: McGraw-Hill Book Co.
1984   *The Legacy of the Roaring Sea. The Evolution of Javanese Gamelan.* Book 2. Wilhelmshaven: Noetzel.
1988   *Paragon of the Roaring Sea. The Evolution of Javanese Gamelan.* Book 3. Wilhelmshaven: Noetzel.

HUGHES, DAVID
1988   "Deep Structure and Surface Structure in Javanese Music: A Grammar of *Gendhing Lampah*." *Ethnomusicology* 32/1: 23–74.

KARTOMI, MARGARET
1973   *Macapat Songs in Central Java.* Oriental Monograph Series no. 13. Canberra: Australian National University Press.
1990   *On Concepts and Classifications of Musical Instruments.* Chicago: University of Chicago Press.

KEELER, WARD
1975   "Musical Encounter in Java and Bali." *Indonesia* 19: 85–126.
1987   *Javanese Shadow Plays, Javanese Selves.* Princeton: Princeton University Press.

KINGSBURY, HENRY
1988   *Music, Talent and Performance: A Conservatory Cultural System.* Philadelphia: Temple University Press.

KIPPEN, JAMES
1987   "An Ethnomusicological Approach to the Analysis of Musical Cognition." *Music Perception* 5/2: 173–96.
1992   "Tabla Drumming and the Human-Computer Interaction." *World of Music* 34/3: 72–98.

KOENTJARANINGRAT
1985   *Javanese Culture.* Singapore: Oxford University Press.

KOSKOFF, ELLEN
1988   "Cognitive Strategies in Rehearsal." *Selected Reports in Ethnomusicology* 7: 59–68.

KOSKOFF, ELLEN, ED.
1992   *The World of Music.* 34/3: Ethnomusicology and Music Cognition.

KUNST, JAAP
1949   *Music in Java.* 2 vols. 2d ed. The Hague: Martinus Nijhoff.

KUSUMADILAGA, K. P. A. [OR MAS SASTRAMIRUDA?]
1981   *Serat Sastramiruda.* Trans. [Indonesian] Kamajaya. Jakarta: Departmen Pendidikan dan Kebudayaan.

LAKOFF, GEORGE
1987   *Women, Fire, and Dangerous Things: What Categories Reveal about the Mind.* Chicago: University of Chicago Press.

LANE, EDWARD O.
1860   *An Account of the Manners and Customs of the Modern Egyptians.* 5th ed. Edward Stanley Poole, ed. London: John Murray. Republished by Dover Publications, 1973.

LASKE, O. E.
1977   *Music, Memory, and Thought: Explorations in Cognitive Musicology.* Ann Arbor: University Microfilms.

LERDAHL, FRED, AND RAY JACKENDORFF
1983   *A Generative Theory of Tonal Music.* Cambridge, MA: MIT Press.

LINDSAY, JENNIFER
1992   *Javanese Gamelan: Traditional Orchestra of Indonesia.* 2d ed. Singapore: Oxford University Press.

LYSLOFF, RENÉ T. A.
1990   "Shrikandhi Dances Lengger: A Performance of Music and Shadow Theater in Banyumas (West Central Java)." Ann Arbor: University Microfilms.

MCDERMOTT, VINCENT, AND SUMARSAM
1975   "Central Javanese Music: The Pathet of Laras Sléndro and the Gendèr Barung." *Ethnomusicology* 19/2: 233–44.

MCLEAN, MERVYN
1968   "Cueing as a Formal Device in Maori Chant." *Ethnomusicology* 12/1: 1–10.

MCLEOD, NORMA, AND MARCIA HERNDON
1980   *Ethnography of Musical Performance.* Norwood, PA: Norwood Editions.

MARCUS, SCOTT
1989   "The Periodization of Modern Arab Music Theory: Continuity and Change in the Definition of *Maqamat.*" *Pacific Review of Ethnomusicology* 5: 33–48.

MARSUDI
1983   "Gender Panerus Slendro beserta Titilaras Cengkoknya." Surakarta: ASKI. Trans. Kent Devereaux in *Balungan* 3/2 (1988): 24–35.

MARTOPANGRAWIT, R. NG.
1979/80 *Sulukan Pathetan dan Ada-ada Laras Pelog dan Slendro.* Surakarta: ASKI.

1984   *Catatan-catatan Pengetahuan Karawitan*. Trans. Martin F. Hatch. In Becker, Judith, and Alan Feinstein, eds., *Karawitan*, vol. 1, pp. 1–244. Originally published in 2 vols. Surakarta: Akademi Seni Karawitan Indonesia, 1975.

MERRIAM, ALAN
1964   *The Anthropology of Music*. Evanston: Northwestern University Press.

MLOYOWIDODO, R. NG.
1977   *Gending-gending Jawa Gaya Surakarta*. 3 vols. Surakarta: Akademi Seni Karawitan Indonesia.

MOORE, GERALD
1950   "The Accompanist." In Elkin, Robert, ed. *A Career in Music*, pp. 95–115. London: William Earl and Company.

MORO-MYERS, PAMELA
1988   "Thai Music and Musicians in Contemporary Bangkok: An Ethnography." Ann Arbor: University Microfilms.

NATTIEZ, JEAN-JACQUES
1991   *Music and Discourse: Toward a Semiology of Music*. Trans. Carolyn Abbate. Princeton: Princeton University Press.

NEUMAN, DANIEL
1974   *The Cultural Structure and Social Organization of an Artistic Tradition*. Ann Arbor: University Microfilms.
1980   *The Life of Music in North India*. Detroit: Wayne State University Press.

NKETIA, J. H. KWABENA
1974   *The Music of Africa*. New York: W. W. Norton & Co.
1989   "Musical Interaction in Ritual Events." In Collins, Mary, David Power, and Mellonee Burnim, eds., *Music and the Experience of God*, pp. 111–24. Edinburgh: T. & T. Clark.

NOJOWIRONGKO, M. NG. (ATMOTJENDONO)
[1954]   *Serat Tuntunan Padhalangan*. Ngajogjakarta: Kementerian P. P. lan K.

PEMBERTON, JOHN
1987   "Musical Politics in Central Java (or How Not to Listen to a Javanese Gamelan)." *Indonesia* 44: 17–30.

PERLMAN, MARC
1983   "A Grammar of the Musical Genre *Srepegan*." *Asian Music* 14/1: 17–29.
1992   "American Gamelan in the Intonational Garden of Eden." Unpublished paper delivered at the University of California, Berkeley.

PERTL, BRIAN
1992   "Some Observations on the *Dung Chen* of the Nechung Monastery." *Asian Music* 23/2: 89–96.

POERBAPANGRAWIT, RADÈN MAS KODRAT
1984   *Gendhing Jawa*. Trans. Judith Becker. In Becker, Judith, and Alan Feinstein, eds., *Karawitan*, vol. 1, pp. 409–38.

POERBATJARAKA, PROF. DR.
1987   "Raden Inu Main Gamelan: Bahan Untuk Menerangkan Kata Pathet."
        Trans. Stanley Hoffman. In Becker, Judith, and Alan Feinstein, eds., *Karawi-
        tan*, vol. 2, pp. 261–84.

POLANSKY, LARRY
1985   "Tuning Systems in American Gamelan." *Balungan* 1/2: 9–11.

POWERS, HAROLD
1980   "Language Models and Musical Analysis." *Ethnomusicology* 24/1: 1–60.

PRESSING, JEFF
1988   "Improvisation: Methods and Models." In Sloboda, John, ed., *Generative Pro-
        cesses in Music: The Psychology of Performance, Improvisation, and Composition*, pp.
        129–78. Oxford Science Publications. Oxford: Clarendon Press.

PROBOHARDJONO, R. NG. SAMSUDJIN
1954   *Sulukan Pelog baku kangge njuluki Padalangan wajang Gedog*. Solo [Surakarta]:
        Budhi Laksana.
1984   *Serat Sulukan Slendro*. Trans. Susan Pratt Walton. In Becker, Judith, and Alan
        Feinstein, eds., *Karawitan*, vol. 1, pp. 439–523. Originally published 1966,
        Sala [Surakarta]: Ratna.

RACY, ALI JIHAD
1983a   "Music in Nineteenth-Century Egypt: An Historical Sketch." *Selected Reports
        in Ethnomusicology* 4: 157–79.
1983b   "The Waslah: A Compound-Form Principle in Egyptian Music." *Arab Stud-
        ies Quarterly* 5/4: 396–403.
1988   "Sound and Society: The Takht Music of Early–Twentieth Century Cairo."
        Selected Reports in Ethnomusicology 7: 139–70.

RAHN, JAY
1978   "Javanese Pelog Tunings Reconsidered." *Yearbook of the International Folk Music
        Council* 10: 69–82.
1983   *A Theory for All Music*. Toronto: University of Toronto Press.

RICE, TIMOTHY
1987   "Toward the Remodeling of Ethnomusicology." *Ethnomusicology* 31/3:
        469–88.
1988   "Understanding Three-Part Singing in Bulgaria: The Interplay of Theory
        and Experience." *Selected Reports in Ethnomusicology* 7: 43–57.

RICKLEFS, M. C.
1974   *Jogjakarta under Sultan Mangkubumi, 1749–1792*. London: Oxford University
        Press.

ROUGET, GILBERT
1985   *Music and Trance*. Trans. Brunhilde Biebuyck. Chicago: University of Chi-
        cago Press.

RUCKERT, GEORGE
1994   "The Music of Ali Akbar Khan: An Analysis of His Musical Style through

the Examination of His Composition in Three Selected Ragas." Ann Arbor: University Microfilms.

RUSSELL, ROSS
1971   *Jazz Style in Kansas City and the Southwest.* Berkeley: University of California Press.

SANTOSA
1979   *Palaran di Surakarta.* [Surakarta]: Sub Proyek ASKI.

SCHUMACHER, RÜDIGER
1980   *Die Suluk-Gesänge des Dalang im Schattenspiel Zentraljavas.* 2 vols. NGOMA: Studien zur Volksmusik und Aussereuropäischen Kunstmusik, vol. 7. Munich-Salzburg: Musikverlag Emil Katzbichler.

SCHUTZ, ALFRED
1976   "Making Music Together." *Collected Papers 2: Studies in Social Theory,* ed. Arvid Brodersen. The Hague: Martinus Nijhoff. Vol. 2, 159–78. Originally published in *Social Research* 18/1 (1951): 76–97.

SCHUYLER, PHILIP D.
1979   "Music Education in Morocco: Three Models." *World of Music* 21/3: 19–31.

SHANKAR, L.
1974   "The Art of Violin Accompaniment in South Indian Classical Music." Ann Arbor: University Microfilms.

EL-SHAWAN, SALWA
1980   "The Socio-Political Context of al-Mūsị̄ka al-'Arabiyyah in Cairo, Egypt: Policies, Patronage, Institutions, and Musical Change (1927–77)." *Asian Music* 12/1: 86–128.

SINDOESAWARNO, KI
1984   "Faktor Penting Dalam Gamelan." Trans. Stanley Hoffman. In Becker, Judith, and Alan Feinstein, eds., *Karawitan,* vol. 1, pp. 389–407.
1987   "Ilmu Karawitan." Trans. Martin F. Hatch. In Becker, Judith, and Alan Feinstein, eds., *Karawitan,* vol. 2, pp. 311–87.

SLOBIN, MARK
1992   "Micromusics of the West: A Comparative Approach." *Ethnomusicology* 36/1: 1–87.

SLOBODA, JOHN A.
1985   *The Musical Mind: The Cognitive Psychology of Music.* Oxford Psychology Series no. 5. Oxford: Clarendon Press.

SLOBODA, JOHN A., ED.
1988   *Generative Processes in Music: The Psychology of Performance, Improvisation, and Composition.* Oxford Science Publications. Oxford: Clarendon Press.

SOEKANTO, SASTRODARSONO
1966   *Teori Nabuh Gamelan.* Surakarta: Kemudawati.

SORRELL, NEIL
1990   *A Guide to the Gamelan.* Portland: Amadeus Press.

STONE, RUTH
1982   *Let the Inside Be Sweet.* Bloomington: Indiana University Press.

SUANDA, ENDO
1985   "Cirebonese Topeng and Wayang of the Present Day." *Asian Music* 16/2:
        84–120.

SUGARMAN, JANE
1988   "Making Muabet: The Social Basis of Singing among Prespa Albanian
        Men." *Selected Reports in Ethnomusicology* 7: 1–42.

SUKAMSO
1992   *Garap Rebab, Kendhang, Gender, dan Vocal dalam Gendhing Bondhet.* Surakarta:
        STSI.

SUKERTA, PANDE MADE
1979/80*Rebaban Karawitan Bali.* Surakarta: ASKI.

SUMARSAM
1975   "Gender Barung: Its Technique and Function in the Context of Javanese
        Gamelan." *Indonesia* 20: 161–72.
1984a   "Gamelan Music and the Javanese Wayang Kulit." In Morgan, Stephanie,
        and Laurie Sears, eds., *Aesthetic Tradition and Cultural Transition in Java and Bali,*
        pp. 105–16. Madison: Center for Southeast Asian Studies, University of
        Wisconsin.
1984b   "Inner Melody." In Becker, Judith, and Alan Feinstein, eds., *Karawitan,* vol.
        1, pp. 245–304.
1987   "Introduction to Ciblon Drumming in Javanese Gamelan." In Becker, Ju-
        dith, and Alan Feinstein, eds., *Karawitan,* vol. 2, pp. 171–203.
1992   "Historical Contexts and Theories of Javanese Music." Ann Arbor: Univer-
        sity Microfilms.

SUPANGGAH, RAHAYU
1988   "Balungan." *Balungan* 3/2: 2–10. Trans. Marc Perlman.
1991   "Some Thoughts on Learning to Play Gamelan." Paper delivered at the
        conference Indonesian Music: Twentieth Century Innovation and Tradi-
        tion, University of California, Berkeley, September 27–28.

SURAJI
1991a   *Gendhing Beksan dan Pahargyan.* Surakarta: STSI.
1991b   *Onang-onang, Gendhing Kethuk 2 Kerep Minggah 4 Sebuah Tinjauan Tentang: Garap,
        Fungsi Serta Struktur Musikalnya.* Surakarta: STSI.

SURJODININGRAT, WASISTO, P. J. SUDARJANA, AND ADHI SUSANTO
1972   *Tone Measurements of Outstanding Javanese Gamelan in Jogjakarta and Surakarta.* 2d
        rev. ed. Jogjakarta: Gadjah Mada University Press.

SUSILO, HARDJA
1984   "Wayang Wong Panggung: Its Social Context, Technique and Music." In
        Morgan, Stephanie, and Laurie Sears, eds., *Aesthetic Tradition and Cultural*

Transition in Java and Bali, pp. 105–16. Madison: Center for Southeast Asian Studies, University of Wisconsin.

1987   "Improvisation in Wayang Wong Panggung: Creativity within Cultural Constraints." Yearbook for Traditional Music 19: 1–11.

SUTTON, R. ANDERSON

1978   "Notes toward a Grammar of Variation in Javanese Gendèr Playing." Ethnomusicology 22/2: 275–96.

1979   "Concept and Treatment in Javanese Gamelan Music with Reference to the Gambang." Asian Music 11/1: 59–79.

1982   "Variation in Javanese Gamelan: Dynamics of a Steady State." Ann Arbor: University Microfilms.

1984a   "Change and Ambiguity: Gamelan Style and Regional Identity in Yogyakarta." In Morgan, Stephanie, and Laurie Sears, eds., Aesthetic Tradition and Cultural Transition in Java and Bali, pp. 221–46. Madison: Center for Southeast Asian Studies, University of Wisconsin.

1984b   "Who Is the Pesindhèn? Notes on the Female Singing Tradition in Java." Indonesia 37: 119–34.

1991a   Traditions of Gamelan Music in Java: Musical Pluralism and Regional Identity. Cambridge: Cambridge University Press.

1991b   "Individuality and Writing in Javanese Music Learning." Paper delivered at the conference Indonesian Music: Twentieth Century Innovation and Tradition, University of California, Berkeley, September 27–28.

1993   Variation in Central Javanese Gamelan Music: Dynamics of a Steady State. Center for Southeast Asian Studies, Monograph Series on Southeast Asia, Special Report no. 28. DeKalb: Northern Illinois University.

SUYENAGA, JOAN

1984   "Patterns in Process: A Glimpse of Java through Gamelan." In Morgan, Stephanie, and Laurie Sears, eds., Aesthetic Tradition and Cultural Transition in Java and Bali, pp. 83–104. Madison: Center for Southeast Asian Studies, University of Wisconsin.

SWEENEY, AMIN

1987   A Full Hearing. Berkeley: University of California Press.

TENZER, MICHAEL

1991   Balinese Music. Berkeley: Periplus Editions.

TUCKER, MARILYN

1991   "Schnaut Worked Years for Isolde Debut in America." San Francisco Chronicle, October 18, p. D13.

TURINO, THOMAS

1989   "The Coherence of Social Style and Musical Creation among the Aymara in Southern Peru." Ethnomusicology 33/1: 1–30.

TURNER, JONATHAN

1988   A Theory of Social Interaction. Stanford: Stanford University Press.

VAN GROENENDAEL, VICTORIA MARIA CLARA

1982   Er Zit Een Dalang Achter De Wayang. Amsterdam: De Goudsbloem.

VAN NESS, EDWARD C., AND SHITA PRAWIROHARDJO
1980   *Javanese Wayang Kulit.* Singapore: Oxford University Press.

VETTER, ROGER
1984   "Poetic, Musical and Dramatic Structures in a Langen Mandra Wanara Per-
        formance." In Morgan, Stephanie, and Laurie Sears, eds., *Aesthetic Tradition
        and Cultural Transition in Java and Bali,* pp. 163–208. Madison: Center for
        Southeast Asian Studies, University of Wisconsin.
1986   "Music for 'The Lap of The World': Gamelan Performance, Performers and
        Repertoire in the Kraton Yogyakarta." Ph.D. diss., University of Wiscon-
        sin, Madison.
1989   "A Retrospect on a Century of Gamelan Tone Measurements." *Ethnomusicol-
        ogy* 33/2: 217–28.

VITALE, WAYNE
1990   "Interview [with] I Wayan Dibia: 'The Relationship of Music and Dance in
        Balinese Performing Arts.'" *Balungan* 4/2: 16–22.

WADE, BONNIE
1984a   *Khyal.* Cambridge: Cambridge University Press.
1984b   "Performance Practice in Indian Classical Music." In Gerard Béhague, ed.,
        Performance Practice: Ethnomusicological Perspectives, pp. 13–52. Westport, CT.:
        Greenwood Press.

WARIDI
1985/86 *Proses Kumulatif Unsur-Unsur Musikal Dalam Diri Empu Karawitan II Bapak RL
        Martopangrawit.* Surakarta: ASKI.

WARSADININGRAT, K. R. T.
1987   *Wédha Pradangga.* Trans. Susan Pratt Walton. In Becker, Judith, and Alan
        Feinstein, eds., *Karawitan,* vol. 2, pp. 1–170. Originally published in 6 vols,
        typescript. Surakarta: SMKI, 1972.

WEISGARBER, ELLIOT
1968   "The Honkyoku of the Kinko-Ryu: Some Principles of Its Organization."
        Ethnomusicology 12/3: 313–44.

WONG, DEBORAH
1991   "Across Three Generations: A Solo Piece for Thai Gong Circle." *Balungan*
        5/1: 2–9.

ZHANG, WEI-HUA
1994   "The Musical Activities of the Chinese American Communities in the San
        Francisco Bay Area: A Social and Cultural Study." Ann Arbor: University
        Microfilms.

DISCOGRAPHY

COMMERCIAL RECORDINGS

Pangkur Pamijen. Kusuma, KGD 018, n.d.

Aja Lamis. Kusuma, KGD 069, n.d.

Gandakusuma. Lokananta, ACD 131, n.d.

Palaran Gobyog. Vol. 2. Lokananta, ACD 144, n.d.

FIELD RECORDINGS

KS3 = Radio Broadcast at KONSER, Surakarta, Nov. 4, 1983.

KS13 = Recording of *gamelan gadhon,* Surakarta, May 15, 1993.

SU1–5 = Recordings of *sulukan* made in Surakarta, 1983.

Index

References to Javanese musicians' roles are listed by instrument; e.g., *gendèr* refers to the instrument and the player. Italicized page numbers refer to definitions of terms